W9-CJN-884

MUNICH

Henri Noguères

MUNICH

'PEACE FOR OUR TIME'

Translated from the French by Patrick O'Brian

McGraw-Hill Book Company

New York   Toronto   London

*Europe, like an artichoke, was ready
to be eaten leaf by leaf*
J. PAUL-BONCOUR

Contents

Contents

Illustrations

Photograph numbers 7 and 8 are reproduced by kind permission of *The Times;* the others by kind permission of The Keystone Press Agency

Maps

Introduction

At dawn on that Thursday, September 29, 1938, the whole of Europe was under arms.

Never had the rising tide of danger seemed so relentless, not even in the summer of 1914, whose memory was haunting so many minds. The question that men (men of good will or not) were asking themselves was not whether there was a risk of a spark setting fire to the powder-barrel, but rather whether it was still possible to get the fuse out of the bomb that might go off at any moment.

In London the civil defence volunteers were feverishly digging air-raid shelters in the City itself and piling up sandbags in front of the windows of the public buildings, while the men of the Home Guard were getting anti-aircraft guns into position, although helmets were all the military equipment they had been given. Four proclamations calling up the Royal Navy's reserves had been signed by King George VI the day before at Buckingham Palace.

In France the *Journal Officiel* of that morning published the decree authorizing the application of the measures provided by the law dealing with the organization of the country in time of war. But several categories of reservists had already been mobilized. Those belonging to '*tranche 8*', recalled by placards posted up on the afternoon of the day before, had joined their units during the night, and this had brought the number of men with the colours to 1,221,000.

Nazi Germany was living in the expectation of a general mobilization: it had been announced and then put off. But in fact for months past the Wehrmacht, facing west, had been occupying the works of the Siegfried line, which Dr Todt was building with ever increasing speed. But it was above all in the east that the troops were massed, concentrations planned long before for the carrying out of Operation Green, the invasion of Czechoslovakia; and they were ready there to charge at the first sign the Führer should give. What is more, the generals appointed to the command of the ten armies entrusted with Operation Green had been named since September 18.

Fascist Italy, Nazi Germany's ally, had not yet officially called up her reservists. But all day long the day before the people in the streets of Rome had noticed the little green army liaison cars hurrying about the city and stopping in front of certain doors. Every time the same thing happened: an officer got out, handed the concierge an envelope and went away again after giving final instructions: it was the distribution of the individual notices of recall to the reserve officers of the mountain units.

In Prague general mobilization was an accomplished fact five days old, that is to say, ever since London and Paris had, not without reservations, informed the Czechoslovak cabinet that they could no longer advise against such a measure.

For their part the Poles were making ready to cross the Czechoslovak border and seize Teschen. And the Red Army, on a war footing, was prepared to intervene. The Hungarians denied having carried out a general mobilization, but admitted that 'mobilization measures had been put in force in the regions along the Czechoslovak frontier'. Belgium herself had thought it necessary to call up six classes of reservists to strengthen her covering arrangements.

And yet while the columns were filling the roads and the passenger trains were standing motionless for hours to let the troop convoys go by (forty men, eight horses), and while the testing of the sirens reminded the civil population with a sad howling insistence of the dangers of a war in which no one could be sure of being spared, the nations, all the nations in Europe and the whole world, suddenly began to believe in peace.

Why? Simply because on that morning of September 29 four men had set out to take part in a meeting; and when this meeting had been announced the afternoon before it had caused hopes to spring up that were in proportion to the danger that men saw darkly before them.

In response to the invitation sent out by Hitler, the Chancellor of the Third Reich, Neville Chamberlain, His Britannic Majesty's Prime Minister, Edouard Daladier, the premier of France, and the Duce, Benito Mussolini, head of the 'imperial' government of fascist Italy, had agreed to come to the rendezvous at Munich.

It had happened very suddenly.

On the twenty-sixth Hitler had announced that the German general mobilization would take place in forty-eight hours, that is to say at precisely two o'clock in the afternoon of the twenty-eighth. And he had added that if between now and then Prague had not accepted all Germany's conditions, the Wehrmacht would enter Czechoslovakia by force.

After that ultimatum it had seemed that there was no longer anything that could stop the whole of Europe going up in a blaze. By the morning of September 28, the D-day of the German mobilization, nothing had happened to allow any hope of an improvement in the situation.

Yet in the evening of the same day hope of peace had taken the place of the dread of approaching war.

How had it come about, and what had been the sequence of events that could bring Europe to the brink of a fresh conflict less than twenty years after the armistice had put an end to the Great War?

How, by whom, and at what price had the situation been reversed – a reversal without which this September 29 would no doubt have been the first day of the second world war, an advance of eleven months in history's calendar?

To answer these questions we must recall to mind those six months from March to September, 1938, from the Anschluss to Munich, which saw the birth and the development of the German-Czechoslovak crisis.

Only then will it be possible to join Hitler, Mussolini, Chamberlain and Daladier, the 'big four', on their road to Munich, and to attempt the reconstruction of their meeting in the Führerhaus that day.

CHAPTER ONE

The Austrian dress-rehearsal

Word of honour · England steps in · Who is to be the horseman and who the horse? · Russian pessimism

FRIDAY, March 11, 1938 . . .
Since dawn the world, powerless and racked with anxiety, had been watching Austria's last convulsions.

All day long a continual series of dispatches and telephone calls reached the chanceries, the press agencies and the newspaper offices:

Three German army corps are concentrated on the Austrian frontier . . . The plebiscite has been postponed . . . Schuschnigg resigns . . . Nazi ultimatum: Miklas is given two hours to appoint Seyss-Inquart chancellor . . . Miklas resists . . . Seyss-Inquart is setting up a provisional government . . . he has asked for the help of the German army . . .

At nightfall crowds gathered in Paris, London, New York, gazing up at the news on the electric lights or at the flashes posted up outside the great newspaper offices: they were waiting for the latest news from Vienna, or even more, perhaps, from Berlin, since from then onwards it was in Berlin that the decisions which might determine peace or war were taken. But the only news that came through from Berlin that evening was of a kind that surprised even the most blasé listeners: the only thing that was mentioned was a splendid, ostentatious party. For in Berlin, while Austria's fate was being settled, they were dancing. They were dancing in Berlin, and it was Göring who led the ball.

It is true that he had sent out his invitations long before, but he had thought it sound policy not to cancel them in spite of the sudden, violent development of the Austrian crisis: so more than a thousand guests – officers, diplomats, high-ranking Nazi dignitaries, Berlin society – crowded under the great chandeliers of the *Haus der Flieger*, as though nothing out of the ordinary had happened during the day.

The dancing couples revolved to the allusive rhythm of Viennese waltzes: nothing was wanting but a Salvandy to repeat his historic remark more than a century after he had first uttered it: for indeed, the dancers in Berlin in 1938, like those in Paris in 1830, were dancing upon a volcano.

As the evening wore on most of the Wehrmacht and Luftwaffe officers quietly vanished, one after another, called back to their posts, either with their units or on various staffs. For their part the attachés and the embassy secretaries did no more than disappear from time to time: they were keeping in touch by telephone and they came back to the party to tell their ambassadors (who were all there, to the last man) how the situation was developing – or at least to tell them what they had learnt about it.

The most nervous and anxious of all the diplomats accredited to Berlin appeared to be Dr Mastny, the Czechoslovak minister. It was easy to see why this should be so, for on February 20, less than twenty days before, Hitler had made a speech in the Reichstag – a speech that announced the impending settlement of the Austrian affair but that also included a warning directed at Czechoslovakia.

'There are more than ten million Germans living in two of the states which have a common frontier with us,' the Führer had said. 'It is intolerable for a great power to know that just beside it its blood-brothers are continually suffering the bitterest torments because they feel themselves part and parcel of the whole undivided nation ... It is for the German Reich to protect those Germanic peoples along our frontier whose own efforts are not capable of assuring them political and spiritual freedom.'

Ten million? To reach this total Hitler could only have added the three million Sudeten Germans to the seven million Austrians.

Two states having a common frontier with Germany? Austria was one of them; Czechoslovakia was the other.

On that same February 20, in London, Anthony Eden, disagreeing with the prime minister, Chamberlain, on the attitude that should be adopted towards the Italian and German dictators, had left the Foreign Office. He had at once been replaced by Lord Halifax. This resignation and the selection of a new foreign secretary who was in favour of the policy of appeasement may not perhaps have acted as a catalyst in the Austrian affair, but there is no sort of doubt that it made its progress much easier. Was it not reasonable to fear that after

Austria it would inescapably be Czechoslovakia's turn – and that very soon?

Word of honour

Unable to bear it any longer, Dr Mastny went up to Göring, who was happily swaggering about, plastered with orders and decorations, in the middle of an animated group. An unexpected diplomatic conversation of the highest importance between the two men was to take place – a conversation that was given a strange, soothing background by the violins of the orchestra.

'Dr Mastny,' said Göring, 'sought me out; he was much worked up and he was trembling. He asked me what was going to happen that night, whether we were going to enter Czechoslovakia as well. I gave him a short account of the position and said to him, "No, it is solely a question of the annexation of Austria; it does not concern your country in the least, above all if you do not busy yourselves in the matter." He thanked me, and went off, apparently to telephone.'[1]

Mastny did, in fact, go and give Krofta, his foreign minister, an immediate account of this conversation and of the assurances offered by Göring. Having received, for his part, the assurance that Czechoslovakia would not mobilize, the minister at once returned to the *Haus der Flieger*.

'A little later,' Göring went on, 'he came back, even more worked up, and I had the feeling that he was too moved even to understand me clearly. In the presence of other people I then said to him, "Your Excellency, pay close attention to what I say: I give you my personal word of honour that it is solely a question of the Anschluss of Austria and that not a single German soldier will go near the Czechoslovak frontier. See to it that Czechoslovakia does not mobilize, for that would worsen the situation." He agreed.'

The French ambassador, André François-Poncet (who certainly appears to have been one of the 'other people' in whose presence this conversation took place), confirms the statement and adds fuller detail to Göring's account.

'M Göring then repeated to him what he had told him before, adding that he was speaking not only for himself personally but also in the name of the Führer, who, being away from Berlin for some time, had given him full powers.'[2]

In addition to these assurances, the Czechoslovak minister was to be given many more. At noon the next day Göring telephoned Mastny to tell him that the German troops had been ordered not to go within fifteen kilometres of the Czechoslovak frontier.

Lastly, at half past five in the afternoon of that same March 13, the Czechoslovak minister was summoned by Neurath, who was then the foreign minister of the Reich. Neurath, speaking in the Führer's name, renewed the 'soothing assurances' that Göring had already lavished on his visitor. Mastny took advantage of the opportunity to state 'that his country should remain perfectly calm, being entirely confident of her allies' good faith and of their support in case of need.'[3]

England steps in

Jan Masaryk,* the Czechoslovak envoy in London, skilfully set himself to extract the utmost possible profit from this diplomatic conjuncture. As early as March 12 he made this suggestion to Halifax, 'Marshal Göring has given our minister in Berlin the explicit assurance that the Reich has no intention whatever of interfering with Czechoslovakia's independence. The German minister in Prague has made the same declaration to M Krofta. Why should not my government officially inform the Foreign Office of this double intimation? Such a démarche would allow you to take official notice of it and subsequently to send Berlin a note in which the British government would record the assurance thus given to Czechoslovakia.'

And indeed the next day the Czechoslovak note specifying the assurance given by Göring and Neurath in Berlin, and by Eisenlohr, the German minister to Prague, and repeated again by Mackensen, the secretary of state, was handed to the Foreign Office. Halifax immediately sent Nevile Henderson, the British ambassador, to call upon Göring, who confirmed what he had said, adding that he in no way objected to his declarations being made public. The only reserves he expressed were on the subject of the arbitration treaties, which, he said, 'concerned the Chancellor and Herr von Neurath, and whose scope was not thoroughly known to him personally.'

The result was that finally, on March 14, Neville Chamberlain was able to tell the Commons, 'I am informed that Field-Marshal Göring on March 11 gave a general assurance to the Czech minister

* Son of Tomás Garrigue Masaryk, the founder of the Czechoslovak Republic and its first president.

in Berlin – an assurance which he expressly renewed later on behalf of Herr Hitler – that it would be the earnest endeavour of the German government to improve German-Czech relations. In particular, on March 12, Field-Marshal Göring informed the Czech minister that German troops marching into Austria had received the strictest orders to keep at least fifteen kilometres from the frontier. On the same day the Czechoslovak minister in Berlin was assured by Baron von Neurath that Germany considered herself bound by the German-Czechoslovak Arbitration convention of October 1925.'

For his part François-Poncet went even farther in setting out the assurances that Göring had given. On March 15, in a telegram to the Quai d'Orsay, the French ambassador, having confirmed Göring's consent to public reference to his assurances, said that he was able to assert that the Germans had promised his British colleague to with-draw their troops from Austria 'before the plebiscite of April 10'.

It is a fact that Marshal Göring expressed himself very clearly . . . but according to him he had exercised a certain mental reservation. Later, recalling his conversation with Mastny and giving details of it, he was to say, 'I never said to him "I give you my word of honour that we shall never turn our attention to Czechoslovakia"; but he was asking me for explanations concerning that incident only and for that single period, and I gave him an explanation valid for that period; for I had already plainly stated that sooner or later, in one way or another, a solution of the problem of the Sudeten Germans would have to be reached. I never bound myself by my word of honour, because that would have been impossible, since I had already made a previous declaration in the opposite sense. I was asked for an explanation dealing with the occurrences immediately at hand – the Austrian affair. With a clear conscience I was able to give him the assurance on my word of honour that Czechoslovakia should not be touched on that occasion, for we had not yet taken any decision to set a date for Czechoslovakia or the solution of the Sudeten German problem.'[4]

Who is to be the horseman and who the horse?

Since the Nazi machine had set itself in motion to carry the German nation's *Weltanschauung* into effect, France and the French govern-ment had scarcely entered into consideration at all. There was an excellent reason for this: for it so happened that between Thursday,

March 10, and Sunday, March 13 – that is to say between Hitler's making up his mind to carry out the Anschluss and the Führer's triumphal entry into his native Austria – France had no government.

The legislative body was half-way through the period for which it had been elected: on the first day of its sitting, in May, 1936, it had been marked by the victory of the Front Populaire; but after governing for a year Léon Blum had been obliged by pressure from the Senate to hand over the reins to Camille Chautemps. Chautemps had just been forced to resign in his turn, for his Socialist supporters had refused their consent to his financial programme. And the President of the Republic did not call upon Léon Blum again until three days had passed in consultations – the three days of the Anschluss.

Paul-Boncour, who succeeded Yvon Delbos at the Quai d'Orsay, therefore found himself, as far as Austria was concerned, faced with a *fait accompli*. The case was not yet the same for Czechoslovakia, but Paul-Boncour was conscious that quick action was essential. As early as March 14, therefore, he summoned Osusky, the Czechoslovak minister in Paris. 'If Czechoslovakia were attacked,' he told him, 'France would unfailingly carry out the engagements that arise from our treaty of October 16, 1925, which confirms and more clearly defines that of January 25, 1924 . . . I assure you of this.'

At the same time the new foreign minister asked Charles Corbin, the ambassador in London, to inform the British government of the attitude taken up with regard to Czechoslovakia – and to make inquiries about Chamberlain's intentions.

Paul-Boncour was perfectly aware that this eagerness to reassure Czechoslovakia 'did not tend in quite the same direction as the policy then pursued by Mr Chamberlain'. But he thought that nevertheless the 'gentleman of the British government' could not bear him any ill-will for having thus spontaneously reaffirmed the French government's intention of honouring its signature.

'Like our neighbour at Valançay,'* writes Paul-Boncour, 'I think that the alliance between England and France is as necessary as that between the horseman and the horse. But, like him, I think we must try not to be the horse. As a continental power, with a common frontier with Germany that has always been in dispute and that was, since the remilitarization of the Rhineland,† threatened once more, for us the defence of Czechoslovakia's independence was a matter of

* Talleyrand; the Chateau de Valançay had belonged to him.
† March 7, 1936.

vital concern. We were going to ask England's intentions having already made up our minds; we were not asking in order to find out from her reply what position we should adopt; and I was persuaded that she would be the last to be surprised by this.

'I was not mistaken. I owe this tribute to Mr Chamberlain, that even if our position did not exactly comply with his policy, he was too upright to take advantage of it to minimize the value of the obligations which M Flandin and I had managed to have accepted, two years earlier, as confirming and strengthening those of Locarno.'[5]

And indeed when Chamberlain addressed the House of Commons once more on March 24 he listed Great Britain's international engagements and noted that among them there did not figure automatic assistance to France in the case of her being called upon to support Czechoslovakia in virtue of the Franco-Czechoslovak bilateral agreements of 1925; but he nevertheless added,

'When peace and war are concerned, legal obligations are not alone involved, and, if a war broke out, it would be unlikely to be confined to those who have assumed such obligations. It would be quite impossible to say where it would end and what governments might become involved. The inexorable pressure of facts might well prove more powerful than formal pronouncements, and in that event it would be well within the bounds of probability that other countries besides those which were parties to the original dispute would almost immediately become involved. This is especially true in the case of two countries like Great Britain and France, with long associations of friendship, with interests closely interwoven, devoted to the same ideals of democratic liberty, and determined to uphold them.

A delicately-shaded taking up of position, to be sure; but one which nevertheless did not close the door upon the possibility of British intervention.

Russian pessimism

This same speech, however, did close another door – that of the League of Nations, before which Litvinov, on March 17, had suggested opening a debate to find the best way of blocking the road to German aggression for the future. Chamberlain recalled this proposal and totally rejected it as being of a nature to make the situation worse rather than helping to improve it.

It must be added that the People's Commissar for External Affairs had few illusions about the reception that his proposals would meet with. The day before Chamberlain's speech, on March 23, he confided to the American ambassador Joseph Davies that he was entirely certain that Czechoslovakia would cause difficulties during the summer.

'It is to be feared,' added Litvinov, 'that Czechoslovakia may voluntarily yield to Germany's demands out of a want of confidence in France and because she is entirely surrounded ... furthermore, France has not the least confidence in the Soviet Union, and the Soviet Union has not the least confidence in France.'[6]

And when Davies asked him what forecast he could give on the basis of this pessimistic appraisal, the People's Commissar answered flatly, 'I foresee a fascist peace imposed by Germany and Italy ... The middle states, Rumania, Yugoslavia, Bulgaria, Hungary and Czechoslovakia, are all terrified, and the only thing that might prevent the total reign of fascism over Europe would be a change of government or of policy in Great Britain.'[7]

There was no question, for the moment, of either the one or the other: the British Conservatives, in spite of the opposition of Winston Churchill, who had just joined Anthony Eden, were firmly settled in power. And Halifax's presence at the Foreign Office showed Chamberlain's determination to change ministers if he had to, but not policy.

The only problem, therefore, was to know, in this month of March, 1938, whether Litvinov's gloomy forecast was to be fulfilled or not, whether Germany, after the Anschluss and in spite of Göring's 'word of honour', would attack Czechoslovakia: and whether the happenings in the days and the months to come would confirm Guido Zernato's saying, 'Austria is a little world in which History gives her dress-rehearsals.'

CHAPTER TWO

Czechoslovakia in 1938

Frontiers and minorities · The centrifugal forces · Konrad Henlein · The diplomatic situation of Czechoslovakia · Thirty-two divisions ... and the guns of Skoda

THERE was a catch-phrase that was so often repeated in 1938 that in the end it came to be accepted as a self-evident truth: 'The Czechoslovak state is an artificial creation of the Treaty of Versailles.'

This was a convenient summary in more ways than one, particularly in that it allowed those who spread it abroad to sleep well by night and to digest their meals in peace; for the Treaty of Versailles, less than twenty years after it had been signed, had a bad press. Wilson's successors had seen to that. And making this parallel between the Czechoslovak republic and the showy, fragile structure built up by the winners of the first world war amounted to the same thing as excusing, or even better, justifying, all harsh treatment of the Czechoslovaks, or just plain indifference towards them.

Yet there were some men during 1938 who spoke out to correct this over-simplified and only partially true description; and these were men who could not be suspected of repeating the themes of a campaign organized by the left or the extreme left. For example, in Great Britain there was Churchill, and in France André Tardieu.

'Who is there who remembers,' exclaimed Tardieu on May 6, 1938, in *Gringoire*, of all papers, 'that the creation of Czechoslovakia dates not from the Treaty of Versailles of June 28, 1919, but from the war, one of whose aims it was, and from the armistice with Austria on November 3, 1918, of which it was one of the conditions?'

And Tardieu recalled that as early as December 30, 1916, and January 10, 1917, the Allied governments were setting 'the liberation of the Czechoslovaks at present subject to foreign rule' among their war aims; that in the summer of 1917 the French and English governments had recognized the Czechoslovak National Council as an allied government; and that they had entrusted Tardieu himself with the recruiting of three Czechoslovak brigades in the United States – brigades that were subsequently to take their part in the common effort and the common sacrifice.

Furthermore this 'Czechoslovak nation' was by no means so much of a merely intellectual concept as some people chose to believe, a pseudo-nation raised up for the requirements of the Allied cause. It had a long, splendid, and painful history running down through the centuries from the days of the ancient Moravian emperors; of Wenceslas, the Bohemian king of the legends, the Saint Wenceslas whose feast-day is celebrated so zealously in September every year in Prague; of John Huss, whom the Council of Constance condemned; and of the luckless heroes of the White Mountain.

To be sure, during these thousand years the Czechoslovak nation had more often been subject than free, more often conquered than conquering. The Czech and the Slovak Slavs had never lacked oppressors to hate from the time of the Hungarian conquerors of the tenth century to that of Franz Joseph, with the Bohemian Germans, upheld by the fathers of the Council of Constance, coming between them. But is not this the most certain way of bringing a nation's soul into existence?

'We existed before Austria and we shall continue to exist after her,' wrote the Czech historian Palacky, an outstanding figure in the struggle against the Teutons – against the Habsburgs; and he wrote it in 1876.

Throughout the first world war Masaryk and Benes did their utmost to fulfil Palacky's words; and on the day of the signature of that Austrian armistice referred to by Tardieu they could feel that they had succeeded.

Frontiers and minorities

On December 21, 1918, Tomás Garrigue Masaryk, the first President of the Czechoslovak Republic, made his entry into Prague. Czechoslovakia, a new state but an old nation, already had a capital, a device – the double-tailed lion – and a motto, which was the same as John Huss's, *Pravda Svitezi!* – truth above all. In short, it no longer lacked anything but frontiers.

The Czechs and the Slovaks had been united a thousand years before, in the time of the Moravian empire, and only then. Since those days, and including the three centuries when both had been under Habsburg rule, the Czechs had been subject to Austria and the Slovaks to Hungary. And between these two sets of people of the same race, whose destinies had run in different directions for too long, even neighbourly intercourse had not always been devoid of unpleasantness. But for all that, and thanks to the personal initiative of Masaryk, who was himself the son of a Czech coachman, a former serf, and of a Slovak maidservant, the decision to join the two peoples in a single state had been taken even before the winning of the common victory.

On June 30, 1918, the Czech and Slovak immigrants in the United States reached a solemn agreement in Pittsburgh, recognizing that the Slovak people should have a wide degree of internal autonomy. This document could not be binding on the elected representatives of the whole Czechoslovak nation when in due time they should come together to make their decisions; but it did nevertheless possess the merit of establishing the desire of the Czechs and the Slovaks to join together – a junction based upon the application of the principal of nationalities, and one which made the justification for the dismemberment of Austria-Hungary derive from this same principle. But Eduard Benes, the new Czechoslovakia's able spokesman at the peace conference, so managed it that once the application of the principle of nationality was accepted in favour of his country, the conference also took into account other, and directly contradictory, principles, based upon historical, geographical, economic and even strategic considerations. This inevitably resulted in delicate problems arising from the ethnic minorities.

So that the Czechoslovaks should have the protection of the Bohemian mountains, the bordering zones of Germany, inhabited for the most part by the Teutonic 'Sudeten Germans',* were included within the frontiers of the new republic. In the same way, in order to satisfy Czechoslovakia's Danubian aspirations, various stretches of territory with a predominantly Magyar population had been taken from Hungary. An open conflict with Poland on the subject of the coal-basin of Teschen (or Cieszyn, as the Poles called it) was to end in an arbitration by the ambassadors' conference on July 28, 1920.

* They had chosen this name themselves: it is that of one of the chains of mountains in their region. (See map 2, page 104.)

It was a judgment of Solomon, and naturally it pleased nobody, least of all the Poles, who saw 139,000 of their people obliged either to acquire Czechoslovak nationality or to emigrate, whereas only 85,000 were returning to the Polish fold.

Finally, the population of Czechoslovakia according to the figures of the last census, that of 1930, was made up as follows:

Czechs	7,447,000
Germans	2,231,600
Slovaks	2,309,000
Magyars	691,900
Ruthenians	549,000
Poles	81,700

The Czechoslovak state 'reproduced the racial jig-saw puzzle of the Austro-Hungarian empire in miniature'.[1] As Mussolini was to say, in his speech at Treviso on September 21, 1938, it was not merely a Czechoslovakia, but a 'Czecho-germano-polono-magyaro-rutheno-rumano-slovakia'.

It was a state that enclosed within its own frontiers elements whose mixture might become explosive at any moment.

The centrifugal forces

But although this was the composition of the country, Czechoslovakia had nevertheless shown, during the twenties and the beginning of the thirties, that it was born a viable state. This was no doubt to be attributed to the economic and geographic considerations that had been taken into account at the time when the frontiers were fixed. For indeed, at the cost of an agrarian reform which was a bold one for that period and of a severe financial policy, the granary of Slovakia and the industrial complex of Bohemia-Moravia complemented one another admirably. To a certain degree Czechoslovakia had become the pilot country for the middle European states; it was well-balanced and prosperous, and some of its neighbours, with Austria first among them, were in its debt.

The republican form of government installed itself smoothly. In 1935 Benes quite naturally succeeded Masaryk. And yet the question of the minorities was only partially solved, for Czech centralization was rigid in its working, and in an unfederative system the exercise of democratic rights did not provide the minorities with an absolute guarantee that their linguistic and cultural particularities should be maintained.*

What is more, each of these minorities except the Slovaks was under the influence of the brother-nation in which it originated, even when the creation of Czechoslovakia had not cut the minority off from the main body, which was particularly the case with the Sudeten Germans.

As for the Slovaks, they made up a sufficiently numerous body in themselves not to need to look beyond the frontiers. But they were by no means untouched by the propaganda of an autonomist party which based itself upon the Pittsburgh agreement – an agreement that had remained a dead letter. Furthermore, since by far the greatest number of them were Catholics they were susceptible to the influence of an episcopacy and a clergy that looked with a most unfavourable eye on both the atheism of the majority of the Czech working-class and on the neo-Husite character of the Czechoslovak Church, which was founded in 1919.

Nevertheless, in spite of a lurking ill-temper and a few outbursts of high feeling, the Slovak question was never one which might have been expected seriously to endanger Czechoslovak unity. For a long while the spokesmen and propagandists for Slovak autonomy themselves, the bishops Hlinka and Tiso, only thought of complete secession as a last resource.

'The Slovak nation wants to live,' Hlinka used to say, 'even if it must be at the price of the existence of the Czechoslovak Republic.'[2]

But gradually, as the political agitation grew in the regions inhabited by the Sudeten Germans, the Slovak autonomists saw in it the beginning of Czechoslovakia's dismemberment, and their own aims therefore changed. They entered into contact with the other ethnic minorities; German agents worked upon the Slovak autonomists and gave them material help.

One day, at the beginning of 1938, Hlinka received a Polish journalist, and during the interview he made some observations that revealed the connexions established between the Slovaks and the Germans. This journalist, Roman Fajans,[3] asked him 'whether, faced with the German danger, it would not be better for the Slovaks as well as for the Czechs, to forget these family quarrels and join together against the common enemy.'

---

* Yet it must be observed that in Prague there was a German university as well as higher technical colleges in which the teaching was carried on in German.

'What German danger?' asked Hlinka, with an air of astonishment and an ironical smile. 'I am not aware of any German danger in Slovakia. The Germans scarcely threaten us. And the rest does not interest me . . .'

The rest? That is to say Prague, Benes – in short, Czechoslovakia. Now as it happened 'the rest' could already no longer overlook or underestimate the German danger.

In point of fact, the discontent of the Sudeten Germans had made itself plain in the very first days of the Czechoslovak Republic. The regions bordering on the Bohemian quadrilateral that these Teutonic people had come to inhabit in the course of the centuries had never been joined to Germany, except perhaps in the time of the Holy Roman Empire. But the Habsburg dynasty was Teutonic. And when Austria-Hungary collapsed the Sudeten Germans had strongly hoped that they should be attached to the German Republic, in spite of the fact that it is scarcely usual to grant territorial gains to the side that loses.

As early as June 1, 1920, Lodgman, the president of the German parliamentary group, speaking in parliament in Prague, stated, 'The Germans of Bohemia, Moravia, Silesia and Slovakia have never expressed the desire to unite themselves with the Czechs and to form the Czechoslovak Republic with them. For this reason they will never cease to call for the right of self-determination and they will look upon it as the vital principle of all their activities and of their attitude with regard to the said republic.'[4]

These declarations, however, were to remain tolerably ineffectual for many years. The Czechoslovaks' attempts at assimilation were only partially successful, but administrative centralization had a greater effect. Benes even succeeded in gaining the support of a section of the German representatives in parliament for a considerable time and in inducing certain outstanding men from the German Agrarian, Christian Socialist and Social Democrat parties to join the government.

When Hitler and National Socialism came to power in Germany it had the effect, from 1933 onwards, of progressively changing the three million Germans into a homogeneous bloc, with a firm organization and structure, whereas before they had been unorganized, and their attachment to the German 'motherland' had scarcely shown itself in anything more than a sentimental manner.

On May 19, 1936, at the general election, the Sudeten German

Party of SdP, a body which was not officially a branch of the Nazi party but which openly proclaimed its loyalty to Hitler and its adherence to the principles of National Socialism, won virtually the whole of the German vote and went into the Prague parliament with a strength of forty-four members.

Konrad Henlein

It is worth looking closely at the activities of the SdP, for they were to play a decisive part in the development of the Sudeten crisis.

There was already a Czechoslovak Nazi party before 1933; this was the DNSAP, and it had been officially disbanded a little after Hitler became chancellor. For a short period it had been turned into the *Sudetendeutsche Heimatfront*, the Sudeten German Patriotic Front, and then it had given birth to the SdP.

Its leader, Konrad Henlein, was a bank clerk; he was often referred to as a gymnastics instructor, simply because he had learnt from the example of the Sokols and had begun recruiting under the cover of a gymnastic society.

The Führer of the Sudeten Germans scarcely ever left the district of Carlsbad, Marienbad, Asch, and Eger, where he applied Hitler's methods on the spot. His armed bands exercised what amounted to a parallel authority, compelling by terror the use of German alone, forcing the shopkeepers to display photographs of Hitler and Henlein prominently, smashing the windows of those who were unwilling, marking the houses of suspects . . .

Carrying on his inquiry, Roman Fajans went to Carlsbad to watch one of those huge demonstrations which were organized by the Nazis and to which the whole population was 'invited' from time to time.

'This former gymnastics instructor, a fairly big, fair man with spectacles, hardly differed in outward appearance from the thousands of other Sudeten Germans,' states Fajans. 'His way of speaking had nothing extraordinary about it. He perpetually repeated the same boring and senseless demagogic slogans, directly against all truth and irritating to any objective observer. And yet the ecstatic crowd roared madly, carried away by a wave of enthusiasm. But what sent the crowd into this state must have been a mysticism quite unlike that which Henlein was serving out to it. The operative mysticism came from far away, from beyond the frontiers; and it was always the other, the "great"

31

man that these hysterical thousands were seeing instead of this humble gymnastics instructor.'[5]

A few days later Fajans went from Carlsbad to Eger, for he wanted to see what Konrad Henlein was like off the platform. The Führer of the Sudeten Germans gave the reporter from the *Kurjer Warszawski* an appointment at the 'Brown House', a Nazi centre modelled on all those in Germany – and in Austria too, even at this date.

'Henlein,' says Fajans, 'was the incarnation of hypocrisy . . . He acted the part of an angel of peace. He assured me that the Sudeten Germans had not the least wish to break away from the Czechoslovak Republic . . . ' But Henlein had a very curious notion of his 'work' for Czechoslovakia: in particular he insisted upon the setting up of a positive German 'state' within the Czechoslovak state. His ambition was the creation and legalization of a completely autonomous German community, not territorial but racial. This amounted to saying that any Czechoslovak citizen whom the Sudeten Nazi leaders should designate as being of 'German blood' should belong to this community. This community would have special rights and privileges. It would be allowed to maintain all kinds of direct contacts with the Reich. It was under these conditions that Henlein declared himself ready to 'collaborate loyally' with the Czechoslovak Republic. He also talked a great deal about his unbounded liberalism. According to him the members of his party were very good and ardent Catholics. They were not even anti-Semitic.

> 'He devoted a large part of his statement to the persecutions which, according to him, "the poor Sudeten Germans" had to suffer from the Czechs. "They are throttling our industry, because it is not Czech," he assured me. "They are killing it by taxation and administrative measures. For example, Germans are not allowed to set up certain industries in various parts of the country. No German factory may export more than a strictly limited quota of its products to foreign countries. We do not have enough schools, they are suppressing even some of those that do exist. Czech gaols are filled with unjustly imprisoned Germans." '[6]

In fact, as Fajans was himself able to establish during his stay in Czechoslovakia, the number of Germans imprisoned on political grounds throughout the whole of the Sudeten region scarcely amounted to a few dozen. And in spite of the persecution that

Henlein complained of, both Sudeten industry and commerce remained unusually flourishing.

While Henlein stayed on the spot and watched over the maintenance of his fellow-countrymen's morale, Dr Sebekowski, the head of the SdP's propaganda bureau and the real force behind the movement (as well as its thinker), had his headquarters in Prague itself, in a splendid building called the *Deutsches Haus*. He too was very anxious to back up the fiction of a SdP that was wholly independent of Germany and that wished to remain strictly within the bounds of Czechoslovak legality.

The truth of the matter was that since 1936 the Sudeten German Party had been drawing from the special funds of the *Volksdeutsche Mittelstelle*, an organization that was directly dependent on the Wilhelmstrasse. Contact with Eisenlohr, the German minister to Prague, was maintained by Karl-Hermann Frank, a German member of the Czechoslovak parliament and to some degree the parliamentary leader of the party: and it was Frank, also, who drew the monthly subsidy of 15,000 RM – a sum, it must be added, whose inadequacy was very soon pointed out by Henlein.*

Nevertheless, the Germans, as they always did where agents abroad were concerned, supervised the activities of the SdP and its leader very closely indeed. To be sure, the transmitter of the German secret service in Czechoslovakia, directly attached to the political section of the SD†, sent on the 'valuable information' that Henlein gathered for it – indeed there were times when it was necessary to set up special direct telephone lines to Berlin from the Czechoslovak-German frontier to deal with the abundance of material! But at the same time, as Walter Schellenberg, the head of the Nazi counter-espionage, has revealed, 'Heydrich had charged a special branch with the task of keeping a close watch on the Sudeten German Party and on Henlein.'[7]

The diplomatic situation of Czechoslovakia

With the Nazi canker thus eating into her, not only on her German borders but even in her capital and her parliament, could Czecho-

---

* The SdP drew 12,000 RM a month, paid in Prague through the German legation, and 3,000 RM received in Berlin by the 'Bürger Office', which acted as the party's agent. By a decision taken at the Wilhelmstrasse on August 23, 1938, the Bürger Office's subsidy was raised to 5,500 RM.

† SD, the initials of the *Sicherheitsdienst* (security service).

slovakia at least reckon upon outside support at the moment when the magnetism of Hitler's Reich for the Sudeten Germans should become really threatening?

It is in fact possible to sum up Czechoslovakia's diplomatic position in a single phrase – and to emphasize its uncomfortable nature – by observing that although she had powerful allies they were a great way from her frontiers, whereas her potential enemies, on the other hand, were all her nearest neighbours.*

In a somewhat complex manner Czechoslovakia formed an integral part of the general system which had been set up by the democratic nations after the Great War and which very gravely bore the name of 'collective security'. Czechoslovakia had joined the League of Nations.† On January 25, 1924, she had signed a treaty of friendship and alliance with France. And as a supplement to the Locarno Pact, the two countries, on October 16, 1925, had also signed a second treaty of mutual assistance in the event of either of them suffering from a violation of the engagements that had been concluded that day with Germany. This second treaty specifically stated that if such a violation should be accompanied by the unprovoked use of force, aid and assistance should be immediate.‡

Czechoslovakia had also signed a mutual assistance pact with the USSR on May 16, 1935. This very special kind of pact reproduced the main clauses of the Franco-Soviet pact that had been signed a fortnight earlier; but added to it there was this suspensive condition: 'At the same time the two governments recognize that the engage-

---

* See map 1, page 16.

† Benes had even been the president of the 'sanctions assembly' in 1935, at the time of Italy's aggression against Abyssinia. This explains Mussolini's pertinacious hatred of Czechoslovakia.

‡ Professor Joseph Barthélémy, who was, it is true, a specialist in constitutional and not international law, maintained (*Le Temps*, April 12, 1938) that these two treaties were no longer in force; this provoked a vigorous reply from André Tardieu. 'Joseph Barthélémy bursts out, "All this amounts to nothing. For it is all based on things that are dead. The pact is dead! Locarno is dead! Everything that goes with them is dead!" Joseph, you are wrong. For it to be true, France would have had to denounce Locarno: now as Mr Butler, the Under-Secretary of State at the Foreign Office, said the other day, "Locarno is still in force." ... Because Germany has violated the Treaty of Versailles a score of times, are we going to proclaim that Treaty dead? In any case, to return to central Europe, it is not for the France of 1938, the heir of the France of 1914, to profess, with regard to treaties she has signed, the theories of Herr von Bethmann-Hollweg on "scraps of paper".'

It is worth noting that for his part, in recalling Joseph Barthélémy's 'legal proof', Georges Bonnet, in *De Washington au Quai d'Orsay*, says, 'I did not share this opinion.'

ments of mutual assistance shall have effect only in so far as help shall be furnished by France, to the party that is the victim of an aggression, when the conditions anticipated by this pact obtain.'

As well as these, President Benes had signed the agreements with Yugoslavia and Rumania that were known as the Little Entente, but their prime intent was, in effect, to cut short any nascent desire to restore the Habsburgs.*

So much for the friends. As for the others, they surrounded Czechoslovakia, hemmed her in and harassed her with territorial claims based on the irredentism of the ethnic minorities: Beck's Poland claimed Teschen, Horthy's Hungary wanted a far-reaching rectification of the eastern frontiers, and lastly Germany . . .

And yet no. At the beginning of 1938 Germany was, at least in appearance, still one of Czechoslovakia's best-behaved neighbours. It was not by mere chance that Henlein and Sebekowski feigned to act on their own initiative alone, to receive neither subsidies nor directions from the Third Reich, and to keep their opposition within the bounds of legality and loyalty.

Germany set forth no precise claim with regard to Czechoslovakia, and Benes could display a certain degree of optimism. After all, not so long before Germany had been making advances to him!

In 1936 two secret envoys, Count Trauttmansdorf and Dr Haushofer junior, had been sent to Prague by Hitler. They had offered Benes a German guarantee to respect Czechoslovakia's territorial integrity on condition that Czechoslovakia should renounce intervention in the event of a Franco-German war. And when Benes recalled the obligation that arose from the Franco-Czechoslovak treaties, the Germans replied that what the Führer was above all *not* asking for was the denunciation of these treaties – he was simply suggesting to Benes that when the time came he should refrain from applying them.

In the autumn of 1937 there was a fresh approach, carried out this time by a highly-placed German military figure; its object was to let the President of the Czechoslovak Republic know that 'if he wanted to take advantage of the Führer's offer he had better be

---

* This, it must be added, was a ruling consideration with Benes. In 1938 Daladier recalled having met Benes in 1933 and hearing him say, 'Rather the Anschluss than the Habsburgs!'

35

quick, because events would shortly be taking place in Russia rendering any help he could give to Germany insignificant.'*

In fact Hitler was carrying on according to his usual method, always doing his utmost to deal with one problem as far as possible before starting on another. Now at the beginning of 1938 Austria had to be settled first.

To be sure, President Benes was aware of this. But for all that he could not prevent himself showing a certain degree of optimism. When Roman Fajans asked him whether he did not think that the Reich would end by using force, the President of the Czechoslovak Republic answered, 'There cannot be a war between Germany and Czechoslovakia. Such a war would be impossible. We should at once have a general outburst if it were to happen. It is quite certain that the world would not abandon us in the event of a German attack. It would be too monstrous, too ridiculous and too dangerous for the world itself.'[8]

'It was just as if I were hearing Chancellor Schuschnigg speaking,' comments Fajans gloomily. But then, after a moment of silence, Benes went on, 'If I am mistaken, however, and if the unbelievable were to happen and we were left alone, face to face with Germany, the outlook would be appalling, not only for Czechoslovakia but for the whole of Europe. A war breaking out would never remain a localized struggle between Germany and Czechoslovakia; but it would always, and in every case, be a European, if not a world-wide, war. To be sure, it might not burst out on all fronts at once. There would no doubt be a kind of short truce . . . But that would not in any way change the essence of the matter. And let no one blame us in that case if the guns of Skoda fire on Paris, just as they did in 1914–1918.'[9]

---

* It was to Churchill that Benes gave this account, when he went to see him at Marrakech in 1944. (W. Churchill, *The Second World War*, vol 1, *The Gathering Storm*.) The 'happenings' that were presently going to take place in Russia were none other than the purge of 1937, which, as everyone knows, chiefly affected the high command of the Red Army. When he was writing his memoirs Churchill could still say that this ruthless purge was 'perhaps not needless'. Today it is known how the whole business was fabricated by the German intelligence service. But it is true, as Churchill points out, that Benes, unaware that the Germans were making use of him, was then able in all good faith to warn his ally Stalin and tell him of Tukhachevsky's alleged 'contacts' with Germany. And Churchill also observes that from then onwards Stalin felt personally indebted to President Benes.

Thirty-two divisions . . . and the guns of Skoda

However much Benes might believe that this war was impossible, or at the utmost suppose that it would very quickly turn into a world-wide struggle, he was still compelled to make ready for it. And to make ready for it with all the more care in that a mere glance at the map of Europe was enough to show both the remoteness of those who should in certain contingencies be Czechoslovakia's allies and the proximity of her potential enemies.

In the event of war, even if the pacts came into operation, even if 'collective security' fulfilled all the hopes of the statesmen of the democratic countries, even if France opened a front to the west of Germany, and even if Russia succeeded in forcing the Poles or persuading the Rumanians to let the Red Army pass, a considerable period would necessarily remain, and during this time Czechoslovakia would have to rely primarily upon herself.

Still, this outlook was not of a kind to have a very serious effect upon Benes's optimism, for from a purely military point of view his country's potentialities for defence were by no means trifling, and in the last few years they had made striking and rapid progress.

At this time General Faucher had been at the head of the French military mission – a mission to which he had belonged for more than twenty years – in Czechoslovakia for a considerable while and he had been one of the chief figures in the building up of this military power. Better than anyone else, and more objectively than a Czechoslovak, he could bear witness to the work that had been done.[10]

'At an earlier period,' he says, 'there were twelve divisions in Czechoslovakia, grouped in higher commands by province . . . Seven army corps were formed, two in Bohemia, two in Moravia, three in Slovakia. The number of divisions was raised from twelve to seventeen but the divisions from then on had three infantry regiments, six in Bohemia, four in Moravia, seven in Slovakia. The high proportion kept for Slovakia . . . means that the Czechoslovaks rightly looked upon Slovakia as the inner stronghold of the country's defence, but without therefore wishing to give up Bohemia or Moravia a priori, in spite of their somewhat exposed geographical position.'

General Faucher also emphasizes the attempt at modernization that had been undertaken.

37

'The formation of four regiments of infantry for holding fortified positions, a new creation corresponding to the fortifications which will be referred to later.

'The formation of four tank regiments. Up until then tanks had only existed as patterns . . .

'The formation of four "fast-moving" divisions, which were to replace the three old-fashioned cavalry brigades. . . .

'This was still not all that could be desired, but we were coming nearer to a more modern concept.

'Air force. The number of regiments was raised from four to six.

'Equipment. The bringing into service of new types of ordnance – a new field-gun, a new light and very satisfactory light machine-gun (so satisfactory indeed that it was adopted by the British), and above all a very considerable increase in war-reserves . . .

'The mobilization of industry had been prepared long before, but now preparations were carried much farther. Most of all, decentralization was pushed on as far as possible, without waiting . . .

'The most important war industry in Czechoslovakia was that of the Skoda works at Pilsen, little more than thirty miles from the frontier. They could not stay there. Branches of Skoda had therefore been set up, some of which had underground factories, in the north of Slovakia.'

The fortifications, which were undertaken in 1935, were an important factor in Czechoslovakia's military potentialities.

'On the northern frontier of Moravia and the north-east of Bohemia,' continues General Faucher, 'important works, comparable to those of our Maginot line, were set up. In other places there were lines of casemates to block the main routes into the country . . .

'I have sometimes heard it said that it was the French who created the Czechoslovak fortifications. This is not quite the case. We must not exaggerate. We did help the Czechoslovaks as much as we could: there was no sort of doubt that it was quite against our interest to let them flounder and there was no sort of doubt that we should let them take advantage of our experinece.

'A Czechoslovak mission was sent to France. At the ministry of war they were shown how France had worked out her fortifications and the underlying principles of the works; and they were taken to see the most interesting parts of our organization. For questions of technical detail, two French officers, a major and a captain, were put at the disposal of the Czechoslovak ministry of defence. Theirs was a purely technical role.'

Lastly, the setting up of a solid holding-force reflected the transition of the Czech nation and armed forces to a footing of war.

'There were seventeen divisions in time of peace, and in principle these were doubled on mobilization, but one or two were wanting, so that in fact there were thirty-two. To these must be added the troops in the fortifications and the various army formations. This force was based upon natural defences and upon fortifications, most of which were already usable.

'The high command was young, but it had not been wasting its time since 1919 ...

'The men were very well trained. Of course, I may have looked upon them with too favourable an eye; indeed, I probably did, for one cannot live and work with an army for twenty years without coming to feel a kindness for it. I therefore discount my views to some extent; but I was not alone in forming a favourable judgment of the Czechoslovak army. Great French leaders came to visit it on several occasions – there was Pétain in 1929, Marshal Franchet d'Espérey in 1930, General Gamelin in 1934 and General Schweisguth, the assistant chief of staff, in 1936.'

As for the morale of the people and the army, in 1938 it was higher than it had ever been before.

'From 1933 onwards,' General Faucher goes on, 'the signs of depression that had earlier been apparent in Czechoslovak public opinion quickly disappeared. Not only were the very heavy financial and other burdens set on the people accepted without complaint, but they were accepted with relief, and the people even called for them. I myself have gathered much evidence, not only in military circles and from civilians in Prague, but also in the provinces. The manoeuvres were a favourable opportunity for getting into touch with the people.'

CHAPTER THREE

The vice tightens

*The Daladier-Bonnet team · Operation Green · The Franco-British con-
versations of April 28 and 29 · A diplomatic fortnight*

In Paris Blum's government, which was formed on March 13, was
only to last for a brief interlude.

The factors of an economic and financial nature which had
already compelled the socialist leader to resign once still applied,
just as there was still a majority in the Senate that was hostile to the
Front Populaire. To this, after the Anschluss, there was to be added
the beginning of a split in the left wing, starting with the Socialist
left, over the problems of international policy. A split that only grew
the wider as the Czechoslovak crisis developed.

Yet in this area the attack was carried out primarily by the right
and extreme right wing opposition, whose leader in parliament was
undoubtedly Pierre-Etienne Flandin.

The former prime minister, taking up the arguments urged by
Joseph Barthélémy in his article in *Le Temps*, unvaryingly maintained
that the most recent Franco-Czechoslovak treaty, a consequence of
the Locarno Pact – and signed, furthermore, on the same day –
had become null and void since the treaty of Locarno had ceased to
exist.

But Czechoslovakia was not yet a matter of such burning concern
that it was possible to arouse a great body of public opinion about it.
The enemies of Léon Blum and the Front Populaire therefore tried
to embarrass the government in another direction: they launched a
violent attack based upon an untrue report which was being deliberately spread abroad by the *cagoulard** Loustaunau-Lacau (who
only a little while before had belonged to Pétain's departmental
staff) – a report which led people to believe that at a meeting of the

---

* A member of an extreme right-wing organization: they wore hoods – *cagoules*.

defence committee the head of the government and his foreign secretary had advocated the sending of two divisions into Spain.

Spain had certainly been mentioned at the meeting, but it had been mentioned in relation to the new situation that now faced Czechoslovakia as a result of the Anschluss. The presence of quite considerable numbers of German and Italian troops on Spanish territory did indeed justify Blum's double question – in the first place, how great a threat would these Axis forces amount to on the French Pyrenean frontier in the event of war; and in the second, how vulnerable were they, in case the French were to think it preferable to undertake nothing in the east until they had made sure of their security in the south.

As for the two divisions, it had been decided, at General Gamelin's request, to move them down to cover the Pyrenean frontier as a prudential measure and because of the rapid advance of the united troops of Hitler and Mussolini. Furthermore, the vote in the Senate that refused Léon Blum the powers he was asking for to enable him to carry out a financial policy that included the regulation of foreign exchange brought about a fresh ministerial crisis on April 9, and put an end to the controversy. And Paul-Boncour, who had called for the prosecution of Loustaunau-Lacau, presently observed, without surprise, that the case had been dropped.

The Daladier-Bonnet team

It is true that any slight inclination to entrust power once more to a government that genuinely reflected the majority which the elections of May 3, 1936, had produced, was done away with on April 10 by the setting up of Daladier's government.

The Front Populaire had had its day. And by a curious paradox the man whose coming to power meant that this death-certificate could be drawn up had never ceased to be directly and personally involved in the exalting adventure of the Front Populaire during these last months. He had been one of those who originated the anti-fascist union immediately after February 6, 1934, and he had then helped in winning the elections of May 1936 and had taken office in Blum's and Chautemps' governments. He was one of those who marched in the front rank in all the great popular demonstrations – from the Bastille to the Place de la Nation – greeted by crowds giving the clenched-fist salute and chanting alternate verses of the Marseillaise and the Internationale – one of those who had so often been hailed by the working classes.

In point of fact, although the Front Populaire majority had fallen to pieces, it was very difficult to abide by the old concepts of left and right in regard to the essential problem – peace at any price or the deliberate acceptance of a certain risk of war.

Was the right wing, in its sympathy for the 'strong régimes' of Hitler and Mussolini, prepared to make every concession? Perhaps so; but Paul Faure, the secretary-general of the SFIO, was advocating a pacifism that in fact resulted in the same end. And together with him there were many Socialists; the trade-unionists of the Belin school; the school-teachers, who kept Delmas at the head of their union; the intellectuals of the committee of vigilance; the Socialist students . . .

And yet did not the greater part of the left wing still favour resistance, firmness, respect for international obligations, if only out of anti-fascism? Perhaps it did; but who could claim that Paul Reynaud, Georges Mandel or André Tardieu were to be described as left-wing, to say nothing of Henry de Kérillis?

In fact the line of cleavage that was coming into existence in France was based upon other criteria. And for his part Daladier found himself obliged to make a choice of the very first importance when, in setting up his government, he had to pick a foreign minister.

On Sunday, April 10, Daladier invited Paul-Boncour, the foreign minister in the outgoing cabinet, to meet him in the red and gold drawing-room of the ministry of war in the rue Saint-Dominique. Paul-Boncour gave the new prime minister the main outlines of the policy that he would pursue if he were to stay at the Quai d'Orsay.

> 'If, after Austria, we let Czechoslovakia fall, it will be Poland's turn tomorrow. Can we have that? If not, do you not think that we should be in a weaker position to defend Poland, once there is no Czechoslovakia any more, nor the Czechoslovak army, nor the Bohemian plateau, that military position which is so strongly fortified today and where the fate of Europe has already been at stake three times?'[1]

Paul-Boncour went on urging his cause, recalling the Russian alliance, the mistaken notions about the Maginot line, the necessity for putting up with the burdens of a series of alliances once they were signed, as well as accepting the advantages.

A few hours later Daladier telephoned Paul-Boncour to let him know his decision. 'I have been thinking. The policy that you outlined to me is a very fine policy, thoroughly worthy of France: I do not think that we are in a position to undertake it. I am going to have Georges Bonnet.'

'Since you choose to follow the other policy,' replied Paul-Boncour, 'you could not make a better choice.'[2]

It did indeed appear to have been the choosing of a policy. And yet P.-E. Flandin, obsessed by his longing for a Franco-Italian rapprochement, was to blame Daladier for the fact of evading this very choice. 'There was an underlying disagreement between the Socialists and the Radical-Socialists,' he writes, 'and it showed itself upon all occasions. M Georges Bonnet therefore felt himself embarrassed by the open anti-fascism of M Léon Blum and his friends. A choice ought to have been made between the interests of France, which in foreign policy required a rapprochement with Italy even at the cost of a change of majority in home policy, on the one hand, and on the other, the party-interest that required the Front Populaire to remain in power. Throughout the entire duration of his government M Daladier was unable to bring himself to make this choice.'[3]

Although the more subtle Debu-Bridel, a journalist and Tardieu's confidential friend, also deplores (though for other reasons!) Daladier's shrinking from the choice, he does so in a more delicately shaded manner, and one furthermore which lets it be understood that a 'certain choice' was nevertheless made, if not proclaimed.

'The choice of G. Bonnet, however, showed a total change in our foreign policy, and this was borne out by the telephone call to Paul-Boncour.

'What is serious is that this change was never positively stated. Far from it, for in his ministerial declaration Daladier once more affirmed that France would stand by all her international engagements and would fulfil her obligations. Georges Bonnet did not express himself in any other fashion, and when the Czechoslovak government grew uneasy he reassured them. President Benes could in all good faith believe that J. Paul-Boncour's declaration had lost nothing of its worth.

'France was only playing the part of steadfastness. She was deceiving Czechoslovakia and bluffing England. Germany alone, thanks to

43

G. Bonnet's confidences to F. de Brinon and Claude Jeantet, was aware of our sudden change of mind.

'But no doubt – and this is the only explanation – Daladier was acting the part to himself, as he was acting it to Benes and Mandel and the Communists.

'What a choice to have to make! He had not yet had the intellectual courage to make a decision. He put off any kind of solution.'[4]

At all events, no one will deny that in entrusting Georges Bonnet with Paul-Boncour's post Daladier had certainly chosen a man whose personal qualities would arouse violent reactions; and that, furthermore, as much in liberal right-wing circles in France and abroad as among the people who were called 'left-wingers'.

General Gamelin: 'M Georges Bonnet became foreign minister. In my opinion this last appointment was exceedingly unfortunate, for he never stopped playing an equivocal part . . . He was a very intelligent man, but he had no deep convictions, and it might even be said no morals. In everything he saw his own immediate personal interest alone, and he had a natural taste for intrigue. On several occasions I was able to establish that one could never trust what he said. It must be added that he had a considerable influence, if not authority, in political circles. This certainly had a cramping effect upon Daladier, who was obliged to reckon with him. In the great questions that were to confront us, particularly on the moral plane, M Georges Bonnet's heart (if that is an expression which can be used in reference to him) was fundamentally with Laval. In Daladier's ministry, which did in fact include several men of real merit, he was an evil leaven.'[5]

Jean Zay, the minister of education: 'The intention of abandoning Czechoslovakia and Poland if they were attacked, that is to say, of repudiating the solemn engagements undertaken by all our governments since 1920, and the determination to leave Germany completely free to do as she wished in the east and in central Europe dated from long before the crises of September. It was an already-established and thoroughly-considered basic attitude, and its chief exponent inside Daladier's ministry was the foreign minister himself, M Georges Bonnet. Perhaps he would not be blamed for it if he had announced it openly. The cabinet would have made its choice. But he pursued this scheme in a secret

44

manner, at the same time making a display of ostensible adherence to the official line of conduct of the government of which he was a member.'[6]

Winston Churchill: 'Many of us had the sensation that Bonnet represented the quintessence of defeatism, and that all his clever verbal manoeuvres had the aim of "peace at any price".'[7]

Eduard Benes: 'Bonnet's reputation was that of a gambler and an unblushing and shameless grafter for whom all roads were good so long as they led to the place he wished to reach. As a minister he sent instructions by telegram or letter that were in line with the government's official declarations. At the same time he gave diametrically opposite orders by word of mouth. He was a priori against any diplomatic or military resistance to Hitler's expansionism. What he would have preferred to anything was an armed struggle between the Nazis and the Bolsheviks.'[8]

What were the reasons that had induced Daladier, apart from purely political considerations, to pick Georges Bonnet rather than some other member of parliament of the same group?

'I chose M Georges Bonnet as foreign minister,' said Daladier, 'because in 1932 he had presided over the Stresa conference on the economic reconstruction of central Europe and because when he had been appointed ambassador to Washington by Léon Blum's government he had been able to gain the undoubted esteem of President Roosevelt, Sumner Welles, the assistant Secretary of State, and the political circles, as well as a fortunate influence over them.

'In his second government Léon Blum invited him to be ambassador a second time. The choice of M Bonnet was very favourably commented upon in the foreign papers, particularly those of America and England and Soviet Russia too.'[9]

If that is indeed what Daladier thought of his foreign minister, what was Bonnet's opinion of his political chief?

A few days after his arrival at the Quai d'Orsay Georges Bonnet asked Pierre Lazareff, the editor of *Paris-Soir*, to luncheon at Carton's, in the Place de la Madeleine. Lazareff noted down the gist of his conversation[10] with the new foreign minister, particularly what Bonnet said to him about Daladier.

'A strange man, Daladier; difficult to know. If he is popular with the army it is because he has always backed up the general staff, letting them do what they like and never going against their plans. If he is accepted by the Socialists and the right wing it is because both the one set and the other are out of power by reason of the parliamentary majority, and both suppose that they can govern through him, for he is a hesitant man and susceptible to influence. Besides, Daladier is clever enough to make both hope that he will indeed govern with them. Furthermore, Daladier has the appearance of a strong man. He will be very good at giving the country (forgetful of the bad days) the impression that France herself is strong. As we are weak, what I for my part fear most is that although this country may be taken in, Hitler will not . . .'

As for his policy, Georges Bonnet defined it for his companion; and it cannot be said that he was not frank. 'Don't let us go in for heroism; we are not up to it . . . The English will not follow us . . . As foreign minister I am determined to play my part fully, and it consists of finding a solution before the minister of war has to take one. France can no longer allow herself a blood-letting like that of 1914. Our population figures are going down every day. And finally the Front Populaire has reduced the country to such a state that it must get ready for a sensible convalescence – a rash movement might be fatal.'

Where Czechoslovakia was concerned, therefore, Georges Bonnet showed himself reticent to say the least. He chose to remember only those parts of Chamberlain's declarations that allowed reserves on Great Britain's part to be detected, and he finished by saying, 'When you state that you are not sure that you will fight, but that "perhaps for all that" you may fight, believe me, a man like Hitler understands that he is simply being asked not to act in such a way that we shall be forced to fight him. Moreover, I think this English policy both intelligent and wise.'

On April 12 Edouard Daladier presented his government (in which the Socialists did not take part) to the Chamber of Deputies. It was almost unanimously approved – 576 votes to 5. No government in the whole history of the Third Republic had ever had so many. During the night he was voted full powers in financial matters by 574 to 8. And two days later the Senate carried the same two votes, this time unanimously.

The vice tightens

Operation Green

Whether it was good or bad, the Daladier-Bonnet team therefore had behind it an amount of parliamentary support that at least in theory assured it of a remarkable degree of international attention.

It was going to need it, for even before Hitler had 'digested' Austria he was already deeply concerned with passing on to the next chapter and with making his arrangements for the beleaguering of Czechoslovakia – arrangements that were at the same time to cause her disintegration.

The Führer had already said to General Franz Halder on March 12 as they sat in the car that was bringing him back in triumph as a conqueror to his native land, 'This is something that will thoroughly embarrass the Czechs.'

The first of the decisions that Hitler took to 'embarrass' the Czechs even more was to tighten the links that attached Henlein to Germany, even if this did mean making them less secret.

The decision, moreover, accorded with the 'little cock's'* most fervent wishes. On March 17 Henlein begged Ribbentrop to arrange 'a personal conversation in the very near future with the Führer' for him.

On March 28 his hopes were fulfilled: Hitler saw Henlein at the Chancellery for three hours, Ribbentrop† and Rudolf Hess being there too. The next day, March 29, there was a meeting to see how Hitler's basic decisions should be carried into effect. On the German side (if such a distinction can really be made) there appeared Ribbentrop, minister of the Reich, Mackensen, the secretary of state who was to be appointed ambassador to Rome a few weeks later, Weizsäcker, the under-secretary at the Wilhelmstrasse and Mackensen's successor-designate, Eisenlohr, the minister plenipotentiary at Prague, Stiebe, a minister, Tvardovsky, Altenburg and Kordt, counsellors at the ministry of foreign affairs. The SS Obergruppenführer Lorenz of the Volksdeutsche Mittelstelle and Professor Haushofer, who had initiated Hitler into the mysteries of geopolitics, were also there.

The Sudeten Germans, the delegates of the SdP, were, apart from Henlein, Karl-Hermann Frank, Dr Kunzel and Dr Kreisel.

* Henlein means little cock in German; and as long as the Prague government had it in its power to forbid the swastika effectually Henlein's followers used the cock as their badge.

† Joachim von Ribbentrop succeeded Baron von Neurath at the head of the German foreign ministry on February 4, 1938.

The report drawn up at the end of the meeting stressed the political watchwords that had been given to the SdP. The party was to 'see that Sudeten Germans did not join the government, and at the same time gradually to increase the number of claims submitted, setting them out with a continually greater exactness. During negotiations it must be made abundantly plain that the only body negotiating with the Czech government is the SdP and not the government of the Reich.'

Furthermore, 'With a view to future collaboration, Konrad Henlein has been required to keep in the closest possible contact with the minister of the Reich and the head of the Volksdeutsche Mittelstelle, as well as with the German minister in Prague, who represents the foreign minister of the Reich in that city. The task of the German minister in Prague will consist of supporting the claims of the Sudeten German party semi-officially, and above all, during private conversations with Czech statesmen, of showing that these claims are reasonable, yet without at any time exercising the slightest influence upon the scope of the party's requirements.'

Now that Hitler had ensured that he should be served according to his wishes inside Czechoslovakia, he was able to turn his personal attention to the military side of the question. Yet he did so only in the first days of April, for the consequences of the Anschluss, especially the plebiscite that had to be organized in Austria, still occupied him for some while. But on April 21 he summoned General Keitel, telling him to bring the file on Operation Green with him.

This code-name referred to a plan that Hitler and his generals had already discussed several times. Blomberg* had begun to work out Operation Green as early as June 24 of the year before: it was nothing less than a plan for the invasion of Czechoslovakia. On November 5, 1937, Hitler had let it be understood that the general staff might produce a complete version of Operation Green in 1938.

Now this was an accomplished fact. And Operation Green was perpetually improved, recast and made more exact as the abundant information came in from all of the general staff branches at the daily urging of Major Rudolf Schmundt, the head of the Führer's military department.

This conversation between Hitler and Keitel on April 21 was only a first exchange of opinions on Operation Green. But even at this

* Marshal von Blomberg had been replaced at the war ministry by Marshal Keitel on February 4, 1938.

stage the Führer gave Keitel to understand that he inclined towards one of the proposed versions, and this was Solution 3; perhaps he preferred it because it touched his nostalgia as a former soldier, reminding him of the outbreak of the first world war – it was simply a question of having an incident to justify a lightning-stroke.

What did Keitel think of the murder of Eisenlohr, the German minister? Would that not be a splendid *casus belli*?

Keitel was far too orthodox (or too wanting in imagination) to accompany Hitler into these realms. He even wondered whether the Führer were speaking seriously.

It is Göring once again who provides a more reassuring account of the business. According to him[11] there was not the least question of deliberately slaughtering the unfortunate Eisenlohr (whose zeal, by the way, might perhaps have diminished if he had known that his assassination was under discussion); they were merely looking into the not improbable case of the murder of the German minister by the Czechoslovaks in the event of a demonstration in front of the legation, for example.

This meeting devoted to Operation Green had another consequence. It brought a very brisk reaction from General Beck, the chief of the general staff of the army, whom Hitler had kept out of it: he was told by Keitel, and in a high state of wrath he drew up a memorandum in which he set himself firmly against the plan for invading Czechoslovakia, objecting both to its basic principles and to its technical military aspects.

The Franco-British conversations of April 28 and 29

Faced with the increasing tension caused by the recrudescence of Henlein's activities, the French and English, during the last days of April, saw that it was urgently necessary to harmonize their policies.

Daladier and Bonnet, accepting Chamberlain's invitation, flew from Le Bourget on April 27 and landed after a flight of fifty-five minutes at Croydon, where they were welcomed by Lord Halifax and Charles Corbin, the French ambassador.

As soon as this voyage had been decided upon, Daladier had sent General Gamelin, the chief of the general staff, a hand-written note. 'Let me know exactly what military action France can initiate against Germany to help Czechoslovakia, it being understood that mobilization is only the first move.'[12]

When he reached London the premier had Gamelin's answer in his brief-case.

Note on possible action by France in favour of Czechoslovakia.

I There is no military agreement whatever as a complement to the assistance pact, at the adoption of which the military authorities did not take part.

II France can take steps first on her own territory which at the same time constitute a safety-measure and a threat and which progress from giving the alert to setting up a state of security, thence to the taking up of covering positions and lastly complete mobilization.

III Upon the government's decision the French land and air forces can then carry out offensive operations in the conditions provided for in our operational plans.

It is certain that the power of our offensive action will depend on whether our forces are or are not obliged by Italy's attitude to remain in the Alps and in North Africa.

IV The effectiveness of our help to Czechoslovakia will also depend on the possible assistance that may be given her by the other two powers of the Little Entente (Rumania and Yugoslavia), the USSR, Poland and the British Empire. But these are questions which arise primarily on the diplomatic level.' Gamelin.[13]

This, then, was the military information that Daladier had at his disposal when, after an evening spent 'at home' in the embassy, the French ministers arrived at 10 Downing Street the next morning.

The whole of the first day was devoted to the relations of the British and the French with Italy and Spain.

Only one firm point emerged: there was agreement on the principle of military co-operation as far as the air forces and the navies were concerned.

In the evening the royal family invited Daladier and Bonnet to Windsor Castle. To emphasize the strength of the *entente cordiale* this invitation was not confined to dinner: the Queen had rooms made ready for her guests, who were thus able to enjoy the royal hospitality until the end of breakfast the next day.

After dinner a Scottish orchestra came and played traditional French tunes while Daladier and Bonnet, guided by the King and Queen, walked through the drawing-rooms and galleries to admire the royal collections.

It seems that Daladier's chief recollection of that evening (apart from 'the graceful curtsies of the young princesses Elizabeth and Margaret') was the Queen's particularly friendly greeting on his arrival, 'How brave you are, M Daladier'. Yet it must be said that although the premier was very pleased with the kindness, he appears to have spent a great while wondering whether it had a hidden meaning.

For his part, the practical (or the chilly) Georges Bonnet was delighted at the sight of huge logs blazing in the Gothic fireplace when he went to his bedroom.

On the next day, April 29, the talks at last reached the heart of the matter. The theme for discussion was the Czechoslovak affair. Had some of those French politicians who blamed Daladier and even more Bonnet for their lukewarmness in supporting Czechoslovakia been at these talks they would have been filled with pleasure (or perhaps with confusion), for Bonnet and Daladier vied with one another in pleading Benes' cause. But these politicians would also have been rigid with anxiety, for the Englishmen's attitude left very little hope that there would be any action that might effectively counter Hitler's plans for attack.

Indeed, despite the warmth of the official welcome, the British ministers displayed all the more reserve in that fundamentally they shared the views of their adviser, Sir William Strang of the Foreign Office, who had a tolerably poor opinion of the representative character and of the efficacy of the new French government – to say nothing of the sincerity of its spokesmen.

'Unlike the British Government, the French Government were deeply divided,' writes Strang, 'with Georges Mandel and his friends all for resistance and Georges Bonnet and his like all for surrender, and with Edouard Daladier . . . torn between the two, leaning towards a robust policy, but lacking the resolution to hold to it. The result was that, while the declared policy of France was to stand by her obligation, a very different impression was given by what French ministers said behind the scenes, whether in social gatherings or to foreign representatives.'[14]

The official record of the talks during this 'Czechoslovak day' includes a series of statements that really deserve to be quoted from beginning to end. However, we must be satisfied with taking the most immediately relevant passages.

'M Daladier in no way denied Germany's strength, but he was of the opinion that the advantages of her present military position were over-estimated.

'The Czech army was by no means to be despised, and it was very well officered. It was true that the annexation of Austria allowed Germany to outflank its fortifications, but the Czechs could counteract this by a fresh alignment of their forces.

'As to the USSR, to which Lord Halifax had just alluded, M Daladier also thought that the Soviet army had probably suffered from the consequences of the violent changes and the summary executions of these last months. But for all that it still had the most numerous air force on the continent and its potentialities for war and its reserves of war material were vast . . . The French premier believed that strength of will was the essential question. Britain and France could make a fresh attempt at conciliation, but if the Czech concessions had no effect they must not allow the destruction of Czechoslovakia.'

Before this the French premier had recalled the actions successively perpetrated by Germany, and he had forecast the stages that were yet to come.

In his reply[15] Chamberlain did not mince his words.

'If he had understood M Daladier correctly, the latter was of the opinion that, if, at this juncture, we were to speak to the German government with sufficient firmness, then there would be no war, for either Germany would not be able or would not care to brave the united forces of France, Great Britain and Czechoslovakia, and such assistance as might be obtainable from outside sources. He considered that this was what the Americans in their card games called bluff. It amounted to advancing a certain declaration in the hope that the declaration would prevent the events we did not wish to occur. But it was not a certainty that such action would be successful. It might be true that the chances against war were a hundred to one, but so long as that one chance existed we must consider carefully what our attitude must be, and how we should be prepared to act in the event of war . . .

'Mr Neville Chamberlain admitted that after the invasion of Austria he too had feelings resembling those of which M Daladier had spoken.* How far should one yield before savage displays of strength? Had not the moment come when certain risks should be incurred to stop them? At first the Prime Minister thought that the Czechoslovak question might perhaps provide the opportunity for a declaration of the kind the French premier had suggested. But the more one looked at the military situation the more one saw that it abounded in difficulties; if such a declaration were to end in war it was impossible to see how Czechoslovakia could be preserved, how the country could be spared from invasion or its army from being broken to pieces. No doubt this army had great qualities; but as M Daladier had himself pointed out, its fortification had already been outflanked since the Austrian Anschluss,† and one had but to glance at the map to see that Czechoslovakia was surrounded on three sides. The staggering speed with which Germany had invaded Austria was quite enough to show the dangers that threatened the Prague government.'

The Prime Minister therefore advised prudence. 'If it was thought necessary to tell Germany that further expansion on her part would not be tolerated, and that if all else failed war would be declared to stop it, yet still a favourable moment from the military point of view must be chosen, and this did not seem to be the case at the moment.'

And having painted a gloomy picture of what a war would entail (and having uncandidly announced that he agreed with what M Daladier had said on the increasing power of the defensive position) Mr Neville Chamberlain categorically asserted, 'At the present moment British public opinion would certainly not accept the undertaking of such responsibilities and it would not be prudent for the government to go beyond what is acceptable to public opinion.'

There is nothing very surprising, therefore, in Chamberlain's conclusion, as it is given in the official minutes.[16]

'It was obviously impossible entirely to exclude the possibility of a war, for circumstances might arise in which things more precious would be at stake than wealth, or life, or property; but

---

* A little farther on the Prime Minister even said that 'it made his blood boil to see Germany getting away with it time after time and increasing her dominion over free peoples'.

† This observation, which was often repeated during and after the Czechoslovak crisis, may be compared with General Faucher's statements on the fortifications and the very special importance attributed to the Slovak redoubt, which had not been 'outflanked' after the Anschluss.

it must be resorted to only as a last recourse – it must not be entered upon lightly. The Prime Minister had taken part in one war, and he had seen how impossible it was for anyone to come out of a war stronger or happier. It was therefore only in the case of unavoidable necessity that one should submit to it. Mr Neville Chamberlain stated that he was entirely against any notion of a preventive war.'

It was Georges Bonnet who undertook to answer the Prime Minister – though at the same time he declared that he did not wish to do so. First the foreign minister recalled the state of affairs that was in preparation – Czechoslovakia wiped off the map of Europe, Teschen given to Poland, and Slovakia, provided with some kind of autonomous status, given back to Hungary; and then he went on,

'In such an event, what would be the attitude of France? There is no possible doubt about the matter. M Daladier has stated that the French government would scrupulously abide by the obligations to give aid and assistance that are contained in the 1925 agreements. France must honour her word and her signature. Great Britain, who teaches her school-children the importance of this kind of duty, will be the last to be astonished by this attitude and the first to value it as it deserves.'

It did appear that no progress could be made. And the 'glum' atmosphere, as Bonnet says, which persisted throughout luncheon, seemed to make this more sure.

Yet in the afternoon, after fresh and equally unavailing exchanges, Chamberlain asked whether he might consult with his ministers. The consultation seemed endless to Daladier and Bonnet, but nevertheless it allowed Chamberlain to come back in the end with a plan for a compromise 'which we discussed although it appeared that we should inevitably have to accept it,' says Daladier, who sums it up thus:

'The two governments should tell Benes of their wish to see a peaceful settlement between Prague and the Sudeten Germans brought about as quickly as possible.

'The British government would inform Berlin that it had advised the Czechoslovak government to be moderate and that it thought a friendly solution possible. It would warn the German government of the dangers of violent action during the course of peaceful negotiations.

'The only advance that I could note after that long day of talks,' ends the French prime minister, 'was that England no longer held aloof from Czechoslovakia, and that she, together with ourselves, accepted joint action, though solely on a diplomatic level.'[17]

For his part Bonnet observes, 'It would in fact have been a mistake to entertain any illusions about Great Britain's undertakings with respect to France! . . . We said, "If we are united Hitler will give way." And the English ministers replied, "We are ready to try this experiment with you. If our joint diplomatic action is successful, so much the better. But take notice that we are not required to go beyond that." '[18]

Towards the evening the two French statesmen went to Croydon, where the pilot of their military aeroplane, Major Rossi, was beginning to grow uneasy because of the forecast of fog over the Channel. But the aeroplane, gaining height, eventually thrust its way through the clouds overhead and reached the blue sky.

'At that moment,' observes Bonnet sadly, 'I thought that we should find it harder to make our way out of the murky business that we had just entered upon with our English friends.'

A diplomatic fortnight

Diplomatic activity was the keynote of the two weeks that followed the Anglo-French conference, both for the Axis and for the democracies.

On May 3 three special trains left the Anhalter Bahnhof: it was Hitler making an official journey to Italy. Five hundred people went with him, among them half the German government. The journey was to tighten the bonds of friendship between the two dictatorships; it was a journey to pay the thanks that Mussolini had so thoroughly deserved by his immobility at the time of the Anschluss;* but it was also a journey undertaken for the sake of prestige, one intended to convince the Italians of their ally's strength and wealth.

The theatrical producer Brenno von Arent, guided by Frau von Ribbentrop, had especially designed a most surprising full-dress uniform that the German diplomats were henceforward to wear: for the daytime it was navy blue with gold buttons and braid, set off for ceremonial occasions by silver aiguillettes, a sash and a dirk; for the

---

* 'Duce! I shall never forget what you have done for me': this was Hitler's telegram to Mussolini from Linz on March 13.

evening a dark blue coat, its lapels deeply embroidered with silver leaves, and a sword 'which we never took off, even for banquets', says Schmidt, the Wilhelmstrasse interpreter who accompanied Hitler, 'because it was impossible to get it out of its sling.'[19] And the whole was crowned, on all occasions, by a Prussian cap.

Those for whom this charming fancy-dress was designed called it their admiral's uniform; but Schmidt, who was by no means persuaded of its beauty, was of the opinion that when he and his colleagues were dressed up in it they more closely resembled level-crossing keepers.

In Hitler's suite these sartorial questions took precedence over all other concerns for ten days on end. 'The Chef du Protocole at the foreign ministry has laid down the manner in which we were to be dressed for every hour of the day with the utmost precision. Often, as we were going from one Italian town to another, we had to change our tail coat for our day uniform, the knightly cloak for the admiral's greatcoat, the dirk for the sword, so that our compartment was far more like the wings of a studio during the shooting of a film than an ordinary sleeper.'

But Hitler's attempts to impress his confederate were outshone by the astonishing display of Italian splendour – the coach-ride through a Rome lit up with Bengal lights and cressets, a naval review that included a 'ballet' of a hundred submarines diving all together and reappearing at the same second, each immediately firing a gun, the trumpets of *Aïda* at the opera-house, receptions in the royal palaces . . .

While all this was going on, the French and British diplomats in Berlin and Prague were carrying out the démarches that their heads of government had agreed upon in London; though it appears that they did so without much conviction. The clear-minded, disillusioned Coulondre, the French ambassador to Moscow, speaking confidentially to his American colleague Joseph Davies, said,

'The British Foreign Office has very mildly warned Berlin that if France should go to the help of Czechoslovakia a very serious situation would arise; that Great Britain should then feel obliged to consider whether she should support France; and that it could not be said whether she might not do so. That is not at all the kind of talk that Hitler can understand. To speak in this way is in some degree to give backing to the view that Ribbentrop is perpetually expounding to Hitler – the view that "whatever happens, Great Britain will not fight".[20]

For his part Léon Noël, the French ambassador in Warsaw, whom Daladier and Bonnet had entrusted with a 'semi-official and confidential' mission of inquiry in Prague, sent back findings which also justified the gloomiest outlook: Benes had not concealed from him that he had 'no hope whatsoever of being helped by his allies of the Little Entente'. On his side, replying to the Czechoslovak leader's questions, the French ambassador could only confirm Poland's disappointing attitude. Both of them had established that in the military field nothing had been undertaken that would make effective co-operation with the Russians possible.[21]

But it was the problems within Czechoslovakia that were giving the head of state the most immediate anxiety, and chief among these was the hardening of the attitude of the Sudeten German party since the conference of March 28. All advances and all the attempts at conciliation that had been undertaken at the prompting of the French and British were met by fresh demands, each harder to satisfy than the last.

Henlein had thoroughly understood Hitler's orders, and he was carrying them out scrupulously. On occasion he meekly asked for more detailed instructions; but he was so full of his subject that he could himself supply the answers without any sort of hesitation.

Speaking to the SS Obergruppenführer Lorenz one day, he asked, 'What should I reply if, under pressure from the foreign governments, Czechoslovakia should suddenly accept all our demands and ask in return that the SdP should join the government?'

'We are not at that point yet!' said Lorenz, rather surprised. 'There will be long and difficult negotiations before that question will arise.'

'Yes, but I have to have instructions. Suppose that at the moment when the question does come up I cannot get in touch with Germany.' And as Lorenz did not answer, Henlein provided his own reply, going on, 'It is quite simple. If Czechoslovakia agrees to all my demands I shall answer yes, but I shall insist upon an alteration in her foreign policy, and that is something that the Czechs will never accept.'

On May 9, furthermore, Henlein announced that the negotiations that had been going on with the Prague government were broken off. But the 'Führer of the Sudeten Germans' nevertheless still kept his party's structural links with Germany secret. At the end of this first fortnight of May he even made a quasi-official journey to England – it is true that this visit was preceded, though the British did not know it, for the secret was well kept, by a halt at Berlin and a long talk with Ribbentrop and Weizsäcker, who gave him a detailed note on what he was to say in his talks with the English.

In London Henlein was received by Sir Robert Vansittart, a high official in the Foreign Office. But Ribbentrop had very cunningly suggested that he should also ask to see Winston Churchill. A meeting was therefore arranged at Morpeth Mansions, with Sir Arthur Sinclair there and Professor Lindemann as interpreter.

Although he was not 'seduced', Churchill was impressed by the constructive and indeed reasonable nature of what his visitor had to say to him. Henlein recommended that in Prague there should be set up a central parliament which should, by the rule of the majority, democratically govern foreign policy, defence, finance and communications: the regions in which the ethnic minorities lived should be allowed internal autonomy, but everywhere the fortified works could be occupied by 'Czech troops'. All elections, those for the local or regional bodies as well as those for the central parliament, should be carried out freely. In the German-speaking provinces the chief officials should be required to speak German, and a share of the taxes gathered by the central government should be put at the disposal of the provinces. Finally, if problems of border-delimitation should arise, they should be submitted to the arbitration of an international tribunal.

Jan Masaryk was told of this by Churchill, and 'he professed himself contented with a settlement on these lines'.[23]

A feeling of optimism therefore began to prevail in London, where the renewal of the negotiations between Henlein and the Prague government, expected for May 17, was confidently awaited.

On the way back, and openly this time, Henlein stopped at Berlin in order to be received by Hitler, who had returned from Italy some days before.

The diplomatic fortnight came to an end. It had also included a session of the council of the League of Nations, beginning on May 9 at Geneva. During the actual sitting the debates had touched only upon the legal problem raised by Swiss neutrality in relation to sanctions and, once again, the Abyssinian affair – a discussion in which the Negus took part. But in the lobbies Georges Bonnet had important interviews, particularly one in which he was able to broach the Czechoslovak question with Litvinov, during a relaxed and friendly conversation.

'The French government,' said Bonnet,[24] 'are uneasy about the possibility of a clash between Prague and Berlin. In such an eventuality France would help Czechoslovakia . . . but it is essential that she should know what the USSR would do.'

Litvinov at once replied, 'If France fulfils the obligations towards Czechoslovakia arising from her assistance pact, the USSR will also honour the obligations of her own pact.'

'But from the practical point of view, how will you be able to help Czechoslovakia, since you have no common frontier? It stands to reason that you will be forced to send your troops or your aeroplanes across Polish territory or Rumanian territory . . . Is the USSR ready to oblige these two countries to consent?'

Litvinov's answer was perfectly clear. 'No. My government will neither go through nor fly over Polish or Rumanian territory unless it obtains the consent of Poland or Rumania . . . We have not the least desire to find ourselves at war with these two countries. But,' added the People's Commissar, 'for her part France has a treaty of friendship with the one and of alliance with the other. So it is she who is best placed for obtaining this right of passage.' And Litvinov suggested that it might well be easier with the Rumanians than the Poles.

When he left Litvinov the French minister therefore at once drew his Rumanian colleague aside – this was Comnenus, who, like Bonnet, was an old Geneva hand.

Both very soon reached agreement on the gravity of the German threat, as they did upon the necessity for obtaining the support of Poland. But as soon as the delicate question of Russian troops passing through Rumania, or merely of aeroplanes using Rumanian airspace, was touched upon, Comnenus grew formal. 'No Rumanian government could tolerate it,' he told Bonnet. 'The entry of the Russians would at once bring about the entry of the Germans, and my country would immediately become one huge battlefield.'

All that remained was to sound Poland. But Bonnet knew Beck, and he nourished few illusions. Nevertheless, Léon Noël, who had just returned to his post at Warsaw after his brief mission to Prague, was to ask the question.

CHAPTER FOUR

The May crisis

Prague mobilizes · The British démarches · Henderson changes his tune

MEANWHILE, as the month of May wore on, so the situation became more tense in the Sudetenland, where the campaign for the municipal elections set for Sunday, May 22, was in progress.

As for Hitler, he continually ruminated upon Operation Green. Schmundt, his immediate assistant for military questions, was now daily badgering the Oberkommando der Wehrmacht, the OKW, for the information that the Führer required.

'How many divisions are there that can thrust into Czechoslovakia at twelve hours' notice?'

'Twelve,' answered the OKW.

'What are their numbers?' insisted Schmundt. And they had barely time to answer before he was asking something else. 'This Czech "Maginot line" – the Führer wants to know all about it – the size of the works, where they are, the troops that are holding them . . .'

Hitler needed all this information to make a well-based decision on the new version of Operation Green that Keitel was to produce for him on May 20. And on that day the Führer, at Obersalzburg, did indeed receive the plan that had been worked out after the meeting of April 21.

At the same time there arrived in Berlin a telegram from Eisenlohr in which he gave an account of the 'uneasiness' displayed by the Prague government over the German troop concentrations in Saxony.

What was this uneasiness based upon?

On May 18 agents of the Czechoslovak intelligence service had reported the massing of troops and suspicious movements at certain points near the Bohemian frontier. The troops concerned were SS units, and later this allowed Hitler, juggling with words, to assert

60

that 'the Wehrmacht' was not in any way concerned. Yet the Wehrmacht was also carrying out movements in east Germany – but after all it is possible that these may have been, as they were said to be, mere episodes in the spring manoeuvres. At all events, a Leipzig newspaper of May 19, which reached Prague the next day, spoke of German troop movements in the frontier region.

Prague mobilizes

Did the Czechoslovak general staff content itself with this information, or had it had more exact intelligence?* In any case one thing is certain, and that is that Benes personally considered the situation serious enough to warrant partial but immediate mobilization.

It was a mobilization that went no further than the occupation of the fortified works, but it was one that was carried out in satisfactory (and in some aspects unexpected) conditions.

'All my Czechoslovak comrades I saw after this covering operation,' said General Faucher, 'told me with one accord that the whole thing had passed off in a remarkable and even, from a certain point of view, a rather cheerful manner . . . At that time there was great excitement in the Sudetenland and the Germans there were heart and soul for Hitler. They were expecting to see German troops arrive and it was Czechoslovak soldiers that appeared. For a moment they were stunned. Then when their astonishment was over they set themselves to organizing the working arrangements and the lodgings with the utmost goodwill. Even more, some of them volunteered to help the troops cut down trees to barricade the roads.'

This was more than enough to bring Henlein's fury to the boiling point – all the more so since this show of strength might adversely affect the results of the next day's elections.

A frontier incident that chanced most happily for them allowed the Sudeten German party to recover control of the situation: two

* William L. Shirer, in *The Rise and Fall of the Third Reich*, a book full of well-authenticated detail on the activity of the secret services, states that the origin of the report received by the British and Czech secret services according to which German troops were concentrating on the frontier has never been discovered. He suggests a theory, however: the Czech or British services may have intercepted telegrams going between Obersalzburg and Berlin, whether they had to do with the new version of Operation Green or with the OKW's answers to Schmundt's questions.

of Henlein's followers, riding a motorbicycle, crossed the frontier at Eger, and when they were summoned to stop by the Czech soldiers they refused to obey. A sentry opened fire. The two Sudeten Germans were killed.

The men of the SdP were able to organize immediate demonstrations, and to prepare an enormous funeral for the two 'victims of Czech barbarity'.

The British démarches

The news from Czechoslovakia set off sudden and intense diplomatic activity in Berlin. As early as the twentieth Henderson had asked Keitel, 'how much truth there was in these stories'. In spite of a flat denial, the British ambassador, rendered uneasy by fresh details that came in during the night, asked for an interview with Ribbentrop on the twenty-first.

It was a stormy meeting: a too-well-informed English paper had unwisely fathered the official denial made public by the embassy on Keitel. Now this happened just at the moment when Ribbentrop and Keitel were on the worst possible terms.

'Since this is the way things are,' said Ribbentrop, by way of an opening, 'I am going to give instructions that no military information of any kind is ever given to you again.'

For once Henderson was not inclined to put up with unpleasantness. 'Very well,' he said sharply, 'I shall therefore conclude from your attitude that the information which General Keitel did in fact supply me with is inexact. I shall at once inform my government of this.'

Ribbentrop instantly flew into a Hitlerian rage. 'Two more Germans have been murdered near Eger by these Czech swine . . . but believe me, whether you like it or not, all the Czechs shall be wiped out! All, do you hear me? Women and children too.'

'I am perfectly willing to agree that the death of these two Germans is most regrettable,' said Henderson, 'but if one reflects upon the hundreds of thousands that a war would kill . . .'

'We are not afraid of war,' shouted Ribbentrop. 'Every German worthy of the name is ready to die for his country!'[1]

Schmidt, the interpreter, who was a witness of this unusual scene, explains it partly by the anger that the Keitel incident had aroused. But according to him there was also Ribbentrop's particular enmity for the English. 'Ribbentrop was very much set against the English,' he says, 'because at the time when he was ambassador to London his arrogant manners had not answered with them at all. He gave free vent to his resentment in his talks with Henderson who, as a gentlemanly Englishman of the old school, was often bewildered by the German minister's churlish manner of speaking, and who, as a diplomat, was not of the calibre to return coarseness for coarseness.'[2]

Nevertheless, Ribbentrop did succeed in making this diplomat 'of the old school' lose his temper. Henderson reminded the German minister that France had exact obligations to fulfil with regard to Czechoslovakia. And he added that 'His Majesty's Government could not guarantee that they would not be forced by events to become themselves involved.'[3]

On that same day Henderson returned twice to the Wilhelmstrasse. And twice he displayed a firmness that was neither characteristic nor customary in him.

The next day Henderson was all the more sorry that he had let himself be carried away because he learned from a reliable source that although there might have been some German troop-movements on the Czechoslovak frontier, there was nothing that allowed the use of the expression 'concentrations', still less the quoting of the figures of eight to ten divisions, as General Krejci had done at Prague.

For as it happened, before going to see Ribbentrop on the twenty-first, the ambassador had asked his two military attachés, Colonel Mason MacFarlane and Major Strong, to carry out a reconnaissance over a great area of Saxony and Silesia. The one had driven seven hundred miles and the other five hundred in twenty-four hours without seeing the slightest signs of unusual or significant German military activity. Most of the military attachés belonging to the other embassies and legations in Berlin had also made journeys of the same kind, and they too had drawn a blank.

An incident that happened at the same time shows how, with the May crisis reaching its highest point, the psychological tension induced people to interpret the most trifling facts in the gloomiest way: this was the incident that Henderson calls 'the story of the special train'.

The British naval attaché was about to take his annual leave, together with his family, and another member of the embassy asked him to look after his own children for the journey. As there was no room to be had in the train the railway company agreed to add an extra carriage on the condition that it should be fully occupied. Two other people from the embassy then decided to send their families as well, and this, by filling up the remaining seats, meant that the carriage could be ordered.

Henderson only learnt about the matter at noon on May 21, when he was coming back from the Wilhelmstrasse: François-Poncet was waiting for him outside the gates of the British embassy to ask him whether there was any truth in the rumour going around Berlin diplomatic circles that the evacuation of the whole British colony – and that by special train – had been decided upon.

Towards evening the Foreign Office (warned by what mysterious grapevine?) telephoned Henderson and asked him to interfere and cancel the departure of the 'special train'. And a few minutes later Weizsäcker spoke to the British ambassador and begged him 'not to create panic' in the diplomatic world.

The only thing to do was to cancel the order for the carriage and to suspend all departures of the embassy staff until further notice.

That same evening, during an official dinner, a violent explosion suddenly drowned the voices, and in a facetious tone (he admits himself that better jokes could be made) Henderson said to François-Poncet, 'The war seems to have begun.' It was in fact an old Berlin hotel being demolished for reasons of town-planning.

A few months later Göring, to whom the remark had been reported as having been made in all gravity, chaffed Henderson, saying, 'You were yourself pretty scared during the May crisis.' But when the ambassador protested, saying that he had only meant it as a joke, even if it was a wretchedly thin one, the Marshal put him at his ease by observing, 'As for me, when I heard the first explosion I said to myself "There we are; those cursed Czechs have begun it!" '

Henderson changes his tune

Was it because he felt that he had given in too soon to war psychosis? Was it because the business of the 'special train' weighed upon his conscience? Or was it because of the negative reports from his military attachés? Was it quite plainly because he felt that he had failed in what he had never ceased to think of as his true mission, that is to say to work for the 'natural' union of the British and the Germans against the communist menace? At all events, from May

22 onwards Henderson abandoned all firmness. Indeed, he went very, very much farther than that. For, being instructed to deliver a personal message from Halifax to Ribbentrop, he did so in a manner and in terms that could, it seems, have had no other object than that of depriving the message of all its meaning.

Halifax had written,[4] 'His Majesty's Government are exerting all possible influence at Prague for avoidance of further incidents and will continue to do so, and I earnestly hope Herr von Ribbentrop will do anything he can on his side to secure patience at this critical time. If resort is had to forcible measures, it is quite impossible for me or for him to foretell results that may follow, and I would beg him not to count upon this country being able to stand aside if from any precipitate action there should start European conflagration. Only those will benefit from such a catastrophe who wish to see destruction of European civilisation.

In any case prospects of understanding and cooperation between our two countries would be gravely jeopardised by any action that would appear to English opinion as wantonly destroying chances of peaceful settlement.'

On the twenty-second Henderson asked to see Ribbentrop in order to give him this message. But he was told that the minister 'was not coming to the office that day'. The ambassador then fell back on Weizsäcker, the secretary of state. As soon as Henderson had gone Weizsäcker drew up a minute summarizing the conversation for Ribbentrop. If the foreign minister of the Reich had retained a certain degree of uneasiness as to the British attitude after the stormy interviews of the day before, Weizsäcker's minute would have comforted him. There are no diplomatic expressions to describe a more complete collapse. As for the immediate task with which Henderson had been entrusted, his manner of carrying it out seems to have come very close to disavowal.

'The Ambassador added by way of commentary,' wrote Weizsäcker,[5] 'that Herr von Ribbentrop might take the letter in the sense in which it was written and intended, namely, as a personal and friendly appeal. Halifax considered the situation to be very grave, but earnestly hoped that we, the parties concerned, might all be stronger than fate. We should not let it get out of hand, for then the only ones to profit would be the Communists. Henderson then went on to say that, in conformity with Berlin's suggestions, very strict instructions had been issued to the British Minister in Prague to exert strong pressure in that quarter. He, the Ambassador, could add, in confidence, that in Paris they were dismayed at the irregular and unagreed mobilisation measures and were advising the Government in Prague to cancel them. Henderson was sceptical when I rejoined that, according to one of our information reports, Benes was acting in agreement with Paris. He did not believe in the existence of French intriguers who had Benes in their power . . .

Henderson agreed of his own accord that such a thing as the deployment of eight to ten divisions in Saxony was completely out of the question, because that of even one single division could not be concealed from anyone with present-day transport columns.'

It may be that Paris had been 'taken aback' by the Czechoslovak mobilization; but there is no doubt that Paris would have been taken even more aback had it learnt of the kind of remarks that the ambassador of Great Britain had thought fit to append to 'the gravest of warnings' that Halifax had sent the German government. Yet 'gravest of warnings' was the description that the Foreign Secretary gave to his démarche.

It is true that this description appeared in a note which the ambassador, Sir Eric Phipps, handed to Georges Bonnet during the night of May 22–23 – a note which, on the part of the British government (markedly given to the hesitation-waltz) constituted another 'warning', and one no less grave.

'It is of utmost importance that French Government should not be under any illusion as to attitude of His Majesty's Government, so far as it can be forecast at the moment, in the event of failure to bring about peaceful settlement in Czechoslovak question.

His Majesty's Government have given the most serious warnings to Berlin, and these should have prospects of success in deterring German Government from any extreme courses. But it might be highly dangerous if the French Government were to read more into those warnings than is justified by their terms.

His Majesty's Government would of course always honour their pledge to come to the assistance of France if she were the victim of unprovoked aggression by Germany. In that event they would be bound to employ all the forces at their command.

If, however, the French Government were to assume that His

Majesty's Government would at once take joint military action with them to preserve Czechoslovakia against German aggression, it is only fair to warn them that our statements do not warrant any such assumption.'[6]

In short, to make use of the curious expression that Chamberlain employed on April 28 at the London conference in his reply to Daladier, Great Britain had ended by making up her mind to do 'what Americans, in their card games, call bluffing'.

Still, the Prime Minister might have been asked whether to his knowledge the Americans, 'in their card games', had invented any word other than 'cheat' for the player who, while his partner is bluffing, deliberately shows his hand to the other side, as Henderson had just done.

On the evening of May 22 the threat of war was not yet set aside. This was to happen the next day, however, and that in the most unusual manner, by Hitler's own personal decision. On the twenty-third he sent his orders from Berchtesgaden to the Wilhelmstrasse; Benes' diplomatic representative in Berlin was sent for at once and told that the German Reich was entertaining no aggressive intentions against the Czechoslovak Republic whatsoever, and that it denied the untrue statements that had been spread abroad on the subject of alleged troop-concentrations in Saxony and Silesia.

The incident was closed. The 'May crisis' was over.

Meanwhile, in the municipal elections, Henlein had won practically every vote in all the cantons of the Sudetenland.

CHAPTER FIVE

Lord Runciman appears

After the storm · Runciman's mission

HITLER had not taken this 'sensible' decision frivolously. It was his reason (the exception proves the rule) that had obliged him to do so. The Führer had had Keitel's draft for Operation Green since April 21, and in the light of the information that he had ordered Schmundt to collect, he did not think that the affair was ripe. So it was better to wait and to move only when success was sure.

Henlein had been sent for to Berchtesgaden in the utmost secrecy at the crucial moment of the crisis and told of what was going on; he was now awaiting fresh instructions for the next phase. He was to get them very quickly, for during the days immediately following the end of the May crisis, Hitler felt his fury mounting within him.

Its best nourishment was, without any sort of doubt, the newspapers of the European and American democracies. Indeed, the publicity given to Halifax's bluff produced a campaign in which insolent delight mingled with foolish exultation: *The dictator has given way . . . he has given way before England's firm words and the democratic powers' determination . . . From now on it is known that Hitler can be stopped – and we know how to set about it, too. The threat of a coalition has made the aggressor draw back . . . Collective security has proved its worth.*

These phrases (and no one knew better than he that they had nothing whatever to do with the facts) had the power of setting Hitler beside himself with rage. How could it be otherwise since they accused him of planning what in fact he had planned, thus unmasking his batteries, and ridiculed him by claiming that all that had been needed was for England to wave a wooden sword to force the master of the Third Reich to surrender?

On May 28 the Führer was back in Berlin. He had done with

68

brooding in his Obersalzburg eagle's nest, and his sullen reflections were now to be expressed in pitiless determination.

He called a decisive conference on Operation Green at the Chancellery and summoned the heads of the three services and the general staff, Göring, Raeder, Brauchitsch, Keitel and Beck, as well as Ribbentrop and Neurath. Jodl took notes.

As an opening stroke Hitler announced, 'Czechoslovakia shall be wiped off the map!' Then, turning to the file Keitel had prepared, the Führer criticized it on a certain number of points, approved others, and drew up the main lines of a directive whose aim was to be done with Czechoslovakia, whatever the circumstances, by October 1 at the latest.

And before dismissing his colleagues Hitler set Keitel a rigorous time-limit: the directive, in its final shape, was to be submitted to the Führer for signature within forty-eight hours.

For this day, May 28, Jodl wrote in his diary,

'The Führer's intention of not touching the Czech question for the moment has been altered as a consequence of the strategic concentration of Czech troops on May 21, which took place without any threat from Germany and without the slightest reason that could justify it. Because of Germany's deliberate moderation this has resulted in the Führer's losing face, which he is determined not to put up with a second time. New orders have therefore been given for Operation Green (attack upon Czechoslovakia), to be signed on May 30.'

Jodl might also have added (for the decision was not without its importance, even if it were only because it was to cost Germany nine million marks) that on the same day Hitler determined to entrust Dr Todt with building the 'West Wall' opposite the Maginot line, to guard against any hostile reaction on the part of the French.

On May 30 Keitel put the last touches to the final version of Operation Green. And Hitler signed it.[1]

'It is my unalterable decision to smash Czechoslovakia by military action in the near future . . .

'It is essential to create a situation within the first two or three days which demonstrates to enemy states which wish to intervene the hopelessness of the Czech military position, and also provides an incentive to those states which have territorial claims upon

Czechoslovakia to join in immediately against her. In this case the intervention of Hungary and Poland against Czechoslovakia can be expected, particularly if France, as a result of Italy's unequivocal attitude on our side, fears, or at least hesitates, to unleash a European war by intervening against Germany.'

After the storm

As it always happens after a period of very great tension, the weeks that followed the May crisis were unusually calm.

On May 31 Bonnet received a long dispatch from his ambassador in Warsaw; it only reported what was already known. 'It would be quite illusory to expect any Polish government whatsoever to be a party to Soviet military intervention, with the Russians passing through Polish territory.'[2]

Marshal Smigly-Rydz entirely confirmed this four days later, when he received Léon Nöel in audience. At the same time Robert Coulondre, the French ambassador in Moscow, was gathering important complementary intelligence during a personal talk with Litvinov. The People's Commissar had just heard from the Soviet intelligence service (which was usually well-informed) that the Polish and Rumanian staffs were negotiating an agreement to oppose the passage of Russian troops if the need should arise.

But even more than the perfidy of France's ally, Poland, it was the attitude of France herself that was engaging Litvinov's mind.

Coulondre understood this preoccupation all the more in that he shared it, for he knew what it was based upon: on several occasions, and especially when Bonnet had received him at the Quai d'Orsay on May 20, he had himself urged that staff talks between the French, Czechoslovaks and Soviets should begin. But in spite of his repeated approaches it had been impossible for him to get an exact answer on this point. His uncertainty matched that of the man he was talking to.

'However discreet a foreign minister has to be,' writes Coulondre, 'there are times when his partner must know what kind of game is being played. But in M Georges Bonnet's eyes was the USSR still his partner?'[3]

As for the English, they were growing impatient. Chamberlain had had the Czechoslovaks told that he advised them to come to a friendly understanding with Henlein as quickly as possible, and he expressed astonishment that his advice had not produced more effect. His vexation was echoed in a memorandum sent by Lord Halifax to Bonnet:[4]

'We have good reason to believe that during his conversation with Dr Hodza* on May 30, Dr Kundt† put forward in detail the propositions outlined by Herr Henlein during his London visit, and that accordingly the question of foreign policy, reparations, and 'Weltanschauung' did not figure in the proposals. We understand further that Dr Hodza promised to let the Sudeten Party know at the end of this week whether or not he could negotiate on this basis.

These proposals commended themselves as reasonable here to persons of widely differing political thought‡ and I think it of the highest importance that the Czechoslovak Government should accept them as a basis of discussion, since in my belief it should not be impossible to reach a solution along these lines. I have reason to know that if a settlement is very much longer delayed, there will be increasing danger of a serious and perhaps disastrous deterioration in the situation.

In these circumstances we must leave Dr Benes in no doubt that if such a failure to reach an early settlement should result from the unwillingness of the Czechoslovak Government to move along lines that seem reasonable here, this would exercise an immediate and adverse effect upon the interest taken in the problem in this country and upon the sympathy felt for the Czechoslovak Government in their treatment of it.'

The beginning of the turn could not have been more distinct, nor the preparation for the shifting of responsibility more obvious.

Bonnet meekly fell into step with Halifax. On June 9 he summoned Osusky, the Czechoslovak ambassador to Paris, and having drawn a dismal picture of the diplomatic situation – the USSR, Poland, Rumania – he urged him to go to Prague and give Benes personally an aide-mémoire confirming the Quai d'Orsay's agreement with the attitude of the Foreign Office. 'To delay negotiations and the reaching of a settlement on this basis,' Bonnet told Osusky, 'would mean the Czechoslovak government's running the risk of losing the advantages

---

* Prime minister of the Republic of Czechoslovakia.
† One of the SdP members of parliament.
‡ Alluding particularly to Churchill's favourable reaction after Henlein's visit.

of a situation which, although it is favourable at the present time, is nevertheless at the mercy of the next fresh incident.'[5]

At the same time Nevile Henderson was confiding the real meaning of this sudden haste to Ribbentrop. 'If Germany proceeded to sudden action in Czechoslovakia before all diplomatic possibilities of a peaceful adjustment of the conflict had been exhausted, that might lead France to intervene. In that case Britain's position would be difficult.'[6]

Whereas if Prague did not succeed in coming to an understanding with Henlein, the position would be quite different.

Ribbentrop could not but approve: was he not aware that since April 29 Henlein had had orders 'gradually to increase the number of demands put forward' expressly in order to prevent the settlement of the quarrel by friendly means? A fact that was quite enough to explain why still another fortnight could go by without the negotiations between the Sudeten Germans and the Prague government making the least advance.

It is interesting to compare the use that each opposing side made of this time in the most important field, that of military preparation.

On July 1 Fierlinger, the Czechoslovak ambassador to Moscow, showed Coulondre an account that Osusky had just sent him from Paris from which it appeared that for the moment the French government were not carrying on with the plans for Franco-Soviet military talks 'in order not to arouse the susceptibilities of the English Conservatives'.

Coulondre's disappointment had two aspects: he naturally found it unpleasant to learn of his government's decisions only by this roundabout way, but he was above all 'saddened at being obliged to record the uselessness' of his efforts.

At the beginning of July, too, the German general staff hastened their work on the final stages of Operation Green. On July 7 Keitel had the general strategic directives approved by Hitler.[7]

'There is no danger of a preventive war by foreign states against Germany . . .

'The settlement of the Czech question by my own free decision stands as the immediate aim in the forefront of my political intentions. I am resolved, as from October 1, 1938, onward, to make full use of every favourable political opportunity for the realisation of this aim . . .

Since even a war started against us by the Western States *must*, in view of the present situation, begin with the destruction of Czechoslovakia, the preparation for war *from the point of view of a strategic deployment* with the main effort by the Army and the Luftwaffe against the West is no longer the primary one.'

In this document there is therefore an examination of the various possible forms of intervention after the beginning of Operation Green – France, Great Britain, Russia and even Poland. But it was made perfectly clear that the study of these eventualities was purely theoretical and that action on the part of the states mentioned would be 'contrary to forecast'.

The next day Göring in his turn summoned his colleagues in the air ministry and told them that Hitler had ordered him to establish an armaments programme so huge that it would make all earlier efforts seem trifling. He said that these orders required him to bring an air force five times the size of that originally provided for into existence as quickly as possible, to increase the speed of rearmament in the army and the navy, and to concentrate all his efforts on offensive weapons, particularly heavy guns and tanks.[8]

And since it was more than ever necessary to delude the enemy, Hitler joined the diplomatic game in person, with his usual feeling for dramatic effect. He had already made use of Princess von Hohenlohe as an intermediary in his secret contacts with Lord Rothermere; now, half-way through July, the Führer caused her to tell Halifax that he was sending a personal messenger to England. And on July 18 his own aide-de-camp, Captain Wiedemann,* reached London in the utmost secrecy.

Lord Halifax received him in his private house with only one other person present, Sir Alexander Cadogan, the Under-Secretary of State: the Führer's envoy stated that he was the bearer of 'a message of good will'. 'Since there is no essential disagreement to set our two countries against one another and since the other difficulties can be settled without resorting to war, the Führer would like to see the Czech affair dealt with amicably, which will be quite easy if everyone sets about it with good will.'

Captain Wiedemann gave it to be understood that the Führer had been wounded by the coldness with which England had received

---

* Captain Wiedemann had been Corporal Hitler's platoon commander during the war.

his advances up until now ... Perhaps Marshal Göring might consider coming to London ...

'The finest day of my life,' replied Lord Halifax, 'will be the day when the Führer walks into Buckingham Palace by the King of England's side.'[9]

For Chamberlain and Halifax Wiedemann's conciliating tone and his account of Hitler's good intentions were so many points of justification for their policy. Why did the Prague government have to be so slow of comprehension, and why did it so stubbornly delay the peaceful settlement longed for by one and all?

As soon as Wiedemann had gone, Chamberlain, whose confidence had been restored by Lord Halifax's sanguine report, returned to an idea that had already been put forward and rejected once – the sending of some leading figure to Prague who would look into the matter on the spot and who might then be able to suggest a 'friendly compromise' that should finally settle the quarrel between the Czech government and the Sudeten Germans.

Runciman's mission

On July 19 the King and Queen of England disembarked from the yacht *Enchantress* at Boulogne. It was an official visit, and one entirely devoted to the display of regal splendour by the Republic.

Yet by making the most of a brief pause before luncheon on the twentieth, Halifax, Daladier and Bonnet were able to have a quick discussion on the international situation. It was now that the British minister told the two Frenchmen that Lord Runciman, entrusted with a 'mission of inquiry and research' by Chamberlain, would shortly leave for Prague. Daladier and Bonnet at once agreed to this step.

Did Bonnet think of suggesting that a French mediator should accompany Lord Runciman at this juncture? In a confidential message to Ribbentrop, Hencke, the German chargé d'affaires in Prague, asserted that he did.[10]

'Kundt, the member of parliament and chairman of the SdP parliamentary group, who as you know has been appointed head of the SdP delegation to the talks by Henlein, has sent me the following confidential political information, which he has received from an agent. Kundt describes this agent, who, moreover, is a non-Aryan, as a tested source and one that can be relied upon: for many years the agent has worked with the French Professor Brunet on legal matters and for this reason he knows him extremely well. Professor Brunet is quite well known in France as a politician who belongs to the minority, and he was under-secretary of the treasury when that ministry was under Georges Bonnet, the present foreign minister. In his turn Professor Brunet, who has been well acquainted with the Sudeten question for the last twenty years and who has frequently shown exceptional understanding with regard to the German racial group, is friendly with M Bonnet. Professor Brunet has made use of the agent I speak of when he wishes to send requests and information to Kundt, the SdP spokesman.

'This agent also has contacts with the former British minister of transport* and other English politicians.

'The agent was recently in Paris and London, where he had extensive discussions with Professor Brunet and the Englishmen he knows, especially the minister of transport.

'Professor Brunet, in view of his talks with Bonnet, the foreign minister, and Daladier, the premier, told the agent that the French government were thinking of sending him, Brunet, to Prague as a French mediator to accompany Lord Runciman. Brunet had desired the agent to find out Kundt's views on this subject. The agent, assuming this to be Kundt's opinion, took it upon himself to state that for the moment the journey would not be opportune. It seems that Kundt has confirmed this point of view.'

Is this information to be regarded as sound? There certainly were real connexions between Brunet and the SdP leaders.† It is therefore possible that there had been discreet feelers put out towards Brunet – indeed some people have gone so far as to assert that he did in fact carry out various semi-official missions during the summer of 1938. Matters were not carried much farther, however, and at the moment

* The Rt Hon Leslie Burgin.

† In his book *Ci-Devant* Anatole de Monzie recounts an incident that he witnessed on September 21, 1938: Bonnet, speaking to the French minister in Prague on the telephone, was told that Dr Benes was trying in vain to reach Dr Kundt, also by telephone. Upon this René Brunet took a little notebook out of his pocket and remarked 'I know Kundt: he has a private number. Here it is.' He did in fact produce a telephone number that M Benes had been unable to discover.

when Runciman was making ready to leave there was no talk of René Brunet.*

On the twenty-sixth Chamberlain made a statement in the government's name in the House of Commons on the Czechoslovak question.

'Time has shown that a settlement can scarcely be reached without outside help. It is under these conditions that the British government, in answer to a request by the Czechoslovak government, have agreed to propose that someone with the requisite experience and abilities should go and study the problem on the spot and do his utmost, if necessary, to suggest a way of bringing the negotiations to a successful conclusion.

'Obviously the person entrusted with this inquiry and this mediation will be independent of the British government, as he will be, indeed, of any government. He will act solely in his own name, and clearly it will be necessary for him to have at his disposal all the information and facilities that are needed in the accomplishment of his task.

'I cannot state that a proposal of this kind will necessarily bring about a solution, but I really do think that it will have two important results.

1 To a considerable extent it will allow public opinion to become acquainted with the facts.

2 It may, and I hope it will, lead to the problem, which up until now has seemed to have no answer, growing less insoluble, thanks to the influence exercised by a mediator of this kind.

'It need scarcely be said that such a task will be exceptionally delicate. The government are therefore very glad that Lord Runciman has agreed to undertake it. He has agreed upon the single condition of being assured of the Sudeten Germans' confidence. I venture to hope that he will obtain it, as he has obtained that of the Czechoslovak government.'

* He was under discussion during September, however. On the sixteenth Hencke, the German chargé d'affaires in Prague, telegraphed to the Wilhelmstrasse, 'Yesterday Kundt had a conversation with the French professor Brunet, who said that on the instructions of Bonnet and Daladier he had been sent to Czechoslovakia as a private observer. Paris did not have a sufficiently clear notion of Runciman's activities and had therefore set up their own system of information, all the more so since M de Lacroix seemed to be following the Czech line entirely.'

It was this that Henderson was required to explain to Ribbentrop. But the German foreign minister received him somewhat coldly: since Runciman's mission had been publicly announced in England before the German government had been informed, the Germans would regard the whole matter as 'a purely British affair'.

On August 3 Lord Runciman arrived in Czechoslovakia, where the government had by no means begged for his coming, in spite of what Chamberlain said in the Commons. William L. Shirer, who was passing through Czechoslovakia, attended his press conference and observed in his diary, 'Runciman's whole mission smells.'

What kind of a man was this Runciman?

A British businessman, close on seventy, who had throughout his life collected chairmanships of boards of directors. He belonged to the Liberal party, but that did not prevent him from being as fundamentally reactionary as most Conservatives. Lloyd George, who would doubtless not have chosen him for so delicate a mediation, said of him, 'he would make the thermometer drop, even at a distance.' And Coulondre, the French ambassador, who had met him five years earlier at the London economic conference, has this charming description of him, 'I can still see him, occupying the chair at the commission on trade. Clean-shaven, impassive, buttoned up tight in a black morning coat, with his head perched on top of a prodigious stiff collar, he seemed to have dropped out of a page of Dickens and still to be feeling his fall.'[11]

When he arrived in Prague the 'mediator' (who lacked any real powers of mediation, it must be added) was favourably received by virtually all the newspapers. The Prague government was ready to help him. As early as July 28 Hodza said to Eisenlohr, the German minister in Prague, 'I am very glad of Lord Runciman's coming. He may find a way out in a situation that has become impossible. I shall do everything possible to help him against ill-intentioned minds, and I shall do so not in the interest of any one of the parties but in that of peace and the future.'[12]

Germany persisted in taking no notice of the Runciman mission. But this was only a tactical attitude, chiefly imposed by an anxiety to prove that Henlein was acting without receiving orders from Berlin.

Ribbentrop's reception of Henderson made Halifax uneasy about the success of the British venture, and he wrote personally to Hitler's foreign minister to make a somewhat mean apology for indiscretions

77

which originated in England and which provided Ribbentrop with an excellent excuse for refusing to use his influence with the Sudeten German party.

Halifax urged Ribbentrop to 'encourage and support' the undertaking. Ribbentrop nevertheless stubbornly refused to change his point of view. And by way of emphasizing his determination he personally initialled a note that pointed out that Runciman was a 'private British citizen' with whom the German chargé d'affaires in Prague was not to collaborate directly in any circumstances. 'If the British government have anything whatsoever to communicate to us,' the note continued, 'let them do so by way of London alone, never by way of Runciman through Eisenlohr.'

But if officially the Wilhelmstrasse held aloof from the British mission, it meant to be thoroughly informed of Lord Runciman's smallest movements. Weizsäcker told Eisenlohr to keep the Wilhelmstrasse up to date on the mission's activities, and Runciman's talks and intentions, as precisely and as quickly as possible, 'so that Germany may be able to intervene with the Sudeten Germans and if need be in London even before Runciman's plans are born'.

And, having reminded Eisenlohr 'that he must neither seek direct relations with Runciman nor yet withdraw from them if they arose naturally', Weizsäcker finished by emphasizing that 'Runciman must of course be kept in a state of fear lest the Czech question should take on a dangerous aspect if his proposals do not satisfy the Sudeten Germans.'

Henlein and the SdP, on the other hand, did enter into contact with the 'mediator'. How could it have been otherwise, since as early as July 27 the British minister in Prague had taken the trouble to give Kundt official notice of Runciman's mission, and that in terms that could not but gratify the Sudeten German leaders? 'The British minister's approach,' telegraphed Eisenlohr to Ribbentrop, 'seems to show that the British government consider the SdP as an interlocutor treating with the Czech government on a footing of equality.'

This had indeed appeared on August 3, when Runciman's train stopped at the platform in Prague. Newton, the British minister, had taken the precaution of giving the chief men of Henlein's party notice of Runciman's arrival and had offered to introduce them to him. The SdP members of parliament Kundt and Sebekowsky were therefore at the station.

Runciman had scarcely stepped out of his carriage before the officials were hurrying towards him: Benes had sent his chef du protocole, who was accompanied by several members of the government and of parliament. The chef du protocole introduced them to Runciman one after another. When it was the turn of the SdP delegates, on the other hand, Newton took over according to a well-concerted plan and asked Kundt and Sebekowsky to come forward. After a few friendly words to Runciman, Kundt ended by saying, 'I welcome you in the name of the German people of the Sudetenland.'

This shows whether the mission was begun under fortunate auspices or not.

But very soon the Prague government began to feel the gravest uneasiness as to the impartiality of this curious 'mediator'; for with deliberate intention Runciman kept in far closer contact with the men of the SdP than with the Czechoslovak government. It is true that the Sudeten Germans had taken their measures to keep in continual touch with Chamberlain's envoy. They knew his ways, they understood the social circle in which he moved and his tastes, and they did not confine themselves to the appointment of a political delegation led by K. H. Frank; they also entrusted a wealthy nobleman and a great landowner, Prince Ulrich Kinsky, with the setting up of a 'society' delegation. And the activities of this body soon showed that it was uncommonly effective.

Many hereditary landowners, determinedly hostile to the Prague government and particularly to their agrarian reform, answered the call of Prince Kinsky and of Prince Max von Hohenlohe, whom Hitler had already made use of at the time of the Anschluss.*

Runciman, who loved hunting, fishing and golf, and who was used to big fashionable gatherings, was overwhelmed with invitations to the most splendid country houses, where great shooting parties and receptions were organized in his honour. It was at the Hohenlohes' palace, at Rothaus, that he met Henlein, and it was when he was staying with Prince Kinsky or the Dietrichsteins that he 'studied the German-Czechoslovak dispute' as he fished for trout or paced the golf-links.

Meanwhile a political delegation undertook the task of convincing

* A certain number of Bohemian nobles belonging to the oldest families, however, among them another Kinsky, remained faithful to Czechoslovakia and after Munich went so far as to sign a protest.

the 'mediator's' colleagues, Ashton-Gwatkin and Messing, during endless working sessions.

Rumours about the contacts that Runciman was making and about his good understanding with the Sudeten Germans began to reach London and Paris; but far from causing any anxiety, they raised exactly the same hope both at the Foreign Office and the Quai d'Orsay.

On August 9 the German ambassador in Paris was received by Georges Bonnet, and in the account that he sent to Ribbentrop after this conversation he summed up Bonnet's remarks on the Runciman mission thus:[13]

'For his part Bonnet still thought the sending of Runciman a sound and prudent measure, in spite of the Czechs' attempt at making him appear an open friend of the Germans. In this matter of the Sudeten Germans it was necessary to go to the extreme limit of concessions, even if this did not suit the Czechs.

'From a theoretical point of view the Runciman mission might have the following results:

 1 The solution might satisfy both sides, the Czechs as well as the Sudeten Germans. This hypothesis might virtually be left out of account.
 2 The Czechs might agree but not the Sudeten Germans, in which case it would be necessary to find the means of coming to an agreement.
 3 The Sudeten Germans might agree but not the Czechs, in which case the Czechs would have to be brought to accept the Runciman plan whether they liked it or not . . .'

At this very time Halifax was writing to his ambassador, Henderson,[14]

'We have consistently exercised our influence at Prague to facili-tate the early discover of such a solution which, of course, must be one to give satisfaction to the legitimate aspirations of the Sudeten section of the population. Lord Runciman's mission as an inde-pendent investigator and mediator will, we hope, prove what it was intended to be, namely, a practical and effective factor in enabling such a solution to be arrived at . . .'

In short, Halifax and Bonnet were counting upon Runciman to come to conclusions favourable to the Germans and thus to bring the Prague government to give way all along the line. It therefore seemed to them a good sign that the resumption of direct negotiations between the SdP delegation and a special commission of the Czechoslovak government was announced as being imminent.

Yet one single cloud remained – that which had prompted the British minister's letter to his ambassador: the Germans' military preparations were beginning to cause comment, and this just at the moment when it seemed that everything was to be settled so happily 'by peaceful and friendly means', those very means that Hitler, speaking through Captain Wiedemann, had said that he preferred.

CHAPTER SIX

Priority for Operation Green

*Help in the kitchen · Operation Green crystallizes · Military counter-measures ·
No fresh Verdun! · The Prague talks · The Western powers blunder again
and again*

IN spite of the optimism that the first 'results' of the Runciman
mission aroused at the Quai d'Orsay and the Foreign Office it was
clear that the disturbing information sent in by the military attachés
could not be entirely overlooked.

Halifax did not hide his disappointment.

'On the top of this, and following upon the decision to complete
the system of western fortifications in the shortest possible time,
comes the news that it is intended to bring an unusual number of
formations of the German army up to war strength for special
training next month and to prolong thereafter the service of men
who would normally be released. Although the British Military
Attaché has been very courteously informed of these measures, he
has not been given any explanation of their necessity at this
particular juncture, other than that they are intended to test the
efficiency of the war organization.'

In Berlin itself François-Poncet was collecting the material for a
complete report for his minister. He was already in a position to draw
a disturbing picture of the Germany of the beginning of August
1938. 'Germany has taken on the look of war. Work on fortifications
is pushed on feverishly; hundreds of thousands of workmen are
employed upon them. The mobilization of the workmen for these
undertakings is carried out by means of sweeps and levies of the
utmost rigour.'

The ambassador went on to describe the fortified lines set up
parallel with the French frontier, the labours undertaken by way of

infrastructure, particularly the widening of certain roads, and the measures of mobilization that had been decreed and the steps taken for the stock-piling of army stores or motor-fuel. François-Poncet's inference was perfectly clear: 'Everything is going on as though autumn were to bring the Reich a war.'

And indeed it was a question of that, for while the repercussions of Hitler's decisions were beginning to change the outward appearance of Germany and the country's life in this way, the working out of Operation Green went forward briskly in the secret recesses of the general staff.

But at the same time some very odd currents began to move in the topmost reaches of the German army. There had already been the first appearances of discontent with the Führer's plans – the memorandum that General Beck, chief of the general staff, handed Brauchitsch, the commander-in-chief, on July 5, was one of these. Since then Beck had sent his immediate chief further warnings, also drawn up – not without courage – in writing. Each time Brauchitsch had been impressed by the arguments of his chief of staff, but until this juncture his innate timidity had prevented him from passing these observations on to Hitler, as Beck asked him.

A fresh memorandum from Beck dated July 16 would no doubt have shared the same fate if its author had not obliged Brauchitsch to convoke the commanding generals on August 4 to hear the memorandum read out. Although they did not yet dare to set foot on the path of rebellion, the highest-placed and most senior members of the Germany army did not conceal their agreement with Beck's criticism of the plan for the invasion of Czechoslovakia. Wilhelm Adam, the general chosen for the western theatre of operations, had particularly stressed the fact that at the moment when Operation Green was to come into effect he would in no event have at his disposal adequate means to stop the French army lying opposite him. In short, the generals were of the same opinion as Beck: at all costs it was essential that the army should find a way of opposing this adventure.

Now at last Brauchitsch summoned up his courage. He went and read Beck's memorandum to the Führer. But the result was exactly the opposite of what had been reckoned upon. Hitler, informed by Brauchitsch of the support for Beck in the highest ranks of the army, at once summoned the officers who were second in command to the chiefs who had taken part in the meeting of August 4: they were to

83

come to the Berghof on August 10. And at the Berghof Hitler argued his case for three hours on end – 'The greatness of Germany . . . brothers in race . . . three million Germans oppressed by the Czechs.' There were indeed some discordant notes, particularly when General von Wietersheim, who, as it happened, was Wilhelm Adam's chief of staff and who, like him, had an exact knowledge of the situation on the French frontier, coldly observed that he could not hold out against the French for more than three weeks.

Hitler furiously interrupted Wietersheim. 'I assure you, general, this position will not only be held for three weeks, but for three years if need be!'[2]

When Beck was told of what had happened at the Berghof on August 10 he at once decided to free himself from responsibility and to resign. Hitler was cunning enough to accept his resignation, but only under certain conditions: at all costs there was to be no public knowledge of this alteration in the high command of the German army, coming as it did when international tension was at its height. Neither the German people nor their possible enemies nor those who might or who probably would be their allies were to know that the general staff was going through a crisis.

Out of soldierly feeling Beck agreed, and no one noticed that gradually General Halder replaced him in all his functions.

From cowardice, intellectual idleness, or merely from habit of discipline, most of the other generals fell back into line. Yet a few, who were already on the road to conspiracy, went on meeting, and they did not give up the notion of undertaking some action that should spare Germany from the adventure towards which the Führer's 'genius' was dragging her.

Although Beck's resignation did not bring about the reactions among the commanding generals who had taken part in the meeting of August that the chief of staff had hoped for, it did at least make him an ideal leader for the conspirators.

Let there be no mistake: these men were by no means anti-Nazis whose convictions dated from the earliest times; on the contrary, most of them had until then made use of the régime just as much as it had made use of them. Their reaction was neither that of pacifists nor that of anti-Fascists. Except for a few earnest Christians such as Halder, who was later to join the plotters, these Nazi generals rose against Hitler because they considered Operation Green untimely and dangerous. Had the matter seemed to them technically feasible they would probably not have criticized it at all. Apart from Beck and Halder outstanding members of the conspiracy were the generals Erwin von Witzleben, Erich von Brockdorff, Ahlefeld and Höppner, and above all the head of the *Abwehr*, Admiral Canaris.

Although they had not yet clearly settled their plans for a rising they had in mind a military putsch that should coincide with the launching of the attack upon Czechoslovakia. Nevertheless they still had to know whether the Western powers would, in this event, open a western front. Furthermore, the English and French had to be told of Hitler's plans.

No doubt in ordinary times it would have been enough to sound out the British and to warn them (since it was to the British the conspirators had decided to turn rather than to the French)* by speaking to their ambassador in Berlin. But by now no one in German political or military circles was ignorant of the degree to which Henderson, moved no doubt by anti-Communism, had personally involved himself in diplomatic activities that led to closer relations with the Nazis. Both for reasons of security and of effectiveness, therefore, it was impossible to count upon him.

From this there arose the decision, which was taken shortly after August 10, to send a completely reliable envoy to London. Edward von Kleist, the man chosen, reached London on August 18 and he was received first by Vansittart and then by Churchill. He revealed the plans for the invasion of Czechoslovakia both to the one and to the other, and he told them of the reaction of the German generals. He asked them both to use their influence so that Great Britain should take up an unequivocal attitude with regard to the Nazis.

Winston Churchill, whose personal views on these very questions kept him out of the government's counsels, gave Kleist an encourag-

---

* There is no question but that the English were warned. It is no less certain that they did not think it worth while to pass on this information to their French allies. 'At all events,' wrote Daladier in *Le Nouveau Candide* of September 14–21, 1961, 'it was a pity that we were never told of the German conspirators' confidences and that when they had warned London they did not think it useful to warn Paris too!' Yet the Quai d'Orsay was not entirely without intelligence of what was going on. An 'important figure' in the Germany embassy in London (this probably refers to Theodor Kordt) had steadily kept Mailland, a French journalist (the same who was to become Pierre Bourdan), informed of the Nazi plans and particularly of the dates laid down for the operation against Czechoslovakia. Of course this information was at once passed on to the French embassy in London by P. L. Bret, who was running the London branch of the Agence Havas and who was Pierre Mailland's chief. (See P. L. Bret, *Au feu des événements*.)

ing letter, which he carried back to Berlin. Its text, copied out by Canaris, was known to the Nazis a few days later.

Sir Robert Vansittart, acting officially in his capacity as the government's diplomatic adviser, sent Chamberlain a fairly detailed report, and one that was interesting enough to make the Prime Minister decide to recall Henderson to London for consultation.

As well as Kleist's mission, the conspirators sent London a second warning, as a safety measure, by means of the British military attaché in Berlin; but this had to pass through Henderson, and he so glossed it that it was deprived of all meaning.

Nevertheless it cannot be denied that London was warned, and that not once but twice. And even if it is possible to remain doubtful about the effectiveness of the conspiracy properly so called, the first part of the warning (that is, on the decision to invade Czechoslovakia at the end of September) did deserve to be taken into consideration.*

Help in the kitchen

Hitler was not in the least impressed by English protests as to the untimely nature of the military preparations, nor was his ardour damped by the crisis in the high command of the German army: he ran straight along the road that he had marked out for himself, without swerving from it by so much as an inch.

In order that his Operation Green should develop in the best possible conditions, it was necessary that the countries which had any kind of interest in sharing the spoils should range themselves on Germany's side as early as possible: furthermore, it was desirable that Czechoslovakia's allies should give up all idea of helping her before they had made even a show of doing so. The best way of gaining this double goal was still a display of German might, so

* Since the war there has been a great deal of discussion about the nature of these opposition groups consisting of German soldiers and sometimes of civilians, and about their means of action. There is no doubt that the attempt of July 20, 1944, showed that although this military opposition may have been badly organized and badly led it did include some determined men in its ranks. Yet who can tell whether the little group that existed in 1938 (and which was only later to be re-inforced by the forceful, driving men who organized and carried out the attempt of July 20, 1944) would have been capable of moving into action in September, 1938? At all events it is impossible to take on trust every single account that has been published since the war, or even the evidence produced at Nuremberg, whose intention was only too obviously to prove the existence of an anti-Nazi 'resistance' which brought together enough picked men to give a prevision of the leaders of the new German state – and of a new Wehrmacht.

that the one set of countries should be anxious to join the stronger side and that the others should take care not to interfere lest they be overwhelmed.

The publicity given to the recent measures and the 'appearance of a country at war' which struck foreign observers in Germany were already in themselves ways of displaying German military strength. But there were other ways as well, and Hitler decided to organize highly spectacular manoeuvres. Army manoeuvres close to Danzig, for Poland had to be induced to come firmly over to the side of those who attacked Czechoslovakia. Naval manoeuvres, which were both to impress England (always attentive to anything that happened by sea) and to decide the Hungarian leaders, who were the Führer's guests for the occasion.

On August 22 Hitler went to Kiel, accompanied by Horthy, the regent of Hungary. Naval review. From Kiel the party moved on to Heligoland, a very large and exceedingly modern maritime fortress. Naval manoeuvres: a hundred and ten men-of-war, thirty-seven submarines and the brand-new *Gneisenau* went through their paces before the Hungarian guests and the military and naval attachés of the entire world. Then, back on the mainland, the Führer's guests were treated to an immense display of armour and motorized equipment.

Although the chief aim of these manoeuvres was to show the striking German war-machine, political talks did take place aboard the man-of-war *Patria*. Some indeed were not without immediacy – there was question, for example, of the possibility of Hungary coming in against Czechoslovakia, the intervention being linked to the beginning of Operation Green.

Ribbentrop asked Weizsäcker to draw up an *aide-mémoire* on the German-Hungarian talks.[3]

'While not keeping silent on his misgivings as to the British attitude, he (Horthy) nevertheless made it clear that Hungary intended to cooperate. The Hungarian Ministers* were and still remain more sceptical, for they realise more strongly the direct danger to Hungary's unprotected flanks.

M. Imredy had an interview with the Führer in the afternoon and was most relieved when the Führer stated to him that, in this particular case, he required nothing of Hungary.† He himself did

* Imredy and Kanya.
† Underlined in the original.

not know the precise moment. He who wanted to sit at table must at least help in the kitchen.'

And Weizsäcker ended by summing up the Hungarians' state of mind in these words:

'(a) Hungary is glad at not having to expect from us demands in the form of an ultimatum, and
(b) Hungary is convinced that she will not be able to intervene until some 14 days after the outbreak of war.'

Ribbentrop had another political conversation, also on board the *Patria* and also relating to Czechoslovakia, but this time with an Italian, the ambassador Attolico. Attolico, without any diplomatic beating about the bush, went straight to the heart of the matter. 'The Duce has given me instructions to ask the German government the approximate date at which they think they will start their action against Czechoslovakia.'

As Ribbentrop gave nothing away, the ambassador went on, 'The Duce attaches an especial importance to receiving this information. As you may well imagine, an action of this kind will necessarily entail certain consequences for Italy. This time my government would like to avoid being caught unawares by events.'

This was an open reference to the Austrian affair. Ribbentrop would have liked to avoid irritating the representative of the 'great Italian ally', whose anxiety was, after all, understandable. But in this Czechoslovak business Hitler had determined to play a cautious game and to trust his secrets to no one. When one is the attacker the effect of surprise is too valuable for one to run the risk of an indiscretion. The reply of the foreign minister of the Reich was therefore civilly evasive. 'No date has yet been settled for the expected action. I can simply assure you that the German government will not tolerate a repetition of the incidents of May 21! If the Czechs provoke us again, we shall march . . . Tomorrow? In six months? Only in a year? What I can promise you is that if the situation enters an acute phase or if the Führer has to take a decision, we shall warn the Duce by the quickest possible means: whatever happens, the Italian government shall be the first to be told.'

While Hitler in person was doing the honours of his fleet, entertaining his present and future allies, Göring, with General Milch to help him, displayed the might of the Luftwaffe to a delegation of

French airmen. Aircraft-construction factories, formation flights, the performance of particular aeroplanes. The point of the operation was to gain prestige; Göring carried it through handsomely and its results exceeded his hopes.

At the end of the French airmen's short stay Göring received them at Karinhall, and he asked General Vuillemin, the head of the French air force, 'What will France do if war breaks out between Germany and Czechoslovakia?'

Without hesitation the Frenchman replied, 'France will keep her word.'

But a quarter of an hour later, when Vuillemin, still dumbfounded by what he had just seen, was saying goodbye to François-Poncet, he said, 'If there is a war at the end of September, as you say there will be, not a single French plane will be left after a fortnight.'

When he reached Paris on August 24 the commander-in-chief of the air force at once went to see Gamelin, Guy La Chambre, Georges Bonnet, Daladier and President Lebrun, and repeated the same observation. It was an observation which from then onwards was to have a terrible weight when it was a question of taking decisions that might entail serious consequences from a military point of view.*

Operation Green crystallizes

Now if the note that Jodl submitted for the Führer's approval on that same August 24 was anything to go by, the time when these decisions would have to be taken was not far away.

This note shows a quite remarkable effrontery on the part of the man who wrote it. It particularly states that 'Operation Green will be set off by an incident in Czechoslovakia that will provide Germany with an excuse for military intervention.'

And Jodl adds,

'If, for technical reasons, it is desirable that the incident should take place in the evening, it will not be possible for the next day

* Pierre Lazareff says of General Vuillemin, 'General Vuillemin, who was a pilot promoted from the ranks, had behaved courageously during the first world war. After that he had acquired a great deal of popularity by taking part in long-distance flights and by leading the *Croisière Noire*, a rally for military aircraft across French Africa. The Vuillemin family had been friendly with Georges Bonnet's family for a long time, and the general, his wife and their children spent their holidays near Arcachon with the foreign minister, his wife and their son.' It would appear that this was in fact at Saint-Georges de Didonne, near Royan.

to be D-day: this will have to be the day after. We must at all events act on the principle that nothing that might give away our mobilization must be done before the incident, and that after it we must act with the utmost possible speed.

'The intention of these notes is to show how closely the incident concerns the Wehrmacht and how necessary it is that the Wehrmacht should be told of the Führer's intentions in good time, insofar as it is not the *Abwehr-Abteilung* itself that is entrusted with arranging the incident.'

When he drew up this note Jodl supposed that he was playing the Führer's game entirely, in opposition to Halder, Beck, Canaris and the other conspirators who were against Operation Green. But what he did not know was that as it happened he was no more than a tool in their hands. For their chief concern was to get Hitler to agree that the OKW should be told of the beginning of the operation early enough, in any case the day before. Now it was Halder who had asked this, and he had asked it in order to have the necessary time to attempt a *coup* against Hitler at the very moment when the invasion of Czechoslovakia should begin.

Matters had not yet reached this point, however.

In these last days of August it was clear that nothing would stop Hitler: he had scarcely left the *Patria* before he was scouring the roads. On the twenty-sixth the Führer, accompanied by Jodl, Himmler and Dr Todt, went to inspect the fortifications that were hastily being built over against the French frontier.

He was shown the fortified zone by General Wilhelm Adam, who commanded the western theatre. Adam had not changed his opinion since the half-secret meeting of August 4. He had not changed his opinion and he had only one wish – to make it clear to Hitler.

At last the general was granted a direct personal conversation with Hitler in his car during part of his journey. As soon as he was alone with the Führer Adam criticized the 'West Wall' and particularly pointed out that in no event could he either hold it or defend it with the forces at his disposal. But he only succeeded in sending Hitler off into one of his epic rages and in the end he was told that a man would have to be 'a despicable fellow, not to hold these fortifications for as long as it should be required'.

In any case, the journey of the Führer and his suite did not pass unnoticed by the French and British intelligence services, any more than the army manoeuvres, the naval reviews and the demonstrations of air-strength.

Military counter-measures

Although they were confident that peace would be maintained, the Western statesmen nevertheless reached the point of thinking that 'something ought to be done about it'.

On August 25 M Massigli, sent by Georges Bonnet, came to see General Gamelin in Paris. 'The minister desires me to ask you what measures you think of taking, with the rumours that are going about concerning all these German military preparations.'

'Our whole system is ready,' replied Gamelin. 'We only have to press a button to set it in motion.'[4]

And three days later, among his letters, Daladier found a note in which the chief of the general staff submitted a series of proposals to him:

1 The recall of the recently liberated conscripts who had served in the fortified or defensive regions and sectors.*

2 The principle of retaining the class that should be due for release at the end of September.†

3 Additional calling-up of men on the reserve, particularly as regards the formations assigned to these fortified regions and sectors as well as to the military regions.‡

4 The calling-up of a certain number of training units.

These measures were intended to provide a covering force; they were submitted to the cabinet on September 2 and approved. And the same day General Colson was entrusted with telling the German military attaché, General Kühlenthal, that the strengthening of the German positions obliged France in her turn to take these steps.

On September 2 also there were important diplomatic talks on the possible intervention of the Red Army. In Moscow, Litvinov received Payart, the French chargé d'affaires, and they both took note of the fact that Poland and Rumania were still opposed to any passage of

---

* This class was, of course, released a month or six weeks earlier than the field formations, so that the young soldiers called up and sent to fortress formations might be given a preliminary training before the older soldiers belonging to the rest of the army left. (General Gamelin's note.)

† After the Munich agreement this class was released in October; but it was recalled in March, 1939 (General Gamelin's note).

‡ Especially for the anti-aircraft formations. (General Gamelin's note.)

Russian troops through their territories. The People's Commissar maintained an attitude of strict respect for international law. Furthermore, he did not think it an unproductive position. 'In view of the negative attitude taken up by Warsaw and Bucharest', he said, 'as I see it there is only one way out – an appeal to the League of Nations. Once Geneva authorizes flying over these countries everything takes on a different aspect. In my opinion everything should be done to warn the Council of the League, so that the machinery of Geneva should be ready to set itself in motion as soon as the aggression occurs.'[5]

At about the same time in the day the Soviet ambassador in London, Maisky, was paying Winston Churchill a visit at Chartwell. It was a friendly visit, but its meaning did not escape Churchill. 'It was clearly intended,' he writes, 'that I should report what I was told to His Majesty's Government.'* At Chartwell Maisky too argued in favour of the matter being brought before the Council of the League, which, in Moscow's view, was the only organization that was capable of influencing Rumania's decision.

No fresh Verdun!

On the following day, September 3, the preparation of Operation Green made a fresh advance during a conference at the Berghof. Hitler had summoned Brauchitsch, the gunner General Keitel and Major Schmundt: in the minute that he wrote immediately after this meeting Schmundt, the Führer's aide-de-camp, reproduced the atmosphere of the conference as exactly as he could – in other words he set down a long monologue by the Führer.

Only one other person presumed to express a few timid reservations: this was Brauchitsch, who spoke of the condition of the motorized divisions, the reinforcements, and the leaders' want of training.

But the irritated Führer brushed these defeatist reasons to one side. And once again he completely overturned the plan set before him.

So the staff wanted to entrust the main push to the Second Army? 'An attack in this strongly fortified area,' decided Hitler, 'would mean a terrible flow of blood, and a task that could not be carried out. Perhaps Verdun all over again! Who can tell?'

* Churchill did this at once, drafting a note for Lord Halifax.

It was in the Tenth Army's sector that the attack had the greatest chance of succeeding. One single army, but that in the heart of Bohemia, and the business would be over. All the motorized and armoured divisions were therefore to be attached to the Tenth Army and used in the thrust. Let it not be forgotten that the enemy opposite the Tenth Army was not behind concrete positions all along the line ... Moreover, it should be easy, in this region, to recruit Henlein's followers. Uniforms for them would have to be provided ...

Brauchitsch jotted this down. He went on with the reading of his plan: 'The field units will march on September 28. From that date onwards they will be ready for action –'

Hitler stopped him. 'No! The troops will be assembled two days' march away. Secrecy is essential. You will see that the movements are camouflaged in all sections. As for D-day, it will be quite enough if the OKW knows it at noon on September 27.'

The Prague talks

With his mind at ease, Hitler could prepare his attack for the last days of September: Henlein on the spot was doing all that was necessary in Czechoslovakia to make the crisis evolve according to the orders that he had received and that had been repeated to him at Berchtesgaden on September 1. For his part, Runciman was letting himself be manipulated by the Sudeten Germans as they chose. And the Western chanceries, which would persist in believing in the possibility of a negotiated settlement, helped to weaken the Prague government's diplomatic position, and, which was still more serious, their military position.

The tactics of the Sudeten German party's delegation in its talks with the English 'mediator' were quite simple. Friedrich Bürger, Henlein's representative in Berlin, had defined them as early as the first day.

'The Sudeten German Party's tactics consist in cramming the British with information and with very copious documentary evidence in the form of memoranda, articles, and published literature.

'At the first preliminary discussion on the trend of the information, K. H. Frank stated as the slogan of the delegation:

93

' "It is the duty of the Sudeten German Party to convince His Lordship (Runciman) that the nationality problem in Czechoslovakia cannot be solved within the State, and that the Czechs are in no way prepared to make concessions of a kind that could lead to a real pacification of the State. His Lordship must take away with him the impression that the situation in this state is so confused and difficult that it cannot be cleared up by negotiation or diplomatic action, that the blame for this lies exclusively with the Czechs, and thus that the Czechs are the real disturbers of peace in Europe." '[6]

Lord Runciman was naturally reserved and his bringing up had made him circumspect; he scarcely let it be seen how much this 'poisoning' was affecting him. But Lady Runciman's behaviour revealed the state of mind that was prevalent among those who accompanied the 'mediator'.

Hencke, the German chargé d'affaires in Prague, observed it at a reception given at the British legation. 'Lord Runciman has not breathed a word on the Sudeten German question either to foreign diplomats or to me. But on the other hand, Lady Runciman's conversation shows remarkable understanding of the Sudeten German cause, and she has spoken of the Bolshevik influence in Czechoslovakia.'

As well as this 'conditioning' of Lord Runciman and those close to him, the SdP delegates carried on their negotiations with the Prague government. It may easily be imagined in what spirit they did so. Yet during the first days of September their task had grown difficult, for in spite of the accusations put out by the Nazi propaganda Benes had firmly taken the path of concession. No doubt this was more by way of demonstration for the English and the French than from any hope of reaching a peaceful settlement.

As early as August 30 the head of the Czechoslovak state had handed Kundt and Sebekowsky, the SdP delegates, proposals so liberal that they had positively staggered Hencke. Benes, indeed, had observed that he was not opposed to a public statement by the SdP that the eight demands of Carlsbad were satisfied. He would so handle matters that the Czech press should not have a biased reaction to statements of this kind.

Frank described the proposals as 'quite ample, to be sure, but still not enough'.

As for Kundt, he thought that their being brought into effect might in fact mean 'the fulfilment of the Carlsbad demands'.

These 'quite ample' proposals had therefore succeeded in shaking even the steadiest of Henlein's lieutenants; nevertheless they still seemed insufficient to the British government, which, according to Bonnet, was 'very displeased that Prague should still, at the eve of the Nuremberg congress, not have laid down a programme that should satisfy the Sudeten Germans' fundamental claims'.

So on September 4 Newton, the British minister to Prague, called upon the head of the Czechoslovak state and spoke to him of this 'displeasure'. The tone of the conversation was of such a kind that it left Benes very little hope of ever being upheld by Great Britain, who, as Newton told him, 'would prefer the Carlsbad programme to war' if she had to choose.

Benes then determined to go to the uttermost limit of concessions. Shirer had come to Prague to follow the succeeding stages of the crisis on the spot, and under the date of September 5 he wrote, 'President Benes, realizing that a decisive step on his part was necessary to save the peace, convoked the Sudeten leaders Kundt and Sebekowsky to Hradschin Palace and told them to write out their full demands. Whatever they were he would accept them. "My God," exclaimed the deputy Sudeten leader, Karl Hermann Frank, the next day, "they have given us everything!" '[7]

Indeed, the German chargé d'affaires was obliged to record that Benes had gone very far – much too far.

'Both from this proposal and also from statements by President Benes and the Prime Minister, it can be assumed with comparative certainty that Benes, as well as the Government, is endeavouring to come to a draft agreement with the Sudeten German Party, so as to demonstrate to world public opinion that the Government was going thus far in the interests of peace to accept and to realize in practice Konrad Henlein's eight Carlsbad demands, within the limits of the sovereignty, integrity, and unity of the State ... If the Sudeten German Party does not wish to put itself, and thus also the German Reich, in the wrong, the Sudeten German Party must eventually accept such an agreement which, outwardly and in its essential content, covers the most important principles of the Carlsbad demands.'[8]

Optimism shone out in Paris and London: at last Benes had given way! Henceforward the Sudeten Germans were satisfied in every respect ... yet when Benes received Lacroix, the French minister, and told him of the concessions that he had just made – concessions that went 'beyond the limits that ensured the Czechoslovak state's integrity' – the diplomat only spoke of moderation and conciliation, just as though it was still for the Prague government to make the first advances in this field.

'Unless conciliation is carried to the farthest point,' he told Benes, 'it would be impossible, in the event of a rupture, for the French government to find the backing of French public opinion for a war with Germany, with France not being attacked by Germany and England standing aloof because of the fact that the French frontiers are not threatened.'[9]

So the French thought it helpful to urge Benes to show a conciliating attitude on the very day he had yielded everything. For their part, the Sudeten Germans knew very well what to make of it. They knew not only who it was who had made the first steps towards the other side, but also who it was who had gone the whole length of the road. And, as the bridge-playing English say, they felt that they were being squeezed.

To get out of this disagreeable situation Henlein turned to the oldest, best-tried method – that of distracting attention (and of suddenly changing the data of the problem) by bring up a new fact; and this, of course, could only be a provocation. It was impossible to murder Eisenlohr, for he was on leave; besides this was an eventuality that had been contemplated only for the moment when it should be a question of opening hostilities. In order to justify breaking off the negotiations the SdP would be satisfied with a minor incident, so long as it was well handled.

On September 7, at Moravska-Ostrava, or as the Germans call it, Mährisch-Ostrau, some SdP deputies who had come to look into the arrest of eighty-three Sudeten Germans, imprisoned for gun-running and spying, got into a quarrel with Czech policemen. One of the deputies even succeeded (according to his own account, at all events) in being struck with a whip by a Czech police officer.

This was more than enough. While Runciman, who was genuinely distressed, sent one of his close associates, Major Sutton-Pratt, to the spot as an observer, the SdP delegation informed Benes and Hodza that the negotiations were broken off 'until the affair should be settled'.

The great point was to gain a few days so as to allow Hitler to make use of the platform of the National-Socialist Party congress, which was opening at Nuremberg. It would be very surprising if, after this congress and the speech that the Führer intended to make at it, there should remain the slightest chance of finding any area of agreement in Czechoslovakia.

Yet this speech was not made until September 12, although the opening session of the congress took place on the fifth.

The Western powers blunder again and again

During the very first days of the Nuremberg congress Paris, London and Washington made a certain number of more or less inept moves, which rendered the democracies' weaknesses obvious and which strengthened Hitler in his conviction that he did indeed have a free hand to act when and how he chose in Czechoslovakia.

The first blunder was made by Georges Bonnet as early as September 4. It was all the less excusable (if indeed it was committed in good faith, as Bonnet asserts it was) since he had been ambassador to the United States and had been picked by Daladier as foreign minister particularly because of his knowledge of American reactions.

On September 4 Bonnet went with William Bullitt, the American ambassador in Paris, to La Pointe de Grave, where a memorial to the American soldiers who fell in Europe during the first world war was to be unveiled. Banking on the ambassador's love of France, Georges Bonnet urged him to slip a few words on the United States' active solidarity into his speech. The reserve that Washington had shown when Bullitt submitted the first draft to the State Department should have warned Bonnet to be cautious. But, on the contrary, he pressed for a version which, even in an attenuated form, should still let it be understood that America might find herself drawn into a fresh conflict, at the side of her allies of 1917 and 1918.

In the end Bullitt, with the agreement of the State Department, said, '. . . as I said on February 23, 1937, if war broke out in Europe no one could state or foretell whether or not the United States would be drawn into such a war.'

And, so that there should be no mistake about the meaning of these words, Bonnet added, when it came to his turn to speak,

'Neither your leaders nor ours have ever accepted the idea that war was inevitable, and neither your leaders nor ours have ever accepted the idea that they could remain unmoved in the event of a conflagration threatening to wreck a civilization in which your country, like ours, has its share . . . I am therefore touched, but not surprised, when your fellow-countrymen often tell me that if France were attacked once again, once again they would come to defend her.'

In addition to this Bonnet, referring to the Czechoslovak crisis, stated, 'In any event France will remain faithful to the engagements that she has undertaken.'

This simple phrase at once stirred up eddies which spread to the very heart of the French government. One of Daladier's ministers, Anatole de Monzie, who was also one of the leaders of the 'pacifist' tendency, immediately showed his disapproval. He came within an ace of calling Bonnet a militarist and a sabre-rattler.

'This sentence did not form part of the text that we were shown when he left,' writes Monzie angrily. 'Who asked for it to be added? Under whose influence? I cannot find out who is responsible for this untimely and therefore dangerous addition – so untimely and so dangerous. It is impossible to get a valid explanation from Georges Bonnet. Apparently neither Daladier nor Léger is involved. Maybe it is only a detail in small-scale history, but history on the great scale is watching us. What adds to the strangeness of this incident is the fact that it was Chautemps and Bonnet, the most cautious of all, who were the only ones to stress the Franco-Czech pacts. Blum himself has spoken in a reserved manner in all circumstances. As for Daladier, up to the present moment he seems impregnable. I remember his observation of July 31 – "I do not want to act the part of Don Quixote." '[10]

And Anatole de Monzie, still referring to this blameworthy phrase, went on to suggest that the 'addition' must have been made 'during the journey, somewhere between Paris and La Pointe de Grave'. When one knows that Georges Mandel, one of the ministers most firmly resolved to support Czechoslovakia, by force if need be, was at La Pointe de Grave, it is not difficult to imagine who it was that Monzie held responsible for this alteration 'during the journey'.

But Georges Bonnet is much clearer on this point that Anatole de

Monzie would have us suppose. 'I drove down from Paris to Bordeaux alone,' he states, 'and I therefore had no one travelling with me to prompt me to say what I did on France's engagements. This had been drafted at the Quai d'Orsay, and it was the result of collective work with Léger and my colleagues.'[11]

Yet presently these words faded into the background and appeared less important, less heavy with consequences, than those uttered by Bullitt. Indeed, in spite of 'his knowledge of American political circles and his personal relations with the President of the United States', Bonnet, as far as American public opinion and Roosevelt's reactions were concerned, had committed a two-fold psychological error.

The Americans were divided on the question as to whether a possible intervention in Europe would be opportune or not; and although Roosevelt had said that he was in agreement with the text that Bullitt had read, he did not have the power to set the United States on a road that might lead to war without a vote of Congress, above all if he were not sure of expressing the unanimous feeling of the nation. So during his press conference on September 9 he made statements that were both a disavowal of Bullitt and at the same time an involuntary encouragement to Hitler to carry on fearlessly with his policy of aggression.

'To include the United States in a Franco-British front against Hitler,' said Roosevelt, 'is a political columnists' interpretation, and it is a hundred per cent wrong.'

And a few minutes later the president said, 'Ambassador Bullitt's speech does not constitute a moral engagement on the part of the United States towards the democracies.'

The diplomatic venture undertaken by Bonnet thus confounded its author and brought about two separate disadvantages, the first being a solemn reaffirmation of France's determination (whereas Bonnet could not have been less determined) and the second a display of American isolationism. Very soon afterwards a third and no less disastrous consequence appeared, for a few days later the American government wrote to Daladier to say that if war were to break out the Neutrality Act would forbid the delivery of the aeroplanes that had been ordered in the United States as early as May.

And what of the English?

They too, during the first days of the Nuremberg congress, had provided the Germans with good reasons for pursuing the course they had chosen; and they had provided the Czechoslovaks with grave motives for fearing the worst. For on September 7 *The Times* published a leader that startled the entire world. It included the following lines:

'If the Sudetens now ask for more than the Czech Government are ready to give in their latest set of proposals, it can only be inferred that the Germans are going beyond the mere removal of disabilities for those who do not find themselves at ease within the Czechoslovak Republic. In that case it might be worth while for the Czechoslovak Government to consider whether they should exclude altogether the project, which has found favour in some quarters, of making Czechoslovakia a more homogeneous state by the cession of that fringe of alien populations who are contiguous to the nation to which they are united by race.'

A taking up of a position of this kind allowed the Germans henceforward to present the dismemberment of Czechoslovakia as an idea originating in England. It would, nevertheless, have had no more than limited repercussions if it had come from any other newspaper. But for many years it has been assumed (and apparently not without reasonably solid evidence) that *The Times* expresses notions that arise in the Prime Minister's immediate circle. The same paper had already, in June, launched a preliminary *ballon d'essai* on the same subject. And even at that time English political circles took it to be the expression of an idea that originated in 10 Downing Street.

After the leader of September 7 the Foreign Office put out a clarifying statement. But the telegram that Theodor Kordt, the German chargé d'affaires, sent to Ribbentrop on the eighth emphasized the merely relative worth of this denial and thus gave a true reflection of the opinion of the well-informed English.[12]

London, September 8, 1938.

Last paragraph of yesterday's *Times* article caused great sensation in London. General opinion that idea of cession of Sudetenland to Germany, to prevent threat of world war, inspired by Government. Foreign Office denied this view first in press conference at midday and then in evening in form of official statements. Statement says:

'. . . that a suggestion appearing in *The Times* this morning to the effect that the Czechoslovak Government might consider as an alternative to their present proposals the occasion [*sic*] of the fringe of alien population in their territory in no way represents the views of His Majesty's Government.'

Later official *démenti* was result of direct intervention by Masaryk, Czechoslovak Minister here, who twice called at the Foreign Office for this purpose.

Daily Telegraph and leading provincial papers attack *Times*, particularly on grounds that Sudeten German attitude would be stiffened by *The Times* article.

According to reliable information, *The Times* article was certainly not inspired by the Foreign Office. The possibility exists, however, that it derives from a suggestion which reached *The Times* editorial staff from the Prime Minister's entourage. Supporting this view is fact that *The Times*, in today's leading article, 'The Threat of Force', maintains its opinion, even though in less pronounced form.

Part Two

ON THE SLOPE

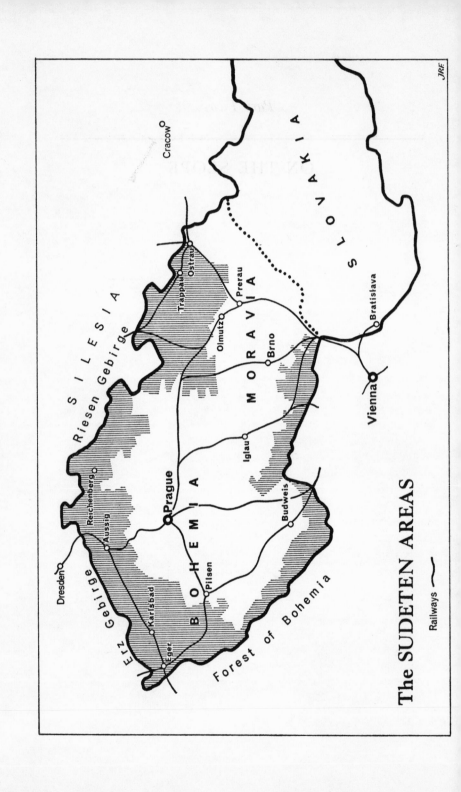

The SUDETEN AREAS

Railways ⌒

CHAPTER ONE

The road to Berchtesgaden

The evolution of public opinion · Military measures · The speech · Henlein goes into action · The Prime Minister and the gangster · From Croydon to Berchtesgaden · A tête-à-tête · Everything is smoothed over

THE swastika hung over the beginning of this month of September, which saw the preparation, the opening and the first sessions of the Ninth Congress of the German National-Socialist party at Nuremberg. Racked with anxiety Europe once more watched this show put on for her benefit. For days on end the continent remained in suspense, waiting for the speech upon which its fate was to depend – war or peace. In short, the film director Goebbels once more showed the extent of his virtuosity; he succeeded in winning the whole world's attention and in keeping it fixed day after day upon this vast moving shot which first embraced Germany and then gradually narrowed down to Nuremberg, the Nazis and their heavy boots thundering in the streets, the army parade, the march-past of the Workers' Front . . .

After the stadium with its three hundred thousand uniformed men and its red sea of banners and its hundreds of floodlights all converging on the platform, the last shot was of a single man, motionless and silent while the hysterical crowd's *Sieg Heil* rose towards him, and finally this man's ravaged, tormented, grimacing face, in the grip of a positive delirium of words.

But this last act was arranged only for the evening of September 12, and for the intervening week the congress was to 'carry on with its work'; the keynote, this year, was the historic mission of the Third Reich, whose duty it was to gain justice for all those Germans who were still cut off from the Fatherland.

By way of symbol, Hitler had caused the emblems of the Holy Roman Empire, the crown, the sword and the orb, to be taken out of the Hofburg and brought to where the congress was meeting.

According to a custom that was already several years old, foreign delegations had come to Nuremberg to attend the congress – and above all the parades that formed its essential complement. The interpreter Schmidt, whose duties particularly required him to look after these foreign 'sympathizers', observed that there had never been so many of them. Indeed, among the English he noted the presence of Lord Stamp, Lord Clive, Lord Holenden, Lord Brocket, Lord McGowan and Norman Hulbert, MP; there were several Frenchmen and there were representatives from many other foreign countries.

Naturally Franco's men, the 'Spanish brothers in arms', were at Nuremberg too. But Schmidt was very much surprised by the conduct of the Spanish ambassador, who, says he, was one of those who was most deeply concerned at the situation. The interpreter adds, 'He often said he was afraid of seeing France, on the outbreak of hostilities, putting an end to the Franco régime with the help of the Spanish left-wing parties.'[1]

Meanwhile, although Hitler was certainly taking part in the sessions of the congress and although he accepted the requirements of the programme arranged by Goebbels – the banquets, parades and demonstrations – he nevertheless did not forget Operation Green.

On the evening of September 9 he summoned Brauchitsch, Keitel and Halder, together with Captain Engel and Captain von Below. The conference went on until the dawn of the tenth, and once more Major Schmundt, the Führer's aide-de-camp, drew up the minutes.

The new Operation Green was beginning to take shape. It was Halder, the chief of the general staff, who outlined it. Objective: to prevent the Czech army from withdrawing from Bohemia-Moravia. Defeat the army. Bring about a quick decision. The objective may be attained by means of a pincer movement attacking in the direction of Olmütz and Brünn, carried out by the Second and Fourteenth Armies. Difficult transport problem in Austria, the chief thrust therefore in the Second Army's sector.

Thus the general staff, showing a surprising stubbornness, in spite of Hitler's orders six days earlier,* persisted in wishing to entrust the Second (and not the Tenth) Army with the main effort. The most that could be said was that this pincer movement in which the

* See above, p. 92.

Fourteenth Army was to take part had been added to the original draft; it had not been mentioned at the Berghof on September 3.

Dealing with these experienced strategists, Hitler gave a display of both a certain degree of flexibility and of an immovable obstinacy. According to Schmundt's account he even took advantage of the occasion to read them a lecture.

'There is no doubt that the planned pincer movement is the most desirable solution and should take place. But its success is nevertheless too uncertain for it to be depended on. Especially as a rapid success is necessary from a political point of view. The first week is politically decisive, within which a far-reaching territorial gain must be achieved.

'Our artillery (21cm howitzers) not adequate against the fortifications. Where an attack is expected the element of surprise is ruled out.

'Besides, from experience it is difficult to abandon an action which achieves only partial success. More and more units are thrown into breaches and "bleeding to death", which must be avoided, sets in. (Verdun!!) . . .

'If pincer movement has no success, Tenth army will open way for Twelfth Army, bringing strong forces into the heart of the country. If both operations are successful, this means the end of Czechoslovakia.'[2]

The end of Czechoslovakia, that was what the members of the Nuremberg congress cheered the next day, September 10, when Göring addressed them.

'A trifling piece of Europe,' he said, 'is making life unbearable for mankind. The Czechs, that vile race of dwarfs without any culture – nobody even knows where they come from – is oppressing a civilized race; and behind them, together with Moscow, there can be seen the everlasting face of the Jewish fiend!'

A few hours later on the same day Benes spoke to the Czechoslovak nation on the radio. William Shirer was still in Prague, and he describes the atmosphere in the city.

'But Benes' broadcast of the same day took no notice of Göring's diatribe; it was a quiet and dignified appeal for calm, good will and mutual trust.

'Underneath the surfaces, though, the Czechs were tense. I ran into Dr Benes in the hall of the Czech Broadcasting House after his broadcast and noted that his face was grave and that he seemed to be fully aware of the terrible position he was in. The Wilson railroad station and the airport were full of Jews scrambling desperately to find transportation to safer parts. That weekend gas masks were distributed to the populace.'[3]

The evolution of public opinion

No more than twenty-four hours remained before the contents of the Führer's speech would be known. But through a sudden change in the situation all the news that reached Hitler in the course of these twenty-four hours was of a kind to make him ponder, all the more so since it showed not so much a stiffening attitude on the part of the governments (which might easily be explained by purely political factors) as a development of public opinion in the democratic countries.

There were various reasons for the alteration noted by the German diplomats. Among them may be mentioned the irritation caused by the show of strength at Nuremberg and the publicity given to the German military measures; but above all public opinion in France, England and even the United States had the same reaction at the sight of Benes's concessions and the dilatory attitude and obvious bad faith of Henlein and the leaders of the Sudeten German party.

It was a fact that the Prague government, after the incident at Moravska-Ostrova, had given a favourable reply to all the demands of the SdP, but the latter had put off the resumption of talks until September 13, that is to say until the day after Hitler's speech.

The off-hand manner in which the SdP leaders received the concessions, fundamental to the problem, that Benes had granted, was considered all the more shocking since there had been great hopes of this attempt at conciliation.

Kundt's ponderous joke – 'Benes had yielded us ninety per cent; but when you cut a man's head off, he too still has ninety per cent left. And what he lacks is important, whatever they may say' – made nobody laugh.

In a telegram sent to the Wilhelmstrasse and at once relayed to Nuremberg the counsellor von Selzam summed up British public opinion and the attitude of the press.

'Whole press agrees unanimously that Czech proposals to Sudeten Germans are extremely far reaching and that attitude of Czech Government gives no justification whatsoever for German action by force . . .

'British public opinion is accordingly reckoning with the possibility of a war. It is convinced that, after serious loss of prestige during the last few years, Britain could not allow unilateral German action by force against Czechoslovakia. It considers the security and freedom of the Empire would be threatened if Britain did not give active assistance to Czechoslovakia and France in this event.'[4]

As far as France was concerned, it was Brauer, the chargé d'affaires, who sent a telegram summarizing the position before the Führer's speech. He divided his report into five sections.[5]

'(1) Daily increase of nervousness and fear of war in broadest sections of the population is unmistakable . . .

'(2) Fear repeatedly expressed that determination of Western Powers to resort to military intervention in favour of Czechoslovakia in event of German attack upon latter not sufficiently clearly understood in Germany.'

Then come two sections devoted to the press. One mentions the few leader-writers who called for fresh concessions on the part of the Czechoslovaks – Paul Faure in *Le Populaire*, Fabre-Luce in *La Journée industrielle* and Le Boucher in *L'Action française*; the other describes the reactions of certain journalists after the appearance of *The Times* leader.*

Finally, the last section, in spite of its cautious circumlocution, plainly gives it to be understood that French public opinion had evolved since the May crisis and that the papers opposed to any kind of intervention in Czechoslovakia were now only a minority.

'(5) Despite fact that Government stresses determination not to shrink from military intervention in the event of German attack on Czechoslovakia and great majority of press follows same line, yet isolated voices – even though less numerous than early this year – are heard which draw attention to senselessness of unleashing a world war on account of Czechoslovakia. Especially the provincial press and, in particular, the Alsatian press publish articles of this sort.'

* See above, p. 100.

In the United States, less than forty-eight hours after Roosevelt had disavowed Bullitt at his press conference,* Thomsen, the German chargé d'affaires in Washington, warned his government against undue optimism. '. . . In spite of this, the basic attitude of American foreign policy has not altered. If, in the event of German intervention in Czechoslovakia, England and France take up arms against Germany, it is upon their side that America will range herself.'

Selzam, the counsellor in the London embassy, caught an echo of the same note during a conversation with Joseph Kennedy, the American ambassador. And this was all the more important since Kennedy was notoriously opposed to intervention and in favour of every concession. Besides, he did not conceal his personal feelings as he spoke to Selzam.[6]

'Kennedy told me he had always been of the opinion so far that, in the event of warlike developments in the Sudeten German question, Britain would make every effort not to become involved in the conflict. He had completely altered this opinion of his within the last 72 hours, particularly as a result of conversations which he had had with Chamberlain and Halifax yesterday.† . . .

'To my question as to how America would act in the event of a European conflagration in which Great Britain was involved, he replied that firm assurances by Roosevelt to the Government here (as was stated in the press) could not be given for Constitutional reasons. They would naturally endeavour "to keep America out of the war", as in the last World War. He himself had two‡ sons and would work for this. He was, however, convinced that America would nevertheless intervene in the end. Feeling in America had never yet been as anti-German as was the case at present, and in his opinion very wrongly so, for Hitler had done wonders in Germany.'

Furthermore Kennedy had to acknowledge that Roosevelt had told him to 'assure Chamberlain that he approved of his attitude'. Now it so happened that this attitude had been made public by a semi-official note, an 'authorized statement' which the Foreign Office gave the press during the morning of September 11. It ended with sentences of the first importance.

* See above, p. 99.
† Selzam's note is dated September 12.
‡ The ambassador Joseph Kennedy had four sons, the second of whom, John Fitzgerald, became President of the United States of America.

'In no event could Great Britain remain indifferent to a conflict in which the integrity of France might be threatened.

'It is of primary importance that the German government should entertain no illusions upon this matter and that they should not suppose that a rapid and victorious campaign in Czechoslovakia could be begun without bringing about the possibility of intervention by France and subsequently by Great Britain.'

This text was published by the Paris evening papers on September 11 and by the whole of the press the next day, and it at once caused an immense sensation. The Paris papers' headlines, which in many cases spread right across the front page, revealed much of the underlying feeling on this subject.

Le Petit Parisien: England has spoken.
Le Populaire: The British government do away with all uncertainty.
Ce Soir: England is with us!
L'Epoque: The forces of peace close their ranks.

Yet there was a question that arose from this communiqué: did it exactly reflect the British government's attitude?

Georges Bonnet had already asked this question in advance, for on September 10 he invited Sir Eric Phipps, the British ambassador, to the Quai d'Orsay, and said to him, 'Germany may attack Czechoslovakia tomorrow. If she does, France will mobilize at once. She will turn to you and say, "We march: do you march with us?" What will be the answer of Great Britain?'

Sir Eric reported this conversation to Lord Halifax the same day. The next day, the eleventh, the Foreign Office communiqué was handed to the press. And yet in spite of the closeness of the dates it was not a question of a public answer to Bonnet's inquiry of the day before. Indeed, on the twelfth the British Foreign Secretary sent the ambassador a reply which was couched in terms far less sharp and distinct than those of the 'authorized statement'.[7]

'So far therefore as I am in a position to give any answer at this stage to Monsieur Bonnet's question, it would have to be that while His Majesty's Government would never allow the security of France to be threatened, they are unable to make precise statements of the character of their future action, or the time at which it would be taken, in circumstances that they cannot at present foresee.'

There is a certain irony in comparing these shifty and evasive words with the message that Kordt, the German chargé d'affaires in London, sent to Ribbentrop on the subject of the Foreign Office communiqué.[8]

'It amounts to a definite statement of British policy, the seriousness of which can no longer be doubted. The possibility can be discounted that such a far-reaching definite statement could have been made only for the purpose of intimidation. The complete change which British public opinion has undergone during the last fortnight places British government in a position to implement tomorrow the policy announced today.'

Military measures

So before he finally drafted his speech Hitler had had very grave warnings from his own diplomats about 'the sudden change in public opinion' not only in England but in the other democratic countries. And unless he were to trust in more direct sources of information than those of the Wilhelmstrasse, he was to suppose that the governments themselves were following the same line of development as public opinion in their countries.

Furthermore he had additional information, all pointing in the same direction, on the military measures being taken in Great Britain and France.

On the tenth Siemens, the German naval attaché in London, had been received by Rear-Admiral T. A. Troup. 'Admiral,' asked Siemens, 'are the newspaper articles about the mobilization of the English fleet true?'

'They are true as far as concerns the minesweepers and the minelayers.'

'And are these the only mobilization measures taken by the Royal Navy?'

'Yes, the only ones,' replied Troup.

But Siemens did not leave it at that. 'I can therefore report to my admiralty that these are the only steps?'

'You put me in an embarrassing position, with your report . . . I am not a diplomat! I must make inquiries . . .' And the admiral asked his visitor to leave him alone for ten minutes – that is to say, to give him time to telephone. Even before these ten minutes were over he confirmed what he had said before. 'Yes, these are the only steps.'

'Then, admiral, how do you explain that the *Royal Oak* and the fourth torpedo-boat flotilla are heading for Portsmouth and not for Scapa Flow, as it had been arranged? At least that is what I see in *The Times*.'

'That is not a question of mobilization measures,' Troup protested. 'These ships have new captains and crews aboard; they are going to carry out exercises.'

Siemens showed that he was not taken in by this. 'That explanation may do for the public. But I am a naval officer, and I should have to be given something rather easier to believe.'

Of course the Wilhelmstrasse at once received a detailed account of this conversation; and the report also went to the minister of war and the commander-in-chief of the navy of the Third Reich.

In the same way Kühlenthal, the military attaché in Paris, had been summoned by General Gamelin, who, 'because of their personal relationships and in the name of the soldierly comradeship that he had always felt for him', told him of the intensification of the military measures being taken in France – the cancelling of all leave, the recall of those on furlough, the dispersal of naval depots and training centres, and other preparatory steps.

General Gamelin particularly stated that these measures still constituted part of the first stage of the security arrangements (state of alert, first level). He added that no unattached forces and no classes had been called upon, but that large-scale calling-up of several classes of reserves was going to take place.

These military problems with which the French were faced were the subject of important talks during the day of September 12, that is to say a few hours before the Nuremberg speech. At five in the afternoon, after the meeting of the cabinet, the three most important men in the army, General Gamelin, the chief of the general staff, General Georges, the general appointed to the command of the north-eastern theatre of operations, and General Bilotte, posted to the Alpine theatre, were received by Daladier in his dual function of head of the government and minister of war.

With slight differences of emphasis, the three generals agreed in considering that a strong thrust with a view to breaking through could not usefully be mounted at the beginning of the hostilities against the Siegfried line. Reckoning up the strength of both sides they maintained that even if Germany were committed in Czechoslovakia and even if she had to protect her Polish flank, she could still have troops between the Rhine and the Moselle that, as far as numbers went, could be compared to the French.*

The view of the military leaders, summed up by General Georges and noted down by General Gamelin, was therefore

(a) to be prudent in decisions aimed at committing the first French troops beyond the frontier.

(b) to preserve liberty of movement for the main body of the army, so that it might either be stationed ready for a counter-thrust on the wings (Luxemburg, Belgium and the Jura), or that it might go over to the offensive as soon as coalition should bring about a certain equality between the opposing forces.

Yet all three were of the opinion that in the event of a German attack upon Czechoslovakia, French intervention would cause such a threat to the Siegfried line that Hitler would be obliged to concentrate his reserves there, and that to that extent the Czechoslovak army would be relieved.

The speech

At last there came the hour, dreaded by some and hoped for by others, the hour of the closing speech of the Nuremberg congress.

Hitler arrived at two minutes to seven, and it took him twelve minutes to pass through the ranks of his followers, under a continuous roar of *Sieg Heil*! Meanwhile, by a well-managed movement, the banners of the National-Socialist formations had been gathered together under an immense swastika.

The orchestra could scarcely be heard, in spite of the number of players and the great wealth of brass; it had time to play the *Badenweiler* and then the Nibelungen march. After that it began the Meistersinger overture but suddenly stopped: the time was ten minutes past seven, and Rudolf Hess had just stepped on to the platform. It was he who had the duty of announcing that the Führer was about to speak.

Hitler began by recalling the National Socialist party's struggles at length. He adorned his speech with dull gleams of ponderous humour that delighted his hearers – a very easily pleased audience.

* We have seen (p. 90) that this was not the opinion of 'the neighbour over the way', the German general Wilhelm Adam, in command of the Western theatre.

Speaking of the time when the Nazis seized power the Führer said, 'They were waiting for the moment when the drummer (that meant me) should be replaced by the real statesmen (that meant the others).'

But it must be said that on that evening even the fanatics in brown shirts were anxious, and they were unable to delight as much as they usually did in this new display of their idol; for they too were waiting for the speech's essential passage. They were waiting for what Hitler was going to say about Czechoslovakia. At last it came.

'What forces us Germans to take part in this question is quite natural: among the majority of nationalities oppressed by the Czech state there are also three and a half million Germans.

'About as many men of our own race as the whole population of Denmark. These Germans are also God's creatures; the Almighty did not make them in order that they might be handed over, by a political interpretation of Versailles, to a foreign power that they detest. He did not create the six million Czechs to supervise the three million Germans and keep them under their thumb, still less to browbeat and torment them.'

Then came the usual refrain about the 'persecutions' suffered by the Sudeten Germans.

'The Sudeten Germans' wretchedness is indescribable. The Czechs want to wipe them out. They are being intolerably and shamefully oppressed. Three and a half million members of a nation of close on eighty million do not have the right to sing songs that the Czechs happen to dislike. They are beaten until the blood flows, just because they wear white stockings, which do not appeal to the Czechs. They are terrorized, and misused because their way of greeting does not please the Czechs, or else because they do not greet the Czechs but salute one another. Every time they indulge in a display of their national life they are hunted down like so much game . . .'

And now there appeared the warning to the democracies.

'No doubt all this ill-treatment leaves a great many of those who represent the democracies unmoved. No doubt many of them look upon it with approval, since it is only a question of three and a half million Germans.

'I shall only say to the representatives of these democracies that it does not leave us unmoved, and that if these tortured people ask us to come to their help and to secure their rights it shall be done. The pariah status of these men must come to an end . . . I have not claimed that Germany should have the right to oppress three and a half million Frenchmen nor that three and a half million Englishmen should be handed over to Germany to be trodden under foot, but I do claim that the oppression of three and a half million Germans in Czechoslovakia should stop, and I demand that in its place there should be the right of self-determination.

'We should be sorry if this were to disturb or damage our relations with other European states, but the blame does not lie with us!'

Thanks to the radio everyone throughout the world, from the heads of state to the humblest citizens, was able if not always to understand this speech then at least to hear the Führer's harsh voice, and above all the frequent interruptions of the huge crowd, which responded to every stress in the flood of words, cheering the Sudeten Germans, booing 'the Czechs' and the democracies, endlessly applauding the Führer.

And as soon as the peroration was over and even before the last ovation had come to an end, the translation began to come over on the press agencies' tickers.

Everywhere, even in Prague, the first reaction was almost exactly the same – a sigh of relief; for there had been no ultimatum. No denunciatory summons. At the most the assertion of close solidarity (which everyone was aware of) between the Third Reich and the Sudeten Germans.

Among the democracies, therefore, the speech led to the belief that a fair and peaceful solution might still be sought for – and found.

And, taking his ear from the loudspeaker of the set to which he had been listening for an hour and a half, Mussolini himself, who prided himself on his knowledge of German, observed, 'I had expected a more threatening speech . . . Nothing is lost.'

Henlein goes into action

So the evening of September 12, from which the worst had been feared, ended in comparative euphoria. But on the other hand the day of the thirteenth was to give rise to the most extreme anxiety.

For that morning it was learnt that Hitler's speech had given the signal for a rising in the Sudeten regions of Czechoslovakia. The paramilitary formations of the Sudeten German party had everywhere gone into action, attacking police and gendarmerie stations, while demonstrators tried to seize railway stations, post offices and public buildings.

To restore order the Prague government, which was in continuous session, was finally obliged to declare a state of siege and to proclaim martial law in several Sudeten districts at noon.

Henlein's reply came at once. It assumed the form of an ultimatum.

'The Executive of the Sudeten German Party sets on record that a large number of Sudeten Germans have been killed and injured by State authorities and Czech frontiersmen. In view of this situation the Executive of the Sudeten German Party cannot see its way to negotiate freely and unhindered with the Government regarding the rights and destiny of the Sudeten German element, unless the Government adopts the following measures:

'(1) The proclamation of martial law is to be rescinded at once.

'(2) The State Police will be withdrawn from all districts where the majority of the population is German. The exercise of the powers of the police is to be transferred to mayors and magistrates of communes, who are to arrange for the establishment of the corresponding substitute authorities for the maintenance of peace and order.

'(3) The gendarmerie and all other instruments of the SOS. are to be limited to their normal functions and their normal strength. They are, at the same time as the State Police are withdrawn, to establish good relations with mayors and magistrates of communes in order to avoid further bloodshed.

'(4) All military formations are to be confined to their quarters and in purely military premises and barracks. They are to be kept away from the civil population.

'If these demands by the Sudeten German element, designed to create a normal situation in which negotiations can alone be conducted, are not accepted, enacted, published, and in particular broadcast by radio within six hours, the Executive of the Sudeten German Party will disclaim any responsibility for further developments.'

At the same time it was learnt that the Sudeten delegates had finally abandoned their initial series of demands. From now on it was no longer a question of being satisfied with the 'eight points' of Carslbad – which had in any case been accepted by Benes. What the Sudeten Germans – following *The Times*' suggestion – were now claiming was a plebiscite.

At the end of the day the casualty-list of the riots provoked by the SdP became known: twenty-one dead, of whom twelve were Czechoslovaks (nine being gendarmes) and nine Germans. It was impossible to count the wounded, for most of them, at least on the Sudeten German side, refused to have themselves looked after at the first-aid posts. On their side the Czechoslovaks had a hundred and seventeen wounded – three soldiers, seventeen gendarmes, eighty civilians, fifteen policemen and two treasury officials.

Throughout almost the whole of the day the governments had been in continuous session in London and Paris. In the evening, convinced that it was necessary to initiate some move such as the general conference that Bonnet suggested or at all events a joint Franco-British discussion, Daladier telephoned Chamberlain.

The connexion was bad, and this added still more to the dramatic nature of the conversation. Daladier suggested to Chamberlain that there should be a direct approach to Hitler, conceived in terms that should emphasize Franco-British unity: but Chamberlain's answer cut all discussion short, and without enlightening Daladier as to the Prime Minister's intentions, it left him in a state of perplexity the whole night long.

'Some time ago,' said Chamberlain, 'I came to a resolution. I believe it to be useful . . . I cannot tell you anything yet, but I will let you know about it a little later.'

The Prime Minister and the gangster

The resolution that the Prime Minister had reached was to cause utter amazement throughout the world. One of the first to know of it was the Führer's interpreter. On the morning of September 14 he was brought a short message to translate into German.

> In view of the increasingly critical situation, I propose to come over at once to see you, with a view to trying to find a peaceful solution. I propose to come across by air, and am ready to start tomorrow. Please indicate earliest time at which you can see me,

and suggest place of meeting. Should be grateful for very early reply.

Neville Chamberlain

This message was dated London, September 13, 1938, 23.00 hours.

Less than two hours earlier, at 21.18 hours, another message had been sent to the Wilhelmstrasse, also from London. It came from Kordt, the chargé d'affaires, and it contained most valuable information about Chamberlain's state of mind at the moment at which he decided to suggest this meeting to the Führer.[10]

'Prime Minister's press secretary informed German press correspondents that Chamberlain felt disappointed and hurt by Führer's speech. Chamberlain considered European war to be unavoidable if matters were allowed to run the same course as hitherto. He was still prepared today to examine far-reaching German proposals, including plebiscite, to take part in carrying them into effect, and to advocate them in public.'

Including the plebiscite! There was the key word, already uttered before the event, the key word that was to prove to Hitler that he had always been right and not his advisers, his generals, and his diplomats; he had always known that the Western statesmen would give way, that they would put up with whatever he was determined upon, with or without war, and that they would abandon Czechoslovakia after having asserted their determination to defend her up until the last moment.

The fact that Chamberlain, a gentleman of close on seventy, should offer to come the whole way to meet the Führer, that he should make his press officer officially announce that he did not consider the plebiscite a solution that was a priori to be set aside, that he should even suggest helping in its organization – were not all these so many signs of a game already won beforehand?

Without showing any undue haste, Hitler replied after a few hours that he would be happy to receive the Prime Minister the next day, September 15, at Berchtesgaden. And at the end of the day the news was made public throughout the world. It must be said that it aroused an almost unanimous enthusiasm: tension had reached such a pitch that it seemed as though the race towards war was henceforward obliged to follow its relentless course. This move of the Prime Minister's was so unusual, so obviously far outside the ordinary smooth diplomatic procedure, that everyone regarded it as something that might be able to put a new face on what they had already almost accepted as inevitable.

The popular reaction in England went beyond any heights that British exuberance had ever reached – and although this exuberance is not often shown, it is none the less comparable to the most striking of Mediterranean outbursts. During the whole of the afternoon of the fourteenth a vast crowd, even larger, according to the 'experts', than that which gathered there at the time of Edward VIII's abdication, had been massing in and around Downing Street. In the course of the day a government communiqué had been announced; then it was put off until later. And suddenly, in the evening, when journalists from all over the world were beginning to wonder whether they had been waiting for nothing, the Prime Minister's chief press officer appeared, with a piece of paper in his hand.

Yves Morvan* was there for *Le Journal*.

'The terms of the communiqué which announced Mr Neville Chamberlain's sensational decision,' he writes, 'positively amazed the journalists; many of them had been deeply convinced that Great Britain would go a long way to preserve the peace; a few, in spite of all opposition, had maintained that as far as the conciliating and peaceful approach were concerned, the British government had not said their last word. But even so . . .

'Some had continually given out that England would shun any spectacular threat, yet they had not dared to prophesy that she would go so far in a spectacular invitation to keep the peace.

'At the sight of the journalists running for the telephones and the policemen clearing a way for them, the crowd grasped that something extraordinary had happened, and surged forward. Suddenly the news was flying from mouth to mouth along Whitehall. Cheering broke out. It is no exaggeration to say that all those who were there at once understood the immense contribution that has just been made to peace . . . the news, spreading by word of mouth, was already making its way through the heart of London . . .'

In Paris the headlines of the papers were enough to show the people's

* *Le Journal*'s special correspondent in London in 1938, Yves Morvan was better known as Jean Marin. He used this name as part of the BBC's war time French team and still uses it as Director of the *Agence France Presse*.

relief. Political circles were very happy to learn that in the afternoon Chamberlain had telephoned Daladier and that the two men had had a friendly and hopeful conversation.

In Berlin the news had a bomb-like effect. The moderates and the trimmers in the Führer's entourage, who could not see Operation Green's D-day coming nearer without intense anxiety, were filled with hope; but since they knew their master well they were also aware of their hope's fragility.

At all events they took the matter seriously. Schmidt himself, surfeited though he was with international meetings and talks 'on the highest level', suddenly changed his view.

'That same evening I left for Munich in a perfectly common-place special train, with no uniform; and I had the feeling that this time I was not merely going to act as an extra in some international demonstration, but that I was going to play a part, modest yet not without importance, in one of the great dramas of History. "Gather your wits together," said Weizsäcker, the secretary of state, in the train, "for tomorrow at Berchtesgaden it will be a question of war or peace." '[11]

There were other Germans who for the most part had been genuine Nazis, but who were beginning to find it hard to stand the régime, the vulgarity of its dignitaries and the madness of its leader; and the news of Chamberlain's coming spread consternation among them. It suddenly multiplied Hitler's prestige tenfold; and it did so at the very moment when the conspirators were intending to look for the army's and the people's support in order to put an end to the 'Bohemian corporal'.

The former Nazi Gisevius, an officer of the police services (of the Gestapo, to put it plainly), who had become one of the prime movers in the plot, does not hide his disappointment.

'Each of us tried to explain the thing in his own way: Schacht, deeply moved, paced up and down his office, striking his forehead every two minutes. "Can you conceive such a thing? The Prime Minister of the British Empire coming to see this gangster!"

'Nebe overwhelmed me with reproaches, saying that once again I had given him false hopes. "Don't you see that the others want no part of it [sic]!"

'Oster put on an appearance of unconcern, but he prevented me from going to see Canaris, for at the Abwehr the atmosphere was too heavy. The most painful side of it was that Witzleben himself was shaken . . .'[12]

Lastly, at Prague the announcement of the meeting between Hitler and Chamberlain was received without enthusiasm. It came at a time when fresh news of the serious disturbances caused by the SdP was coming in from the Sudeten regions; at Haberspirk, in the Talkenau district, the Sudeten Germans had taken the gendarmerie post by storm, had seized grenades, two machine-guns and cases of ammunition, and had then fought a pitched battle with the gendarmes sent as reinforcements. At Cheb there had been firing between the police armoured cars and the men of the SdP barricaded in buildings used as the party's centre. At Schwaderbach, on the German frontier, two thousand rioters had imprisoned the Czech gendarmes and customs-officials.

As martial law was continued and extended to other districts, Henlein registered the fact that no notice had been taken of his ultimatum, and early in the morning he issued a communiqué which announced the final breaking-off of the negotiations and the disbanding of the SdP delegation that had been set up to meet the representatives of the Prague government.

Then at the end of the morning the Führer of the Sudeten Germans received the members of the Runciman mission at Asch: they were without Lord Runciman, who for his part was enjoying Count Czernin's splendid hospitality at the chateau of Petersburg with Lady Runciman – hunting, social delights, the reception of a delegation of young Sudeten Germans wearing white stockings and giving the Hitler salute . . .

Henlein, accompanied by the Deputies K. H. Frank and Kunzel, officially told Runciman's colleagues, Ashton-Gwatkin, Peto and Henderson, of the breaking-off of negotiations; he added that they could only be resumed when the gendarmerie and the police were withdrawn from the Sudeten territory, and that in that event the basis of the talks would no longer be the Carlsbad programme but the right of the Sudeten Germans to self-determination, that is to say, to join the Reich.

After this Henlein quietly and illegally crossed the frontier, fixing his headquarters at Selb, in Bavaria. Here he drew up a proclamation addressed to 'the Sudeten Germans and to the whole world'.

'. . . At this hour of anguish I come before you, before the German people and before the whole civilized world to cry "We want to live as free Germans! We want peace and work to come back to our fatherland! We want to return to the Reich!"

'May God bless us, as He blesses our rightful struggle!'

Henlein then sent a message to Hitler, telling him where he stood, for the purposes of the meeting next day. Relying upon the statements that the members of the Runciman mission had made to him, Henlein asserted that according to all likelihood Chamberlain would propose union, and assuming this to be the case he added two conditions that the Prime Minister should have to accept.

1 No plebiscite, but immediate handing-over of the territories whose population was more than fifty per cent German.
2 Occupation of these territories by German troops within twenty-four hours (motive: to put an end to the murders by Czech fanatics).

Of course, only part of this news was yet known in Prague. Henlein was still thought to be at Asch, and nothing whatever was known of his message to Hitler. But what was known, either by official channels or by rumour, was quite enough to make the Berchtesgaden meeting seem ominous.

So during the evening there was a spontaneous demonstration in the streets of Prague. Thousands of men and women marched up in procession towards the Hradschin Castle, Benes' residence, to show the head of the state that he might count on the people's will to resist.

This knowledge that the people were behind him was the most valuable and the most useful stimulant for the President of the Czechoslovak Republic. He had great need of it, for he nourished few illusions as to the outcome of the direct talks that were beginning.

When Sauerwein, the special correspondent of *Paris-Soir*, came to ask him what he thought of the meeting at Berchtesgaden, which was announced for the next day, Benes replied, 'Peace is still possible. Everything depends on the price that you and the English will agree to make us pay. But let Chamberlain and Daladier remember that we can only draw cheques upon their accounts . . .' And after a thoughtful pause the head of the state added, 'Poland and Hungary are thinking only of rushing in for the spoils of our Czechoslovakia.

As for Stalin, he will only move if the democracies prove to him that they are not trying to manage affairs so that in the end the USSR will be left alone, grappling with Hitler, which is what he is afraid of.'[13]

From Croydon to Berchtesgaden

On September 15, the day of that meeting which the whole world's press had already before the event described as historic, Neville Chamberlain made his first flight at eight o'clock in the morning, aboard a Lockheed Electra, the fastest machine in the British air lines.

All the way from 10 Downing Street to Croydon an extraordinarily thick crowd, considering the time of day, greeted and cheered 'good old Chamberlain'. And at Croydon many outstanding figures, headed by Lord Halifax, welcomed the Prime Minister and went with him as far as his aeroplane. Among the people at the airfield there was Lord Londonderry, who was known for his friendly relations with Hitler and Ribbentrop. While the steward was taking charge of the Prime Minister's modest baggage (a travelling-bag, an attaché case and a leather brief-case), Lord Londonderry was seen to go up to Chamberlain, and the two exchanged a few words in an undertone.

When he mounted the steps Chamberlain, with the BBC microphones in front of him, made this short statement. 'I am going to see Chancellor Hitler because the situation seems to me of such a kind that discussions between him and me may have useful consequences. My policy has always been to try to ensure peace. The prompt acceptance of my suggestion encourages me to hope that my visit today will not be without results.'

Two colleagues accompanied the Prime Minister; his closest adviser, Sir Horace Wilson, and the head of the Central European section of the Foreign Office, Sir William Strang.

Less than four hours later, on the stroke of noon, the three Englishmen stepped out of the Lockheed on Munich aerodrome, where Ribbentrop and the interpreter Paul Schmidt were waiting for them.

'I stood the voyage very well,' said Chamberlain to Ribbentrop, 'though we had bad weather for part of the way, and this is the first time I have ever flown!'

They drove in an open car from the aerodrome, through Munich to the station, and this allowed Chamberlain to observe that the people of the town had turned out in large numbers and that they welcomed him warmly. More warmly, remarked Schmidt without dissatisfaction, than they had welcomed Mussolini a year earlier.

A special train was standing in Munich station, with steam up. Hitler had put his own dining-car at his visitor's disposal, and a single long table had been arranged in it. Chamberlain, with Wilson and Strang, sat on one side of it, Ribbentrop, Henderson and Schmidt on the other. The journey was to last three hours – three hours in which the train of the 'messenger of peace' continually passed military convoys – troop trains, guns, war material of every kind.

A few miles from Berchtesgaden the rain began to fall. The low-hanging cloud shut out the mountain-tops. Suddenly it became very dark, with a storm rumbling in the heights.

At the foot of the stairway leading to his home Hitler came forward, alone, to meet his guest.

A tête-à-tête

It was the first time that Neville Chamberlain had actually seen the Führer: September 15, 1938, was undoubtedly a day of discoveries for this Englishman on the edge of seventy. To tell the truth, Hitler rather disappointed him.

'Half way down these steps stood the Führer bareheaded and dressed in a khaki-coloured coat of broadcloth with a red armlet and a swastika on it and the military cross at his breast,' wrote Chamberlain. 'He wore black trousers such as we wear in the evening and black patent-leather lace-up shoes. His hair is brown, not black, his eyes blue, his expression rather disagreeable, especially in repose, and altogether he looks entirely undistinguished. You would never notice him in a crowd and would take him for the house-painter he once was.'[14]

After a few welcoming words the two men introduced their assistants to one another. Chamberlain noticed only one face – 'General Keitel, a youngish, pleasant-faced smart-looking soldier'. The great room into which Hitler first brought his guest, the room in which the Führer had already received the Duke of Windsor, some years before, and then Lloyd George, was of the most striking proportions. And inevitably the huge sheet of plate-glass that took up the whole of the far window and which gave out on to a magnificent display of mountains drew all eyes. But the weather was too cloudy for the view to be really at its best. Still, the room provided Chamberlain with a very good opening – all the more so as Hitler, who seemed to him diffident and nervous, did not set the conversation going. The two men, with the interpreter Schmidt, now sat down at a little table where tea was served.

'I have often heard of this room,' said Chamberlain, 'but it is much larger than I had expected.'

'It is you that have big rooms in England,' said Hitler politely.

'You must come and see them some time.'

'I should be received with demonstrations of disapproval.'

'Well perhaps it would be wise to choose the moment,' suggested Chamberlain subtly.

At that, noted the Prime Minister, 'H. permitted himself the shadow of a smile.'

This short and not very original opening of the conversation took up the time allotted for the ceremony of tea, and suddenly Hitler, who soon appeared to his guest less and less shy, asked Chamberlain what procedure he would prefer.

'Would you like two or three of our assistants to take part in our talks? Of course I am not referring to Herr Schmidt, who will be there as interpreter, but for that reason belongs to neither side.'

This question did not find Chamberlain unprepared. 'If it is convenient to you,' said the Prime Minister, 'I should prefer a tête-à-tête.'

It was Hitler's turn not to be surprised. For indeed, as Schmidt points out, all this was the result of a little plot: it had been agreed, with the Führer's consent, that Ribbentrop should not be included in the meeting. It was thought on both sides that the presence of the foreign minister would constitute an obstacle to a peaceful settlement between England and Germany! Hitler was perfectly aware of the wounds that Ribbentrop's vanity had received in London, and this agreement, worked out by Henderson and Weizsäcker with Göring's approval, had his consent. Schmidt, then, was the only man to go up to the first floor with Hitler and Chamberlain.

Chamberlain had been rather shocked during tea by a nude which hung in the hall on the panel nearest him, and he observed that in the big antechamber on the first floor there were also fine paintings by Italian and German masters – and several of them were nudes, too.

On the other hand the simplicity of the room into which Hitler now led him was a surprise to Chamberlain: no decoration, 'not even a clock', merely an unpretentious pedestal table upon which there stood two bottles of mineral water ('which he didn't offer me,' observed Chamberlain), three chairs round the table and a sofa along one wall. That was all. It was here that the three men were to sit and talk for three hours.

Chamberlain began first; he started by recalling that he had always advocated closer relationships between Great Britain and Germany. But the deterioration of the relations between the two countries made him uneasy ... Overcoming his impatience Hitler listened. He even put in some polite words to compliment Chamberlain and to tell him how much he appreciated his having undertaken this journey. After this the Führer came to the heart of the matter and went on for a long time; indeed, after his own fashion he gave an account of the entire history of the German-Czech crisis. With increasing passion and vehemence the Führer recalled the treaty of Versailles, the League of Nations, Germany's relation with her neighbours and with the great powers; he listed the grievances that Germany could bring forward against England ...

Schmidt listened, translated and took notes; but he also watched Chamberlain, for it was always interesting to see the effects of Hitler's speeches on the face of a hearer who was not accustomed to his eloquence.

'The English minister listened attentively. His brown eyes often gazed at Hitler. Nothing in his typically English face with its bushy eyebrows, pointed nose and energetic mouth under a little black moustache let one see what was going on behind his high forehead, topped with slightly greying hair. It was the same attitude as that of his brother, Sir Austen Chamberlain, when he was engaged with Stresemann at Locarno or Geneva. Yet he did not seem to have the "fish's blood" of that British Foreign Secretary. He quickly broke in to contradict certain points in Hitler's account, made the classic reply on the freedom of the press with a friendly, almost soothing, smile, and looking Hitler squarely in the face he asserted that he was prepared to look for a solution on all the points that the Germans complained of, but that in all circumstances resort to force must remain out of the question.

' "Force?" burst out Hitler, "Who is it who talks about force? It is Herr Benes who is using force against my fellow-countrymen in Sudetenland. It is Herr Benes who mobilized in May, and not me!" '15

But it was useless for Hitler to raise his voice. Chamberlain would by no means follow him on to this ground; on the contrary, he remained quite calm and did his utmost to bring Hitler back to the discussion of facts and principles. Thus the Führer brought up his theories on racial unity again and his ideal, which had always been to give Germany back those children who had been torn from her, and when he reached the three million Germans living in Czechoslovakia, having spoken of the seven million Germans of Austria, at this point Chamberlain interrupted him. 'Hold on a minute.'

Surprised, for he was not used to being stopped in mid-harangue like this, Hitler gazed at Chamberlain, understanding for the first time perhaps that he had opposite him a man over whom he could not exercise the same power as that which he had possessed over all those whom he had hitherto summoned to this cell at Berchtesgaden. But Chamberlain was already carrying on with what he had to say.

' "There is one point on which I want to be clear and I will explain why: you say that the three million Sudeten Germans must be included in the Reich . . ."

' "Yes!"

' "Would you be satisfied with that and is there nothing more that you want? I ask because there are many people who think that is not all: that you wish to dismember Czechoslovakia."

' "If by that you mean that I want to include not only the Germans in the Reich but also the Czechs, you are mistaken," said Hitler. "I do not want the Czechs at any price. On the other hand, I admit that I should not feel myself safe as long as a treaty between Czechoslovakia and the Soviets were to continue in force. Furthermore, when the Sudeten Germans have returned to the Reich the other minorities will want to secede in their turn – the Poles, the Hungarians, the Ukrainians . . . Believe me, what will be left of Czechoslovakia after that will be so small that I shall not have to worry about it any more!" '

And now Hitler, with renewed vigour, launched once more into his indictment of the Czechoslovak government, which had been making war upon the unfortunate Sudeten Germans for these last ten years, and which, during the days just past, had reached the point of massacring whole populations of innocent people.

' "Entire villages have had to flee into Germany; there are more than ten thousand refugees here already ... places with three thousand inhabitants have undergone gas-attacks, and there are already over three hundred dead! I shall not tolerate such things any longer. I said this at Nuremberg, and it will be seen that I was not uttering mere empty words!"

' "Why not make a joint appeal to both sides so that they may carry on with their talks in a calmer atmosphere?" suggested Chamberlain.'

Hitler would have none of it, any more than he would hear of an armistice between the Czechoslovaks and the Sudeten Germans.

' "Anyhow, the whole thing has been going on for too long! Now matters must be settled. And before long I shall settle them myself, in one way or another; I am ready to take the risk of a war rather than see this state of affairs last any longer!" '

Schmidt, an unmoved witness of this outburst, observes,

'It was the first time that this expression "*so oder so*" was used during an interview with a foreign head of state, and on this occasion as upon all the others that came after, it amounted to an extremely threatening danger-signal. I naturally translated it as "one way or another", its exact English equivalent, but on that day as on later days it really meant "surrender by the other side or invasion, the use of force, solution by battle".

'Chamberlain, who had listened up until then with the utmost calm, now grew heated in his turn. "If I have rightly understood you," he said, "you are determined to march against Czechoslovakia whatever happens!" Then, after a momentary pause, he went on, "If this is what you meant to do, why did you let me come as far as Berchtesgaden? In these conditions the best thing for me to do is to go away again as quickly as a I can. All this no longer seems to have any point." '[16]

The Prime Minister was on the very edge of going through the motions of getting up and taking his leave.

Everything is smoothed over

Hitler hesitated, thought, remained silent for a few seconds, and then suddenly 'his whole manner changed' as Chamberlain notes – and

Chamberlain was by no means the least surprised by the effect his threat had produced. After this every thing went along very quickly. Chamberlain gives an account of it.

'He quietened down then, said if I could assure him that the British government accepted the principle of self-determination (which he had not invented) he was prepared to discuss ways and means. I said I could give no such assurance without consultations [with the cabinet, the French, and Runciman]. My personal opinion was that on principle I didn't care two hoots whether the Sudetens were in the Reich or out of it according to their own wishes, but I saw immense practical difficulties in a plebiscite. I could, however, break off our talk now, go back and hold my consultations and meet him again. That is a possible procedure, he said, but I am very sorry that you should have to make two journeys. Then I asked him how the situation was to be held in the meantime and he promised not to give the order to march unless some outrageous incident forced his hand.'[17]

All that remained to be done was to draw up a short communiqué for the papers: 'The Führer and Chancellor of the Reich has had an interview at Obersalzburg with the British Prime Minister today which has allowed a broad and sincere exchange of views on the present situation. The Prime Minister is returning to England tomorrow to confer with the British cabinet. In a few days another meeting will take place.'

Yet the day did not come to an end without an incident that somewhat marred the euphoria reflected by the communiqué; it was an incident in which Schmidt, in spite of himself, was involved. For that evening he was working at the fair copy of his analytic report at the Grand Hotel in Berchtesgaden, where the English were staying, as well as Ribbentrop and Schmidt. From time to time Henderson came to ask how the work was getting on, for Chamberlain was waiting impatiently for the text. Suddenly, taking advantage of the fact that Henderson had just left the room, Ribbentrop burst into the interpreter's room. 'What's all this? Do you think you are still at Geneva? At Geneva, where secret documents were given to anyone who asked for them, and everybody was as matey as a styful of hogs* . . . but it is not the same in National-Socialist Germany.

* Schmidt gives an account of the scene, and in his original German this expression is in French—*amis comme des cochons*.

These notes are reserved exclusively for the Führer! Do your best to remember that.'

The unfortunate Schmidt could do nothing but try to find a plausible explanation for telling Henderson and Chamberlain that they were not to count upon having his report. It must be said that the Prime Minister took it badly. 'You can tell the Chancellor from me that in these circumstances I shall have my own interpreter with me, if it so happens that we have another meeting.'

The next day the Englishmen went back to Munich by the auto-bahn and then on to Oberweisenfeld, where the plane that they had left exactly twenty-four hours earlier was standing.

Even before the Lockheed Electra had landed in England, all the German heads of mission throughout the world received a short message from the Wilhelmstrasse which said all that was worth saying about the Berchtesgaden meeting. 'The Führer has stated to Chamberlain that . . . it is no longer a question of granting the Sudeten Germans autonomy, but solely of the cession of the Sudeten-land to Germany . . . Chamberlain has indicated his personal approval.'

CHAPTER TWO

The first surrender

Franco-British discussions · The 'Franco-British' plan · Who was preventing Czechoslovakia from mobilizing? · Prague accepts · Rosenfeld's testimony · The frightened men · Churchill in Paris · Benes surrenders

NEVILLE CHAMBERLAIN gave the British cabinet, which met on the sixteenth, as soon as he returned, a detailed account of the meeting at Berchtesgaden, and ended by saying, 'Clearly everything rests upon Hitler's word. Can we trust in it? For my part, after this personal contact, I think we can: I have the impression that he is one of those men who are to be trusted once they have given their word.'

Before this, in the presence of his ministers, the Prime Minister had defended the Sudeten Germans' right to self-determination; and thus, without delay, he had begun those consultations that he had told Hitler he considered essential – consultations with the British government, the French and Lord Runciman.

Runciman, hastily recalled to England, took the ordinary plane from Prague at one o'clock in the afternoon and reached Croydon at four, a little later than Chamberlain, who had left the Munich aerodrome at 12.48.

His complete report on his mission, which had lasted forty-five days, was not yet ready in its final shape; but Lord Runciman was nevertheless in a position to tell the cabinet of his conclusions. These went well beyond what Chamberlain had personally accepted at Berchtesgaden and even beyond what Hitler had demanded during his conversation with the Prime Minister.

The British 'mediator' was seen by the government as soon as he arrived in England, and he did not conceal his preferences.

'I have a great deal of sympathy for the Sudeten Germans' case. It is a hard thing to be governed by a foreign race, and I certainly

132

have the impression that for the last twenty years the Czechoslovak régime in the Sudetenland, although it has not been an active oppression and certainly not a "terrorism", has been characterized by a want of tact and understanding, and by petty intolerance and discrimination, to such a degree that the resentment of the German population was inevitably moving in the direction of revolt. The Sudeten Germans also felt that in the past they had been given many promises by the Czechoslovak government, but that these promises had been followed by little performance or none. The experience that they had had prompted an attitude of open mistrust with regard to the leading Czech statesmen.'*

Thereupon Lord Runciman listed the Sudeten Germans' chief grievances against the Czechoslovaks: the appointment of 'Czech' civil servants in the German districts, the establishment of 'Czech' colonists by means of the agrarian reform, the building of 'Czech' schools for the children 'of these invaders' . . .

'I believe,' said Runciman, 'that for the most part these complaints are justified.'

After he had recalled the hopes that the rise of Nazism in Germany now aroused among the Sudeten Germans, Runciman reached the point of concrete proposals.

'It has become quite clear to me that these frontier districts between Czechoslovakia and Germany, in which a considerable majority of the population is Sudeten German, should at once without delay be given the right of full self-determination. There is a real danger and even a risk of civil war if a state of uncertainty continues.

'Consequently there are very powerful reasons for a policy of immediate and energetic action. I think that any form of plebiscite or referendum would be a mere formality as far as those zones where the Germans predominate are concerned. A very great majority of their inhabitants desire amalgamation with Germany.

'The unavoidable delays that a plebiscite would entail would only excite popular feeling, and this might have very dangerous consequences.

'That,' ended Lord Runciman, 'is why I think that these

* During his meeting with the members of the British government Runciman confined himself to reading the 'selections' from his report that were to be published in *The Times* on September 29.

districts should at once be transferred from Czechoslovakia to Germany, and furthermore that steps for their peaceful transfer, including measures for the safeguard of the population during the period of transfer, should immediately be taken by agreement between the two governments.'

For the regions in which the population was not German in its majority but where there were nevertheless many Germans Lord Runciman suggested 'local autonomy within the Czechoslovak Republic.'

Finally, as regards Czechoslovak foreign policy, the 'mediator's' conclusions were also in agreement with the extreme attitude of the SdP.

'Lastly, I recommend:

'1 That the Czechoslovak government should forbid those parties or persons who have deliberately encouraged a policy hostile to Czechoslovakia's neighbours to continue their activities in Czechoslovakia, and that if necessary legal steps should be taken to put an end to this activity.

'2 That the Czechoslovak government should so amend their relations with foreign powers that their neighbours should have the assurance that they should in no circumstances attack them and that they should not, by reasons of their obligations towards other states, take part in any aggressive action against them.

'3 That the chief powers, acting in the interest of European peace, should give Czechoslovakia guarantees of assistance in the event of unprovoked aggression against her.

'4 That a commercial treaty on a preferential basis should be negotiated between Germany and Czechoslovakia, if this appears advantageous to the economic interests of the two countries.'

In short, it seemed that Lord Runciman's main preoccupation was to guard Germany against a possible attack by Czechoslovakia. The landed gentry of Bohemia, who had 'taken care of' the Runcimans for forty-five days, had certainly wasted neither their money nor their time. They had paid out the rulers of Prague for the agrarian reform.

Franco-British discussions

After the cabinet and Lord Runciman, Chamberlain still had to consult the French. On September 17, when the ministers of Daladier's government were having lunch at Rambouillet with the President of the Republic after a cabinet meeting in the morning, a message came from Chamberlain, inviting Daladier and Bonnet to come to London 'to hear an account of the Berchtesgaden meeting'.

The next day the French premier and the foreign minister once more took the plane at Le Bourget together. And as soon as they reached Croydon they went on by car to 10 Downing Street.

Chamberlain was waiting for them, and he had invited the three other members of the inner cabinet, Lord Halifax, Sir John Simon and Sir Samuel Hoare. Some high civil servants were also to be present at the talks – Sir Alexander Cadogan, Sir Robert Vansittart and William Strang.

The Franco-British meeting began with a long monologue by the Prime Minister – a detailed account of the Berchtesgaden talks and an analysis of Runciman's report of the day before.

Although Runciman had come to the conclusion that the frontier districts with a 'considerable majority' of Germans should be transferred to Germany, Chamberlain was still personally in favour of a plebiscite. The French, on the other hand, were categorically opposed to a plebiscite. Some of their arguments were not without weight. 'If you agree that a plebiscite should be organized in the zones inhabited by a considerable majority of Germans,' said Daladier, 'how will you prevent the other minorities from claiming the same thing? A plebiscite would open the way for a series of operations of exactly the same kind in Ruthenia and Slovakia and in the regions where there are Hungarian and Polish minorities, and there will be no Czechoslovakia left!'

On the other hand, part of the French ministers' argument had a somewhat specious air; for in order to reason against the plebiscite Bonnet and Daladier recalled the attitude of the Czechoslovak government, which was resolutely hostile to this form of going to the country. Yet paradoxically enough this attitude on the part of the Prague government appeared to them an excellent justification for carrying out the transfer of certain territories to Germany without plebiscite! It is true that in doing this both Daladier and Bonnet say that they were acting in agreement with Benes's more or less secret wishes.

But although they agree in saying that this initiative started with Benes, they differ entirely upon how his wishes became known.

According to Daladier it was not only a matter of direct communication, but of one that had been brought to his knowledge that very morning, with the Franco-British conference in view.

'On Sunday morning,' he writes, 'before I left for London, M Blumel, Léon Blum's former principal private secretary, called on me. He brought me a note that Benes had just had delivered to him by a Czech minister, M Neczas. In no circumstances was it to be revealed that Benes was its author. But he thought it might facilitate negotiations in London and give rise to a compromise. The note proposed the cession to the Reich of three salients in the frontier districts, the one at the north-west corner, the second on the north-east of Bohemia and the third along Silesia. The attached map showed that these territories amounted to three thousand square miles. They were peopled by close on a million inhabitants, and the plan also provided for an exchange of populations.'[1]

Léon Blum has confirmed that he sent André Blumel to Daladier, but he gave a somewhat less sketchy analysis of Neczas' démarche: Neczas, said Blum, came to him, and speaking on behalf of Benes said, 'Matters have now reached such a pitch that England and France are going to ask us to make concessions. I am sending you a map upon which Daladier may see by the actual tracing of our military works and fortifications the ultimate line beyond which we should look upon Czechoslovakia as delivered up and lost.'[2]

On the other hand, according to Bonnet (who does not breathe a word about Blumel's approach nor about Neczas' communication) the suggestion concerning the cession of the 'salients' was made to M de Lacroix, the French minister, by Benes, on September 15. Benes, furthermore, observed that this was a plan that Masaryk himself had meditated upon during the preliminary work for the Treaty of Versailles.

'M de Lacroix,' states Bonnet, 'thanked M Benes heartily. At two in the morning on the seventeenth he sent us a long telegram in which he told us of this plan, which might, as he rightly observed, help us in finding a conciliatory solution at the meeting that we were going to have in London with the English ministers, and avoid the plebiscite that Prague dreaded.'[3]

M de Lacroix does not agree. And he says so with a scarcely diplomatic distinctness.

'Towards the middle of September I asked M Benes whether he did not envisage a solution that might put an end to the crisis. After a fairly long silence he replied that in 1919 he had contemplated the possibility of not including some small regions lying on the north-west and the south-west of Bohemia within the frontiers of his country. But he at once added that this recollection had nothing to do with the negotiations now being carried on and asked me to beg the French government not to take note of it.

'I telegraphed an account of this conversation to M G. Bonnet, strongly advising that it should be kept secret. Now it is my impression that it was at once communicated to the British government at the time of the meeting in London which took place at about this period. I have never forgiven our government for this indiscretion.

'More than that, in going through the foreign ministry's archives I have since found out that my telegram had been so tampered with that it might be supposed that the recollection which Benes called to mind was a solution that he put forward.'[4]

In all events, 'Benes's proposal', or what was advanced under that name by the French ministers, was not thought adequate by Chamberlain, who had come back from Berchtesgaden firmly convinced that Hitler would not be satisfied with 'half-measures'. But, as Daladier candidly observes, this proposal 'did strengthen the point of view of Chamberlain and the English ministers'.

Nevertheless, Daladier and Bonnet agree in claiming the authorship of the formulae upon which the agreement between the French and English was finally based – 'the replacement of the plebiscite by the plain cession of a given territory, and the obtaining of a formal guarantee of the new Czechoslovak frontiers from England.'

With regard to the first point, it was still necessary to decide upon the territory that was to be ceded.

'All the Sudeten territories having a German majority of more than fifty per cent,' proposed Chamberlain.

This was going even farther than Runciman had suggested, for he had only spoken of those regions 'with a considerable German majority'. It also meant taking no notice of the map which Benes had had delivered to Daladier and which showed the ultimate limit beyond which Czechoslovakia might be looked upon as 'delivered up and lost'.

The Frenchmen protested, argued, and gave way.

Daladier and Bonnet looked upon Great Britain's engagement as an important concession that they had wrung from the British government: what is more, the British had to go into the next room and hold council separately in order to agree to it. In fact it was merely a matter of adopting one of Lord Runciman's conclusions.

At one in the morning the agreement was brought into being, with the reservation that the French cabinet had to consult upon it, and a communiqué was handed to the press. 'The British and French ministers have come to a complete agreement upon the policy to be followed with a view to facilitating the peaceful solution of the Czechoslovak problem: they hope that it will be possible for them to envisage a more general settlement in the interests of European peace.'

The 'Franco-British plan'

At ten in the morning on September 19 the French ministers, under President Lebrun, met at the Elysée.

It was Daladier who assumed the task of giving an account of the deliberations of the Franco-British conference in London. He emphasized the 'double victory' won by Bonnet and himself: 'no plebiscite: British guarantee'. And he read the note whose wording had been settled the day before and which now only lacked the approval of the French government to become the 'Franco-British plan' submitted to the Prague government.*

The government's discussion was short. Yet it would not be true to say that it was non-existent.

Anatole de Monzie, a most strenuous supporter of peace at any price, thus sums up the arguments which his friends brought to bear on the ministers whom Daladier's account had left unconvinced.

'Some reserves were expressed. Daladier seemed to be wavering as to what attitude to adopt in the sequence of events. Bonnet denied the possibility of a war for us: he evoked the generalissimo's opinions. At this point Guy La Chambre, whom we were begging to give his views, brought forward the direct testimony of General Vuillemin, one of whose recent reports he read out. There was no doubt about it! It would be madness to go to war, in any event whatever, with so weak an air force against the reserves of the

* See p. 391, appendix I.

138

Luftwaffe. Somebody urged that we should take the Czech strength into account, and even the support of the Russians. But who could count on the USSR with any certainty? Bonnet established that even if she could, Russia did not want to commit herself: his diplomatic intelligence was entirely convincing – so convincing that after he had spoken, no one dared press the matter any further.'[5]

Who was preventing Czechoslovakia from mobilizing?

The Czechoslovak army and the support that it might possibly receive was therefore discussed; and apparently it was judged that Czechoslovakia's military position would not allow her to resist. It might have been as well to state clearly that her defensive potentialities had deliberately been lessened by the desire of the Western governments, and of the French government in particular. For with the aim of avoiding any 'provocation' that might anger Hitler (who was at this time openly concentrating thirty divisions on the Czechoslovak frontier) the Daladier government increased their démarches and their pressure, making use of their position as 'military ally' to prevent the Czechoslovaks from taking the steps required for their own safety.

On this point General Faucher's evidence is positive. 'These activities of the Prague government were the object of increasingly frequent and increasingly irritating interference and recriminations from Paris. I was the witness of some of this interference, carried out by M Bonnet over the telephone, which was obviously very incautious.'

As early as September 15 General Faucher wrote Gamelin a personal letter* in which he took notice of the incomprehensible reactions from Paris to the precautionary steps taken by Prague; and he took this opportunity to point out that all his earlier requests concerning essential Franco-Czechoslovak military co-operation had received no answer other than a mere acknowledgment.

On the eighteenth General Faucher wrote another letter to the chief of the general staff, an official letter. This time the head of the French military mission was sending a positive SOS to Paris. In it he said,

'President Benes has just spoken to me about the situation. The

* See p. 393, appendix II.

German attack may be launched very soon. Now to comply with the desiderata of the British and French governments the army has not taken essential military measures. The army runs the danger of finding itself in a very unfortunate position. This state of affairs cannot go on, and the decree for mobilization will become imperative in twenty-four or at the latest forty-eight hours' time. I beg for an immediate reply.'

As soon as he received this message Gamelin put the essence of it into a letter addressed to Daladier and given to Massigli at the Quai d'Orsay, so that the premier, then in London, might be told of it at once.

'In three or four days at the latest the German forces will be in a position to attack Czechoslovakia,' Gamelin's letter ended. 'As early as tomorrow Hitler may lay his cards on the table and put forward increased demands. If Czechoslovakia has not been able to strengthen her defence measures, in what kind of a position will she be from the military point of view and what kind of responsibility will rest upon us in this respect? At all events, in the case of a general war she will not play her part of holding a considerable proportion of the German forces before her for an appreciable time.'[6]

Not only had this responsibility been assumed, and not only had the French government done nothing to 'allow' the Czechs to mobilize (for it was indeed in these terms that the problem stood), but at the very moment when it was a question of knowing whether or not Czechoslovakia was to be sacrificed, the French statesmen who had quite deliberately kept her in a state of inferiority and diminished resistance based their arguments for the policy of abandonment which they were advocating upon those military inadequacies *for which they were directly responsible.*

It appears that no one spoke of this particular aspect of Franco-Czechoslovak relations during the cabinet meeting of September 19. And who indeed could have spoken of it except Daladier and Bonnet, who were the only ones who knew about it?

It is therefore easy to understand that there was no great difficulty in obtaining the ratification of the London agreement. For his part Anatole de Monzie was exultant. 'The Franco-British plan was unanimously adopted in its wording and in its spirit. I asked that mention should be made of this unanimity in the communiqué, and this was agreed to. If it were unanimous, the communiqué would be of such a nature that it would bring the country and Mr Chamberlain the comfort of our real or apparent understanding.'⁷

Prague refuses

In accordance with the procedure that had been arranged in London, once the consent of the cabinet had been obtained Bonnet summoned Osusky, the Czechoslovak ambassador in Paris, and handed him the 'Franco-British plan', urging that the Czechoslovak government should unreservedly approve it.

In the same way, Jan Masaryk was received in London by Halifax. As he came away from the meeting the Czechoslovak minister exchanged a few disillusioned words with the French journalist Paul Bret. 'Look', said Masaryk, 'here is the Franco-British proposal, or rather the Franco-British summons. I was expecting an ultimatum from Berlin, but not from Paris and London.'⁸ And when Bret had reached the part that dealt with the proposed new international guarantees Masaryk added bitterly, 'With that we shall really have nothing to fear any more! But still, it is a pity that your country insists upon our giving up our alliance with her just at the moment when our need for it would have been the greatest. I doubt whether it will bring her good luck.'

In Prague the French and British diplomatic representatives in their turn went to make the simultaneous approach to Benes that had also been laid down in the scenario agreed upon by the governments of the two countries.

The Czechoslovak statesmen were faced with the most dramatic choice that had ever been before them since the birth of their country. Upon the decision that they were to take there might perhaps depend the immediate beginning of the war; but from the choice of a certain kind of peace there might also depend the total disappearance of Czechoslovakia, at a more or less early date.

Meeting in the Hradschin Castle with Benes as chairman, the ministers and the heads of the army examined the structure of the problem without complacency and without mistaking their wishes for reality.

The situation inside the country, to begin with.

The people of Prague were solidly behind Benes. And every evening more people took part in the demonstrations in the streets of the capital that were meant to assert the population's will to resist.

But opposed to this by no means unimportant mass, the centrifugal forces urging the ethnic minorities out of the Czechoslovak community were growing more numerous – the example of the Sudeten Germans was catching. The Czechoslovak citizens of Polish or Hungarian origin did not attempt to hide their desire for secession. Not without uneasiness, Prague heard of the visit of the Hungarian leaders, Imredy and Kanya, to Hitler, and of the simultaneous visit that the regent Horthy made to Göring.

Furthermore, the SdP's clandestine propaganda in Slovakia had had the effect of reviving what had been no more than smouldering fire.

As for Henlein and his chief colleagues, they had set up a volunteer unit, the Sudeten commando, at the castle of Tandorg, near Reuch, on German territory not far from the frontier. While it was waiting for the D-day of Operation Green this body was given various missions of a provocative nature; it had 15,000 men, equipped with light military material suitable for guerrilla warfare. The first information gathered by the intelligence service of the Czechoslovak army on the activities of this commando listed, for September 19, several violations of the frontier between Germany and Czechoslovakia and the carrying out of acts of violence and sabotage in the frontier districts where there was a Sudeten majority.

The military situation was no less dramatic.

General Faucher's distress signals had remained unanswered: President Benes was anxious, whatever it might cost, to commit no 'fault' which might supply France, that strangely lukewarm ally, with an excuse for the desertion that was felt to be impending; he had not chosen to override France and decree general mobilization.*

* It was only the next day, September 20, that Daladier set about answering Gamelin's message. In the course of that day Gamelin received the following note:
'I beg to acknowledge your letter of September 19, which states that in the event of a general war Czechoslovakia would not be in a position to hold a considerable proportion of the German forces before her, because she has not taken defence measures. It is your opinion that from this point of view our responsibility is engaged. As a consequence of your note, I should be grateful if you would let me know, with the utmost urgency, what steps you would think of taking. Daladier.'
Gamelin at once instructed General Decamp to reply to Daladier, 'The Czechoslovak high command is the only body in a position to give an exact answer. If Czechoslovakia is attacked by Germany she cannot defend herself without total mobilization. The whole question therefore lies in knowing whether from now on France and England wish to leave Czechoslovakia complete, unconditional freedom of action. This lies outside the scope of the French military command.'

Finally, when they looked at their country's situation from the diplomatic point of view on this nineteenth day of September, 1938, Benes and his colleagues were forced to acknowledge that their isolation had never been so complete.

Rightly speaking, Czechoslovakia had only two allies, France and Russia. And of these two the latter would step in only if the first had already intervened. Now not only was it France who was trying her best to force a positive hara-kiri upon the Prague government, but for several months it had been clear that one of the reasons that was making the French government shrink from the obligations of the Franco-Czechoslovak treaty was the prospect of finding themselves allied with the Soviet Union in a European conflict.

These reserves on the part of the French government towards the Russian alliance were so obvious that the French ambassador in Moscow, Coulondre, writing on the same day, observes not without bitterness, 'Just what is happening? We are kept in utter ignorance of the development of the crisis. It seems that as far as London and Paris are concerned, Moscow is no longer in Europe.'

England was not allied to Czechoslovakia; but in Prague it had been hoped that Franco-British solidarity (and even the solidarity between democracies – why not?) would finally come into play against Hitler. Nothing whatever was left of that hope now. Chamberlain had taken the path of direct talks with Hitler. He was waiting for Benes's reply to go back to Germany and bring the Führer what he had promised him at Berchtesgaden.

As for the United States, which had nevertheless been Czechoslovakia's godparent at Versailles, nothing better was to be hoped for than a message from Roosevelt, which hid a complete inability to intervene in European affairs under the expression of the worthiest intentions.

So Czechoslovakia was alone. Alone, and yet by the absurd play of her alliances, deprived of the freedom of organizing her own defence.

On the other hand, the German colossus opposite her was openly and even ostentatiously carrying out military preparations which were quite clearly on the scale of an invasion.

The Italian ally and accomplice would not even have to step in. But in any case the solidarity of the Axis was total. Mussolini had just published a 'Letter to Runciman' written by himself, in the *Popolo d'Italia*, which made his attitude perfectly clear.

'. . . just as there is no Czechoslovak nation, so there is no Czechoslovak state . . . the "elements" of the Czechoslovak family come from different races that cannot bear one another. They are animated not by a centripetal but by a centrifugal power. Only force keeps them together. If this force were to cease, the phenomenon of Czechoslovakia's falling apart would be inevitable and irresistible.'

And at the same time the coalition of vultures was seen to be forming, ready to swoop on Czechoslovakia as soon as Hitler's Germany should have taken the initiative of war before the eyes of the world: Poland and Hungary would not let more than a few hours go by before moving into action. Thus, if a war were to break out, it would do so on three sides, almost at the same moment.

An objective analysis of the position therefore did not seem to leave the Czechoslovak leaders any freedom, any choice: all the factors of the decision called for the same answer – acceptance of the 'Franco-British plan', which was no more than a disguised ultimatum and which gave sanction to a desertion which already existed as a fact.*

And yet against all logic Prague did not give way.

The Western powers' note had been handed in by Lacroix and Newton during the afternoon of the nineteenth. The evening and the night and then the morning of the twentieth went by without the smallest indication reaching London or Paris as to the outcome of the discussions that were going on without a pause in the Hradschin Castle.

Finally, at 13.30 hours, a first telephone call from Lacroix told Bonnet of the development of the situation.

'M de Lacroix telephoned the minister at 1 hour 30† that the Czech government appeared to be wavering between two solutions, the acceptance in principle of the Franco-British plan, with certain reservations nevertheless, and the proposal of arbitration.

'M Georges Bonnet at once asked M de Lacroix to intervene in the most urgent manner and to make President Benes understand that it was a matter of losing no more time and of giving an exact reply to the Franco-British note.

* This, at all events, was the conclusion that Léon Blum reached in his leader in *Le Populaire* of September 20, 1938. This is a leader that is both famous (for it treated of the 'cowardly relief') and little known, since it is usually placed just after Munich and not nine days before. (See p. 395, appendix III.)

† It was in fact 13.30 hours.

Lord Runciman and
President Benes at a
meeting in Prague Palace
in August

Hitler advancing to meet
Mr Chamberlain when
he arrived at Hotel
Dressel-Godesburg for
their first meeting.
Göring is standing
behind and to the left of
Hitler

The French and British delegations, before the flight to Munich for the first meeting. Lord Halifax, Mr Chamberlain, M Bonnet, M Daladier and M Corbin

Mr Chamberlain with the Cabinet before his second Munich meeting. Among those present are Sir Kingsley Wood, Lord Hailsham, Sir John Simon, Mr Hore-Belisha, Mr Duff Cooper, Mr W. S. Morrison, Lord Halifax, Mr Oliver Stanley, Mr Vincent Massey, Sir Samuel Hoare and Sir Alexander Cadogan

'At the same time M Georges Bonnet begged the British ambassador in Paris to inform the British government of this attitude on the part of the Czechoslovak government, so that they might give their representative in Prague similar instructions.'*

At 15.30 hours there arrived a coded message from Lacroix, sent by telephone to the Quai d'Orsay. The text of this message says a great deal, in spite of its brevity, about the variety of ways of applying pressure (or seduction) suggested by Georges Bonnet.

'The political director has been instructed to tell me that the Czechoslovak government's reply to the Franco-British proposal will be handed to us during the afternoon.

'I made the most of this opportunity by repeating to M Krofta the urgent advice that I gave the President of the Republic during the afternoon of yesterday, and I made use of the guidance that Your Excellency gave me this morning on the telephone, particularly with regard to the economic and financial assistance that the French government were prepared to grant the Czechoslovak government. Moreover I urged the impossibility for Czechoslovakia in the present circumstances of retaining within her [frontiers] an [element] of the population which was now animated by a positive hatred for the state and which, furthermore, had the backing of that huge country Germany. Replying to a question from M Krofta I said that my personal feeling was that the French government would in no event change the point of view set forth in the note that M Newton and I had handed in yesterday.

Lacroix'

The afternoon went by, and still the answer that London and Paris were expecting with mounting impatience did not come. At 19.10 hours another coded telegram from Lacroix.

'A person who may be well informed tells me that the reply that is to be given to us very soon will be if not negative then at least

* Neither this account nor the notes and messages received in Paris during the days of September 20 and 21 provide any guarantee of authenticity according to administrative standards: the papers concerned are documents gathered together by M Georges Bonnet personally and taken away by him. He subsequently placed them in the archives of the Quai d'Orsay. Although M Georges Bonnet has personally guaranteed the exactness of these documents, it has been disputed, particularly by M de Lacroix, who, giving evidence before the parliamentary commission of inquiry into the events occurring between 1933 and 1945, has spoken of 'falsification' and 'mutilation'.

based upon a notion of postponement. It appears that there is speculation on the fall of the French cabinet [and] on the change that Czechoslovak resistance might bring about in French public opinion.

'This person states that according to his informant the [Czechoslovak] leaders' state of mind [might] still be modified by an immediate and very categorical warning from the Paris and London governments.

'He adds that a very plain appeal sent directly by General Gamelin to General Krejci would be more effective than anything. This appeal would explain why the complete and immediate acceptance of the Franco-British [proposal] is [essential]. At 15.20 hours I transmitted the preceding message that your Excellency entrusted me with by telephone. My British colleague made a similar démarche at 14 hours . . .

Lacroix'

Bonnet consulted Daladier as to the timeliness of this approach that might be made by Gamelin to the chief of staff of the Czechoslovak army; and Bonnet says that Daladier agreed with him not to proceed with the suggestion: both were of the opinion that the government could not ask the generalissimo 'to take a political responsibility' in their place.

Perhaps it was all the wiser not to ask, since this spared the ministers the refusal that would have been both likely and justified.

At last, at 21.50 hours,* the message bearing the Prague government's reply reached Paris.

'M Krofta has just handed me the Czechoslovak government's counter-proposal to the démarche that I made yesterday morning together with my British colleague. The latter was received by the foreign minister immediately after me. The Czechoslovak government state that it is impossible for them to accept a solution that has been drawn up without reference to them and that would not, in their opinion, put an end to the conflict, but would on the contrary open the door to new demands from Germany, result in the complete reduction of Czechoslovakia to the state of a vassal, and bring about a loss of balance in the Danube basin and the whole of Europe.

---

* The note on the document deposited by M Georges Bonnet reads 'Received by telephone at 21.50 hours'. In his book *De Washington au Quai d'Orsay*, however, M George Bonnet sets the time of arrival of this message at 21.15 hours.

'They recall the breadth of their most recent concession to the Sudeten Germans, a breadth the Sudetens themselves admit.

'They propose a recourse to arbitration on the basis of the treaty between Germany and Czechoslovakia of October 16, 1926, and end by making an appeal to the alliance of France and to the friendship of Great Britain to ask these two great powers to reconsider the question . . .

Lacroix'

So Benes had not given way! With their back to the wall, the Czechoslovak government, in spite of the promises and the pressure, in spite of the 'financial assistance' on the one hand and the threat of desertion on the other, in spite of the systematic opposition of their 'ally' to the taking of essential military measures, and in spite of the prospect of having to fight on three fronts – that is to say the certainty, in fact, of being crushed – refused to obey the orders of the 'democracies', which were claiming the right of disposing of Czechoslovakia without even having consulted her.

And this heroic decision was not the result of a sudden outburst, it was not a reaction to be ascribed to ill-temper, taken ab irato in a few minutes: more than twenty-four hours elapsed between the notification of the 'Franco-British plan' and its rejection.

Prague accepts

Yet while the news of the rejection of the 'Franco-British plan' was spreading consternation in Paris and London, or more exactly at the Quai d'Orsay and the Foreign Office, in Prague an unexpected face of things was beginning to make its appearance. The starting point of this was a telephone call from Hodza, the prime minister, urgently summoning M de Lacroix.

This call came exactly at the moment when the French minister was drawing up the telegram that announced the rejection of the Franco-British plan. Lacroix finished drafting it and rushed to the prime minister's house. Going straight to the matter, Hodza asked him this question, 'Are you sure that France will back out if it comes to fighting?'

Taken at short notice, Lacroix tried to find a way out. 'Prime Minister, I cannot tell. Would you like me to ask Paris at once by telegram, calling for a firm answer?'

On the slope

'No. It would take too long. I assume a priori that France will not march. If you can obtain a telegram from your government confirming this tonight, President Benes will yield. It is the only way of saving the peace.'

And, replying to an exact question from the French minister, Hodza added, 'Yes. I am acting with the agreement of President Benes and of the general staff, which is of the opinion that a war against Germany, without the support of France, would be the equivalent of suicide.'*

At the Quai d'Orsay Bonnet, with Alexis Léger, the secretary-general, and Jules Henry, the *directeur de cabinet*, by him, was finishing reading the message in which Lacroix reported this conversation when Daladier came in.

The premier and the foreign minister thought of the possibility of a sudden calling of the cabinet.† But the time in which Lacroix wanted an answer was too short – and besides, Lebrun was at Rambouillet.

All at once Daladier and Bonnet decided to telephone him. The call brought Albert Lebrun out of his bed.

* This conversation agrees with the account of the interview given by M de Lacroix before the parliamentary commission of inquiry into the events occurring in France between 1933 and 1945. In giving evidence M de Lacroix said, 'I at once informed the government of this conversation. Now, on examining the archives of the foreign ministry, I have established that M Hodza's first question and my answer, which expressed doubt, have been cut out of my telegram . . . I am of the opinion that the mutilation of my telegram is a serious charge for the French government, for it appears to show that without choosing to acknowledge it, the government were not determined to honour their obligations.'

This, in fact, is how the telegram appears in the documents in the Quai d'Orsay archives that are labelled '*documents Georges Bonnet*'. '[the prime minister] has just summoned me. With the agreement of the president of the republic, he told me, he stated that if I were to come this very night and declare to M Benes that in the event of war between Germany and Czechoslovakia over the Sudeten German question, France, because of her engagements with England, would not march, then the president of the republic would take cognizance of this statement; the prime minister would at once summon the cabinet, all of whose members were already in agreement with the president of the republic and himself to yield. The Czechoslovak leaders need this cover in order to be able to accept the Franco-British proposal. They are sure of the army, whose chiefs have stated that fighting alone against Germany would be suicide. M Hodza states that the démarche that he suggests is [the] only way of saving the peace.

'He wishes that everything should be finished before midnight if possible, or in any case during the course of the night. The prime minister will make the same [communication] to the minister of Great Britain.'

† This is a point upon which M Georges Bonnet dwells particularly, stating that the idea came from him.

148

'We have just received a telegram from M de Lacroix which I am going to read to you,' said the foreign minister. 'Daladier is beside me. Together with him and the under-secretaries of the ministry we have prepared an answer which I am also going to read to you, and we ask you for your consent.'

Lebrun listened to the reading of the two documents without saying anything, then he reacted. 'No; we must reflect. It seems to me that the cabinet will have to be called.'

But Bonnet insisted. 'M Krofta, the Prague foreign minister, asks for a reply tonight.'

'Then,' said Lebrun, 'I give my consent.'[9]

At 00.30 hours the following message was therefore sent to the legation in Prague.

'France, in agreement with England, has set in motion the only procedure that she does in fact consider, in the present circumstances, calculated to prevent the entry of the Germans into Czechoslovakia.

'By rejecting the Franco-British proposal the Czechoslovak government take the responsibility of bringing about Germany's appeal to force. By that very act they break the Franco-British solidarity that has just been established and thereby take away all practical efficacy from French assistance.

'These are warnings that we have already given, particularly in my instructions of July 16 and in my conversation with M Osusky yesterday.

'Czechoslovakia is therefore taking upon herself a risk from which we are conscious of having protected her. She must herself understand the conclusions that France has a right to draw if the Czechoslovak government do not immediately accept the Franco-British proposal.'

As for the British, they telegraphed Newton to go and tell President Benes that the London proposals alone would allow Czechoslovakia to avoid an immediate German attack. And that furthermore if the Prague government persisted in rejecting the Franco-British plan and in calling upon the provisions of the German-Czech treaty, Mr Chamberlain would have to renounce meeting Hitler a second time. After this, naturally, Great Britain would dissociate herself from Czechoslovakia's fate 'in the event of occurrences for which the British government could accept no responsibility'.

In the end it was two o'clock in the morning when the two ministers, Lacroix and Newton, appeared at the Hradschin Castle and asked to speak to Benes, who was asleep and who had to be woken up.

At Lacroix's first words Benes collapsed – 'as if I had hit him with a club', as he said later – and burst into tears. He listened first to the French and then to the British minister and found the strength to tell them that they should be given an anwer a little later.

In fact, as Benes has stated and as everything proves, this double declaration, made in these conditions and so late at night, had indeed had the effect of a blow from a club upon this exhausted man, worn out by fatigue and nervous tension, and who had not been in any way prepared to withstand the shock. For in contradiction to what the prime minister had told Lacroix, Benes knew nothing whatever of Hodza's démarche.

And while the two diplomats supposed that they were bringing the head of the Czechoslovak state an asked for and expected 'cover', they were showing him, with harsh cruelty, the emptiness of the last hopes that he thought he could still cling to.

The simple fact that Benes was already in bed, and sleeping, is enough to prove that he was not expecting this double announcement, that he had not asked for it, and that he had not even been given a hint of it beforehand.

Rosenfeld's testimony

But there is another even more decisive proof – the telephone conversation that took place that same night at about three in the morning between two of Benes's closest associates, Hubert Ripka, the editor of his paper, and Neczas, the minister of state insurance, on the one hand, and the French journalist Oreste Rosenfeld, the Paris editor of Léon Blum's paper *Le Populaire*, on the other.

The man speaking to Rosenfeld* at once told him why he was being rung up. 'The government have met and have just postponed their discussions because the president wants to consult you before taking a final decision. We want to reject the Franco-British proposal. If Hitler attacks us we can hold out for a fortnight. Can we hope

---

* O. Rosenfeld, from whom we have this evidence, cannot state for certain with which of these two he had the essential conversation, for he spoke to both; and as it will be seen he spoke to them twice, at three in the morning and at five.

that in these two weeks of unequal battle a change might come about in French public opinion and in the attitude of the French government, which would allow France to keep her engagements to us and come to our help? President Benes begs you to consult MM Léon Blum and Edouard Herriot urgently. We shall telephone you again in two hours.'

'I knew very well,' said Rosenfeld later, 'what reply I should have to give Prague, since we had not the least hope of making the Daladier government go back on their decision, and since public opinion and even a section of our own SFIO Socialist Party was ready to follow the government out of fear of war. However, as a matter of duty I at once telephoned Léon Blum. He called me back three-quarters of an hour later and told me to tell Prague that Czechoslovakia could not count on so rapid a change in France and her government. When Prague telephoned me again at five o'clock I carried out this painful commission, with a feeling like death in my heart.'

Thus, far from having agreed that the English and French should be asked for a 'cover', Benes still wanted to persist in refusing the London plan, in spite of the desertion notified to him by Lacroix and Newton. Far from being 'in agreement with the general staff'* in looking upon a single combat between Germany and Czechoslovakia as suicide, Benes thought Czechoslovakia could hold out for a fortnight, and he was ready to do so if only he had been allowed to hope for a sudden change in France before the end of that time.

And his will to resist was so firmly based that in spite of the disappointing reply that he had had from Rosenfeld, speaking in Léon Blum's name, Benes had still not given way at half past twelve the next day, and either to gain time or for history he asked Lacroix for a written confirmation of his verbal note delivered in the night.†

* Besides it is very probable that Hodza did not get the general staff's opinion, any more than he had Benes's agreement.

† In various works brought out after Munich, and even after the armistice of 1940, by pro-German journalists or 'historians', Rosenfeld's telephone calls are spoken of. They are mentioned so that the editor of *Le Populaire* may be accused of having rashly urged Benes on to war. It is known that the contrary is the case. On the other hand it is true that Georges Mandel telephoned Prague several times during the crisis, always to persuade Benes to resist. Robert Bollak, who was running the Agence Fournier in 1938 and who was a friend and colleague of Mandel, gives the essence of a telephone conversation which took place while he was present during the days before Munich. As Bonnet complained on the twenty-second that Mandel had telephoned Prague 'to destroy the effect of Bonnet's own communications', it may be supposed that the conversation reported by Bollak was on September 21.

'You are at the head of a free and independent nation,' cried Mandel into the

The frightened men

At five o'clock in the afternoon, however, Benes ceased the struggle: he did not feel that he had sufficient backing from his partners in the governmental coalition to continue fighting on all fronts.

For it is here that we must seek the explanation – the only logical explanation – of the events that occurred during that night of September 20–21: within the Prague government a set of 'frightened men' had gradually been revealed, as they had been in Paris and in London. And the Agrarians, whose leader was Hodza, had been the first to be infected.

As early as September 18 in Warsaw the head of the eastern department of the Polish foreign ministry, Kobylanski, gave Szembeck, the secretary of state, an account of a short stay that he had made in Prague, and told him 'Moscow has launched the watchword "no yielding"; it is supported by Benes *and fought against by Hodza, who is tired and over-wrought.*'[10]

And the Russian Potemkin confirms this. 'Only the influential Czech Agrarian party, led by Hodza, the prime minister, were in favour of the concessions to Hitler's claims that were supported by the British and French governments.'

The steps taken during the night, the invitation to the French and British governments to provide the Prague government with a 'cover' that would allow it to yield to the Franco-British ultimatum – all this was the work of Hodza, and of Hodza alone.*

Furthermore, his manoeuvre led to the result that he hoped for, since in the end the President of the Czechoslovak Republic was obliged to surrender.

telephone. 'Neither Paris nor London has the right to tell you what to do. But if your territory should be violated you must not hesitate for a second to give your army, which is prepared, the order to defend your country. By doing this you would save Europe from Hitlerism, for I can tell you that if you fire the first gun it will echo through the world in such a way that the guns of France and Great Britain and those of Soviet Russia too will in their turn go off, and go off of their own volition. The whole world will follow you and Germany will be beaten in six months without Mussolini; in three months with Mussolini . . .'

After he had encouraged Benes in this way, Mandel rang up Paul Reynaud. 'In spite of everything,' he said, 'I am confident that Benes pays attention to me – more than he does to Georges Bonnet.'

* At no point in his study of the events of the night of September 20–21 does Georges Bonnet take notice of the categorical statements of Benes, who has said that he was never aware of démarches made in his name by Hodza. It might be supposed that even now the former foreign minister would like to profit by the cover of Benes's name.

Churchill in Paris

Yet in the course of that day, September 21, Benes, on two occasions, caught a glimpse of a ray of hope. First he learnt that one of the few British statesmen he knew he could rely upon, Winston Churchill, was making a short visit to Paris to meet the French politicians who were hostile to Daladier's and Bonnet's policy of surrender, particularly the ministers Paul Reynaud and Mandel.

But this visit did not have the consequences that Benes was hoping for. For it is likely that the Czechoslovak president, speculating on the beginning of a ministerial crisis in France, drew the strength needed for resistance from the possibility of a resignation by Paul Reynaud and Mandel, who would probably have been followed by others, such as Champetier de Ribes and Jean Zay.

Now Churchill on the contrary considered the matter in quite another light, and he urged Reynaud and Mandel not to resign.*

'I have always believed that Benes was wrong to yield. He should have defended his fortress line. Once fighting had begun, in my opinion at that time, France would have moved to his aid in a surge of national passion, and Britain would have rallied to France almost immediately. At the height of this crisis (on September 20) I visited Paris for two days in order to see my friends in the French Government, Reynaud and Mandel. Both these Ministers were in lively distress and on the verge of resigning from the Daladier Cabinet. I was against this, as their sacrifice could not alter the course of events, and would only leave the French government weakened by the loss of its two most capable and resolute men. I ventured even to speak to them in this sense. After this painful visit I returned to London.'[11]

The other hope that Benes clung to stubbornly during the afternoon of the twenty-first was that which Litvinov's firm statement to the League of Nations had aroused in him.

Entering upon the Czechoslovak question, although it was not upon the agenda, the People's Commissar for Foreign Affairs, 'who certainly felt that it was his entire policy that was at stake', as Paul-Boncour, also at Geneva, observed, had flatly asserted the USSR's intention of respecting its international engagements.

* Paul Reynaud and Georges Mandel, as it will be seen, finally did resign as a protest against the pressure brought to bear on the Prague government, but only after Benes had accepted the Franco-British plan.

'Czechoslovakia is at present suffering interference from a neighbouring state, which is loudly and publicly threatening to attack her. One of the oldest, most cultivated, most industrious of European nations, one whose independence was won after centuries of oppression, may today or tomorrow be obliged to take up arms once more to protect her freedom.

'An event such as the disappearance of Austria left the League of Nations unmoved. The Soviet government, aware of the implications of this event, as much for Europe as a whole as for Czechoslovakia in particular, officially entered into contact directly after the Anschluss with the great powers and proposed immediate talks on the consequences of this annexation and the joint adoption of preventive measures. To our great regret this proposal which, had it been carried into effect, might have spared us the anguish as to the fate of Czechoslovakia that is now weighing on the entire world, was not valued at its true worth . . . Some days before I left for Geneva, the French government for the first time sought information as to our attitude in the event of aggression against Czechoslovakia; in the name of my government I gave the following reply, which seems to me perfectly clear and unequivocal: "It is our intention to stand by our treaty-engagements and together with France to assist Czechoslovakia according to the means at our disposal. Our ministry of war is from now onwards prepared to take part in a conference with the representatives of the French and Czechoslovak war ministries to consider the measures that the circumstances call for . . . It is only two days ago that the Czech government officially asked my government whether the Soviet Union, in the framework of the Soviet-Czech assistance pact, would bring Czechoslovakia efficacious and immediate assistance in the event of France, true to her engagements, bringing her similar assistance. My government gave a clear and affirmative answer."

'It is not our fault if our proposal was not acted upon. Unhappily other measures were adopted which have led and which could only lead to a surrender of such a kind that its incalculable consequences will sooner or later become disastrous. To avoid a problematical war today in order to have a certain general war tomorrow is not acting in the spirit of the League of Nations Covenant, above all when one wishes to do so in order to satisfy the appetite of insatiable aggressors, and that at the price of the annihilation or the mutilation of sovereign states.'

But a Russian intervention on Czechoslovakia's side remained conditional upon a prior intervention by France or a condemnation of Germany as an aggressor by the council of the League, which presupposed that Czechoslovakia, isolated, would let herself be attacked. The Russian ambassador in Prague, summoned by Benes the same day, was to confirm this interpretation in every respect, and thus at the same time do away with the last illusions of the head of the Czechoslovak state.

Benes surrenders

Nothing was left but to surrender – and to let the Czechoslovak people and the world know the conditions in which this surrender had been forced upon the country. The communiqué published in Prague at the end of the day on September 21 was touchingly dignified.

> 'We relied upon the help that our friends might have given us; but when the question of reducing us by force arose, it became evident that the European crisis was taking on too serious a character. Our friends therefore advised us to buy freedom and peace by our sacrifice, and this in proportion to their own inability to help us . . . The President of the Republic and our government had no other choice, for we have found ourselves alone.'

And Vavrecka, the minister of propaganda, said on the radio, 'Our friends and allies have obliged us to accept conditions that are usually put forward to a beaten enemy. It is not lack of courage that has forced us to take a decision that wrings our heart . . . Let us not judge those who have deserted us at the moment of the disaster: history will make her decision.'

As soon as the news was known in Prague it provoked violent reactions. Once more the people of the capital gathered to demonstrate both their anger and their desire to resist.

Towards the end of the evening the number of demonstrators continually increased, and General Syrovy, the inspector-general of the army, had to come out on to the balcony of the palace to try to calm the crowd.

'We cannot lead a whole nation to suicide . . .'

Only the last word was heard and retained, and at once the demonstrators began a rhythmic shout 'Suicide! Suicide! We want to fight!'

On the slope

The very next day the Hodza government were swept away and a government of national safety under General Syrovy brought in.

General Faucher, tearing up his French passport, asked to be allowed to serve in the Czechoslovak army.

In Paris the news of Prague's acceptance of the Franco-British ultimatum and the terms of the Czechoslovak communiqué, which were known at once and which left no sort of doubt remaining about the nature of the pressure brought to bear by the Western powers, caused a violent wave of indignation in the circles that were opposed to the surrender.

At seven in the evening at the Palais-Bourbon the Communist group carried a motion for the left-wing delegates, whose suspended sitting was to start again in half an hour.

> 'No one will understand, say the Communists, that it could be possible for Mr Chamberlain to go for Herr Hitler's orders a second time without the groups forming the Front Populaire parliamentary majority taking up a definite position on the defence of Czechoslovakia, whose integrity is inseparable from the security of France and of peace.'

Although the Socialist deputies were divided, they ended by passing a motion that severely condemned the government's action by an overwhelming majority.

> 'The Socialist group, convinced that firmness in the French and British governments would have gathered the free and anxious nations round them, whereas their weakness is encouraging the attempts of violence, cannot associate itself with diplomatic action that results in compelling a state, without that state's being consulted and under the threat of an attack, to sacrifice its independence, in materially and morally strengthening the régimes that use violence, in isolating France, in hurrying on the armaments race and thus in aggravating the risks of war.'

Seventy-five Socialist deputies voted for this text. There were only ten against it.

Lastly at eight o'clock the administrative committee of the CGT,* in spite of the existence of an important pacifist current within the trade union movement, passed a motion protesting 'against the pressure brought to bear upon the Czechoslovak government'.

* The General Confederation of Labour.

156

The first surrender

In England too the opponents of the appeasement policy reacted. The Labour Party expressed its 'profound humiliation before this shameful submission to Hitler's orders' and deplored that 'the long British tradition of democracy and justice' should be flouted thus.

The last public demonstration of the day was that of Winston Churchill, who had come back from Paris at the beginning of the evening and who had summoned the journalists at about midnight to give them this prophetic communiqué.

'The partition of Czechoslovakia under pressure from England and France amounts to the complete surrender of the Western Democracies to the Nazi threat of force. Such a collapse will bring peace or security neither to England nor to France. On the contrary, it will place these two nations in an even weaker and more dangerous situation. The mere neutralization of Czechoslovakia means the liberation of twenty-five German divisions, which will threaten the Western front; in addition to which it will open up for the triumphant Nazis the road to the Black Sea. It is not Czechoslovakia alone which is menaced, but also the freedom and the democracy of all nations. The belief that security can be obtained by throwing a small State to the wolves is a fatal delusion. The war potential of Germany will increase in a short time more rapidly than it will be possible for France and Great Britain to complete the measures necessary for their defence.'

Dramatic events at Godesberg

'That is no longer of any use' · *While the Godesberg talks were going on* · *The exchange of letters* · *Ultimatum or memorandum?* · *The bang of the big drum*

'A PEACEFUL solution of the Czechoslovakia problem is an essential preliminary to a better understanding between the British and German peoples; and this, in turn, is the indispensable foundation of European peace. European peace is what I am aiming at, and I hope this journey may open the way to get it.'

Having uttered these words at Heston aerodrome before the journalists of every country in the world, the newsreel cameras and the microphones, on the morning of September 22, Chamberlain for the second time climbed the steps of the plane that was to carry him to Germany.

This time the meeting with Hitler was to take place not at Berchtesgaden but at Godesberg, a spa on the Rhine, near Cologne.

No doubt Chamberlain was less anxious than he had been the week before: not only was he now used to flying but he also knew the man he was going to speak with, and there was every reason to suppose that Hitler would be pleased at the way these few days had been employed.

Yet there were some clouds on the horizon, and these accounted for the lines on the Prime Minister's forehead. The German chargé d'affaires, who had come to the aerodrome, observed this and at once warned Hitler by telegram. 'Chamberlain and those with him are afraid that arising out of the Sudeten German problem properly so called . . . demands may be made concerning the Hungarian and Polish minorities', and, furthermore, 'it is absolutely certain that the opposition is growing' in Great Britain and that the Prime Minister's policy was far from having the unanimous support of the country.

When the Prime Minister's plane landed at Cologne aerodrome at the end of the morning, the arrangements for welcoming it were far more impressive than those of a week before at Munich. This time, it is true, the appointment had been made in advance.

There was 'a galaxy of dignitaries',* a guard of honour and the band of the *Liebstandarte* Adolf Hitler, whose brasses blared out God Save the King. The whole of the route from airfield to Cologne and so to Godesberg was hung with flags – swastikas and Union Jacks – and the people were there in crowds to cheer the 'messenger of peace', who was accompanied by Ribbentrop.

Rooms for the Prime Minister and his suite had been prepared at the Hotel Petersberg, a sumptuous place whose balconies gave on to the Rhine, offering a view of the Hotel Dreesen on the other side of the river, where Hitler was awaiting his guest.

This time Chamberlain had with him not only his usual advisers and the ambassador Henderson, but also two officials from the Foreign Office, an interpreter, Ivone Kirkpatrick, and Sir William Malkin, the head of the legal department.

The Prime Minister was sanguine: he seemed to have forgotten the anxieties that furrowed his brow at Heston. Was he not bringing Hitler exactly what he had asked for? As for Henderson, the favourable way in which the crisis was evolving rendered him poetic.

'The Prime Minister and I,' he wrote later, 'were to spend the whole of the morning† of the morrow pacing the wide balcony, which ran the whole length of the hotel outside the rooms placed at our disposal. It was a lovely autumn morning, and the view was wide and fair to look upon – "where every prospect pleases, and only man is vile". It is a hackneyed phrase, but it is astonishing how often in this world it recurs to one.'[2]

Poetic recollections did not make Sir Nevile forget practical realities however; the ambassador was delighted, almost amazed, to see that each bedroom had a bathroom. And his pleasure was raised to the highest pitch when he observed that these two rooms had been provided, thanks to the care of the hotel proprietor, 'with the special products of Cologne: scent and soap, and bath-salts and shaving requisites'.[3]

Hitler, on the other bank of the Rhine, may perhaps have entertained other thoughts, for his surroundings awoke other memories

* The expression is Iain Macleod's, *op. cit.*
† It was in fact the first part of the afternoon.

for him: it was in this hotel, run by Dreesen, the 'Führer of the German hotel industry', whose Nazi party card bore one of the earliest numbers, that all the decisions for the 'night of the long knives'* were taken. It was from here that the Führer, together with Goebbels, left for Munich to put an end to Roehm – and we know what kind of an end it was.

William L. Shirer had come to Godesberg with all the other foreign newspaper correspondents stationed at Berlin to cover the second Hitler-Chamberlain meeting, and he did not fail to use his talent for observation.

'Hitler was in a highly nervous state. On the morning of the twenty-second I was having breakfast on the terrace of the Hotel Dreesen, where the talks were to take place, when Hitler strode past on his way down to the riverbank to inspect his yacht. He seemed to have a peculiar tic. Every few steps he cocked his right shoulder nervously, his left leg snapping up as he did so. He had ugly, black patches under his eyes. He seemed to be, as I noted in my diary that evening, on the edge of a nervous breakdown. "*Teppichfresser!*" muttered my German companion, an editor who secretly despised the Nazis. And he explained to me that Hitler had been in such a maniacal mood over the Czechs the last few days that on more than one occasion he had lost control of himself completely, hurling himself to the floor and chewing the edge of the carpet. Hence the term "carpet-eater". The evening before, while talking with some of the party hacks at the Dreesen, I had heard the expression applied to the Führer – in whispers, of course.'[4]

At five o'clock in the afternoon, having crossed the river in a ferry, watched by thousands of onlookers crowding the two banks, Chamberlain arrived at the Hotel Dreesen.

'That is no longer of any use'

Hitler was civil, but glum. The incident that Ribbentrop had provoked over the matter of the minutes of the last meeting was still too recent for there to be any question today of putting up with a single interpreter. Schmidt and Kirkpatrick therefore followed Hitler and Chamberlain to the first floor, and the four of them took their places around the green cloth of a long rectangular table in a very large

* The usual expression in Germany for the bloody purge of June 30, 1934.

room, 'somewhat colourless,' says Schmidt, 'like so many that I had seen during conferences with manufacturers in the various European capitals.'

The window, open wide to the balcony, offered a splendid view over the Rhine and the Siebengebirge. But the two statesmen – and this is still Schmidt's observation – 'were scarcely in a mind for all this beauty. Without even glancing at the landscape they at once sat down at one end of the long table.'

Chamberlain began speaking first. He had prepared a long statement and he had no intention of shortening it, since it emphasized the exertions of the British government to win acceptance for the arguments advanced by Hitler at Berchtesgaden, and the success of these laborious negotiations. 'I have succeeded,' said the Prime Minister, 'in causing not only the British and French cabinets but also the Czechoslovak government to accept in principle what you asked of me during our last conversation.'

Chamberlain reminded Hitler that he had said that the settlement of the Sudeten German question was a necessary preliminary. The free option of the Germans in Czechoslovakia for the Reich was henceforward accepted. Even better, the slow and complicated procedure of a plebiscite had been given up; it was the straightforward cession to the Reich of the zones with a German majority that had been decided upon. And the Prime Minister launched into a long and arduous explanation about the population percentages and the various arrangements that might be envisaged according to these percentages.

After this Chamberlain brought up the question of private or public property, for which a compensation formula would have to be found. Lastly he reached the arrangements for the security of the new state and the guarantee of its frontiers, arrangements which were made necessary by the cession of part of the fortifications set up by Czechoslovakia to Germany. 'France and Great Britain', he said, 'will give their guarantee to the new frontier. And I hope that for her part Germany – since, as you have told me, she will no longer have any fresh territorial claim to express – will agree to sign a non-aggression pact with Czechoslovakia.'

Chamberlain had come to an end. Schmidt, his observation as keen as ever, observes, 'When he had finish ed he leaned back in his chair, satisfied, with the air of one who says, "Have I not accomplished a great deal in the course of these five days?"'

Yet before answering Hitler asked a question. 'Am I to understand that the British, French and Czech governments have agreed to the transfer of the Sudetenland to Germany?'

'Yes,' replied Chamberlain without hesitation.

A fresh silence. A fresh pause. Then suddenly, as though he had only just made his decision, Hitler stated in a firm tone, without raising his voice but categorically, 'I am exceedingly sorry, but that is no longer of any use.* I very much regret, Mr Chamberlain, that I am unable to accept these things, but after the events of the last few days this solution is no longer acceptable!'[5]

With a sudden start Chamberlain sat up straight in his chair. He was at once surprised, shocked and very angry, and he did not trouble to hide it. 'What events do you mean? All the requirements that you expressed at Berchtesgaden have been fulfilled! And that has only been possible at the cost of a considerable effort. You do not imagine that I am going to return to London with new proposals to be told once again "That is no longer acceptable"!'

Hitler took care not to answer in the same tone of voice. In a calm, almost mealy-mouthed manner, he recalled the new developments that had occurred in the last five days: he had seen the representatives of Poland and Hungary and had perceived that there could be no true settlement of the Czechoslovak question so long as these countries had not also obtained satisfaction.

'But you told me yourself, you proved to me,' retorted Chamberlain, 'that the claims of the Poles and the Hungarians did not have the same urgent nature as those of Germany! You told me that they could not be looked into until the Sudeten German problem had been suitably dealt with.'

'Certainly,' said Hitler. 'That is why I cannot consider your proposals on the settlement of the Sudeten question: they involve too long a delay. An end must be put to it at once. The German army must immediately occupy the Sudeten territory ceded to Germany. With no formalities.'

Now it was Hitler who was growing heated and raising his voice. He violently renewed his accusations against Benes and found an argument in the change of government in Prague to assert that he could not trust in the promises made by Czechoslovakia.

The discussion had been going on for nearly three hours, and they had reached a deadlock. There was no point in going on.

* *'Es tut mir furchtbar Leid, aber das geht nicht mehr.'*

'The only ray of hope,' says Schmidt, 'was that a meeting had been agreed upon for the morning of the next day, and that at Chamberlain's express request Hitler had renewed the assurance given at Berchtesgaden that nothing should be undertaken against Czechoslovakia during the talks.'[6]

Yet it was a question of a 'ray of hope' that shone on only one of the Rhine's two banks. For Henderson, who went back to the Hotel Petersberg with Chamberlain, says exactly the opposite. 'The first interview at Godesberg thus ended without any reference to a subsequent meeting, and until the late afternoon of the following day it looked as if there might be none'.[7]

While the Godesberg talks were going on

Thus September 22 came to an end, a day in which Chamberlain had naïvely supposed that he was going to gain a diplomatic success and a day whose unexpected course left him, as he expressed it himself, 'deeply shocked'.

Although the eyes of the whole world had been turned towards Godesberg since dawn, in some places the progress of events continued.

In Prague, as we know, Benes had appointed General Jan Syrovy to form a new government. And, although he had to accept his predecessors' consent to the Franco-British plan, the head of the Czechoslovak army was already doing his best to show, by his first actions, that something had changed and that the state's destiny was no longer in the feeble hands of the Agrarians.

The army, the Communists and the chauvinists united in their common will to resist and stood solidly behind the government of national safety, which was scarcely in office before they renewed (but in a tone quite unlike Hodza's) the démarches that had earlier been undertaken in Paris and London to remove any further opposition on their part to the general mobilization of the Czechoslovak army.

Furthermore these démarches were immediately justified by the serious events that had occurred since the night before in the Sudeten zones. For during the night the Sudeten German *Freikorps* had moved into action. At Eger, Franzenbad and Asch the ex-servicemen of the German army, formed into the *Frontkämpferbund National*, had taken over the police services and had induced the loyal forces to remain in their barracks.

What is more, the news had been triumphantly broadcast by the DNB,* the official German agency.

'Swastika flags are flying over the town hall at Eger and over the church. The Sudeten population is busily decorating the houses with flags and flowers. A certain number of Sudeten Germans who had crossed into Reich territory have already gone back to Eger.'

Informed by the Prague government, the Quai d'Orsay told the Foreign Office, and both at once undertook parallel démarches. At this moment Henderson was just arriving at Godesberg, and in his absence Sir George Ogilvie-Forbes, a counsellor at the Berlin embassy, went to the Wilhelmstrasse and delivered a note.

'The French government have informed the Foreign Office that the Sudeten league has crossed the Czechoslovak frontier and has occupied Asch. If this movement is carried on, very serious disturbances must necessarily result. The British government most urgently ask the German government to prevent fresh incursions.'

The under-secretary of state, Woermann, gave a laconic answer, 'No news of this kind has reached me.'

François-Poncet arrived in his turn to make the same complaint. 'I should like to hope that the German government will do everything in their power to avoid incidents that would put the French government in an exceedingly difficult position both as regards French public opinion and other governments.'

'The English have already made exactly the same démarche,' replied Woermann. 'I at once made inquiries, and I think I may tell you quite certainly that the news of the occupation of Asch is a complete fabrication.'

But during the afternoon Sir George Ogilvie-Forbes came back to the Wilhelmstrasse waving a Berlin evening paper that published the DNB despatch under the headline 'The German flag is flying over Asch'. Furthermore, the British diplomat quoted precise facts about incidents that had taken place at Eger and at Asch.

'The free corps has not crossed the frontier at any point,' repeated Woermann, who nevertheless acknowledged that in some places the Sudeten Germans on the spot had taken over the police services.

In point of fact the free corps had received the Führer's direct

* *Deutsches Nachrichten Büro.*

orders to occupy all territory from which the Czechoslovak troops should withdraw. Yet fresh instructions, passed on during the evening by the Volksdeutsche Mittelstelle, stated that 'large-scale operations were to take place only with the explicit approval of the Führer'.

Lastly, there was an increasing reaction in political circles in London and Paris to Prague's acceptance of the conditions imposed by the French and British governments, which even began a change in public opinion.

As a protest against the pressure that had been brought to bear upon the Czechoslovak government in spite of the decision reached in the cabinet, Paul Reynaud, Mandel and Champetier de Ribes handed their resignations to Daladier, 'leaving him the discretion however, because of the gravity of the situation, of choosing the moment at which he should think it possible to make the resignations public'. Paul Reynaud explains why in the end they did not persist in this determination.

'Daladier denied Prague radio's assertions. At the next cabinet meeting Bonnet was in fact to read us the telegram in which M de Lacroix told him of the approach that the Czechoslovak government had made in order to have their own hand forced.

'During the interview Daladier added that the first steps in mobilization were already being taken, that war was coming, and that in these conditions our resignation would be desertion. Faced with such arguments we agreed not to persist in resigning.'[8]

According to Anatole de Monzie, however, the prime minister spoke to the 'pacifists' in his government in quite a different way. Monzie says that he heard of the resignation of Reynaud, Mandel and Champetier de Ribes, and that together with Pomaret he went to see Daladier. They asked the head of the government about his reaction to this defection, and he said that he had 'shown the three touts the door'.

'If they had offered me their resignation,' Daladier is said to have told Monzie and Pomaret, 'I should have accepted it.'[9]

The exchange of letters

When the sun rose upon Godesberg on September 23 Neville Chamberlain was already up. During the night he had come to a decision: he should write to Hitler. The Prime Minister had already made up his mind as to what this letter should contain; he had slept little, and he had had the time to reflect upon it. Yet when he was sitting there on his balcony, with a blank sheet of paper in front of him, he paused: how was he to address the Führer?

In the end the Prime Minister chose an odd mixture of English and German – 'My dear Reichskanzler'.

In its form, observes Schmidt, the letter was very friendly; but for all that it had 'the effect of a bomb' among the Germans.

'. . . The difficulty I see about the proposal you put to me yesterday afternoon arises from the suggestion that the areas should in the immediate future be occupied by German troops . . . I do not think you have realized the impossibility of my agreeing to put forward any plan unless I have reason to suppose that it will be considered by public opinion in my country, in France, and, indeed, in the world generally, as carrying out the principles already agreed upon in an orderly fashion and free from the threat of force . . .

'Even if I felt it right to put this proposal to the Czech government, I am convinced that they would not regard it as being in the spirit of the arrangement which we and the French government urged them to accept and which they have accepted. In the event of German troops moving into the areas as you propose, there is no doubt that the Czech government would have no option but to order their forces to resist . . .'

This 'bomb' was a damp squib at the very most, but it nevertheless brought about lengthy secret conferences between Hitler and Ribbentrop and their advisers at the Hotel Dreesen.

At last, about three o'clock in the afternoon, the interpreter Schmidt came out of the Hotel Dreesen, with a stout brown envelope under his arm. He got into a Chancellery Mercedes, sitting next to the chauffeur; and his appearance caused a sudden wave of interest on both sides of the river among the onlookers and the journalists who were there for all the papers in the world.

When his car, after crossing in the ferry, drew up outside the Hotel Petersberg, he was surrounded by a positive mob. Schmidt pushed his way through, not replying even when an American journalist, an old acquaintance of the League of Nations lobbies, called to him, 'Are you bringing war or peace in your envelope?'

Chamberlain was waiting for the messenger on the terrace in front of his room, 'undismayed, with the calmness of a summer visitor enjoying his holiday,' says Schmidt admiringly.

He handed the Prime Minister the famous brown envelope, and from it Chamberlain drew a long letter – Hitler's reply, which, according to the Führer's instructions, the German interpreter at once translated. Hitler began by recalling Czech 'barbarity' once more. 'This is an intolerable situation, as I have already said, and I am going to put an end to it,' wrote the Führer, and he added, 'Your Excellency assures me that the principle of the transfer of the Sudeten Germans' territory is in itself already accepted. I am sorry that I must here point out to Your Excellency that we Germans have already been granted theoretical recognition of principles in the past.' Then came the inevitable reminder of the treaty of Versailles.

'It is with best will,' continued Hitler, 'and in order that the Czech people shall have no just cause of complaint, that I have proposed, as the future border, in the event of a peaceful settlement, that racial frontier which represents, I am sure, a just compromise between the two national groups and which also takes into account the existence of large linguistic enclaves. But I am ready, in addition, to have a vote taken in the territory as a whole so that later rectifications may still take place, and to comply as far as possible with the genuine wishes of those concerned. From the beginning I have pledged myself to recognize these rectifications. I have furthermore stated that I am willing to let this plebiscite take place under the supervision of either an international committee or a mixed German-Czech commission. Lastly I am ready to withdraw our troops from the most debatable frontier regions while the plebiscite lasts, provided that the Czechs do the same . . .

'Your Excellency assures me that for you in your turn it is impossible to present such a plan to your own government. I, on the other hand, can assure you that it is impossible for me to present any other to the German people. For as far as England is concerned in this event it is, at the most, a question of political imponderables; but for Germany it is a question of the elementary right to security for more than three million men, and the national honour of a great people.

'Your Excellency tells me that it is impossible for the Czech government to withdraw their troops so long as they fear an invasion. I do not understand. For the solution that I am putting forward is exactly that which will cause the reasons for any violent stroke to vanish . . .'

And Hitler ended, 'In any case, if Germany (as now seems the case) does not succeed in making justice triumph for her oppressed brothers in Czechoslovakia by means of negotiation, she is determined to exhaust the only opportunities that remain to her.'

A little more than an hour later, when Schmidt was with Hitler once more, he was surprised to see how anxious the Führer was to know Chamberlain's reactions.

'What did he say? How did he take my letter?'

The interpreter reassured him. 'He did not show any obvious perturbation . . . and he told me that in about an hour Henderson and Wilson would come to bring you his reply.'

And indeed at the end of the afternoon the Prime Minister's two emissaries crossed the Rhine in their turn and appeared at the Hotel Dreesen, where they were at once received by Ribbentrop.

The letter that the two Englishmen brought was shorter than the two before, but its essential paragraphs set a question of procedure to which it was not sure that Hitler would give a favourable reply.

'In my capacity as intermediary,' wrote the Prime Minister, 'it is evidently now my duty – since Your Excellency maintains entirely the position you took last night – to put your proposals before the Czechoslovak Government.

'Accordingly, I request Your Excellency to be good enough to let me have a memorandum which sets out these proposals, together with a map showing the area proposed to be transferred, subject to the result of the proposed plebiscite.

'On receiving this memorandum I will at once forward it to Prague and request the reply of the Czechoslovak Government at the earliest possible moment.'[10]

Ribbentrop, leaving Henderson and Wilson quite doubtful as to the outcome of their approach, went and shut himself up with Hitler and Schmidt.

At last the foreign minister came back.

'But the war party in Germany,' observes Henderson, 'was also not yet finally in the ascendant. Mr Chamberlain's refusal to renew contact had provoked some consternation among the moderates in the German camp, and Hitler, in view of the high

hopes placed by the German people on Mr Chamberlain's intervention, was reluctant to break off the negotiations and anxious
for a further meeting. Ribbentrop was accordingly instructed to
inform us that a German memorandum would be prepared in the
course of the evening and that we would be informed as soon as it
was ready.'[11]

Ultimatum or memorandum?

At half past ten the talks began again, this time in one of the ground-
floor drawing-rooms, for there were more people on both sides:
since Chamberlain had all his colleagues with him the Germans,
particularly Ribbentrop, also wanted to turn out in force.

Hitler began. 'In the first place I should like to thank you, Mr
Prime Minister, both in my own name and in the name of the
German people, for the efforts you have made for a peaceful
settlement of the Czechoslovak problem.

'I realize not only that these exertions have called for a great
deal of physical exertion on your part, but also that your activities
in favour of peace bear witness to real political boldness.

'To be sure, these are difficult negotiations; and in spite of the
fact that we are both of Nordic stock (for my ancestors came from
Lower Saxony) it is still just as hard to find a basis of agreement
in this matter, which our two nations see from different points of
view.

'Nevertheless I hope that it is still possible for us to find a peaceful solution together. If we do reach that point, allow me to say
that a large share of the credit for the success will belong to you.'

Chamberlain could believe neither his eyes nor his ears: opposite
him, instead of the madman he had left the day before, he saw a
honey-tongued diplomat, overflowing with compliments.

The Prime Minister thanked his host and added almost shyly, 'I
note your last remark about a possible peaceful solution with particular pleasure. I imagine that it is your intention to express this
hope in a more concrete fashion – perhaps, indeed, in that note which
we have agreed upon and which is to summarize your proposals?'

The Führer made a gesture, and as if there had been a well-timed
scenario, the note was at once handed to the British, accompanied
by a map; and while Schmidt was getting up to begin the transla-

tion, Hitler uttered a single comment. 'There you will find the substance of the idea and suggestions that I spoke of during our last interview.'

Schmidt translated the memorandum, the essence of which lay in six points.

1 The evacuation by all Czech troops, police, gendarmes, customs-officials and frontier guards of the territory marked on the map as due to be transferred and which is to be handed over to Germany on September 28.

2 The evacuated territory must be handed over in the condition in which it is at present (see details in the appendix). The German government agree that a representative of the Czech government or the Czech army with full powers may be attached to the Wehrmacht supreme command in order to settle the details of the manner of evacuation.

3 The Czech government shall at once send home all the Sudeten Germans serving in the army or the police in the whole of the territory of the Czech state.

4 The Czech government shall free the prisoners of German race who have been arrested for political acts.

5 The German government agree that a plebiscite shall take place in territories that are to be determined between now and November 25 at the latest. The frontier-rectifications arising from the results of this plebiscite will be decided upon either by a Germano-Czech or by an international commission.

The plebiscite itself shall take place under the supervision of an international commission.

All those who were living in the territories in question on October 28, 1918, or who were born there before October 28, 1918, may take part in the voting.

The simple majority of the whole of the persons of both sexes entitled to vote shall be held to express the desire of the population to belong to the German Reich or to the Czech state.

For the purpose of the plebiscite the troops on either side shall be withdrawn from the territories that are to be decided upon. The date and the duration of the plebiscite shall be settled by joint agreement between the German and Czech governments.

6 The German government propose the setting up of a Germano-Czech committee with powers to settle all other details.

The appendix mentioned in clause 2 made these conditions still more onerous.

The handing over of the evacuated Sudeten territory must take place without the military, economic or transport installations having been destroyed or made unusable; the same applies to airfields and other ground installations and all radio stations.

Economic and transport material situated in the designated territory, particularly the rolling-stock, must be handed over intact. The same applies to all public service plants and equipment (gas-works, generating equipment, etc.) Lastly, there must be no removal of supplies, personal estate, cattle, raw materials, etc.

The effect that this text produced upon Chamberlain and the other Englishmen was, as Schmidt observes, 'appalling'.

'It is an ultimatum!' Chamberlain managed to say, at last, 'a *diktat!*'

Hitler gazed at him, surprised and even, as Kirkpatrick says, 'wounded'. 'You are quite mistaken, Mr Chamberlain. This is not an ultimatum. Here, look at the document yourself: you see that it is headed with the word memorandum.'

But Chamberlain was in no mood to appreciate this kind of humour, even if it were unconscious. 'Excuse me,' he said acidly, 'but I attach more importance to the contents than the title!' And the Prime Minister added that such a document, drawn up in such terms, gave its author the appearance of a conqueror; that it left the Czechoslovak government no respite for execution, and that it therefore involved a considerable risk of incidents that might degenerate into a war.

The bang of the big drum

At this point in the discussion a door suddenly opened and one of Hitler's aides-de-camp came in, carrying a piece of paper. Hitler took it, read it, and passing it to Schmidt said in a solemn voice, 'Read this piece of news to Mr Chamberlain.'

Schmidt translated, 'Benes has just broadcast the general mobilization order for all the Czechoslovak forces.'

To tell the truth there was nothing in the dispatch to surprise Chamberlain, since at the end of the afternoon he had telegraphed the Foreign Office himself to say, in reply to Halifax's question, that

Great Britain could no longer oppose this step, although she deplored the taking of it. But there is no kind of doubt that the Prime Minister would far rather not have been there when the news first reached Hitler.

Yet paradoxically it was perhaps this news that allowed the conference to go on. Schmidt explains this unexpected effect by comparing the announcement of mobilization to the bang of a big drum in a symphony.

'After the big-drum bang of Czech mobilization there were two or three long bars of silence in the hotel drawing-room; then gently the violins took up their melody again. Hitler looked thunderstruck. "Of course, in spite of this unheard-of provocation I still hold to my promise to undertake nothing against Czechoslovakia during the negotiations, or at least for as long as you are on German soil, Mr Chamberlain." Slowly the tension began to slacken. The conversation started again. After the "bang of the big drum" its tone was far more subdued. Everybody seemed to breathe more freely after having seen the catastrophe retreat once more.'[12]

A confused argument at once began as to the meaning of this mobilization by the Czechs.

'The question is settled,' said Hitler, 'the Czechs will no longer wish to give up the smallest tract of land to Germany!'

Chamberlain protested; and he also refused to admit that a mobilization might have an 'offensive' character. He observed, furthermore, that Germany had mobilized first.

'No,' said Hitler.

'Yes she did,' retorted Chamberlain.

'The day Germany mobilizes,' replied Hitler, 'you will see what mobilization is!'

But Schmidt had judged rightly: something had changed, and everything seemed less grave, less irreparable. Hitler even brought a pencil out of his pocket and taking the 'memorandum' from Chamberlain he scribbled a few corrections – two or three alterations in the form, meant to lessen the 'conquering' tone that had shocked the Prime Minister, and a change of date, to which the Führer – a most accomplished play-actor – suddenly attributed an immense value.

'For you, Mr Chamberlain,' he said, 'I am going to make a concession. You will be able to pride yourself on being the only man to

whom I have ever made a concession. I am going to change the date:
I shall agree that the ceded territories should only be handed over to
Germany on October 1.'*

Chamberlain very nearly felt that he ought to say thank you. But
he did even better than that: although he was perfectly aware (he
said so himself) that Hitler's alterations to his note were merely
formal, Chamberlain, who had just stated flatly that it was no good
counting on him to pass this 'ultimatum' on the the Czechoslovaks,
went back on his refusal.

'I should like to say that it is not for me either to accept or to
reject your proposals . . . as an intermediary the most I can do is to
see that they are put before the Czechoslovak government.'

This was all that Hitler wanted. And as it was already two o'clock
in the morning all that was left was to take leave of one another,
after a few moments of tête-à-tête conversation, with only Schmidt
to help this time – a conversation in which Hitler thanked Chamberlain 'in words that seemed to come from his heart', and asserted that
this Sudeten German problem was 'the last big question that he still
had to settle'.

* In fact October 1 was precisely the date that Hitler had set as far back as May
28 for the German entry into Czechoslovakia. (See above, p. 69.)

CHAPTER FOUR

The great September manoeuvres

'It was not ignorance' · Partial mobilization in France · Chamberlain torn by indecision · The French attitude · The Czechoslovaks' refusal · Until three in the morning · 'Bonnet discouraged everybody' · Gamelin's viva voce · Chamberlain: a last attempt · Roosevelt telegraphs the Führer · 'By two o'clock on Wednesday at the latest' · Bonnet asks for exact details · Hitler at the Sportpalast · Chamberlain's reply · The 'authorized statement' of the Foreign Office · Wilson sees Hitler again · The interventions increase · An unsuccessful parade · Intrigues and manoeuvres in Paris · The rue Saint-Dominique and the Elysée · Two British notes · 'I do not see that I can do any more' · At the very last hour . . .

WHILE the second meeting between Hitler and Chamberlain was thus coming to a close at Godesberg, Czechoslovakia was mobilizing.

'The mobilization is being carried out with striking orderliness,' wrote General Faucher. 'Our prestige is rising once more. The officers of the mission can show themselves in uniform again.'*

During the evening of the twenty-third those who were listening to the Prague radio could hear the announcer saying every five minutes that an important communiqué was going to be broadcast. Finally, at 22.30 hours, their patience was rewarded.

'Citizens, the government have decided to proclaim general mobilization. All men aged less than forty and specialists of any age must rejoin at once. All officers, non-commissioned officers and soldiers of the reserve and of the second reserve whatever their rank and all men on leave must rejoin their depots without delay. All are to wear used civilian clothing and to have with them their military papers and provisions for two days. The latest

* '. . . but not for long,' added the leader of the French military mission sadly, at a later date.

174

possible date for rejoining their respective posts is September 24 at half past four in the morning.

'All vehicles, cars and aeroplanes are mobilized. The sale of petrol is allowed with a permit issued by the military authorities.

'Citizens! The decisive moment is coming. Success depends upon each man. Let each man put the whole of his strength at his country's service. Be brave and true. Our struggle is a struggle for justice and freedom! Long live Czechoslovakia!'

The mobilization decree was first read in Czech, then in Slovak, German, Hungarian, Ruthenian and Polish. Lastly the national anthem rang out.

A positive fever at once seized upon the entire population. In Prague that night crowds rushed out into the streets. Processions were formed, and groups of demonstrators cheered the reservists as they hurried to rejoin their mobilization centres. Everywhere, whether in public or in private buildings, the civil defence orders were scrupulously applied.

In every home and in many public places the radio was on continuously, with everyone waiting for fresh orders from the government. In fact the Czechoslovaks heard only one more important broadcast that evening – a German station sending out Konrad Henlein's appeal to the Sudeten Germans and to all the ethnic groups 'oppressed by the Czechs'.

'Fellow-countrymen, you know what to think about this mobilization order. No German will fire upon Germans; no Hungarian will fire upon Hungarians; no Pole upon Poles; Benes has not the right to force you to this horrible murder of your own brothers.

'No German will obey his mobilization order. In a little while you will be free.'

'*It was not ignorance*'

The next day all the foreigners who were in Prague on the evening of September 23 described that night of mobilization in the same fashion. The *Petit Parisien*'s special correspondent wired this message to his paper.

'The situation inside the country was wholly transformed by the general mobilization, which was immediately decided upon and at once carried out. The great majority of Czechs interpreted it as a clear-cut determination to defend the country's territorial integrity and as a promise of Franco-British support.

'A few days before I had seen a whole nation weeping. (This is not a figure of speech.) Now, in every family where there was a son, a brother or a father leaving, there was not a tear! Today that holding-back in enthusiasm and that modesty in emotion which I have so often noticed in the crowd, gave way to an almost demonstrative exaltation. The general mobilization which tore more than a million men from their homes was a solemn and virtually a religious celebration.'

And this witness hastens to add that in spite of their enthusiasm the people had no illusions about the trials that were awaiting them. 'It was not ignorance. They knew that the cost would be high. And ninety per cent of the population of Prague believed that the capital would be bombed at once.'

The German military attaché himself, Colonel Toussaint, could not help being impressed. During the night he sent a message to the OKW. 'Calm in Prague. Last mobilization measures taken. Total of men mobilized according to estimates, one million. Army in the field, eight hundred thousand.'

What is more, calmness and discipline, united to patriotic fervour, were not confined to the capital, where the considerable proportion of purely Czech inhabitants made them understandable.

In order to reach the headquarters of the mobilized army General Faucher crossed a great part of Bohemia and Moravia, and he was thus able to see for himself how matters were going on: he was present at requisitioning operations, and in the villages he saw columns of horses led by peasants 'as well as if they had been under military command, and with more care than usual about the rule of the road – a rule that is not always very exactly obeyed in Czechoslovakia'.

Partial mobilization in France

The ill-success of the Godesberg negotiations, which was immediately known in Paris, the hastening of the German military preparations and the easily foreseeable reactions of Hitler after the Czechoslovak mobilization, were so many reasons for the taking of elementary steps for the security of France.

Daladier and Bonnet discussed them during the night of September 23–24, and Gamelin finally had permission to continue with the setting up of the 'strengthened covering' arrangements.

This involved the immediate recall of very large numbers of reservists to the colours – 'about a million men' said Bonnet.

So on September 24, as Frenchmen left their homes in the morning to go to work they saw the white mobilization posters that had been stuck up on the official notice-boards a little before six o'clock.

Immediate recall of certain classes of reservists.

By order of the Minister of National Defence and War and of the Minister for Air, the officers, non-commissioned officers and other ranks of the reserves who possess white mobilization orders or instructions with the figure 2 overprinted on them* will immediately leave, without delay and without waiting for personal notification.

They will rejoin the depots mentioned on their mobilization orders or instructions according to the conditions laid down in those documents.

Saturday, September 24, 1938, 04.00 hrs
The Ministers of National Defence, War, and the Air.

Another poster gave the army the right to requisition, and a decree of the minister of public works gave military traffic priority.

At the same time the navy was taking steps for calling up personnel.

For France the whole of September 24 was a day of mobilization. Everywhere the reservists rejoined their units or depots; there were no flowers in their rifles, but also there were no desertions, no incidents. And what is more, in their dispatches all the diplomats posted to Paris, including those from the Axis, emphasized the excellent manner in which this mobilization was carried out – a mobilization which, although it was only partial, was still on such a scale that they could assert that the French would not baulk at going to war, if they found they had to.

Chamberlain torn by indecision

Chamberlain, back from Godesberg, called his ministers together the

---

* Identical posters, put up at the same time, also recalled the reservists whose instructions were stamped 3. The figures 2 or 3 were underprinted on each poster, covering its entire length.

same evening. During this cabinet meeting, did the Prime Minister suggest that Prague should be 'strongly advised' to put up with the conditions dictated by Hitler?

Two ministers, Duff Cooper and Leo Amery, assert that he did. Sir Samuel Hoare says that he did not, and even states that at a meeting of the inner cabinet (Chamberlain, Halifax, Simon and himself) it had been held that the Godesberg memorandum could not be accepted.

It may in fact be granted that just after Godesberg the Prime Minister was torn in different directions by opposing attitudes of mind.*

It was difficult for him to argue against those who saw an ultimatum, a diktat, in Hitler's 'memorandum' – for had he not been the first to use these words to describe it? What is more he felt that British public opinion was beginning to turn away from the policy of peace at any price. Already during the night of the twenty-third Halifax had sent him a telegram to Godesberg pointing this out. And the results of the last public opinion poll had just confirmed it: the day after the Berchtesgaden meeting the 'anti-Chamberlains' had amounted to 10%; on September 21 and 22, after the French and English had forced the hand of the Prague government to induce them to accept the Franco-British plan, the 10% had become 40%. Now the English papers were unanimous in condemning the Godesberg memorandum; and it was already known in England that Prague had judged it 'unacceptable'.

But on the other hand Chamberlain was more than ever persuaded that it would be madness to plunge into a war. England was not ready: Australia and South Africa had just told her of their desire for peace. Was France herself in any condition to stand up to Germany? And what of Czechoslovakia? How many days would she hold out against a simultaneous action by the German, Polish and Hungarian armies? So that in the end Chamberlain's attitude, that evening of September 24, was expressed by the words, 'Everything would lead me to advise the Czechoslovaks to refuse, if . . .'

And this 'if' led him to argue in favour of the opposite course and to lean towards acceptance.

But the members of the government did not follow him so far – not yet at least. And Halifax himself displayed more than mere reserve.

* This is the view of Chamberlain's most recent biographer, Iain Macleod.

In any case, the British government were not to come to a final decision upon their attitude towards Hitler's memorandum until they knew the views of Czechoslovakia and France.

Once again, therefore, an invitation was sent out to Daladier and Bonnet. They were told of it during the morning of the twenty-fifth, and at about eleven o'clock they received a copy of the Godesberg memorandum and of the accompanying map. At the same time they were asked to be at Downing Street at nine o'clock that evening.

The French attitude

During that Sunday, September 25, Daladier consulted the army's intelligence service and held a meeting of the ministers. The intelligence service's view was very clear.

> 'The Germans, *to begin with*, are asking for a new frontier, to which they will advance their military forces *at once*. This frontier includes territories in which, even according to the German map, the majority of the population is Czech. This is particularly obvious in the Moravian gap . . . the unqualified acceptance of the German memorandum would not only sanction the handing over of *certain* fortifications, but their virtually complete abandonment. It would bring about the throttling of Bohemia and it would favour its separation from Slovakia.'[1]

According to Daladier the cabinet reached their decision quickly. 'The cabinet,' he writes, 'examined the German memorandum and the accompanying map. They were remarkably different both in their spirit and their text from the proposals of the English plan which had finally been accepted by us and to which the Czechoslovak government had resigned themselves. The cabinet rejected the memorandum.'[2]

On the other hand, although Anatole de Monzie acknowledges that 'the meeting was unusually short', he is far less precise as to the decisions that were reached. According to him Daladier and Bonnet were told 'to act for the best'.

It is impossible to decide between them on the basis of the communiqué that was put out after the cabinet meeting, for this merely stressed the government's unanimous 'approval of the declarations that the premier and the foreign minister intend to make at their meeting with the British government in London'.

Yet Georges Bonnet does agree with Daladier in admitting that the French government considered it impossible to recommend the Czechoslovak government to accept the German memorandum.

The Czechoslovaks' refusal

Besides, it would appear that this time the Prague government had not the least intention of accepting Hitler's conditions, even if the French and British were to urge it.

As early as eight o'clock in the morning Benes summoned Lacroix, and in words interrupted by his indignation at the Godesberg memorandum he defined his position. 'I know the difficulties of France and England and I do not wish to increase them. I therefore stand by our acceptance of the Franco-British proposal that was delivered last Monday. But I shall go no further! And in no event shall I agree to the plebiscite, which is merely a way of disorganizing the state. The plebiscite that Herr Hitler wants would give rise to the worst of disorders, blood would flow . . .'[3]

In London a few hours later, Jan Masaryk, the Czechoslovak minister, delivered Prague's official reply to Chamberlain. The note for the British government said, 'Here, in fact, we have an ultimatum of the kind that is usually only presented to a conquered nation . . . We are deprived of the real basis of our national existence. We must give up a large part of our carefully-erected system of defence to the Germans and allow the German army to penetrate far into the interior of our country . . . Our national and economic independence will automatically disappear with the acceptance of Herr Hitler's plan.'

The Czechoslovak government therefore ended by stating that the German memorandum was 'wholly unacceptable'.

'The Czechoslovak nation will never consent to be an enslaved people!' added Masaryk as he handed Chamberlain this note. And as soon as he had returned to the legation he wrote to Prague, 'Chamberlain is really surprised that we should not be prepared to withdraw our troops from the fortified lines on our frontiers. I emphasized the fact that these fortifications were occupied by our troops only yesterday, and that on the advice of England and France themselves; and that we could not evacuate them again today. Chamberlain cannot understand this. It is really a calamity that this stupid and ill-informed man, a nonentity, should be Prime Minister of Great Britain. Still, I am convinced that he will not remain Prime Minister long.'[4]

Having done this, the Czechoslovak minister, who wished to present the British government with a *fait accompli*, so that the scenario of September 20 should be avoided, if possible, gave the press the text of the German note and Prague's reply. This double publication caused a certain amount of commotion in London diplomatic circles, and as a result the German chargé d'affaires, Kordt, telegraphed the Wilhelmstrasse at midnight.

'The Prime Minister has asked me to transmit the following strictly confidential message. "The news that is expected to appear very shortly in the British and foreign papers and according to which it would seem that Czechoslovakia definitively rejects the German note does not amount to the last word to be said on the matter.

' "I hear on undoubted authority that the immediate publication of this note is due to the Czechoslovak legation in London.

' "This step has caused indignation in Downing Street." '

Until three in the morning . . .

Thus at nine o'clock on the evening of September 25, when the French ministers arrived at 10 Downing Street, two of the three governments concerned had already taken up their positions with regard to the Godesberg memorandum – and in each case this was a negative position.

To begin with Chamberlain gave his guests an account of the Godesberg talks, of which they also had the typewritten report.

The Prime Minister cleverly dwelt upon his own reaction to Hitler's memorandum, showed how he had been the first to consider the Führer's attitude 'cruel and unjust', and recalled that he himself had, while he was at Godesberg, acquiesced in Czechoslovakia's mobilization. Having thus put forward the reasons that should have induced him to approve of resistance, Chamberlain was able, with a clear conscience, to come to his second set of arguments – the horrors of war, the weakness of the Western allies . . .

Yet Daladier urged the impossibility of his advising Benes to accept Hitler's ultimatum. 'If, after Austria, we allow the destruction of Czechoslovakia, upon which Göring lavished assurances, what nation's turn will come next? If our two countries were united to resist the rise of Nazism and to stand against seeing the programme in *Mein Kampf* carried through without a fight, would they not bring in other nations after them?'

The French premier then reverted to an idea that had already been put forward on September 18 – that of sending an international committee to the spot.

'Hitler will not agree,' replied Chamberlain. 'He has said his last word.'

'And what if we propose the meeting of a general congress of the nations concerned with the maintenance of the peace?' suggested Daladier.

'Hitler is waiting for an answer of either yes or no. And if it is no, he will invade Czechoslovakia at once. What will happen then?'

'In that case,' replied Daladier, 'France will at once go to the help of her ally.'

'And that will be war.'

That is the point Chamberlain wanted to reach – war. How? With what means, what plans? In what conditions? From that moment onwards the British ministers, who did not seem so much in favour of resistance, who were not so 'tough' as Sir Samuel Hoare claims they were, submitted Daladier, as minister of national defence, to a running fire of questions, all of which had to do with purely military problems.

Daladier began by speaking of the point of view of the French military intelligence, 'which, for once,' said he, 'was not pessimistic.' He stressed the fact that the Czechoslovak army, with its thirty divisions, represented 'an important, well-equipped and well-officered force'. In spite of the Germans' having partly outflanked Czechoslovakia's fortifications since the Anschluss, the intelligence service thought the Czechs could hold out for a month – that is to say, against Germany alone. 'To be sure,' remarked Daladier slyly, 'the British contribution is slight: to begin with it will not exceed an army corps. But the British air force is already strong. And if the Russians come in, they will assure us the mastery of the sky.'

The discussion, firmly confined to the military aspect of the question, went on and on for hours. In short, Chamberlain had already won, since he had induced Daladier and Bonnet to weigh the chances of success or failure in the action to be undertaken, instead of confining themselves to the acknowledgment of the obligations that had been contracted and to the necessity of observing, in the direction of nations, those moral laws that are considered essential in individuals.

In the end the meeting had to break up at three in the morning; but before this Chamberlain had asked and obtained that General Gamelin should be summoned by telephone, so that the next day he might bring the exact technical information for which Daladier had seemed somewhat at a loss.

'Bonnet discouraged everybody'

The next day, September 26, the commander-in-chief therefore flew from Le Bourget at twenty to eight, and at about nine in the morning his plane landed at Croydon, after a difficult crossing of the Channel in bad weather. From Croydon Gamelin went at once to the French embassy, where Alexis Léger and the ambassador Corbin 'prepared' him from the moment he arrived.

'They were not satisfied with the conversations that had taken place the evening before,' observes the general. 'The British felt that they were scarcely ready to go into action, either from the point of view of the air force or from that of the army; they wanted to gain time. The attitude of Poland seemed to them very worrying. The premier was to see Mr Chamberlain again that same morning. I was to go with him. But it was necessary that M Georges Bonnet should not be there: it was he who discouraged everybody.

'The scenario was worked out accordingly. When we arrived at Downing Street M Daladier first went into the British Prime Minister's room alone, asking our ambassador to go with him as interpreter in case of need. M Georges Bonnet and M Léger stayed with Lord Halifax, who had come to join us in the waiting-room. A moment later I was told that Mr Chamberlain asked me to come in. I saw Lord Halifax taking M Georges Bonnet and M Léger into a neighbouring room. I greeted Mr Chamberlain.'[5]

This surprising little ballet brings no comment from Daladier. As for Georges Bonnet, he contents himself with observing, 'There was first a short meeting between Daladier and the commander-in-chief Gamelin and Mr Chamberlain, Sir Thomas Inskip, the British minister for the co-ordination of defence, and General Lord Gort. It was given up entirely to the most technical military questions. I did not take part in it, therefore; nor did Lord Halifax.'[6]

Gamelin's viva voce

As soon as the door closed behind those who made up this 'technical' conference, Chamberlain said a few friendly words to Gamelin and then the latter, 'after a glance at Daladier', began to speak. He opened his brief-case, brought out his maps, and launched into an account which he sums up himself in these terms:

'1 *France's military strength on the ground and in the air*: five million men; about a hundred divisions to start with; a system of fortifications that guarantee us complete freedom of manoeuvre; an inferior air force, but still one that is in a condition to work at short range to support the army.

2 *The German weaknesses*:* the high command, which realizes the dangers. A system of fortifications which is not yet finished. Important shortages of cadres; persisting difficulty in mobilization for want of adequate trained reserves. Difficulties of a long war because of the lack of raw materials, particularly oil. A superior air force, it is true. We shall suffer from that, especially as regards the civilian population; but so long as morale holds out, that will not prevent a happy outcome for our arms.

3 *The Italian weaknesses*: the country's morale. The impossibility of a long-term war.

'Mr Chamberlain broke in, "If we march, Italy will not march." I replied, "Perhaps so. At all events we shall take the offensive; by sea, very quickly; by land (the Alps), as soon as the winter is over."

'4 *Czechoslovakia's possibilities of resistance*: thirty divisions at present being mobilized, against the Germans' forty. If they hold to the north and the south of Moravia the army may be saved, at the cost of abandoning part of the territory. Then the question of Poland arises: if she comes into action, there is a new front.'†

After this conference with the heads of government, General Gamelin went with Sir Thomas Inskip to a meeting attended by the British defence ministers and the chiefs of staff. The French com-

* A subsequent note by General Gamelin, 'Here, of course, it is a question of the position in September, 1938, as we saw it.'

† Subsequent note by Gamelin, 'I did not speak of the Russian attitude. At that time I did not yet know Marshal Voroshilov's reply, which was only shown me at the end of the morning; besides I would not risk broaching this new subject with Mr Chamberlain without M Daladier's prior consent.'

mander-in-chief noted how little those he was speaking to – with the exception of the sailors – were inclined to go to war.

During this second conference of the morning, General Gamelin received an important telephone call from Paris: his chief of staff, General Jeannel, had just seen the Russian military attaché, who, speaking for Marshal Voroshilov, had told him that the Soviets had at their disposal 'thirty divisions of infantry, a mass of cavalry, many tank formations and the greater part of their air force ready to intervene in the west'.

Of course Gamelin at once passed on this information to the British, 'but it was clear,' he observes, 'that the hypothesis of seeing Russia invade Poland scarcely gave our allies any pleasure at all.'

Chamberlain: a last attempt

While General Gamelin was speaking with the British who were in charge of defence, the Franco-British interministerial conference began again in the Prime Minister's room, with the same members as the day before.

Chamberlain at once spoke of the solution which had been agreed by his ministers during the night and which he had been able to submit to Daladier during a few minutes' tête-à-tête before Gamelin's arrival.

'I understand the French position very well,' he said. 'But I want to make one last effort, one last attempt, to try to save the peace. I have therefore decided to send my political adviser, Sir Horace Wilson, on a mission to Herr Hitler. I have given Sir Horace a personal letter to the Führer asking that he should renounce the use of force, since he was sure of obtaining satisfaction in essentials. I suggest to him the setting up of a German-Czechoslovak committee, possibly with a British member, entrusted with settling the problem of the transfer of the Sudetenland.

'In the event of Hitler's not agreeing, Sir Horace Wilson is then to read him this declaration, which sums up our attitude and which has been approved by M Daladier. "The French government inform us that in the case of a German attack upon Czechoslovakia they will stand by their obligations to the full. Should France, in the execution of her treaty obligations, be drawn into hostilities against Germany, the United Kingdom would feel obliged to come to her help." [7]

And to cut short any inclination to reopen the debate of the night before, Chamberlain added, 'As I am speaking to you now, Sir Horace Wilson is actually getting into the aeroplane.'

Roosevelt telegraphs the Führer

Chamberlain was not the only one who wanted to make a 'last attempt' on that day of September 26. At Washington too they had at last reached the decision 'to make an effort', according to the very expression that the ambassador Bullitt used when, twenty-four hours earlier, he suggested that President Roosevelt should take the initiative of calling an international conference. Bullitt's approach was quickly followed by a telephone-call from Joseph Kennedy, the American ambassador to London, to the Secretary of State, Cordell Hull.

'Kennedy,' says Cordell Hull, 'told me about the differences of opinion that had appeared within the British cabinet, Chamberlain still being in favour of "peace at any price" whereas several of his ministers did not wish to have anything more to do with fresh contacts with Hitler, and thought that "it would have to come to war".

'He told me that Colonel Charles Lindberg (who had been so deeply impressed by the power of Göring's air force) had been consulted by the British and had stated that in his view the Germans could easily withstand the combined air forces of all the other countries of Europe put together.' [8]

Then on the twenty-fifth the White House received a message from Wilbur J. Carr, the United States minister in Prague; Benes was speaking through Carr and he most urgently pressed Roosevelt to intervene with the French and British and persuade them not to abandon Czechoslovakia.

These various approaches ended by convincing Roosevelt of the necessity for stepping in personally.

Without going so far as to give formal advice against the taking of such a step, Cordell Hull still did not hide the fact that he scarcely believed that it would do any good. He even feared, in the event of an apparent success, that the democratic nations might come to think that the danger of war had been removed, which would lead them to slow down and diminish the military preparations that the presence in Europe of an aggressive Germany, armed to the teeth, nevertheless rendered essential.

Furthermore, the Secretary of State was afraid that the result of increasing the number of approaches to Hitler would only be an increase in his vanity and megalomania. But the President was of Bullitt's opinion, and he considered that it was necessary to intervene even if there were no great hope of success.

'It can do no harm,' said Cordell Hull. 'And it is wise to fight for peace up until the last moment.'

Roosevelt, Cordell Hull and their advisers therefore set themselves to the drafting of a telegram addressed to Hitler personally, but of which a copy was to be sent to Benes, Chamberlain, Daladier and the principal European heads of government.

The President of the United States drew up this warning: 'The supreme desire of the American people is to live in peace. But in the event of a general war they face the fact that no nation can escape some measure of the consequences of such a world catastrophe.'[9]

But the heart of his message was devoted to a plea in favour of negotiation.

'During the present crisis the people of the United States and their Government have earnestly hoped that the negotiations for the adjustment of the controversy which has now arisen in Europe might reach a successful conclusion.

'So long as these negotiations continue, so long will there remain the hope that reason and the spirit of equity may prevail and that the world may thereby escape the madness of a new resort to war.

'On behalf of the 130 millions of people of the United States of America and for the sake of humanity everywhere, I most earnestly appeal to you not to break off negotiations looking to a peaceful, fair, and constructive settlement of the questions at issue.

'I earnestly repeat that so long as negotiations continue differences may be reconciled. Once they are broken off, reason is banished and force asserts itself.

'And force produces no solution for the future good of humanity.'

On the slope

'By two o'clock on Wednesday at the latest'

A little before five in the afternoon, at the very time that the French ministers were returning to Paris through torrential rain, Chamberlain's special envoy left the British embassy in Berlin together with Henderson and Kirkpatrick for the Chancellery, where Hitler was waiting for him. At five o'clock the three British diplomats were in the presence of the Führer, who was accompanied by the inevitable Paul Schmidt.

'For the first and only time in my presence,' observed Schmidt, 'Hitler completely lost his head.'

It was the reading in German of the letter that Sir Horace Wilson had brought from Chamberlain that caused the explosion.[10]

'The Czechoslovakian Government,' wrote Chamberlain, 'now inform me that, while they adhere to their acceptance of the proposals for the transfer of the Sudeten-German areas on the lines discussed by my Government and the French Government and explained by me to you on Thursday last, they regard as wholly unacceptable the proposal in your Memorandum for the immediate evacuation of the areas and their immediate occupation by German troops, these processes to take place before the terms of cession have been negotiated or even discussed.

'Your Excellency will remember that in my letter to you of Friday last I said that an attempt to occupy forthwith by German troops areas which will become part of the Reich at once in principle and very shortly afterwards by formal delimitation, would be condemned as an unnecessary display of force ...

'The development of opinion since my return confirms me in the views I expressed to you in my letter and in our subsequent conversation.

'In communicating with me about your proposals, the Government of Czechoslovakia point out that they go far beyond what was agreed to in the so-called Anglo-French plan. Czechoslovakia would be deprived of every safeguard for her national existence. She would have to yield up large proportions of her carefully prepared defences and admit the German Armies deep into her country before it had been organised on the new basis or any preparations had been made for its defence. Her national and economic independence would automatically disappear with the

188

acceptance of the German plan. The whole process of moving the population is to be reduced to panic flight.'

As early as the first sentence, when he heard that the Czechoslovaks had found the German proposal 'wholly unacceptable', he turned pale. He nevertheless succeeded in mastering himself until the passage in which Chamberlain, quoting Prague's arguments without commentary, seemed to consider them valid. Violently interrupting the reading, the Führer started to his feet. Before the petrified diplomats, he stamped with rage. 'There's no point at all in going on with negotiations,' he shouted, rushing towards the door.

The English and Germans stared at one another, aghast: if the head of the German state were to leave the room before even having heard the British message, it would be a diplomatic incident, a breaking-off . . . but he did not.

'On reaching the door,' says Schmidt, 'Hitler grasped how impossible his behaviour was, and he came back to his place like a small boy in a temper.'[11]

The interpreter was at last able to begin reading again. The Prime Minister suggested a meeting with the Czechoslovaks.

'A negotiated settlement is still possible, and it is because I clearly remember the conversations that we have had together and because I equally clearly measure the consequences that would arise if a breaking-off of negotiations were to be followed by a settlement by force, that I ask Your Excellency to agree that representatives of Germany should meet representatives of Czechoslovakia for the immediate discussion of the situation that faces us, so as to come to an agreement upon the manner in which the territory is to be handed over. I am sure that these discussions can be brought to a rapid conclusion; and if you and the Czechoslovak government would like it, I am prepared for a British representative to take part . . .'

As soon as he had heard the last words of the Prime Minister's message Hitler burst out again. This time the argument was general, muddled and violent; and over everything was heard the vociferation of the Führer, who was only rendered the angrier by Wilson's apprehensive appeals for calm. He belched out insults against Benes, while Ribbentrop, who had drawn Henderson aside, also spoke of 'Benes the terrorist' and 'the Czech warmongers'. The disconcerted

Wilson, who in any case was totally incapable of standing up to the Führer, gave up arguing. He merely noted this cardinal statement: 'I can no longer allow things to drag on! I expect a reply from the Czechs by two o'clock on Wednesday at the latest.'

Wednesday, September 28, at two o'clock in the afternoon: that is to say, in less than forty-eight hours.

Before he left Chamberlain's envoy did succeed in saying that he intended to remain in Berlin, and he asked the Führer for another audience the next morning.

The essential words which Chamberlain had written and which Daladier had approved, stating that if France were drawn into the war then Great Britain would be beside her, had never been mentioned.

Since Daladier thought that the Prime Minister had included this statement in his letter, he was all the more surprised when he heard how the meeting had gone.

'Sir Horace Wilson,' he writes. 'went no further. No doubt taken aback by this reception, he did not acquaint Hitler with the most important part of the message – the United Kingdom's determination to come to the help of France if she were drawn into hostilities against Germany.[12]

In fact Chamberlain's message had been read from the first line to the last. But the one phrase that had been submitted to the French ministers was not in the letter. Sir Horace Wilson was only to read it to Hitler if the latter 'would not agree to anything'.

By way of compensation, two other approaches, British in origin, were still to be attempted during that day in Berlin, at least one of which had Chamberlain's official backing; and this, it would seem, without the French having been consulted as to their timeliness.

The first was carried out by Sir Frederick Maurice, the president of the British Legion, who was received by Hitler at Chamberlain's request.

With the Prime Minister's agreement, Sir Frederick had come to propose to the Führer that detachments of the British Legion rather than the German army should enter the Sudetenland to see to the carrying out of the plebiscite and the transfer of the zones allotted to the Reich according to the conditions laid down.

Hitler, having paid a tribute to the British Legion, 'whose efforts he had always followed and encouraged with the utmost sympathy', refused: but he willingly accepted Sir Frederick's offer as far as it concerned the territories provided for in point 5 of the memorandum (that is to say, those in which the percentage of the German population did not allow the immediate transfer to the Reich, and which were to be settled only on November 25).

'Sir Frederick Maurice,' said Ribbentrop in a communication to the British government the same day, 'has stated that he is in agreement with this modification of his proposal.'

The other British approach, unofficial, personal and in no way committing the government, came from that magnate of the English press Lord Rothermere, the owner of the *Daily Mail* among other papers and 'friend' of the chief Nazi leaders. It was in the form of a telegram addressed to Ribbentrop.[13]

> London, September 26, 1938
> In the name of our old friendship and our common desire for peace between our peoples, I do urge Your Excellency to use your influence to postpone the decisive movement of October 1 to a later date that time may be given to allay present passions and provide opportunities for reaching adjustments of detail.
> Rothermere
> 14, Stratton House, Piccadilly, London.

Ribbentrop answered this message by a long telegram in which he recalled Hitler's grievance against Benes and then added:

> Even you, my dear Lord Rothermere, will, however, understand, being one of our old friends, that even the Führer's remarkable patience, evident for months in this vital question of the existence or non-esixtence of 3½ million Germans, has its limits.
> ... Germany ... desires peace and friendship with Britain, but if foreign Bolshevik influences gain the upper hand in British policy, Germany is prepared for any eventuality. The responsibility for such a crime could, however, in the eyes of the world, never fall on Germany, as you, my dear Lord Rothermere, know best of all.
> Your old friend,
> Ribbentrop.

Bonnet asks for exact details

As soon as he was back at the Quai d'Orsay, Georges Bonnet summoned the British ambassador in Paris, Sir Eric Phipps.

The conversation that he had with him was rather surprising, since it took place scarcely more than a few hours after the talks in London, and since the French minister's chief concern in it was to ask for precise details – questions that might very well have been asked directly, and in Daladier's presence, when Bonnet had Chamberlain and Halifax opposite him. The points that were in the French foreign minister's mind had all, in fact, appeared upon the agenda of the Franco-British conference.

In the first place Georges Bonnet emphasized the inadequacy of the military assistance contemplated by the British: during the first six months of war, 150 planes and two non-motorized divisions (the support of the British fleet does not seem to have been thought sufficiently important for Bonnet to mention it).

Then the minister asked the ambassador three definite questions.

1 If war breaks out because France has helped Czechoslovakia, attacked by Germany, are the British government ready to decree general mobilization immediately?

2 Are they determined to pass a conscription bill?

3 Do they agree that Britain should pool all her economic and financial resources in a common fund with us for the carrying on of the war?[14]

The ambassador confined himself to writing down these three questions at Bonnet's dictation, and he promised to send them to his government immediately.

Hitler at the Sportpalast

At the beginning of the evening the world's eyes turned once more towards Berlin. This time it was no longer a question of a diplomatic meeting concerning which the journalists would be reduced to guesses. The words that Hitler was to utter – or rather to roar and bellow – would be spoken before twenty thousand people and broadcast on the wavelengths of the entire world. For it was from the platform of the Sportpalast, in front of fanatical Nazis and in a setting of flags, floodlights and guard of honour designed by Leni Rieffenstahl, that Hitler was to tell the German nation of his decisions.

He spoke for more than an hour, pausing from time to time to let the crowd intoxicate itself with *Sieg Heils*.

'Unlike many democratic states, Germany's foreign policy possesses philosophical bases. The aim of the philosophic concept of our nation of the Third Reich is to uphold and to ensure the existence of our German people ... You know this terrible fate that has pursued us for fifteen years, and you know too that if Germany has become great once more in spite of everything, she owes it solely to her own might!'

German might ... The Führer devoted a long passage of his speech to it: his whole policy rested upon it. To begin with Hitler emphasized the reassuring aspects of this policy – friendship with Poland, the hand stretched out to England, the relinquishing of subjects of discord with France: 'Alsace-Lorraine no longer exists for us ... all territorial disagreements between Germany and France are abolished', and lastly the Italian alliance and the return, without bloodshed, of the Austrian bloodbrothers to the fatherland. 'And now before us stands the last problem that must be solved and shall be solved; it is the last territorial claim that I have to make in Europe, but it is a claim from which I will not recede and which, God willing, I will make good!'

There followed an 'historical account' of the Czechoslovak crisis, which provided Hitler with an opportunity for insulting Benes – 'this Herr Benes' – as one head of state had never publicly insulted another. The memorandum? It contained nothing that Benes had not already accepted and promised. And he found it unacceptable! Hitler then listed the 'concessions' that he for his part had agreed to make.

'I was ready to have a plebiscite held throughout the whole of Czechoslovakia. Herr Benes and his friends set themselves against it ... I gave way on that point. I said, "Mr Chamberlain, if you want the voting to take place only in a few disputed districts, let it be so!" I agreed to let an international commission draw the frontier. This very day I stated that I was prepared to invite the British Legion to go into the territories where there was to be a plebiscite to maintain law and order there.'

At last there came the peroration.

'This is the end! I have asked that after twenty years Herr Benes should be made to tell the truth. He must hand back these territories on October 1. Herr Benes has hopes of the whole world

... but I can only say one thing – there are two men face to face, Herr Benes and myself! We are two men of a different make-up. In the great struggle of the peoples, while Herr Benes was sneaking about through the world, I as a decent German soldier did my duty!'

In the course of his speech Hitler had a kindly word for Chamberlain. 'I am grateful to him for all his efforts.' And he solemnly restated what he had already told the Prime Minister at Berchtesgaden and at Godesberg – that as soon as Czechoslovakia should have settled all the problems raised by all her minorities, the Czech state would no longer concern the Reich, 'and I should be perfectly happy to guarantee it, indeed ... We want no Czechs!'

'In four and a half years of war and twenty years of political life no one has ever been able to accuse me of being a coward. I now march before my people as its first soldier, and behind me – this the world should know – there marches a different people from that of 1918 ...

'In this moment the entire German nation is joined with me. Let Herr Benes choose!'

William Shirer heard Hitler's speech from a seat in the Sportpalast just under the Führer, and that evening he wrote –

'For the first time in all the years I've observed him, he seemed tonight to have completely lost control over himself. When he sat down, Goebbels sprang up and shouted into the microphone, "One thing is sure, 1918 will never be repeated!" Hitler looked up at him, a wild, eager expression in his eyes, as if those were the words he had been searching for all the evening and hadn't quite found. He leapt to his feet, and with a fanatical fire in his eyes that I shall never forget, brought his right hand after a grand sweep pounding down on the table, and yelled with the full power in his mighty lungs, "*Ja!*" Then he slumped into his chair, exhausted.'[15]

And Gamelin, who listened to the Sportpalast speech on the radio, considered that it was fiendishly clever, and that it might 'mislead our simpletons'.[16]

Chamberlain's reply

It would appear that it was not only French simpletons that the speech misled.

Indeed, of this long harangue, which was heard on the radio in London and at once translated and passed to the Prime Minister, sheet by sheet, Chamberlain remembered only one phrase – that which concerned him personally. A few minutes after midnight the British people could hear the quavering voice of their Prime Minister.

'I have read the speech of the German Chancellor and I appreciate his references to the efforts that I have made to peace.

'I cannot abandon those efforts, since it seems to me incredible that the peoples of Europe who do not want war with one another should be plunged into a bloody struggle over a question in which agreement has already been largely obtained.

'It is evident that the Chancellor has no faith that the promises made will be carried out. These promises were made, not to the German government direct, but to the British and French governments in the first instance.

'Speaking for the British government, we regard ourselves morally responsible for seeing that the promises are carried out fairly and truly, and we are prepared to undertake that they shall be so carried out with all reasonable promptitude, provided that the German government will agree to the settlement of terms and conditions of transfer by discussion and not by force.

'I trust that the Chancellor will not reject this proposal, which is made in the same spirit of friendliness as that in which I was received in Germany and which, if it is accepted, will satisfy the German desire for the union of the Sudeten Germans with the Reich without the shedding of blood in any part of Europe.'[17]

The 'authorized statement' of the Foreign Office

The next day, September 27, the world's papers devoted their headlines to Hitler's speech and Chamberlain's 'reply'. They also devoted an important place to Roosevelt's appeal.

There was also another article to be found. It was far less prominently displayed in the French papers, but it was to assume a most unusual significance, since, in the absence of the statement that Wilson had refrained from making at his interview with Hitler, it had the merit of clearly defining the allies' position as it was laid down at the London talks. The article was put out as an 'authorized statement' from the Foreign Office.

'It is stated in official quarters that during the last week Mr Chamberlain has tried with the German Chancellor to find a way of settling peacefully the Czechoslovak question.

'It is still possible to do so by negotiation.

'The German claim to the transfer of the Sudeten area has already been conceded by the French, British and Czechoslovak governments. But if, in spite of all efforts made by the British Prime Minister, a German attack is made upon Czechoslovakia, the immediate result must be that France will be bound to come to her assistance, and Great Britain and Russia will certainly stand by France. It is still not too late to stop this great tragedy and for the peoples of all nations to insist on a settlement by free negotiation.'

This statement, attributed to 'official circles', was handed to the journalists at a quarter past nine in the evening of September 26, in London, by an official of the Foreign Office press section. This is a usual practice with the British foreign ministry, which often uses the indirect procedure of the 'authorized statement'.*

The English evening papers, particularly the *Evening News*, published it, furthermore, with the perfectly simple title 'Foreign Office official communiqué'.

Why then did so many of the Paris papers produce it in such a reserved manner? Because there had been an immediate rumour in the editors' offices that the Quai d'Orsay had been surprised at receiving the text, had expressed doubts as to its authenticity, and in any case had questioned its timeliness.

What was one to think of all this? As for the authenticity, the only point upon which there could be any doubt was as to whether the author of the communiqué was Sir Robert Vansittart† or whether Lord Halifax had written it with his own hand.‡ But even if the former were the case, it is certain that the British Foreign Secretary knew of the text and approved it before it was given out.

Moreover, on the twenty-seventh, as soon as London heard of the

* We have already mentioned an earlier 'authorized statement' of the Foreign Office (see p. 111).

† In 1948 J. Debu-Bridel wrote 'It is now established that this text was drafted by Sir Robert Vansittart, the diplomatic adviser, in full agreement with Lord Halifax.'

‡ In 1959 Paul-Louis Bret wrote 'Reginald Leeper – Rex as we called him – the head of the Foreign Office press department, particularly told me that the text had been written by Lord Halifax himself.'

reservations that this communiqué had met with in Paris, both journalists and diplomats reacted with the same energy.

Paul-Louis Bret, of Havas' London office, was one of the first to show his surprise when he received the Paris papers the next morning and saw how his colleagues with one accord had given so little importance to a piece of news that he had at once seen to be of great significance. A few minutes later the head of the Foreign Office press department telephoned Bret: Reginald Leeper asked the chief of Havas in London to come as quickly as possible.

'Do you know,' he said, as soon as Bret came into his office, 'do you know that they are spreading the rumour in Paris that yesterday evening's communiqué is false? I ask you to confirm that it is genuine, quoting the Foreign Office and even using Lord Halifax's name!'

Bret was only too delighted with this confirmation and he did not stay to be asked twice. He immediately handed it on to Havas in Paris. But it was in vain that he waited to see the confirmation reappear in the form of a dispatch sent out by the Paris office. At last during the afternoon the head of the political section, Bassée, telephoned London and asked to speak to Bret. 'This famous "authorized statement" of the Foreign Office,' said Bassée, 'the Quai d'Orsay thinks it is questionable. We have been asked to smother it.'

Bret was furious and he reacted strongly. 'But this is scandalous! Didn't I tell you I guaranteed that it was genuine? One has no right to deceive the public!'

But the only reply from Bassée was a chuckle at the other end of the line. Bret was determined to see the thing through and he telephoned one of his personal friends at the Quai d'Orsay. He did not have much trouble in explaining what he meant: the other man knew all about it and he cut in, 'You are not being any worse treated than the ambassador. Corbin's telegram with the same English statement in it has not been sent to the heads of department either.'

Two days later P.-L. Bret was attacked in *Le Jour* by Léon Bailby, who accused him of being a 'falsifier of news'. Bret at once telegraphed his chiefs: he was resigning so as to be able to sue the libeller. But the reply came immediately, 'There is no point in resigning: you will not be attacked any more; you will be fully indemnified.'

The ludicrous, and painful, ending of this incident must be left to P.-L. Bret himself.

'A few weeks later,' he writes, 'I was summoned to Paris in unusually friendly terms. My detractors in the foreign ministry and at Havas had conceived the idea of making me a chevalier of the Légion d'honneur by way of wiping out "that unfortunate incident". The head of the political section told me the news, smiling broadly. I received it with stony silence. When I left the office I found that the firm had already had the red ribbon put into the button-hole of my overcoat. I tore the ribbon out and swore never to wear it.'[18]

There is still one point, however, that deserves more exact detail: Bret openly calls 'the Quai d'Orsay' into question, accusing it of having wanted 'to smother' the British communiqué. Was it a matter, at this juncture, of a few irresponsible officials in the press section? The head of this section, M Pierre Comert, has made things clear on this point. Not only did he in fact distribute the communiqué, but he too found that he was accused of being a 'falsifier of news'. It was even he who, after a preliminary inquiry, warned Reginald Leeper.

Pierre Comert methodically began by pointing out to the French embassy in London that the 'authorized statement' did not seem to have been sent to the Quai d'Orsay. London's reply was that the communiqué had been wired to Paris as soon as it had been handed to the press. Having asked the embassy to repeat the message Comert then telephoned Leeper and told him what was going on, advising him to come to an understanding with Havas in London. A few hours later, nevertheless, Comert telephoned the London office of the agency directly, and there too he asked for a fresh transmission of the communiqué.

All these efforts were entirely wasted. But Pierre Comert managed to find out why.

'I then made a new inquiry,' said he, 'in Paris this time. The embassy's telegram had indeed been sent. But M Georges Bonnet had prevented it from being distributed in the departments of the ministry and had forbidden Havas to give the press the text of the communiqué, which for the second time their London correspondent had telegraphed to the agency.

'I remember,' ended Pierre Comert, 'that no one who might have played a cardinal part believed in this communiqué. We should have made the most of it; we did not do so, and people like Vansittart and Halifax, who were expecting us to support them as a consequence of the communiqué, found that it had no result.'[19]

So it was not merely 'the Quai d'Orsay' but also the minister in person who is implicated – and that by the departmental official who was directly responsible for the press section.

Besides, Bonnet himself undertakes the task of showing how well founded these accusations were by speaking of his 'surprise' at the sight of the communiqué and of his reactions as soon as he had read it.

'I might well be rather surprised, since three hours earlier the British ambassador himself had been unable to give me any exact information upon the assistance that would be given us, especially about conscription and the mobilization of the army. But Sir Eric Phipps explained to me almost at once that this statement did not derive from the Foreign Office, and that it in no way modified the British government's basic position. The French government should see no more in it than a final attempt at impressing Hitler and obliging him to settle the Sudeten affair by peaceful negotiation. Great Britain's intentions and obligations were still fixed by the British government's notes alone.'[20]

So the French foreign minister was 'surprised' to such a point that he asked the British ambassador for explanations, not because Great Britain refused to come in with France, but because she confirmed her determination to do so!

And this happened during the evening of the very day when the British and French ministers had reached agreement upon a text which the Foreign Office's communiqué did no more than paraphrase and which the French premier, Daladier, rightly thought that he had 'dragged out' of the British.

It is true that this same French foreign minister had already attempted, that afternoon, to induce the British to display reserve and to qualify their promise of support by producing his questionnaire.*

* Other examples of the foreign minister's interference in the realm of information might be quoted. Louis Lévy in *The Truth about France* (1941) speaks of two, the one as typical as the other. On August 24 the English press announced that an official warning would be given to Germany before the Nuremberg congress, and that this warning would clearly show Great Britain's solidarity with France. The next day the German agency DNB denied it. And the same day Havas, urged on by Bonnet, confirmed the German denial in speaking of a Bonnet-Halifax interview. Nevertheless, on the twenty-seventh there was Sir John Simon's speech at

Why did these manoeuvres take place?

Perhaps because Bonnet, like Chamberlain, declined to give priority to strict respect for the obligations France had undertaken over his pessimistic estimate of the forces facing one another. But this does not explain why that estimate should have been systematically pessimistic, even to the pitch of distortion.

May it then have been because of this exact statement in the Foreign Office communiqué – the words about the eventual intervention on France's side not only of Great Britain but also of Russia? That too may well be the case.

At all events it is interesting to observe that at almost the same time, both within the British government and the French, the same kind of realignment was taking place, and in each case it divided the body of supporters of peace at any price (which had hitherto been united throughout) into two separate groups.

Daladier was no longer in agreement with Bonnet: he showed this in London by fighting for a commitment – a commitment whose scope Bonnet at once did his best to reduce by embarrassing the British with over-precise questions. And for his part Halifax was no longer a follower of Chamberlain's policy.

The joint result of Chamberlain's and Bonnet's manoeuvres (though it would seem that they were not preconcerted) was very serious, whatever their motives may have been. And this was made strikingly obvious by the affair of the 'authorized statement'. The allies' firm attitude, agreed upon that morning in London, had no meaning unless it reached Hitler's ears in good time and unless it were quite unequivocal. Now Wilson, in Berlin with exact instructions from Chamberlain, made no mention of it; and Hitler was therefore able to make his Sportpalast speech and assume commitments which could not, for reasons of prestige, be set aside, and this without knowing what their consequences might be.

In the absence of the warning that Wilson was to have given, the Foreign Office communiqué had the merit of plainly expressing the agreement that the ministers had reached that morning. But Bonnet

---

Lanark, which was consistent with the denied news-item. On September 11 Chamberlain and a Foreign Office spokesman summoned the press and said clearly that if France were to be engaged in a conflict, Great Britain would follow. That same evening Bonnet made one of his colleagues telephone the chief diplomatic ournalists (of whom Louis Lévy was one) to ask them to play down this news.

hindered its distribution and Chamberlain deliberately lessened its effect by his speech on the radio.[2]

Wilson sees Hitler again

As it had been arranged, Sir Horace Wilson went back to the Chancellery at the end of the morning, still accompanied by Henderson and Kirkpatrick. During the morning Chamberlain had sent his envoy a message which was no more than a paraphrase of his broadcast the night before, offering Hitler, if he felt that he could not trust in Benes's word, a British guarantee that Prague should carry out the promises that might be made.

Before making this offer Sir Horace, as a diplomat, began by flattering the Führer. 'I watched the demonstration at the Sportpalast as a spectator yesterday. May I congratulate you on the splendid reception that you had there? It must have been a wonderful moment! And let me also say how much the Prime Minister appreciates the references that you were good enough to make to his efforts in favour of peace.'

After this Wilson recalled Chamberlain's declaration. 'The Prime Minister has therefore assumed moral responsibility for the carrying out of the engagements undertaken by the Czechoslovaks. Am I, in this connexion, to carry a message to the Prime Minister? I am leaving for London almost at once.'

'I have nothing to add,' said Hitler in an arrogant tone. 'The Prague government have only the choice between two solutions – to accept the German memorandum or to reject it.' And raising his voice Hitler began to shout, 'I will smash the Czechs! Tell him that I will smash the Czechs!* Prague shall be bombed, the Czech army routed, and Herr Benes will have to flee ignominiously!'[21]

There was nothing left for Sir Horace to do but to carry out (at last!) the most difficult part of his task. 'There is still this that I must say to you: if the Czechoslovaks reject the German note, and if Germany attacks Czechoslovakia, France, as Daladier has stated, will honour her engagements. And if, in this hypothesis, the French armies should be involved in a war with Germany . . . Great Britain would then find herself obliged to go to France's aid.' Sir Horace prudently made things more clear. 'I have not said that the French would attack Germany, but simply that they would fulfil their

---

* '*Ich werde die Tschechen zerschlagen!*'

engagements to Czechoslovakia. Under what form they would do this I cannot say. But if, in pursuit of her treaty obligations, France became actively engaged in hostilities against Germany, the United Kingdom would feel obliged to support her.'

'I can only take note of that position,' interrupted Hitler,' it means that if France elects to attack Germany, England will feel obliged to attack her also. All right! We shall all be at war next Monday. The Czechs, feeling themselves supported, will reject my note; I shall destroy Czechoslovakia; France will attack Germany; England will help France – and all this because Benes has not chosen to accept a note which contains nothing other than the immediate carrying into effect of his promises!'

'I have not said that France would attack Germany,' protested Wilson timidly.

'I have spent four and a half thousand millions on our western fortifications,' continued Hitler without hearing him. 'They can come when they like.'

Chamberlain's adviser seemed inclined to go on with this pointless interchange, but Henderson plucked his sleeve and gave him to understand that all he had to do now was to take leave. But for all that Wilson found means to stay a few minutes alone with Hitler, and promised him to try to bring the Czechs to their senses.*

The three Englishmen had scarcely left his office before the Führer was already ringing for Schmundt and dictating to him an order for the 'moving of Operation Green assault units from their exercise zones to bases for the attack'. The seven divisions affected by this order were to be prepared for action from September 30 with twenty-four hours' notice.

The interventions increase

While Sir Horace was flying to London to give Chamberlain an account of his mission's disappointing results, Hitler received, one after another, a variety of messages whose authors still hoped to make him pause and think.

That same morning Roosevelt had received the Führer's answer to his appeal of the day before.

---

* 'I will still try to make those Czechos sensible': the words are in English in the original of Schmidt's German notes.

'Rest assured,' wrote Hitler, 'that I appreciate the generous intention that lies behind your declarations at its true value and that I fully share your point of view on the unforeseeable consequences of a European war. But it is for that very reason that I am able to decline and that I must decline all responsibility on the part of the German people and its leaders in the event of matters ending with the opening of hostilities in spite of all my efforts.'

And once more Hitler interminably went over his grievances against the Allies, the treaty of Versailles, the Czechs ... And he ended the long harangue with these words.

'It is not Germany's fault if a Sudeten problem exists and if it has given rise to the present intolerable situation. The appalling fate of the people who are affected by this problem means that its solution can no longer be put off. This is why the proposals contained in the German note represent the last chances of a fair settlement by agreement. It is not the German but the Czechoslovak government that henceforth have the power of deciding whether they want peace or war.'

Although this reply from the dictator in fact amounted to a rejection, the President of the United States was from now on determined to increase the number of approaches, and he at once responded to this telegram by a fresh appeal.

'... I was confident that you would coincide in the opinion I expressed regarding the unforeseeable consequences and incalculable disaster which would result to the entire world from the outbreak of a European war. ...

'The present negotiations still stand open. They can be continued if you give the word. Should the need for supplementing them become evident, nothing stands in the way of widening their scope into a conference of all nations directly interested in the present controversy.'

Yet although he justified his intervention, Roosevelt himself defined its limits.

'The government of the United States has no political involvement in Europe and will assume no obligations in the conduct of the present negotiations. Yet in our own right we recognize our responsibilities as part of a world of neighbours.'

At the same time Roosevelt telegraphed Philipps, his ambassador in Rome, entrusting him with a personal and confidential mission to Mussolini, whom the President of the United States asked 'to help so that there might be a continuation of the present efforts to reach agreement on the questions still outstanding by negotiation or any other peaceful means rather than by turning to force'.

For his part the King of Sweden desired the German ambassador in Stockholm to ask Hitler to postpone the fateful limit of October 1 to October 10; otherwise, he said, a world war would certainly break out – and not only would Germany be named the aggressor, but she would meet with such a coalition that she would certainly be beaten.

Furthermore most of the diplomatic dispatches that reached the Wilhelmstrasse during the afternoon brought more disappointment for Hitler than reasons for optimism.

The French mobilization was taking on considerable proportions and it was being carried out with unusual swiftness.* The British were getting ready to put their fleet on a war footing, the Little Entente, faced with the threat of intervention by Hungary, was waking up; Mussolini was indeed speaking of mobilizing, but with the intention of sending his troops to Libya rather than the Alps. And lastly Franco, who owed everything to Hitler and Mussolini, let it be known that he was contemplating the opening of negotiations with London and Paris to have his neutrality recognized. He was already engaging himself not to let any German or Italian forces nearer than 130 kilometres from the French frontier.[22]

An unsuccessful parade

The end of the day was to strengthen Hitler's disagreeable feelings over the flood of bad news, and that in an unexpected manner.

At Goebbel's advice and in order to 'galvanize the people' he had ordered one of the motorized divisions under marching orders to pass through the main streets of Berlin just at the time offices and factories were closing.

---

* At 22.40 hours on the twenty-seventh Kühlenthal, the German military attaché in Paris, telegraphed, 'The French mobilization measures . . . are so advanced that . . . I foresee that the putting into position of the sixty-five first divisions on the German frontier will be finished on the sixth day of mobilization.' From this Kühlenthal deduced that 'any act of force by Germany' would bring about general mobilization and an immediate attack in the direction of Mainz. He also reported the landing of three hundred British planes on French airfields.

'The Germans love military display,' says Henderson,[23] 'but not a single individual in the streets applauded its passage. The picture which it represented was almost that of a hostile army passing through a conquered city. Hitler was deeply impressed. At that moment that he realized for the first time that the cheers of his sycophants in the Sportpalast were far from representing the true spirit and feelings of the German people.'

William Shirer, of course, was in the streets. That evening he wrote in his diary:

'I went out to the corner of the Linden where the column was turning down the Wilhelmstrasse, expecting to see a tremendous demonstration. I pictured the scenes I had read of in 1914 when the cheering throngs on this same street tossed flowers at the marching soldiers, and the girls ran up and kissed them ... But today they ducked into the subways, refused to look on, and the handful that did stood at the curb in utter silence ... It has been the most striking demonstration against war I've ever seen.'[24]

As for Gisevius, he expresses the feelings of the 'opposition'.

'This demonstration was, with regard to foreign countries, an act of intimidation, and with regard to Germany, an act of propaganda: Witzleben was boiling with fury at the theatrical display, and for a trifle he would have set up a battery in front of the Chancellery; yet we could not have asked for anything better, for never yet had the soldiers had such a wretched welcome as they had that afternoon. There were clenched fists in the workers' quarters, and in the middle of the town the people looked ostentatiously away. In the beginning Hitler stood at his "historic" balcony; but seeing that the Berliners did not rejoice and that they watched the parading troops with dislike and disapproval, the popular hero went back indoors, whence he watched the apathetic crowd. His anger broke out against Goebbels. "It is impossible for me to make war with a people like this!" And the propaganda chief replied, "No, Führer; I was down there and I was able to assure myself that all this nation needs is still more enlightenment." ' [25]

Intrigues and manoeuvres in Paris

But if the Führer had been a little more precisely informed of what was going on in Paris during this same day, he might have had some reasons for satisfaction and hopefulness.

The cabinet met at the Elysée, and the discussion, as Bonnet puts it, was 'muddled'. This day did in fact emphasize that difference which had already begun to be felt the day before, between the extreme position of the foreign minister and that of the premier. There were no longer only two tendencies within the government, but three, whose respective leaders were Paul Reynaud, Daladier and Bonnet. And during this cabinet meeting, Daladier suddenly appeared to be nearer to Paul Reynaud than to Georges Bonnet.

Yet this development was still too recent and too unmarked to lead to a break. Did Daladier begin by writing the cabinet's letter of resignation during this meeting, as some have said? Was it because of Albert Sarraut's discreet intervention, 'Wait forty-eight hours', that he refrained? At all events one thing is sure: Bonnet found himself practically isolated, with even his most faithful supporters, Chautemps, Guy La Chambre and Monzie, hesitating to commit themselves completely to his side. Yet paradoxically it was his attitude that won the day in the end, partly because of technical reasons; and the cabinet broke up without having taken other mobilization measures than the recall of a few supplementary classes.

But the most solid support that the foreign minister found in the course of that day was above all outside the government, in trade union circles and among the pacifist left and the fascist or fascist-sympathizing right.

The *Centre syndical d'Action contre la Guerre*,* which had just been formed, increased the number of its communiqués and appeals. These militant trade-unionists relied upon a certain number of Front Populaire parliamentarians. They also stated that various groups were with them, such as the *Comité de Vigilance*, the *Ligue des Combattants de la Paix* and the *Secours International Antifasciste*.

In the Palais-Bourbon these left-wing pacifist elements played their part inside the parliamentary groups of their respective parties; yet there were not enough of them for their point of view to prevail. But on the right and the extreme right wing, in those bodies that were called the 'minority groups' this proportion was reversed. It

* This centre brought together schoolteachers (with their secretary-general Delmas, who had just been re-elected after having declared at a union conference, 'It is better to live as a German than to die as a Frenchman!'), technicians, book-trade workers, metal-workers, underground workers and many of the leaders of the national post-office union.

was from this point, therefore, that the parliamentary offensive of the
pacifists began on the afternoon of the twenty-seventh.

It was a well-led offensive, too; and it is hard to see how it could
have developed as it did unless there had been a contact already
established with Bonnet, for some of the activities of the deputies
and of the foreign minister were strikingly co-ordinated.

The 'delegates of the minority groups', meeting in the Palais-
Bourbon, first had submitted to them a proposal of Pierre-Etienne
Flandin, who, repeating the substance of a letter that he had just
published in *Le Temps*, urged that parliament should be recalled.
Flandin, Piétri and Montigny spoke in favour of this, and it needed
all Louis Marin's authority and the support of his friends in the
Fédération républicaine, Blaisot and Oberkirch, to have the motion set
aside. It would have allowed Hitler to count the 'pacifists' in parliament; and no doubt he would have found that there were more of
them than he had dared to hope for.

But the matter did not rest there. Montigny addressed the minority
deputies and expressed his astonishment at the fact that the map
which Hitler had attached to the Godesberg memorandum should
not yet have been shown to parliament although four days had
passed since the meeting between Hitler and Chamberlain. Then
François Piétri spoke of forgery in connexion with the Foreign
Office communiqué. Upon this Fernand Laurent moved that they
should go to the Quai d'Orsay 'to ask for explanations', and this was
at once decided upon. The 'delegation' was all the more homogeneous in that several of the minority leaders such as Louis Marin,
Camille Blaisot and Oberkirch would have nothing to do with it.
It was composed solely of undoubted 'pacifists' – Montigny, Colonel
des Isnards, Taittinger, Fernand Laurent and Brille.

In fact the dialogue between Georges Bonnet and those friends of
his who came to question him had no other object than that of providing the minister with an occasion for publicly adopting a certain
number of attitudes that might be of service to the cause that he
supported.

What was the point of asking for the Godesberg map?

To let Bonnet assert that Germany had not put forward any new
territorial claim and that therefore there was no basic difference
between the Franco-British plan that Prague had accepted and the
Godesberg memorandum, but only a difference of procedure –
which was precisely what Hitler was saying.

And all the time they were at the Quai d'Orsay the minority delegates went on asking Georges Bonnet questions that were as well chosen as they were cleverly phrased.

'Can the French government guarantee the authenticity of the Foreign Office communiqué?'

'The Quai d'Orsay,' replied Bonnet, 'has received no confirmation on this subject.'

Not only do we know that this was not the case, but also that essentially – which is what counts, after all – the incriminated document (the 'authorized statement' of the day before) did nothing but paraphrase Chamberlain's text, upon whose terms the French and British ministers were agreed. This was a detail that Georges Bonnet did not think worth while giving his visitors.

But there was better to come: as if by chance the minority delegates questioned Bonnet on those very points that he himself had questioned the British ambassador the day before.

'Has the French government exact information as to Great Britain's military co-operation? Has England undertaken to introduce compulsory military service by conscription?'

Bonnet had not yet received Halifax's answer. He therefore did no more than note the question; but in itself the inquiry had the merit of emphasizing the questionnaire put to Great Britain – though it might well have been asked up until then whether the submitting of this questionnaire was in itself a timely act.

Writing of this interview Jacques Debu-Bridel concludes

'Thus, thanks to P.-E. Flandin's exertions, G. Bonnet (according to *Le Jour*)* did not hesitate on September 27

'1 To express a kind of denial of the Foreign Office communiqué and to sow doubt in France as to England's intentions and in England as to France's good faith.

'2 To confirm Hitler's thesis on the comparative moderation of the Godesberg memorandum, which had been rejected by Prague and judged unacceptable by Chamberlain and Daladier.

'Under the pretext of working for peace, this was a very clumsy

---

* It was *Le Jour* of the following day that gave a detailed (and quasi-official) report of the delegation's visit to the Quai d'Orsay. Furthermore, J. Debu-Bridel points out that at the head of *Le Jour*'s foreign policy section there was M A. Piétri, who was a nephew of François Piétri and who was 'reckoned among G. Bonnet's confidential friends and advisers'.

way of playing Germany's game. It may be imagined what kind of a spectacle the recalled parliament would have presented in such circumstances.'[26]

Very clumsy? Is that the word?

The rue Saint-Dominique and the Elysée

After their fruitful visit to the foreign minister the delegates went back to the Chamber. They gave their friends an account of their interview with Bonnet and told them that he had advised them to go and see Daladier and Lebrun. Montigny had had a private conversation with Bonnet before leaving the Quai d'Orsay and he confidentially told his friends that the foreign minister, with a sob in his voice, had said to him, 'Reynaud is mad! We are heading for disaster: I beg of you to do what you can.'

They at once decided to follow Bonnet's advice and to go to ask Daladier for an audience. But at the rue Saint-Dominique the delegation was told that the premier was closeted with Léon Blum, that he was expecting Campinchi after that, and that he could not see the minority's spokesman before tomorrow morning.

Another report – much shorter this time – and another departure, now in the direction of the Elysée, where Magre, the secretary-general, politely but firmly turned the visitors away: the President of the Republic could not receive a parliamentary delegation if it had not first been received by the premier; that was the constitution.

The delegation of the minority groups could only separate until the next day. But its members felt that they had not entirely wasted their time. Some of them even felt that it was because of their activities and the climate that they had succeeded in creating in the parliamentary lobbies that there was the unexpected tone – a tone that they had scarcely hoped for – in the press-statement that Daladier made when he left the ministry of war after having seen Campinchi.

'At the end of this new day of crisis, I should like to make a statement on the international plane: the struggle for peace is not over; the negotiations are going on. Do not imagine that our diplomacy is doing nothing; only today it has been active in several capitals. Do I, as an ex-serviceman, have to say that the government over which I preside will neglect no possibility of maintaining an honourable peace?'

Two British notes

This statement was well received at the Quai d'Orsay: Bonnet was of the opinion that it had 'a much calmer ring'.

François-Poncet's messages from Berlin were far less reassuring: they showed that the German army had completed its preparations and that in twenty-four hours it could cross the Czechoslovak frontier.

As Hitler's ultimatum to Prague expired the next day at two o'clock, perhaps this was the last evening of peace that was now beginning. For Georges Bonnet the first hours of this evening were marked by several visits from Sir Eric Phipps.

The British ambassador brought the French minister his government's reply to the three questions of the day before concerning mobilization, conscription and the pooling of resources.

'In today's circumstances, the factual questions that M Bonnet has asked His Majesty's government will be answered as follows.

'1 *Mobilization*. M Bonnet should refer to the announcement published on September 26 authorizing the call-up of the defence units of the Auxiliary Air Force and this morning's announcement in virtue of which it has been decided to mobilize the fleet as a purely precautionary measure.

'2 *Conscription*. M Bonnet should refer to the declaration made by the Secretary of State at the Foreign Office at the time of the first meeting with the French ministers on April 28 as to the nature of His Majesty's government's participation in a war that would be the consequence of British engagements to France in virtue of the treaty of Locarno.

'3 *A common fund of economic and financial resources*. This proposal raises constitutional problems that can only be decided after parliament has given its consent.'[27]

Bonnet noted these replies without displeasure: they were as evasive and dilatory as could be wished: 'there was still no question of the army', and the British government 'did not commit themselves to decree conscription either', and finally it 'evaded the question of the pooling of economic and financial resources'.

Yet perhaps it might have been more fair to emphasize, as the English (who must have been rather surprised by this curious questionnaire, sent only a few hours after the London conference) had done, that these replies were made only in the *circumstances of the day* – which rendered the questions premature, to say the least.

A second note was intended to secure the British against any ill-timed military action. This is the text, or at least that part of the text Georges Bonnet reproduces.[28]

'The Czechoslovak resistance will not last long: that is the opinion of British military attachés in Prague and Berlin. If therefore our efforts for peace fail and if the German troops enter Czechoslovakia on Thursday, we may expect to be confronted by the *fait accompli* of the occupation of Czechoslovakia very shortly. Meanwhile no declaration and no action on the part of France or ourselves will be able to prevent this rapid and overwhelming result. It is true that we have always borne this possibility in mind. But according to the most recent information we are now forced to look upon it as a reality.

'In these circumstances and in view of the identity of our two countries' interests, it is necessary that all actions undertaken by France to fulfil her obligations or by ourselves to help France should be very closely linked and concerted, above all as regards steps that may immediately and automatically start a world-wide war without in any way having the effect of saving Czechoslovakia.

'We should be happy to learn that the French government agree that no military action whatsoever, and especially no military action of an offensive nature, should be taken except after consultation with the United Kingdom government and with their preliminary agreement.

'This observation does not cover precautionary measures taken by the French army or the occupation of the Maginot Line.'

In fact this text is incomplete. Lord Halifax's note began with the words, 'General Gamelin explained to us on Monday that the Czechoslovak resistance would be of extremely brief duration.' If this was cut off, and if, in the version published by Bonnet, the reference to Gamelin had vanished, it was because of some rather special circumstances which are best dealt with by the person most concerned.

'. . . it remains for me,' says Gamelin, 'to clarify what was a very painful affair for me. I should like to say at once that its sole origin lay in M Georges Bonnet's intrigues.

'I subsequently learnt that in the instructions he sent to Sir Eric Phipps, the British ambassador in Paris, Lord Halifax had expressed himself thus: "General Gamelin explained to us on

Monday that the Czech resistance would be of extremely brief duration. This assessment is disturbing . . ."

'Later I heard that M Georges Bonnet was bringing this up to be able to say that I was against an energetic solution. I therefore took the occasion of a conversation with Lord Halifax to make my position quite clear.'[29]

After this conversation – and this clarification – Gamelin wrote to Daladier to give him an account of it, and he reminded the premier that the commander-in-chief of the French army had adopted an attitude in London that was entirely different from that which had been attributed to him as far as Czechoslovakia's possibilities for defence were concerned. He added that on September 26, furthermore, he had had 'no conversation whatever in the presence of Lord Halifax'.

And the generalissimo concludes, 'No one can doubt the absolute straightforwardness of Lord Halifax. Besides, I have since found out that what I suspected was indeed the case. The remarks that he attributed to me came to him from M Georges Bonnet.'

'I do not see that I can do any more'

In London the evening began wretchedly. Its keynote was an unusually lachrymose speech on the BBC by the Prime Minister.

'How horrible, how fantastic, how incredible it is that we should be digging trenches and trying on gas-masks because of a quarrel in a far-away country between people of whom we know nothing! It seems all the more impossible that a quarrel which has already been settled in principle should be the subject of war.

'I perfectly well understand the reasons why the Czechoslovak government have not thought themselves able to accept the conditions put to them in the German memorandum. It is my impression, after my talks with Herr Hitler, that if only time were allowed it ought to be possible for the arrangements for transferring the territory that the Czech government have agreed to give to Germany to be settled by agreement, under conditions that would assure fair treatment to the population concerned.

'You already know that I have done all that a man can do to settle this disagreement.

'After my visits to Germany I have come to realize how Herr

Hitler feels he must champion the cause of his German brothers, and his indignation at the fact that his claims have not yet been satisfied.

'He told me privately, and he publicly repeated it yesterday evening, that once the Sudeten German incident was settled that would be the end of German territorial claims in Europe.

'I shall not give up hope nor abandon my efforts to maintain the peace so long as there is the least chance of success. I would not hesitate to pay even a third visit to Germany if I thought it would do any good. But at present I do not see that I can usefully do any more in the field of mediation.'

It was a depressing speech from the point of view of his hearers' morale; but how clever it was from that of preparing public opinion for fresh concessions!

In those passages that were meant to bring tears to the eyes of the British citizen there is to be found the basis of the German propaganda themes – the mass of the people's desire for peace, the 'far-away country', the 'people of whom we know nothing', the 'quarrel that has already been settled in principle', 'Herr Hitler's indignation', and above all 'the end of territorial claims in Europe'.

It was all there.

But the emotion that Chamberlain showed in his style, to say nothing of his voice, seems thoroughly false when this text is compared with another document, a letter written by the Prime Minister a few minutes before. Even Georges Bonnet, who has no particular tenderness for Benes, to whom the letter was sent, says 'its severe and official style froze me'.

'According to information received by His Majesty's government, the German forces have received the order to cross the Czechoslovak frontier if the Czechoslovak government have not accepted the German proposals by two o'clock in the afternoon tomorrow. The result of this will be that Bohemia will be overrun and that no action by any other power will be able to prevent it. His Majesty's government cannot take the responsibility of advising you as to what you ought to do; but they are of the opinion that this information should reach you at once.'

At eight that evening, however, the order for the mobilization of the fleet was sent out. This was only made public at 23.38 hours.

On the slope

But before this, at 2230 hours, Chamberlain received a letter whose adroitness was in no way inferior to his own, either in his speeches or his messages. It was a letter as precisely adapted to the Prime Minister's psychology as the Prime Minister's speech had been to the psychology of the average Englishman.

Its author was none other than the Chancellor of the Reich, who was writing personally to his 'dear Mr Chamberlain' and who returned to his argument, this time in a sanctimonious and mealymouthed fashion: he had asked nothing that was not wholly legitimate, he entertained nothing but good feelings for the 'Czechs' – why, alas, had there to be a lack of reciprocity?

In passing, Hitler referred to the 'forces' that Benes was hoping to mobilize, particularly in France and England – those forces which, in his heart of hearts, Chamberlain feared most of all.

And then the last exceedingly shrewd passage which flattered the Prime Minister, quietly prompted him to act, and, a few hours before the expiry of the ultimatum, left the door ajar: 'I must leave it to your judgment whether, in view of these facts, you consider that you should continue your efforts, for which I should like to take this opportunity of once more sincerely thanking you, to spoil such manoeuvres and bring the government in Prague to reason at the very last hour.'

Part Three

THE RENDEZVOUS AT MUNICH

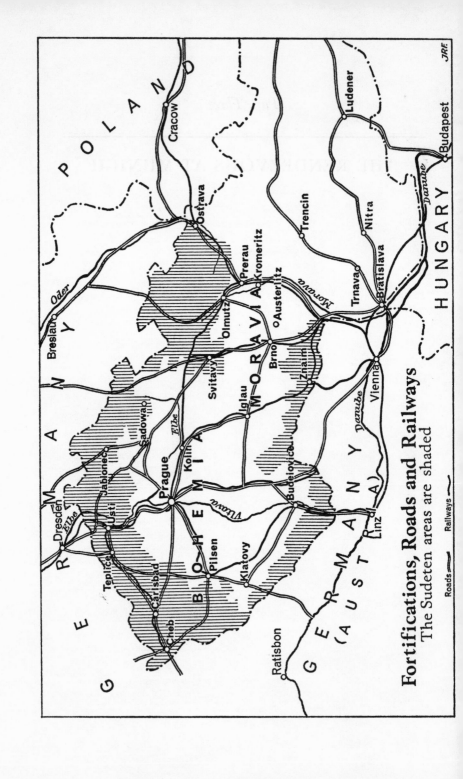

Fortifications, Roads and Railways
The Sudeten areas are shaded

Roads ⚊ Railways ⚊

CHAPTER ONE

The race against the clock

*A few false notes · Lord Perth takes over · Ciano's 'humour' · Göring's
imagination · François-Poncet is at last received by Hitler · Attolico steps in ·
Henderson sees Hitler*

IT does not seem that when Chamberlain received Hitler's personal
letter he at once thought of the international conference that Roosevelt had suggested.

The Prime Minister had another plan in mind: he hoped to succeed
in calming the Nazi ogre's appetite for the time being by giving it a
bone to gnaw. From this there arose a fresh British démarche in
Berlin, which was at once reported to the French government by
Sir Eric Phipps, the British ambassador, who 'came during the night
of September 27–28 to inform the Quai d'Orsay that his government,
in agreement, said he, with Prague, had proposed to Hitler the
immediate entry of German troops into the region of Eger, whose
inhabitants were in a very great majority Germans.'[1]

In agreement with Prague? No one really believed this phrase,
which was put in merely for the look of it.

At all events, it was without the slightest agreement with Prague
that Georges Bonnet in his turn made a higher bid. At one in the
morning of the twenty-eighth the French foreign minister telegraphed new instructions to François-Poncet.

'. . . Sir Eric Phipps has just informed me of a proposal which
his government is submitting to Berlin and which includes the
immediate entry of German troops into the Egerland.

'Please ask your British colleague without delay whether this
proposal is well received.

'If it is not, in order to make a last attempt at avoiding the
irreparable, you will with all haste submit a proposal in the

government's name to Herr Hitler which will repeat the conditions of execution of this last British suggestion and which will comprise the immediate occupation of a greater extent of territory . . .'[2]

It is clear that there was no question whatever of summoning a conference: each was simply doing his best to go farther than the other along the road of concessions.

Nevertheless, a little later Bonnet, who perhaps did not want to be behind-hand if the idea put out by Roosevelt had some chance of being taken into consideration, sent another telegram, this time addressed to Charles Corbin, the French ambassador in London.

'Mr Roosevelt has just proposed the calling of a conference to settle the Czechoslovak question. France will associate herself with this step: so will Britain. But it is desirable that Italy too should support the proposal. Please speak to Lord Halifax on this subject.'[3]

If it was a question of getting Italy to move, why go by way of London and rely upon Lord Halifax to undertake this approach? Simply because the diplomatic relations between the English and the Italians were getting better all the time – a proof of this was the Rome agreement of April 16, which, as it happened, had been negotiated by Lord Halifax himself – whereas in France it had not yet been possible for the foreign minister of Daladier's government, however much he may have desired it, to tighten the bonds with the 'Latin sister' that had been strained by the Abyssinian affair, sanctions, the war in Spain: and the Front Populaire.

But Chamberlain really did not need prompting. It is not even sure that he waited to know about Corbin's approach to Halifax to think that after all the summoning of an international conference might answer Hitler's clearly-expressed wish to see him try something 'at the very last hour'.

During that same night therefore the Prime Minister personally answered the Führer's personal letter. 'I am ready to come to Berlin myself at once,' he wrote, 'to discuss arrangements for transfer [of the territories occupied by Sudeten Germans] with you and representatives of the Czech government, together with representatives of France and Italy if you desire.'*

* 'I only knew about this letter after the event, at the time of the British Blue Book,' writes Daladier in *Le Nouveau Candide*, September, 1961.

At the same time the British premier wrote personally to Mussolini, 'I trust Your Excellency will inform the German Chancellor that you are willing to be represented and will urge him to agree to my proposal which will keep all our peoples out of war.'

Later Chamberlain, speaking of these two letters, said that he was making 'a last desperate snatch at the last tuft of grass on the very edge of the precipice.'[4]

From then onwards there were two distinct lines of diplomatic action being carried on: on the one hand the proposals for the immediate occupation of certain Czech territories, and on the other, the offer to summon a conference. It was still necessary, for either the one or the other to succeed, that Hitler should agree to listen to something besides talk of his general mobilization.

A few false notes

Instructed to make a precise démarche to 'Herr Hitler himself', the French ambassador in Berlin, as early as eight in the morning, asked to be received by the Führer.

'I had had a map drawn,' says François-Poncet, 'upon which the districts whose cession was granted in principle stood out in bright red.* I intended to use it to show him the magnitude of what he could obtain with no outbreak of war.'[5]

Having asked the Chancellery for his audience, François-Poncet telephoned Weizsäcker, the secretary of state for foreign affairs. Ribbentrop was at once informed of this conversation in a 'note from the secretary of state to the foreign minister'.

Berlin, September 28, 1938

This morning, at 08.30 hours, the French ambassador telephoned to tell me that he had been instructed to request a personal audience of the Führer this morning. At the last moment the French government still wished to make an effort to avert the impending misfortune. It was a question of a proposal that went farther than all that the British and French governments had put forward up to the present. Broadly speaking, it would seem that the proposal suggests that German troops should occupy the four sides of the Bohemian quadrilateral, including the territories in

* According to his interpreter, Paul Schmidt, when Hitler talked about the Sudeten crisis afterwards he said, 'Looking at this map you could see at once that it had been prepared by soldiers who knew their job thoroughly.'

which the Czech fortifications stand ... The proposal amounted to something quite new, not only in that it went farther than anything that had been put to us hitherto, but in that it was at present unknown to the Czechs. We, the Germans, were being asked first. If we were to agree, the French government would ask Czechoslovakia to state that she too agreed. If she were to refuse, France would from this refusal draw inferences whose nature the French ambassador did not specify ...

The ambassador was acquainted with the British proposal handed to Herr von Ribbentrop last night and shown to the Führer. M Poncet however is of the opinion that this proposal is of no value.

Weizsäcker

Are we to consider everything in this note as being true, just because it is a memorandum reserved for the Wilhelmstrasse's 'internal use' and not drawn up with a view to publication? Are we, on the other hand, to disbelieve the whole of it, simply because its author, Baron von Weizsäcker, was a minister of the Reich? With these questions there is a grave danger that one may never find an answer.

In any case, it is rather striking to compare this note, speaking of a Poncet-Weizsäcker conversation, with another, emanating from Dr Fritz Hesse, press-counsellor at the German embassy in London, this time, telling – still for Ribbentrop's benefit – of a conversation between Dr Hesse and Sir Horace Wilson on the same day and at about the same time.

London, September 28, 1938, 1030 hours

Sir Horace Wilson talked to me today and spoke as follows. It was simply a matter of giving the Führer's proposal another form: it was that above all that counted for the British government, who were in fact inclined to satisfy the demands in the proposal and to guarantee that the plan should in fact be carried out. But the present form of the plan was such that it was impossible for any democratic government whatsoever, above all the French government, to propose its acceptation by the Czechs. The present plan was, from the psychological point of view, regarded as the application of brute force, for it gave the impression of crushing a nation's freedom. The British government were in fact prepared to satisfy all our demands except insofar as the wholly unbearable military occupation was concerned. On the other hand, any other form of occupation, by the police or by British forces, was possible. If it was impossible to persuade the Führer to give up the total acceptance of his plan, England would make war on us, because democratic liberties would have been violated and because the whole nation would be convinced that everything most precious was at stake. If, on the other hand, we were to give way over the form* the government were prepared to oblige the Czechs and the French effectively to accept all our demands . . .

He emphasized that nothing would be more agreeable to Great Britain than a capitulation on the part of the Czechs that should come from themselves . . .

These few discords in the respective diplomatic tunes of the English and French did not prevent the two ambassadors in Berlin from working in close contact. That same Wednesday morning, September 28, Sir Nevile Henderson was woken by his colleague Francois-Poncet, who told him that he had received instructions at four in the morning to make a communication similar to his own, but to Hitler in person: François-Poncet had therefore already asked for an appointment.

But after this early morning telephone-call the hours went by without the French ambassador's receiving the least reply to his request for an audience. At ten o'clock François-Poncet called Henderson again and told him that 'he feared the worst'. The British ambassador promised to see him at half-past ten. Meanwhile François-Poncet decided to make an approach to the soldiers, on the off-chance: he sent the embassy's military attaché, General Renondeau, to the Wehrmacht general staff, 'there to emphasize the responsibility that the army command would assume in case of war' and at the same time to give notice of the visit that was about to be made to Hitler.

Lord Perth takes over

At the same moment in Rome the British démarche aimed at a European conference was being undertaken by Lord Perth, the British ambassador.

As usual, Ciano took notes.

'10 o'clock. In four hours hostilities were to begin. At that moment Perth telephoned, asking for an audience. I received him

* Underlined in the original.

221

at once. He was very moved and he said that Chamberlain appealed to the Duce to make a friendly intervention in these hours which he looked upon as the last in which peace and civilization could be saved. He repeated the guarantee for the restitution of the Sudetenland that France and England had already offered. I asked Perth if I were to consider the démarche as an official invitation to the Duce to play the part of mediator. "Yes." So there was no time to be lost: the proposal was worth taking into consideration. I told Perth to wait for me in the Chigi Palace. I went to the Duce. He and I at once agreed that it would be impossible to refuse Chamberlain's request.'[6]

So things seemed to be going well: besides, how could Mussolini fail to agree to an intervention that was suddenly to focus all attention upon him and to turn him into the saviour of the peace – perhaps even the arbiter of Europe?

A few minutes later – it was scarcely eleven o'clock – Ciano telephoned the Wilhelmstrasse directly from Mussolini's office and asked for Ribbentrop. The minister was not there, so the operator put the call through to the head of the secretariat, Erich Kordt; speaking to him, Ciano asked to be connected with the Italian embassy, to save time. Bernardo Attolico, the ambassador, was to tell Hitler of the message, which Ciano had wanted Ribbentrop to be the first to hear.

'I telephoned Attolico,' says Ciano. The Italian minister rather childishly attributed to himself a role of the first importance, whereas in fact, and as usual, he had only a very minor part. For it was not he but his father-in-law in person who seized the telephone and talked to Attolico as soon as the ambassador was on the line. The conversation was comparatively short.

'The Duce here. Can you hear me?'

'Yes, I hear you.'

'Ask for an audience with the Chancellor at once. Tell him that the British government have asked me through Lord Perth to mediate in the Sudeten question. The point of difference is very small. Tell the Chancellor that we are behind him, I and fascist Italy. It is for him to decide. But tell him that in my opinion the proposal ought to be accepted. Do you hear me?'

'Yes, I hear you.'

'Hurry!'

Count Ciano went back to the Chigi Palace a few minutes later, and there he found the German ambassador, Mackensen, waiting for him. This was an appointment that had been asked for the day before, to discuss the Spanish affair. Now of course there was no question of talking of anything but Lord Perth's démarche, Mussolini's decision and the instructions that had at once been given to Attolico.

'Do not fail to tell the Führer,' said Ciano again, 'that whatever his decision the Duce will stand by him.'

As Mackensen was leaving Ciano's office he almost ran into Lord Perth, who had just arrived.

During this second interview with the British ambassador Ciano indulged himself in a piece of vulgar facetiousness, one that seems to have delighted him, to judge by the satisfied account of it that he wrote in his 'secret notebooks'.

'I informed Perth that hostilities were to begin today and I confirmed that our place was at the side of the Germans. His face quivered and his eyes were red. When I added that the Duce had nevertheless received Chamberlain's proposal well and had suggested a delay of twenty-four hours, he burst into a sobbing laugh and rushed off to his embassy.

'Shortly afterwards he asked for another audience. He bore a message from Chamberlain to the Duce, and a copy of this message had been sent to Hitler: it concerned a concrete proposal for a four-power conference that should undertake to reach a radical solution of the Sudeten problem within a week. It was impossible to refuse: if Hitler did not accept, he would draw down the hate of the world upon himself, and he would bear all the responsibility for the conflict.'[7]

Once again during that morning the Duce's son-in-law was in contact with Lord Perth, and this was in circumstances that confirm the coolness of Franco-Italian relations.

'It appeared from a telephone-call,' says Ciano, 'that Blondel, the French chargé d'affaires in Rome, was getting ready to make "an approach". None of that: we would not allow France to come and meddle in our affairs. The aspect of the whole question would change and the Germans would quite rightly prick up their ears. I telephoned to Perth. "I hear that France is preparing to step in. I warn you that any approach whatever by Blondel would produce a completely opposite effect. Manage it so that he does not do so. All our work would be endangered." He agreed and undertook to do what I asked.'[8]

Göring's imagination

In Berlin François-Poncet, after his telephone-call to Henderson at ten in the morning, kicked his heels as he waited for a summons from the Führer.

Henderson, on the other hand, did not remain inactive. He at once telephoned Göring and told him about the French ambassador's request for an audience; he also told him that it was a matter of fresh proposals upon which depended war or peace. 'You need not say a word more,' replied Göring. 'I am going immediately to see the Führer.'

Furthermore Marshal Göring claimed to have been immensely active that morning, and he prided himself on having finally swung the decision in favour of peace. But it is clear that his imagination was stronger than his memory, and he managed to confuse the times almost inextricably and to muddle one ambassador with another – all this in order that he might attribute to himself a decisive part in events which in fact seem to have occurred entirely without reference to him.

Göring. 'It might have been half-past six or seven in the morning when the Italian ambassador, Attolico, telephoned to say that he had to see me at once in Mussolini's name. It was a question of the solution of the Sudeten problem. I told him to go and see the foreign minister, but he replied that he had particular orders from Mussolini to talk to me alone first. I met him, at I think it must have been nine o'clock: he then told me that Mussolini was ready to intervene and that it was necessary as quickly as possible to bring about a meeting between Germany (Adolf Hitler) and Italy (Mussolini) in order to provide this question with a peaceful solution.

'Mussolini saw a possible solution and he would at once take all the necessary steps; he begged me personally to use all my influence in this direction. I took the ambassador to the Chancellery of the Reich together with Herr von Neurath, who was not minister of foreign affairs at that time, however, I explained everything to the Führer and used my influence to show him the possible advantages of this agreement, which would bring about a slackening of the general tension. It could not be known whether the other attempts made on the political or diplomatic plane would achieve their end, but if the four western European powers were to meet, that would already be one point gained. Herr von Neurath argued in the same sense and the Führer agreed, saying that the Duce might be telephoned. Attolico, who was waiting outside, did so immediately. Mussolini officially telephoned the Führer, and it was thus that the meeting-place was decided upon – Munich.'*

So it would appear that Göring learnt from Attolico, very early in the morning, the news that the Italian ambassador was only to hear from the mouth of Mussolini himself at eleven o'clock! As to the approach to Sir Nevile Henderson, the *Feldmarschall*, who is supposed to have carried it out, does not even mention it.

Was it true, at any rate, that Göring and Neurath did see Hitler and did plead the cause of peace with him?

Henderson says that it was.

'It is worth recalling the exact sequence of events on that critical day. Göring went to see Hitler between 10.15 and 11.15, and was joined there by Neurath, who had forced his way in uninvited. Both were in favour of a peaceful solution by negotiation. At a meeting of Hitler and his advisers there had been some plain speaking, in which Göring had vehemently accused Ribbentrop of inciting to war. Among other things, it was related that Göring shouted that he knew what war was, and he did not want to go through it again. If, however, the Führer said "March", he would go himself in the first and leading aeroplane. All that he insisted upon was that Ribbentrop should be in the seat next to him. He did say this or something like it, but it was not in the Führer's presence. But I believe that he did call Ribbentrop on

* This highly fictional version of the facts is explained by the circumstances in which Göring produced it: for him, at Nuremberg, it was a matter of placing his activities in the most favourable possible light. It is true, however, that at the time of the crisis of September, 1938, Göring, as opposed to Ribbentrop and Himmler, did belong to the clan of the 'pacifists'. But it seems that this was because he considered war ill-timed and dangerous *at that particular moment*. (Nuremberg, vol IX, afternoon hearing of March 14, 1946.)

that occasion a "criminal fool". Nor, of the various factors which induced Hitler to abandon his idea of a Czech war, was Göring's intervention the least important.'[9]

As it may be seen, there is no longer any question here of establishing a connexion between Göring's démarche and the Italian mediation. And besides, even if the British ambassador does show that he was capable of being impressed by Göring's boastfulness, he is certainly obliged to acknowledge that in this version of the facts there remains a fair amount of rumour.

As for rumours, it seems that these decisive conversations produced great quantities of them. And certain witnesses have provided successive versions which show how difficult it is to come at the truth when each tries rather too hard to attribute the sympathetic role to himself.

Thus the German Ulrich von Hassel, who was familiar with the members of the opposition to the Nazi régime, in the first place records a version of the facts that is fairly close to Göring's, and which comes from another source.

'Yesterday afternoon I stopped at Neugattersieben, at Alvensleben's house. There was Werner Alvensleben there, the famous "Herr V.A." of June 30, let out of prison since then but in compulsory residence in a Pomeranian shooting-box. Rather inscrutable; a conspirator more than a politician. It was interesting to hear that Hammerstein (the general) had told him that Schwerin-Krosigk, the finance minister, had come to see him (or had met him) and still full of excitement had told him every detail of the audience that he said Hitler had accorded him that very Wednesday, September 28. Krosigk, Neurath and Göring had gone to see Hitler to explain very seriously that it was impossible to support the war towards which he was hastening. It seems that Krosigk particularly dwelt upon the fact that we are already at the end of our financial resources and that in any case we could not hold out long. Hitler did not want to listen until the moment when Mussolini's historic telephone-call forced him to compromise.'[10]

But this same Hassel immediately afterwards gives an objective report of another conversation, this time with the secretary of state Weizsäcker, which has quite another ring.

'Weizsäcker was completely overwhelmed by Hitler's methods and by the rash, superficial and unobjective character of his chief, Ribbentrop. Moreover Werner Alvensleben did not report the facts of the twenty-seventh and twenty-eighth exactly, although there was some truth in what he said. Krosigk did not reach Hitler himself, and only gave his opinion in writing. Nor does it appear that Neurath and Göring were there at the time of Mussolini's telephoning. Weizsäcker is furious at Neurath's want of sense of responsibility. The president of the secret cabinet council [*Geheimer Kabinettsrat*] did not stir at the critical moment, but preferred hunting. It was only on Tuesday that Weizsäcker, by dint of telephoning, managed to get him to come: it is true that Neurath claims to have come of his own free will.'[11]

François-Poncet is at last received by Hitler

In fact, and in opposition to the versions given by Göring and Schwerin-Krosigk, nobody among those who surrounded Hitler had yet heard anything of any démarche by Mussolini when Hitler, at eleven that morning, at last decided to see the French ambassador.

The atmosphere in the Chancellery, furthermore, had since dawn been far from favourable to diplomacy. The interpreter Paul Schmidt, a direct witness, scarcely left Hitler at any time during the morning.

'. . . In the corridors and the neighbouring rooms there reigned the animation of the great days. Everywhere, standing or sitting down, there were aides-de-camp, men on private missions, party-members, and soldiers and secretaries of state who had come to accompany their generals or ministers, who were seeing Hitler. Yet these conversations were not carried out in the form of regular conferences. Hitler went through the rooms and talked now with one person, now with another. All who were nearby might come up to him, but no one could utter the slightest word, since Hitler treated each of them, whether he liked it or not, to a long speech on the way in which he himself saw the situation. That morning he made a whole series of little speeches of the Sportpalast kind. It was only with Ribbentrop, Göring or some soldier, generally Keitel, that he went back into his office for a longer talk. Indeed, that day the Chancellery was more like the camp of an army in the field than the centre of an organized government.'[12]

When the French ambassador reached this headquarters full of ebullient activity, he noticed that in the room before that in which Hitler was waiting for him there were little tables laid for a surprising number of guests: someone told him that Hitler had invited the commanding officers of the invasion units to luncheon.

Ribbentrop was already there when François-Poncet was at last brought in to see a 'tense, wrought-up' Hitler with an 'animated face'. Schmidt, the interpreter, was also there 'as a measure of precaution' as he says, for the French ambassador, who had taken a high degree in German, needed no interpreter to make himself understood.

So for once Schmidt was able merely to listen, and to remember, a conversation that he was to recall very exactly[13] 'because of the statesmanlike skill and the extraordinary diplomatic ability with which François-Poncet guided it.'

The ambassador at once began by saying, 'You are mistaken, Mr Chancellor, if you think you can confine the conflict to Czechoslovakia. If you attack that country, you will set fire to the whole of Europe.'

He spoke, as Schmidt observed, with his usual caution, in well-turned, grammatically perfect German, slightly marred by a touch of French accent, which, however, gave still more force to his words.

'Of course,' he went on, 'you are convinced that you will win the war, just as we are convinced that we shall. But what do you want to run this enormous risk for, when you can satisfy your major claims without war?'

Paul Schmidt took an Athenian's pleasure in François-Poncet's dialectic, and he was somewhat disappointed at the weakness of the arguments that the dictator advanced.

'Hitler replied by insulting Benes again, by emphasizing the efforts that he, Hitler, had made to preserve the peace, and by asserting that it was impossible for him to wait any longer.

'François-Poncet did not let himself be put out. He went on showing Hitler the unmeaning side of his conduct in an exceedingly skilful manner, with powerful psychological effect. From the corner of the room in which I was listening to these words and watching the actors at my ease, this battle for peace was a fascinating spectacle, above all when I observed from Hitler's reactions that the scale was leaning slightly in favour of peace. He was no longer blustering; he was finding it hard to work out answers to the splendid French logic of the ambassador's arguments. He was obviously reflecting.'

Ribbentrop could not be present at this performance without irritation – all the more so that for his part he was entirely committed to the 'war at any price' side. Once or twice he tried to intervene – 'and it was not in favour of peace' observes Schmidt – but the foreign minister of the Reich was not a debater of his opponent's class. Here again Schmidt's and François-Poncet's accounts coincide.

Schmidt says, 'Each time [Ribbentrop] was repelled with controlled irritation by François-Poncet, who was perfectly aware that the slightest false note might in these circumstances be perilous.'

And François-Poncet himself, 'Hitler seemed perplexed. Ribbentrop stepped in to weaken the effect of my words. I snubbed him sharply. I was not talking to him, but to Hitler alone. I went on arguing in the most pressing terms.'

Attolico steps in

François-Poncet had spread his cleverly coloured map out on a table, and he was in hopes of 'selling' Hitler the Quai d'Orsay's solution when the sudden appearance of an aide-de-camp in SS uniform broke the charm.

Schmidt anxiously wondered whether this might not be another 'bang of the big drum',* whether the Czechs might not have opened hostilities. But the aide-de-camp pronounced Attolico's name and this at once reassured him, for in Berlin diplomatic and political circles it was well known that the Italian ambassador belonged to the 'pacifist' group. The fact that he wanted to speak to the Führer immediately 'for an urgent reason' might indeed be a good sign.

Hitler got up, and asking François-Poncet to wait for him, went out to receive Attolico in a nearby room. Schmidt, knowing that the Italian ambassador spoke little German and that badly, followed the Führer, as was his duty.

Half an hour had already passed since Mussolini's telephone-call to his ambassador. But Attolico had been very unlucky in his haste: as soon as the Duce's message had been written down he had rushed to his car, without waiting to put on his hat. The chauffeur could not

---

* See above, p. 172.

be found anywhere. Attolico had had to run about looking for a cab to drive him to the Chancellery. 'He seemed utterly out of breath,' says Schmidt, 'and his face was red with emotion. His little intelligent eyes continually darted about behind his thick spectacles.'

As soon as he saw Hitler in the distance he began to shout, in defiance of all protocol, 'Führer! I have an urgent communication for you from the Duce!'

Then, rather more calmly, he put forward the Italian offer of mediation; and furthermore he did not conceal the fact that it was the consequence of a step made by Chamberlain.

'The Duce sends to tell you, Führer, that whatever you decide, fascist Italy will be behind you!'

The ambassador pleaded his case with skill. After all, Mussolini was only asking for the mobilization to be adjourned. And only for twenty-four hours. What is more, the conversation with Francois-Poncet was already beginning to work upon Hitler.

Attolico stopped talking and gazed anxiously into Hitler's face. A heavy silence began: it went on and on.

'It was at this moment,' thinks Schmidt, 'that the decision in favour of peace was taken. It was then a few minutes before noon on September 28, that is to say, two hours before the expiry of the ultimatum that Hitler had pronounced. "Tell the Duce that I accept his proposal," he said – no more.'

It will be observed that there has been no mention of Göring, Neurath or Schwerin-Krosigk in this tight chronological sequence, backed by the direct evidence of the chief actors.

As soon as he had uttered his short but positive reply to Attolico, Hitler came back to the room in which François-Poncet and Ribbentrop had been waiting for him, glaring at one another.

Hitler merely said, 'Mussolini is asking me to postpone things, too,' without thinking fit to inform the French ambassador of his reply. Besides, the interview was coming to an end; it was clear that Hitler's mind was elsewhere. And François-Poncet had an obscure feeling that for the moment he had no further part to play. So a few moments later the ambassador took his leave, taking with him no more than this promise from the Führer. 'I shall have my answer conveyed to you at the beginning of the afternoon.'

On the threshold François-Poncet met Göring and Neurath, and they, says he, made him 'signs of encouragement'. This was an attitude that confirms the two men's opposition to a military adventure whose timing they thought ill-judged. But the lateness of their arrival does away with any argument as to the part Göring and Neurath played in Hitler's decision: this had already been taken, and without reference to them.

In the Führer's anteroom the French ambassador also met the Wehrmacht generals, who were beginning to arrive for the luncheon to which Hitler had invited them. Without waiting, François-Poncet went back to his embassy at once and telephoned Georges Bonnet to give him an account of his interview with the Chancellor and to tell him of Attolico's démarche. The ambassador ended on a note of cautious optimism. When his minister asked him whether, in his opinion, Hitler would keep his general mobilization order for two o'clock in force, François-Poncet merely replied, 'I know nothing about it yet. But my impression is rather favourable than otherwise.'

Sir Nevile Henderson, more fortunate than his French colleague, was already aware that mobilization was postponed. And he had this from the mouth of the Führer himself, who had been delighted at leaving François-Poncet in doubt.

Henderson sees Hitler

The British ambassador had in fact reached the Chancellery scarcely more than a few minutes after François-Poncet had left it. He in his turn had asked for an audience on his government's instructions, for he had received a telegram from London charging him, as he says, 'to give immediately a final personal message from the Prime Minister to Hitler himself.'

This referred to the letter written *the evening before* by Chamberlain in reply to Hitler's personal message (and the delay in transmitting a personal letter from the Prime Minister at a time of full crisis will scarcely fail to be appreciated).

When he reached the Chancellery Sir Nevile had the impression that matters were developing in a satisfactory manner.

'. . . there was an atmosphere of relief in the faces of the less bellicose of the crowd of Nazi soldiers and aides-de-camp who filled the hall. One friend of mine whispered in my ear: "*Das geht besser: halten Sie nur fest*" ("it is going better: only stick to it"). I was at once ushered into Hitler's cabinet room, where I met Göring and Neurath on their way out. I gave Hitler the Prime Minister's message . . .'[14]

In reference to this message, a curious difference between the ambassador's analysis of it and Schmidt's literal translation must be pointed out. For in the place where Henderson merely speaks of the 'representatives of France and Italy',[15] Schmidt, more, shall we say, exact, translates, 'I am ready to come to Berlin at once to discuss ... with you and the delegates of the Czech government, together with representatives of France and Italy . . '

According to Henderson the reading of Chamberlain's message did not occur until after Hitler's announcement, made at the very beginning, of the postponement of the mobilization. 'His first remark to me when I saw him at 12.15, immediately after Poncet, was: "At the request of my great friend and ally, Signor Mussolini, I have postponed mobilization of my troops for twenty-four hours." '

According to Schmidt, on the other hand (and Schmidt was present at this as at the former interviews) Hitler did not say this until the moment the British ambassador took his leave.

This is all the more likely, since between Henderson's arrival and his leaving there was something new, a fact of a nature to induce Hitler to show less evasiveness; for during the British ambassador's visit, as during François-Poncet's, Hitler had left his guest alone with Ribbentrop for a good quarter of an hour while he was once more talking with Attolico who had come 'this time', says Henderson, 'to say that Signor Mussolini himself was prepared to accept the British proposals for a Four-Power meeting which had been telegraphed to Rome.'*

It is obvious that Henderson prefers to forget that for a moment there could have been any question in Chamberlain's mind of *five* powers and not of four.

---

* Henderson certainly mixes everything up. This second visit of Attolico's could not have been to do with Mussolini's 'acceptance' of the British proposals, since the Duce had already taken over these proposals as his own. Yet it is true that for the British ambassador only the 'British proposals' existed.

CHAPTER TWO

The invitation to the journey

Sensation in the House of Commons · At the Palais-Bourbon · Axis diplomacy at work · The last hours of a well-filled day

So Hitler had agreed to grant peace the reprieve of twenty-four hours that 'his great Italian ally' had asked. And at the same time this meant, as Schmidt had felt at once, that he agreed to the Italian, or rather the Anglo-Italian, proposal for the calling of a conference. Nevertheless the conditions were still to be settled, and in the eyes of the German dictator these assumed all the more importance in that his prestige, committed by the ultimatum expiring at two o'clock, was vitally concerned.

In order that his prestige should emerge from this sudden change unharmed and even strengthened, first Mussolini and then the French and English would have to be induced to agree to a certain number of stipulations.

In the very first place (and there was a danger that on this point Chamberlain and Daladier might be less willing to please than Henderson) there could be no question of Hitler's meeting Benes or one of his representatives. The whole of German propaganda had for weeks been based on the theme 'No German-Czech agreement is possible as long as Benes remains at the head of the Czechoslovak Republic. Germany cannot negotiate with Benes because she refuses to believe in his word.'

The conference would therefore have to be a four-power meeting. Otherwise it could not take place. As to the possibility of extending it to include other powers, which would necessarily lead to the inclusion of the Soviet Union among them, it could not even be contemplated. On this point Hitler was well aware that he would meet with scarcely more objection in Paris and London than he would in Rome.

233

Then again, both for reasons of vanity and policy – the impression to be made on world public opinion and the proving of the solidarity of the Axis to France and Great Britain – Hitler very much wanted Mussolini to be there in person. He let this be known with an urgency that was all the more flattering for his partner since it was wholly unnecessary: the Duce had far too much sense of showmanship to neglect such an opportunity for filling the front of the international stage, and of appearing to the world as the messenger of Heaven.

Lastly it was necessary that the conference should take place in Germany, that Chamberlain for the third time and Daladier for the first should make the greater part of the journey; and that Hitler's Germany should be the sole inviting power.

All these points in turn were settled to the Führer's satisfaction, after four visits to the Chancellery by Attolico in less than three hours and twenty telephone-calls between Berlin and Rome.*

With the agreement fixed and confirmed by a final telephone-call, this time between Hitler and Mussolini personally, the Chancellor of the Reich was at last able to give the order to send out the official invitations, at a few minutes before two o'clock – that is to say, while the threat of German mobilization was still theoretically in existence.

It was Göring himself who at once telephoned François-Poncet. 'The Führer proposes the calling of a four-power conference at Munich tomorrow. He begs you to ask M Daladier to attend.'

The French ambassador passed on the invitation to Paris 'without comment'. An hour later François-Poncet was able to telephone back to Göring. 'M Daladier accepts.'

'*Gott sei dank!* Bravo!'

Sensation in the House of Commons

In London, at the beginning of the afternoon and at a time when everybody was still ignorant of the decisions that had just been taken by the two dictators, the House of Commons was sitting to hear the Prime Minister speak on the international situation.

All the members were there, packed on to the benches, as comfortless as those of a tram. In the gallery Queen Mary was to be seen in the front row, together with many peers, including Lord Halifax

---

* Henderson says that 'the telephone operator who handled these calls to Rome was afterwards given two thousand lire by Mussolini in acknowledgment of her services'.

and Lord Baldwin: the diplomatic gallery was full to overflowing.

At five minutes to three Neville Chamberlain, who had been sitting in his place on the right of the Speaker, got up, and he was at once greeted by the 'hear, hear' of his supporters.

In a collected manner the Prime Minister methodically recounted the history of these last days of the crisis; he recalled his own efforts and his fruitless démarches, and this was all without any oratorical show, but rather as if it were the report a chairman reads to his board of directors to explain that everything has been done to put a difficult situation right, but that from now on it seems to him impossible to avoid filing a bankruptcy petition in the next few hours.

Stiff, academic, very upright, with a heavy gold watch-chain across his waistcoat, a stiff collar and a broad black tie, Chamberlain, if he did not look beyond the reach of any emotion, did at least seem incapable of ever letting it show in his face. When he had been speaking for thirty minutes he calmly drank a glass of water that his ministers had solemnly passed along from hand to hand. Then he went on with his speech.

Often the Prime Minister's words were interrupted by applause, and this was by no means all from his side of the House. This applause clearly showed the state of mind of the House, for again and again it greeted the passages in which Chamberlain made it plain that his desire was to give defence of the peace priority over upholding the cause of the Czechs. A positive ovation followed this statement of attitude in particular: 'The British nation would not have followed us if we had wanted to plunge it into war in order to prevent a minority from obtaining its autonomy or even from passing under the rule of another government . . . We decided in favour of mediation.'

The Prime Minister now reached Monday, September 26 – that is to say, two days back – and the failure of Sir Horace Wilson's mission. Suddenly a discreet disturbance in the peers' gallery distracted the attention of some of his listeners. Lord Halifax, who was sitting between Lord Baldwin and the Duke of Kent, was seen to vanish mysteriously, called by one of his secretaries. A few moments later the same secretary reappeared below, in one of the doorways leading into the chamber, and had a sheet of paper passed to Sir John Simon. Sir John, coming back to his seat in front of the Prime Minister, tried in vain to catch his attention. But Chamberlain, unmoved, went on talking; and he noticed Sir John's signs all the less since he had gradually stopped looking at his notes and he was now improvising, speaking in a far less impersonal tone. It was exactly seventeen minutes past four in the afternoon. The Prime Minister had just recalled the ultimatum thrown out by Hitler.

'It was in these conditions that it seemed to me last night that a last effort should be tried. I beg your pardon: I believe I already said "last effort" just now, speaking of the mission entrusted to Sir Horace Wilson. So this time I shall say a *last* last effort. I wrote to Signor Mussolini. Signor Mussolini answered that he had at once had a démarche made by his ambassador in Berlin. After this démarche, Chancellor Hitler agreed to delay German mobilization for twenty-four hours . . .'

A tremor went through his hearers, and a confused murmur began to rise. All the members were talking at once, at first in undertones and then louder. However, with a gesture Chamberlain obtained a comparative silence.

'Whatever view honourable members may have had about Signor Mussolini, I think that they will all appreciate the service that he has just rendered to the cause of peace!'

Profiting by the brief moment of respite caused by the sounds of approval that greeted this tribute to Mussolini, the Chancellor of the Exchequer at last managed to pass Chamberlain the paper that Lord Halifax's secretary had just brought. Chamberlain read it: he read it again. The expression of his face changed all at once, suddenly reflecting his emotion, though one might have supposed that he would be able to master its outward signs, come what may. And in a changed, strangely broken voice, the Prime Minister continued.

'That is not all. I have something further to say to the House yet. I have now been informed by Herr Hitler that he invites me to meet him at Munich tomorrow morning. He has also invited Signor Mussolini and M Daladier. Signor Mussolini has accepted and I have no doubt M Daladier will also accept.'

And while an extraordinary din arose, with all the members standing, shouting, cheering and weeping all at the same time, an unprecedented sight in the history of the British parliament, old though it is, the elderly statesman simply added, as much for himself as for his hearers, 'I need not say what my answer will be.'

Rising above all the other voices, a member could be distinctly heard shouting 'God bless the Prime Minister!' For the first time in her life Queen Mary wept in public without restraint, and the Duchess of Kent and Mrs Chamberlain followed her example: Earl Baldwin, who was sitting beside them, also had his eyes full of tears.

In the public gallery one of the greatest writers and historians of that time, the German Stephan Zweig, watched this extraordinary spectacle, torn between opposing feelings.

> 'At that moment – a fact almost unique in the history of England – the English parliament was no longer the master of its emotions. The members leapt from their seats and shouted and cheered; the galleries were tottering under the jubilation. This venerable house had not trembled with such an outburst of joy for years. Humanly speaking, it was a wonderful sight to see this genuine enthusiasm, caused by the news that the peace might yet be saved, overcoming the correctness and the restraint that the English usually observe with such virtuosity. But politically this outburst was an immense error, for with its great cry of joy parliament and the whole country betrayed all their horror of war and their desire to sacrifice anything, even their own interests, even their prestige, for the love of peace. From the very beginning Chamberlain thus marked himself as the man who was going to Munich not as a fighter for the peace, but as a petitioner.'[1]

Other witnesses of this astonishing scene also judged it severely as they watched. Churchill remained in his seat, and murmured bitterly, 'And what about the Czechoslovaks? Does no one think of asking their opinion?'

In the corridors Paul-Louis Bret mingled with the over-excited crowd.

> ' "What a blessing for England and for the world to have such a man," said a member to me – a Liberal. I looked at him without joining in this gratitude. It appeared to me that one might have said of Chamberlain what Gladstone said of Disraeli, "He was a good man, in the worst sense of the word." '[2]

There was one man in the diplomatic gallery whose eyes were also brimming with tears, but not for the same reason as Queen Mary or Earl Baldwin: the Czechoslovak minister Jan Masaryk, son of the founder of the Czechoslovak democracy, had suddenly come to realize, at the sight of this outburst of collective hysteria, that his country had nothing much more to hope for from the British democracy.

At the Palais-Bourbon

In Paris, at the Palais-Bourbon – one swallow does not make a summer – the atmosphere was far less dramatic, or indeed less melodramatic, than in the House of Commons.

As Wednesday was the day traditionally reserved for committee-meetings, the chamber was empty and the corridors full. At the beginning of the afternoon the journalists and deputies were talking hard, but far less about what might be happening in Berlin, about which almost nothing was known, than about what had happened in Paris that very morning.

The excitement of the day was 'the poster', whose text a few lucky men had been able to copy – unless indeed they had it from the author.

The poster? It had been stuck up on the walls of the capital during the night.

> To the people of France
>
> People of France, you are being deceived. I take upon myself alone the risk of saying so at a time when passions are unloosed and when for weeks and months past hidden forces have set cunning machinery in motion to make war inevitable. Tendentious news, false news – those are the weapons of the men who are urging the country to war. You are being made to believe that Hitler's requirements and what has already been agreed to are separated by an impassable gulf. It is untrue. The only disagreement concerns questions of procedure.
>
> Are the German troops to move into the Sudeten regions that are acknowledged to be German before or after the frontier has been defined? Is France once again to lose a million of her children in a war with such a wretched pretext? But the machinery is at work. The Czech answer must be given before two o'clock. If the Germans decree mobilization there will have to be a reply. And with measure followed by counter-measure it will be war, as it was in 1914.
>
> I have tried to stop this: I asked for parliament to be called. It was refused. I asked that the government should give an explana-

238

tion of its acts, that the official texts and not altered, mutilated texts should be submitted for discussion and criticism by the legal representatives of the democracy, and that each man in the government and in the chambers should assume his own responsibility.

There are no conscientious objectors or cowards in France. If the country is threatened every man will rise up to defend it. All are ready to conquer or die to keep real promises. But patriotism must not be swindled.

The Communist leaders, who serve interests that are not French interests in this tragedy, have demanded my arrest. I would rather be murdered than allow the murder of my country. At this time I can see only one legal way of maintaining peace: let all those who want to save it petition the head of the state against war.

Long live France!

The man who signed this was none other than Pierre-Etienne Flandin, a former premier and the president of the *Alliance démocratique*.

Naturally, this 'Flandin bomb' very quickly aroused many differing reactions. The government ordered the poster to be torn down, not unnaturally thinking it to be calculated to lower the nation's morale, and that at a time when many Frenchmen were already affected by the first mobilization measures.

Furthermore, during the morning there was the news of several sensational resignations: Paul Reynaud, at once followed by several of his friends,* very publicly left the *Alliance démocratique*.

On the other hand a delegation from the parliamentary minority groups was received by the President of the Republic and by Daladier in turn, and on a certain number of points the delegation seemed to have adopted an attitude not wholly remote from the most striking passages in Flandin's poster.

In the corridors of the Chamber of Deputies the spokesmen of this delegation,† having seen those they represented, now told the press about the positions that had been taken up. 'The delegation urged the head of the government to promise not to carry out without previous consultation with parliament either general mobilization or equivalent steps, nor to perform any act committing the country's future.'

---

* Including Louis Rollin, Taurines, Jacquinot and Laniel.

† The delegation, led by Louis Marin, included a score of deputies, among them Montigny, R. Schumann, Taittinger, Philippe Henriot and Temple.

And again, 'The deputies of the minority groups warn the population against the systematic campaign of false news which is welcomed by the papers and even by the radio stations, which tend to tell the public that war cannot be avoided, and to mislead public opinion over facts upon which the fate of the country and the life of its children depend.

'They recall that as France is a democracy, the French must be the sole masters of peace or war.

'They also think it inadmissible that a question which is already settled in principle should be able to bring about a war over the question of the means for carrying out the arrangements.'

Other parliamentary steps were taken, also during that morning and all leading in the same direction, just as though there did indeed exist a 'clever machinery', but one very unlike that denounced by Flandin. For these démarches tended rather to urge the government to 'continue its efforts in favour of peace' – that is to say to go as far as Hitler should insist along the road of concession. Political circles took particular notice of the presence 'in a personal capacity' of four Socialist SFIO deputies together with the *Union Socialiste et Républicaine* delegates, who went in a body to the Hotel Matignon to assure Daladier of their support if he were to persist in the 'policy of peace' of which Bonnet was the author.

As for the former minister of labour, Frossard, he for his part had entrusted Chichery, Daladier's confidential friend and his usual link with parliament, with passing on to the premier a suggestion whose originality (as one must call it) charmed the parliamentary journalists who were in search of something new: it was a question of reverting to Roosevelt's offer of a conference, but of being realistic enough to see that Hitler would never agree to sit at the same table as Benes; this led Frossard to propose a four-power conference, with Germany, England, France and Italy – a conference for which, said Frossard, who had certainly foreseen everything, Mussolini might be asked to take the first steps, should the need arise.

This daring plan had scarcely spread in the corridors of the Palais-Bourbon before Chichery, duly authorized by Daladier, summoned the journalists for an official communication – the announcement of the Munich conference, called by Hitler for the next day at Mussolini's suggestion.

Frossard, surrounded by a great many people, modestly spoke of his

'very lively satisfaction' to the journalists, who were undecided
whether it was his prophetic powers that were to be praised or rather
his sources of information.

Axis diplomacy at work

Hitler's immediate colleagues did not consider their day's work done,
although the decision had been taken in Berlin, and the invitations
had been sent out and the acceptances (returned by London and
Paris with a haste that augured well) received. The group that had
openly showed itself in favour of postponing mobilization and of
calling the Munich conference were not unaware of what was at
stake for them.

Hitler, to be sure, had reached his decision alone. But if he were to
come to regret it he would very soon persuade himself that he had
been prompted to it by others. At all costs, then, it was necessary that
Munich should be a success. Not a success in the absolute sense, not a
conference resulting in the best of compromises and thus in the setting
up of a just and lasting peace, but a success for Germany and for
Hitler. So that Hitler should be convinced that in no case would war
have brought him more, either in prestige or in territorial gains.

This necessity was all the clearer to the Göring-Neurath-Weiz-
säcker group since Ribbentrop did not attempt to disguise his bitterness at the adoption, in his own field, of a solution that he had not
advised – far from it, indeed.

So there was no time to be lost. Matters were made much easier by
the unlimited support that the Italian ambassador, himself deeply
committed since that morning in the same direction, provided for the
'moderates'.

And at the same time this close co-operation with the Italians
strengthened the Axis, which as it happened was itself a creation of
these same 'moderates', and one whose usefulness Hitler would thus
be able to measure.

Weizsäcker took matters in hand and he at once suggested that he,
Göring and Neurath should meet to work out a draft that should
give Germany full satisfaction and that Mussolini could bring
forward at the conference as a 'compromise plan' of his own manu-
facture. Broadly speaking, it was a fairly clever paraphrase of the
Godesberg memorandum.

As soon as the plan was drawn up Göring undertook to show it to

Hitler – for the operation would be pointless unless the draft they had agreed upon received the Führer's full approval.

'All right. It is acceptable,' acknowledged Hitler, having read the document.

All that was to be done now, therefore, was to get it to Mussolini – Ribbentrop, of course, being kept out of the whole business.

Schmidt entrusted Erich Kordt, the head of the Wilhelmstrasse secretariat, with having it translated, for he was none too sure of his Italian and he had himself translated it into French. It was this French text that Weizsäcker handed to Attolico, who managed to dictate it to Rome before six in the evening – that is to say, before the departure of the special train with Mussolini and Ciano aboard.

Besides, Mussolini was all the more inclined to make himself the champion of the German cause at Munich, disguised as a mediator, since after his euphoria of the morning he was affecting to regret his 'magnanimity' towards the democracies. Indeed, speaking to Ciano, who had just accompanied the United States ambassador, the bearer of another message from Roosevelt, to the Palazzo Venezia, the Duce said, 'I am reasonably satisfied because, although the price will be very high, we can liquidate France and England for ever: from now on we have overwhelming proofs of this.'

The Axis diplomats having thus prepared the conference itself, there still remained, in order that the Führer's prestige should be preserved, the work in the field of propaganda, to prevent any 'tendentious' presentation of the meeting of the four, and, above all, of the postponement of mobilization.

During the evening all German ambassadors and heads of mission abroad received this telegram.

'As you will have learnt from the press agency and the radio, the Führer, Mussolini, Chamberlain and Daladier will meet on September 29 at Munich, at the Führer's invitation. The Führer's invitation was issued after the British and French governments had stated themselves to be ready to make important concessions to the German demands. Because of this, the outlook in favour of peace is considerably improved.

'Weizsäcker.'

As for the newspapers, the official DNB agency provided them with a communiqué which originated in the foreign ministry and in which one can also trace the hand of Baron von Weizsäcker, who, in the course of this day, really did show the extent of his abilities.

Berlin, September 28, 1938

The Führer has invited the head of the Italian government, Benito Mussolini, the British Prime Minister, Neville Chamberlain, and the French premier Daladier for talks. The statesmen have accepted the invitation. The talks will take place on the morning of September 29 at Munich.

Today both the British and French governments have submitted fresh proposals with a view to solving the Czechoslovak crisis.

The British Prime Minister Chamberlain has offered to meet the Führer again for a personal interview on this subject. At the same time Mussolini has offered his good offices to try to find an immediate solution. It is totally impossible that the Czechoslovak crisis should drag on any longer; on the contrary, the situation imperatively calls for an immediate solution. Taking this state of affairs into consideration and also having regard to the fact that the proposals expressed hitherto do not do justice to the existing situation, the Führer, guided by the wish to make a last effort to bring about the peaceful transfer of the Sudetenland to the Reich, has invited the heads of the governments of Italy, France and Great Britain for personal talks. It is to be hoped that these talks may even now at the last hour result in an agreement on the measures that must at once come into effect for the transfer of the Sudetenland that has been accepted by the Czechoslovak government.

The last hours of a well-filled day

In the course of this day of September 28, so rich in sudden changes, the world had seen Hitler give up an ultimatum and the British parliament lose its calm – both events of a kind that history had never up until this time scattered with a lavish hand.

In London Chamberlain, before going off to take a rest that in all conscience he might think well deserved, had still to accept an exceedingly disagreeable task: it would not have been possible for him, with Lord Halifax, to refuse to see Jan Masaryk. It was a painful interview: the Czechoslovak minister was above all anxious to know whether the Prime Minister would make the presence of the Czechoslovaks in the conference a necessary condition. Chamberlain, supported by Halifax, replied that there could be no question of doing so: on this point Hitler's attitude was well known and in no event could it be changed.

'If you have sacrificed my country to save the peace of the world,' said Jan Masaryk with a mixture of icy dignity and pent-up anger, 'I will be the first to applaud you. But if not, gentlemen, God help your souls!'[3]

Perhaps Chamberlain was more moved than he let it be seen, for after Masaryk had gone – it was a quarter to seven in the evening – he dictated a personal telegram to Benes.

> 'I shall have Czechoslovakia's interests fully in mind. I go there [to Munich] with the intention of trying to find accommodation between the positions of the German and Czechoslovak governments.'

A few hours later Benes's reply reached Downing Street. Curt. Dignified: and desperate.

> 'I beg that nothing may be done at Munich without Czechoslovakia being heard.'

In Paris Daladier had that very morning caused it to be announced that at the end of the day he should make a broadcast speech. When he fixed this radio appointment the premier thought that he would have to tell the country of grave decisions, perhaps of general mobilization.

When it came to the time he did no more than utter a few cautious, almost evasive, sentences – which were nevertheless relayed by the English, Belgian, Hungarian, Italian and Czechoslovak stations and by the Swiss television.

> 'I had announced that I should speak to the country this evening on the international situation; but at the beginning of the afternoon I was told of a German invitation to meet Chancellor Hitler, Mr Chamberlain and Signor Mussolini at Munich to-morrow. I have accepted this invitation.
>
> 'You will understand that the day before such important negotiations it is my duty to postpone the explanations that I wanted to give you. But before I leave I should like to thank the French

people for their attitude, an attitude filled with courage and dignity.

'Above all I wish to thank the Frenchmen who have been recalled to the colours for the fresh proof of calmness and resolution that they have given.

'My task is hard. Since the beginning of the difficulties that we are now experiencing I have never for a single day ceased to work with all my strength to safeguard peace and France's vital interests. Tomorrow I shall continue this effort with the thought that I am in full agreement with the whole nation in its entirety.'

As for the two dictators, both of them were already in motion, travelling towards the point of their morning encounter – for Hitler had announced that he would go to meet the Duce, and the rendez-vous had been set at the station at Kufstein, on the former frontier between Germany and Austria.

At six in the afternoon Mussolini had taken his luxurious special train at Rome, cheered by a crowd that really seemed for once to have gathered spontaneously. Ciano went with him, as well as a numerous and glittering suite of praetorians in long boots, among whom there were particularly to be seen Alfieri, the minister of popular culture, and Nonis, of the foreign press section. The Duce was in an excellent temper. He dined alone with his son-in-law and he did all the talking. In any case, Ciano knew perfectly well that the best thing to do when the Duce was in form was to let him say his fill. Mussolini went from one subject to another, but often came back to England and her policy; and he was not very civil to either the one or the other.

'When you have a country where animals are adored to such a pitch that cemeteries, hospitals and houses are built for them, and when wills are made in their favour, then you may say that the decadence of that country is a fact. Moreover this decadence arises, among other manifold reasons, from the composition of the English nation: four million surplus women! Four million women without husbands who artificially create a mass of problems to fill their time. Being unable to embrace one single man, they embrace all mankind.'[4]

Hitler for his part left Berlin rather later in the evening, accompanied by Göring and Ribbentrop. Later the *Feldmarschall* was to boast of having thrust himself in. 'I asked Hitler whether I was going with him – or rather I told him that I was going.'[5]

Most of the diplomats posted to Berlin made the journey as well. Attolico took advantage of it to carry on with his 'good offices' mission in the most earnest manner. During the voyage he confidentially told Henderson, for whom he undoubtedly had a strong fellow-feeling, 'The Communists have lost their chance; if they had cut the telephone wires today between Rome and Berlin, there would have been war.'

But a little later his optimism was chilled when he went to see Weizsäcker in his compartment. 'Ribbentrop,' said the secretary of state, 'is determined not to deprive Hitler of his war. Tomorrow he will see to it that the Führer puts forward other, even more uncompromising demands.'

CHAPTER THREE

The four great powers

'This flower, safety' · *'We shall have to fight them side by side'* · *From the Front Populaire to Georges Bonnet* · *At the sign of the Vier Jahreszeiten* · *The mayor of Birmingham* · *At the Führerhaus* · *Hitler was in a hurry* · *'I know what remains for me to do'* · *The 'Italian proposal'* · *What about the Czecho-slovaks?*

LE Bourget, eight o'clock on September 29. That morning a milky fog covered the Paris region; one could barely make out the lowering mass of the hangers. As soon as a machine went on to the runway it was literally swallowed by the obscurity.

A few dozen bystanders at the main entrance to the airport watched the continual arrival of cars with rosettes and pennants bringing important people from Paris to swell the official group in the hall. Among those who were pointed out as they went by were Camille Chautemps, Georges Bonnet, the foreign minister, with his easily-recognized profile, and Guy La Chambre, the air minister, as elegant as an Englishman, escorted by General Bouscat of the air force.

'Presently they will be able to hold a cabinet meeting,' observed one of the watchers. And indeed by this time most of the members of the government were standing round Camille Chautemps.* There were also some high officials there: the prefect of the Seine, the prefect of police, the chief of Air France, the director of the airport, members of several ministers' departmental staffs and lastly many diplomats *en poste* in Paris, starting with the heads of mission of the countries taking part in the Munich conference, except for Italy, seeing that since the Abyssinian affair and the French refusal to recognize the little King Victor-Emmanuel's imperial majesty there had no longer

---

* In addition to Bonnet, Guy La Chambre and Chautemps, there were Gentin, Marc Rucart, Sarraut, Campinchi, Queuille and Champetier de Ribes.

been an Italian ambassador in Paris – nor a French ambassador in Rome.

Gradually there was an increase in the numbers, not only of official personalities but also of spectators, who now amounted to about a hundred, kept at the far end of the hall by good-natured guards and policemen.

Suddenly a murmur ran through the little crowd: he was coming! It was thirty-five minutes past eight. The premier's limousine swung round and drew up in its turn in front of the entrance to the hall. Georges Bonnet and Sir Eric Phipps, the British ambassador, were among the first to welcome Daladier as he got out of his car; but particular notice was taken of the warmth and the length of the handshake that the premier exchanged a few moments later with Herr Brauer, the German chargé d'affaires, before replying to the greetings of the other personalities there.

Without lingering, Daladier, in his dark overcoat and felt hat, crossed the hall for the take-off area, followed by the swarm of officials. The premier paused to acknowledge the cheers of the crowd. 'Long live Daladier! Long live peace!'

To be sure, it was a demonstration that only amounted to a hundred persons; but its spontaneity could not be doubted. These were workers who lived in Le Bourget or close by it, and before going to their factories or building-sites they had come, just to encourage Daladier to do his best for peace. Some women had brought their babies with them, and they held them up in their arms as they too called out, 'Long live Daladier! Long live peace!'

The premier did not attempt to conceal his emotion. He waved his hand, waved his hat . . .

The guard of honour was drawn up on the airfield. White gloves. Clashing of rifles. While the head of the government inspected the airmen those of his colleagues who were to go with him took their seats in the *Poitou*, a silvery twin-engined plane piloted by Durmon. Clapier, the premier's *directeur de cabinet*, Alexis Léger, the secretary-general of the Quai d'Orsay and Rochat, the under-secretary dealing with the European section, walked one after another up the steps and into the aeroplane, where the steward had just arranged a snack on the shelves of the bar – champagne, port, sandwiches and fruit.

In his turn Daladier nimbly went up the little ladder, and stopping for a moment in the doorway replied to the cheers that rose towards him with a last wave of his hand.

A few seconds later, at 8.45 exactly, the *Poitou* took off. In the general rush of ministers in search of their chauffeurs, some gloomy-minded journalists managed to stop General Bouscat and question him.

'General, is it true that the control-tower has sent out grounding orders because of the fog?'

'The QBI? Yes indeed,' replied General Bouscat, who had seen worse, 'but this is only a low-lying fog. Higher up you are in sunlight at once.'

'But what about taking off?'

'Well, the pilot follows a white line drawn from one end of the runway to the other. Not the slightest risk of accident, believe me.'

'*This flower, safety*'

Paradoxically, while a genuine English fog was enveloping Le Bourget, it was a thin rain that was falling on Heston aerodrome, near London. This time there was less mist in the London suburbs than around Paris and the visibility was better; the crowd which gathered along the route the Prime Minister's car was to take from Whitehall to Heston missed nothing of the sight. The people were not sparing in their cheers for the old statesman.

The London correspondent of *Paris-Soir* wrote,

'With its stiff collar, big black tie, slightly too short trousers and of course the inseparable umbrella, Mr Chamberlain's silhouette has become legendary. It is part and parcel of the whole trying period that we have just passed through, and it assures the Prime Minister of a continually-increasing popularity.'

That morning the Prime Minister was able to enjoy the taste of this popularity as soon as he stepped out of the door of 10 Downing Street; he had not yet said good-bye to Mrs Chamberlain, who had come to the doorway to see him off, before the street was already ringing with cheers. It was the workmen piling up the sandbags in front of the Foreign Office windows who were wishing the man whom all England now called the 'man of peace' good luck and a pleasant journey.

There were many governmental, political or diplomatic figures waiting for Chamberlain at Heston, just as there had been for Daladier at Le Bourget. Yet the atmosphere was somewhat different – more relaxed, more normally cordial; and it seemed to reflect an overflowing happiness that was more wholly lacking in reservation.

Here, in the first place, it was not just most of the ministers who had come to see the head of the government off, but every one of them – something, it may be observed in passing, that had never yet been seen in Great Britain. It was Sir John Simon who had taken the initiative in organizing this demonstration of sympathy and solidarity the evening before, and he, as a practical Englishman, had foreseen and arranged everything: not only was Chamberlain also greeted by many friendly faces as he got out of his car, but he was at once led, with cheers, laughter and hearty slaps on the back, to the restaurant where a copious breakfast was waiting for everybody.

There were to be seen Lord Halifax, the Lord President of the Council, the First Lord of the Admiralty, the Chancellor of the Exchequer, the ministers of defence, war, air, the colonies, labour, agriculture and others, together with many members of parliament, the high commissioners of the dominions, the French ambassador, and the German chargé d'affaires.

The Prime Minister's two advisers, Sir Horace Wilson and Sir William Strang, who were presently to leave with Mr Chamberlain, had particular attention paid them.

As at Le Bourget, there were jouranlists, newsreel camera-men and radio reporters, who had come to cover this historic departure. A few minutes later Yves Morvan telephoned an account that reflected the prevailing enthusiasm.

'The premier's face has never beamed so splendidly: making little bows he continually smiled, greeted people and said something pleasant to all those who crowded round him, calling out and cheering all the time.

'The time for departure was getting near. Mr Neville Chamberlain made a short statement which moved those who heard it more than I can say, so simple and lively was its tone. "When I was a little boy," he said, "I used to repeat, *If at first you don't succeed try, try, try again.* That is what I am doing."

'This was a reference to a famous poem, one that all English mothers teach their children.

'After a pause Mr Chamberlain went on, quoting Shakespeare, and really most aptly. "When I come back I hope to be able to say, like Hotspur in *Henry IV*, *Out of this nettle, danger, we pluck this flower, safety.*'

'And as Mr Neville Chamberlain turned round once more in the

250

doorway, the living image of hope, the ministers, the high commissioners and the ambassadors, carried away with enthusiasm, shouted, cheered or waved their hats: we had already seen Lord Halifax at this same aerodrome, at the time of the departure for Berchtesgaden, holding up his well-known bowler towards the aeroplane as it left, but we should never have supposed him capable of shouting "Hurrah" with such youthful fervour, nor of letting his impassive face take on such an expression of happy confidence.

'Presently the aeroplane carrying Mr Neville Chamberlain vanished towards the east once more, the third time, the time that is, according to the fervent wishes of England and the whole world, to ensure the safety of the peace!'

'*We shall have to fight them side by side*'

The Air France plane and the British Airways machine were now both flying towards Germany. The two pilots had been able to set their course for Munich from the start, Marshal Göring, the chief of the German air force, having for this occasion authorised them to fly over forbidden zones that they would otherwise have had to avoid.

Nevertheless Daladier and Chamberlain did not land at Munich until well after the special train bringing Hitler and Mussolini had pulled into the station.

The Führer had reached Munich very early, and, as it had been arranged, he had at once taken the train again to go to meet the Italian dictator. Göring had not left Hitler since the day before, and at ten past nine both of them were at the place fixed for the meeting, the little station of Kufstein.

The two Germans, Hitler wearing a long *feldgrau* greatcoat over his dark uniform and Göring in undress with his marshal's baton in his hand, did not have to pace up and down the platform long; the Italian special train, with a pilot engine running in front of it, steamed into the station scarcely more than a few minutes after their arrival.

Here then, once more together, in Hitler's special carriage, were the two dictators, so close and yet so fundamentally unlike.

Paul Schmidt was present at the conversation during which Hitler and Mussolini finally settled what their joint attitude should be at the conference. This was not the first time that Schmidt had seen the two men together. One day, having attended a talk, he wrote down his impressions. They are valid for this occasion.

'Hitler sat in a rather hunched attitude. When he spoke animatedly the famous lock of hair that so delighted the caricaturists fell over his forehead – a forehead of medium height – and gave him a Bohemian look. When I remember that impression now, the theories, which I only heard of much later, according to which Hitler had Czech blood in his veins do not seem to me at all unlikely; at moments like that I instinctively shifted him into a Slav context. When I used to see him sitting there beside me, with his long dark hair, his slightly retreating forehead, his rather large nose and his very commonplace mouth under the little moustache, when I heard his harsh voice, with its hoarse tone and its rolling r's, when his eyes lit up with passion or shot out a flash of anger that died away the next moment, I did not have the impression of having a typical German by me. He seemed to me to be a product of the cross-breeding that used to be found in the Austro-Hungarian monarchy and which is still to be seen in certain parts of Vienna.

'Mussolini, sitting opposite him, gave a fundamentally different impression. He held himself very upright at all times, rocking a little on his seat as he spoke; and with his Caesar's head he evoked the idea of an ancient Roman, with a powerful forehead, a rugged, forceful chin, thrusting out aggressively beneath the big mouth. His facial expressions were far more lively than Hitler's when he thundered against Bolshevism or let himself go against the League of Nations. His sunburnt face displayed anger, disdain, determination or cunning, each in turn; it was filled with eloquent mimicry, and sometimes as he spoke his large dark brown eyes seemed ready to burst out of their sockets. On this occasion I was once more struck by the exact, crystal-clear form into which he put his thoughts. He did not utter a single superfluous word and everything that he said might have been printed straight away. The difference between their laughs was interesting too. Hitler's always had an after-taste of contempt and sarcasm. He bore the marks of his earlier disappointments and his unfulfilled ambitions. Mussolini, on the other hand, could laugh loud and open-mouthed. It was a liberating laugh and it showed that this man possessed a sense of humour.'[1]

Göring and Ciano, who took part in the day's conversation, were both in favour of conciliation. 'The war cannot take place,' Göring had said the evening before while he was still in Berlin, to his friend Karl Bodenschatz, also a former member of the Richthofen squadron.[2]

On his side, Mussolini would not be sorry to return to Rome as the messenger of peace: the cheers of the day before had shown him the degree to which the Italian people was unwilling to launch into a fresh warlike adventure – particularly as this time it would not merely be a question of overcoming Ethiopians.

It was only Hitler who was still in a bellicose state of mind. He spread out the general staff maps on a table in the saloon: Czechoslovakia, the western fortifications. He showed Mussolini what he was going to have to obtain from the French and English members of the conference – and at once!

Czechoslovakia in her then state retained forty German divisions, just those divisions that he needed to settle accounts with France. 'As soon as the Czechoslovak affair is dealt with I shall only need a dozen divisions to hold this region.'

'The Duce,' observes Ciano, 'listened to him calmly. From now on the programme was decided upon: either the conference would succeed quickly or the matter would be settled by force.'

Hitler went on, 'Besides, the time will come when we shall have to fight side by side against France and England: it would be just as well if this were to come about at a time when the Duce and myself are at the head of our two countries, still young and full of vigour.'

But all this, says Ciano, 'seemed less important than the atmosphere that had in fact come into being – the atmosphere of agreement. The very people who waved all along the railway-line conveyed their delight at the event that was floating in the air.'[3]

A little before eleven o'clock the German-Italian 'pre-conference' came to an end. It was about time, for the train was running into the station at Munich. It was a station hung with great quantities of German and Italian flags; yet here and there a Union Jack or a Tricolour was to be seen. Ribbentrop, even paler and more frigid than usual, was on the platform to welcome the travellers as they stepped out of the special train.

Hitler questioned him curtly. 'Chamberlain? Daladier?'

'They are flying towards Munich: they are not expected before an hour or two.'

The Führer was already leading his guests towards a double row of German soldiers, who presented arms. Mussolini, who was wearing the black uniform of a corporal in the fascist militia, inspected the guard of honour, walking next to Hitler. A few paces behind came Ciano, with Göring and Ribbentrop. Then, in shining boots, black shirts and caps with black silk tassels, came the fascist dignitaries of Mussolini's suite.

Before going to his own quarters, Hitler accompanied Mussolini as far as Prince Charles's palace, an exact reproduction of a Florentine building, where the Italian delegation was to stay. The inhabitants of Munich, obedient to the gauleiter's orders, had decorated their town, mingling the green, white and red of Italy with huge red flags with the black swastika in the middle. And all along the route there were tens of thousands of Germans crowding the pavement on both sides of the street, greeting the procession and enthusiastically shouting *Heil!*

'I did not have the impression,' wrote Georges Blun, the regular correspondent of *Le Journal*, 'that as far as he was concerned the Führer made much mistake about the meaning of the cheers that greeted him, for his face was more irresponsive than usual. Those who said that the Chancellor's expression was tense were exaggerating; but it could clearly be seen that Hitler was in no way deceived as to the real feelings of the crowd that was cheering him nor as to the solemnity of a day that brought him, for the first time and in truly dramatic circumstances, face to face with the heads of both the French and British governments together.'

From the Front Populaire to Georges Bonnet

The silver fuselage of the *Poitou* was now glittering in the rays of a clear sun whose warmth had melted the early mist. At the controls the pilot Durmon followed his course, his mind quite free from anxiety – this would certainly be another straightforward, uncomplicated flight. All that was needed was that the radio-operator Agnus, with his earphones glued to his head, should keep in contact with the outside world.

Behind them, in the body of the plane, Daladier had a bundle of morning papers in front of him. He had found little in the way of discordant notes in them. Apart from the purely news-giving side of the press, which rarely strayed from the path, most of the leader-writers expressed the same hope of peace. In *l'Aube* Georges Bidault wrote, 'At the news that the Western leaders were meeting tomorrow in Munich, hope burst into flower once more.' And the spokesman of the Popular Democrats added this remark, which seemed in advance to ratify the sacrifices that would probably have to be agreed to, 'No doubt easing of the terms will be proposed, as well as greater speed and fresh concessions of pride and prestige. This is legitimate and even necessary.'

Although Léon Blum in *Le Populaire* did not go so far, he did express the same hope, and he urged the negotiators not to destroy any bridge. 'The news of the Munich meeting,' wrote the Socialist leader, 'has aroused an immense wave of faith and hope . . . It would indeed be a crime against humanity to break off the negotiations or make them impossible. The Munich meeting is an armful of wood thrown on to the sacred hearth just at a time when the flame was dying down and in danger of going out.'

So the idealist left wing at last seemed to admit that it was no longer possible to run violently against the pacifist tide that was carrying the whole mass of the people irresistibly along.* It is true that for its part the extreme right was, by its excesses, harming the cause of peace that it claimed to defend. That very night it had been necessary to seize *l'Action française* for incitement to murder – its headline parodied the *Internationale* thus –

> If they insist, the cannibals,
> On making heroes out of us
> The first of all the rounds we fire
> Must be for Mandel, Blum and Reynaud.

As for *Je Suis Partout*, the paper of Gaxotte, Brasillach and Rebatet, it denounced 'the chief Judaeo-French accomplices in the international plot against peace, Georges Mandel and Paul Reynaud'. This same paper never missed an opportunity of expatiating upon the worth of Georges Bonnet.

And yet Bonnet, Mandel and Reynaud were members of the same government, the government that was presided over by the man who was going to speak in the name of France at Munich.

In fact – and *Gringoire* had emphasized this by publishing two sets

---

* At the very time Daladier and Chamberlain were flying towards Munich this tide of opinion had affected Geneva, where the General Assembly of the League passed a resolution in which it declared itself 'convinced that the differences could be solved by peaceful means', and that 'resorting to war, whatever its results might be, did not guarantee a just settlement'.

of caricatures under the two titles of *Those who have urged war* and *Those who have defended peace* – the French government was torn apart. On the one side there were those who were in favour of firmness when confronted with Nazi blackmail – Paul Reynaud, Georges Mandel, Albert Sarraut, Jean Zay, Champetier de Ribes and Campinchi. And on the other Daladier, Bonnet, Monzie, Marchandeau, Guy La Chambre and Pomaret.

There was nothing surprising about these inner contradictions, these divisions that set the one side against the other, to anyone who had followed the political developments in France during the last two years.

Daladier himself had more than once been gravely concerned by the difference between the 'peace at any price' attitude of his foreign minister and his own feelings: what is more, it was hard for him entirely to forget the fact that for many years without a break he had been minister of war,* and that basing his policy upon the weakness of the French army, as Georges Bonnet did, was the same as pronouncing his own condemnation.

Nevertheless, when the premier, five months earlier, preferred Georges Bonnet to Paul-Boncour, he thereby chose 'the other policy', that which today found its expression in this journey to Munich. Georges Bonnet, who remained in Paris, was not the chief person on this voyage; but he was the chief causer of it. And while the *Poitou*, flying over Munich, began to lose height for the landing, Daladier saw the ground coming nearer, and with it the moment of truth at which he would once more and irrevocably have to choose a policy, one which he himself could describe (though was he really sure of this?) as being neither very pretty nor the most worthy of France.

At the sign of the Vier Jahreszeiten

It was precisely a quarter past eleven when the pilot Durmon brought the *Poitou* down perfectly on the Oberweisenfeld aerodrome.

André François-Poncet had come to meet the premier, and he saw 'a broad-shouldered, sunburnt man with his head sunk on his shoulders, his forehead furrowed with lines'. Above all he felt that

---

* He was minister of war for a month in 1925, then for more than a year from the end of 1932 to February 1924, when he was also premier: he returned to the war ministry in May 1936 after the victory of the Front Populaire, and since that time, in spite of the changes of government, he had never relinquished the portfolio.

The signatories of the Munich Agreement. Left to right: Mr Chamberlain, M Daladier, Hitler and Mussolini. Count Ciano is at the far right

Chamberlain talking
to Mussolini at the
Munich conference

Hitler and Mussolini
leaving after signing
the Four-Power
Agreement on the
Sudetenland on 29
September 1938.
Ribbentrop is behind
and to the right of
Hitler

he was 'gloomy and preoccupied', though not less so than Alexis Léger.

Ribbentrop and the secretary of state Weizsäcker welcomed the head of the French government in the Führer-Chancellor's name and accompanied him to his car, though not without having made him pass in front of a guard of honour – protocol insisted upon it, as the 'grave and solemn' Ribbentrop pointed out.

And now there began a surprising adventure for Daladier: only a few hours before he had been in Paris, a Paris where there was just a glimpse of hope, but in which there was still an atmosphere of mobilization and almost of war; now suddenly the premier saw before him a city full of delight and joy, in which every single window had its flag and whose entire population was out on the streets.

Willkommen! Broad streamers welcomed the three delegations from abroad. But it was above all the shouts of the unusually dense crowd that surprised them, and the southern exuberance of which the shouting was the proof. All along the route from the airfield to the Vier Jahreszeiten hotel ('a long-established place with an old and excellent reputation' states François-Poncet) where the French delegation was to stay, the crowd untiringly bawled *Heil! Heil!*

It seemed that a sudden spectacular change was taking place in German public opinion, and that this change was happening under the very eyes of the French premier.

Was this sudden change to be attributed to the certainty that had rightly or wrongly come into existence during the last forty-eight hours that if no other way out were left France would make up her mind to war? This was Jules Sauerwein's opinion.[4] And it might indeed have seemed to be the case, from that morning's *Münchener Nachrichten*, which contained this simple paragraph, whose tone was very unusual in the German press.

'The population of Paris which, with calmness and discipline, has executed all the mobilization measures and which has provided an unprecedented example of dignity, has shown that its true and deep desire is to live in peace.'

At all events it is certain that the man in the street only wanted one thing – to see Daladier, 'the ex-serviceman of '14–'18', and to cheer him; and seeing that for once in a way this wish happened to coincide with the orders given by the gauleiter the day before, there were very few inhabitants of Munich who were not out in the streets.

'The French premier was obviously astonished,' observed Georges Blun, who saw Daladier's car go by as it came from the aerodrome, 'and he stared very hard at what was for him a wholly new kind of sight. He returned the greetings without abandoning an expression that was if not serious then at least grave. One felt that he was, nevertheless, engrossed in his thoughts, and that he had not come to Munich to enjoy himself . . .'

The mayor of Birmingham

Forty minutes after the French plane had landed, the British Airways machine with Neville Chamberlain, Sir Horace Wilson and Sir William Strang aboard appeared over Munich aerodrome.

The British Prime Minister did not have as many reasons as his French colleague for doubting the excellence of the chosen path. Yet Chamberlain was not unaware that though his fellow countrymen overwhelmed him with a general chorus of praise there were some false notes there to disturb it. It was curious to note, too, that in England as in France the old ideas of left and right were inadequate to the task of separating the supporters from the opponents of the foreign policy carried out by Halifax and Chamberlain. The most inveterate enemies of this policy were Winston Churchill and Anthony Eden; yet both the one and the other belonged to the same party as the Prime Minister. As for the fascist Sir Oswald Mosley, he was fighting in the streets to urge the British government to do exactly what they were in the act of doing. This, it may be added, was a form of indirect support that Chamberlain would very willingly have dispensed with.

But although Neville Chamberlain had to contend with various inner difficulties that were related in kind if not in degree to those that assailed Daladier, the head of the British government was not torn, as the French premier was, between his friends of yesterday and his supporters of today. The Edens and the Churchills were rare enough among the British Conservatives.

Whether it was good or bad, the policy of Chamberlain and Halifax, made up of extreme caution in the play of Continental alliances and of concessions to the Germans, 'so unjustly treated at Versailles', was a policy that had continuity.

And then again, the justice of the course of action that had been undertaken, and which would probably reach its full accomplishment at Munich, never seems to have troubled Chamberlain's conscience at all. The only doubt, if he had one, concerned Adolf Hitler. Chamberlain had a most painful recollection of his last meeting with the master of Germany: in spite of a certain fascination, which he still felt against his better judgment, he had been obliged to realize at Godesberg that Hitler did not belong to the same world as himself. André Maurois explains this.

'It was a very strange fate that had brought together the mayor of Birmingham, the chairman of many boards of directors, used to dealing with other businessmen who respected contracts, and the romantic Chancellor of the Reich, who was convinced that his only duties were towards Germany and that a promise made to foreign nations was valid only so long as it was useful to the German people. Neville Chamberlain was the most insular of Englishmen, and before these first meetings he had had no notion of what a man like Adolf Hitler might be. When he was leaving for Berchtesgaden one of my English friends said to me, "Chamberlain does not really believe that Hitler is, like himself, a member of Birmingham corporation; but he does think he is a member of Manchester corporation." This was true.'

In less than half an hour the mayor of Birmingham would be with the Chancellor of the Reich once more; and perhaps he was going to find that Hitler was not worthy of belonging even to the corporation of Manchester.

Meanwhile the ceremonies that had already functioned for Daladier were brought into operation for the British premier: Ribbentrop and the British ambassador, the guard of honour and the journey through the town to the Hotel Regina, the British delegation's quarters, the cheering and the *Heils* of the citizens.

It was close on noon. Unlike Hitler and Mussolini that morning, the two other members of the conference had not yet been able to take counsel together nor to have any direct talks whatsoever. Daladier was at the Vier Jahreszeiten and Chamberlain at the Regina, and it appears that neither the one nor the other thought that any contact was necessary before the opening of the conference.

At the Führerhaus

Noon. Now it was no longer a few tens of thousands of Munich citizens who had left their work with the tacit consent of the gauleiter to form the spontaneous cheering ranks in the streets. It was the town's entire population as the offices and workshops emptied that gathered in crowds along the main streets leading into the Königs-platz and in the square itself to enjoy the spectacle that was offered to them.

And this spectacle was not long in coming. Here, coming from the Regina Palace Hotel and turning into the Königsplatz, was a car, and in it Chamberlain, whose appearance was now so familiar to the Germans, not only because it was particularly characteristic, but also because during the British Prime Minister's two earlier visits to Germany the papers and the magazines had published countless photographs of him.

Chamberlain was the first to enter the Führerhaus, where the conference was to take place. This Führerhaus, which the Nazis had built next to the Glyptothek, was one of those new buildings that made a break with the baroque that Munich had been used to for so long and that displayed the architectural tendencies of the Hitlerite revolution. It was a palace whose lines were Greek but whose proportions were German – a massive and rigid affair. On the cream and pink marble of its bare façade – no bas-reliefs or wedding-cake decorations – a bronze eagle.

A huge central hall sixty-five feet high and a hundred wide led to the great stone staircase that ran up to the reception rooms. Red marble columns, thick wool carpets, vast fireplaces, deep armchairs. Paintings by Gaspar-David Friedrich and Reinhart on the walls. A buffet had been arranged in one of the wide-open drawing-rooms. Chamberlain and his colleagues, Wilson and Strang, were received by Ribbentrop, Weizsäcker and the interpreter Schmidt. Neither the master of the house was there nor any other guests, and for some time around the buffet with its unperturbed footmen in knee-breeches, black coats, silver shoulder-knots, white stockings and silver-buckled shoes, there was that feeling of awkwardness that always accompanies the arrival of the firstcomers at an important reception.

But this chill, which was made all the worse by the dismal appear-ance of the Englishmen, all three of them dressed in black, did not last long: Daladier too was on the way to the Führerhaus, and he was to reach it a few minutes later.

For the moment he was in an open car, travelling through the city to the enthusiastic cheering of the crowd, accompanied by the ambassador François-Poncet and Marshal Göring. For Göring had wished to come in person to fetch the French premier from the Vier Jahreszeiten. Daladier had seen him arrive, 'dressed in a white uniform that emphasized his fatness'. Göring, friendly and smiling, clearly wanted to win over his guest. Succeeding was quite another question, however; but he did seem to have the advantage of a favourable prepossession on the part of François-Poncet, who knew how the *Feldmarschall* had used his influence during the most recent phase of the crisis.

In a second car there were the two other members of the French delegation, Léger and Rochat.

On reaching the Königsplatz the Frenchmen, still escorted by Göring, went into the Führerhaus, climbed the monumental stairs and joined Chamberlain. Quite independently both Daladier and François-Poncet say in exactly the same words that the Prime Minister inescapably called to mind 'an elderly English lawyer'. But the more exact (or less indulgent) François-Poncet completes the description thus – 'greying, bowed, with thick eyebrows and pro- truding teeth, a blotchy face and his hands reddened by rheumatism.'

But already the Frenchmen's powers of observation and critical spirit could turn to fresh victims, for here were the Italians, accom- panied by another National-Socialist dignitary, Rudolf Hess, the Führer's 'permanent deputy', who had also gone to their princely residence to bring them here.

François-Poncet describes Mussolini as 'thick-set, tight in his uniform ['which seemed to me rather too small for him' adds Daladier], with the patronizing expression of a Caesar, very much at home and at his ease, and beside him Ciano, a tall, sturdy fellow, very attentive to his master, more an aide-de-camp than a foreign minister.'

Behind them, vying in gaudiness, gold braid and decorations to such a pitch that it was impossible to tell the soldiers from the civilians, came the Italian officers and diplomats.

Mussolini, says Daladier, came into the room at the head of this brilliant suite 'with a lively step . . . his chest thrown out, his black eyes very active, as if they were running over everything; then very soon he was relaxed and smiling.'[5]

Furthermore, this arrival of many people all at once and perhaps also – why not? – the Duce's emphatic cordiality was enough to do away with all awkwardness. The handshakes had lacked warmth, but now everybody contributed to make the temperature round the buffet rise a little.

It sank again abruptly when the Führer appeared, accompanied by Wiedemann and a few aides-de-camp. Of the 'big three' invited to Munich Daladier was the only one who had never hitherto happened to meet the master of Germany face to face. The French premier's impression at this first encounter is therefore all the more valuable.

'Now, behind all these decorated and uniformed people there appeared Hitler, alone, with his face pale and tense. I noticed his brown hair, and the heavy lock that drooped over his forehead. His dull blue eyes had a hard, strange look, and during the short greetings they suddenly turned upwards.

'He was dressed very simply, like a man of the people, in a khaki tunic with a swastika armband on the right sleeve; and his long black trousers reached down to rather old black shoes. This was my first sight of the man who by trickery, violence and strength had become the supreme dictator of Germany.

'In London I had said and repeated that his aim was to set up his domination over Europe. On seeing him, I thought that I had not been mistaken.'[6]

Hitler was in a hurry

The reason why he had not allowed Ribbentrop to arrange a luncheon more in accordance with the tradition of great diplomatic meetings, and why he had agreed to this frugal collation as a makeshift, was that he was impatient to get to business.

He therefore gave up little time to preliminary civilities – just enough, however, to show, deliberately and ostentatiously, that there existed solid and long-established ties of friendship between the Nazi and Fascist comrades.

Mussolini at once took the cue and came up to the German leaders, who surrounded him directly; and he talked to them as to old acquaintances whom he was happy to see again.

Ciano exchanged a few remarks, that he himself describes as 'insignificant', with Daladier and François-Poncet. Then the Italian minister spoke to Chamberlain. The Prime Minister told him that he would like to talk to Mussolini. 'He thanked him,' says Ciano, summarizing the conversation, 'for all that he had done hitherto. But the Duce did not take advantage of this opening and the conversation died away.'[7]

In any case the time for polite interchange was over: the Führer led his guests to his study.

A discreet process of selection took place, one made the easier by the flexibility of the diplomats of the old school, who in the end almost formed the majority. Ribbentrop and Ciano, both being reigning foreign ministers, followed their masters by right. Neither Halifax nor Bonnet was there, but Léger and Wilson took their places. The ambassadors, François-Poncet, Henderson and Attolico, waited and then observed that they were not expected to take part in the work of the conference, at least not at the opening session. There was nothing for them to do but to stay at the buffet.

Meanwhile the nine men – for the Führer's interpreter was of the number – took their places at a round table, one which Schmidt saw was 'too small once again'. It was an old story: Hitler could not bear either big tables or real desks. He would have nothing but low, narrow tables or pedestal tables, and each time Schmidt lamented the discomfort to which he was condemned.

The room in which the conference was to take place from the beginning to the end was rectangular, and impressive in its size. As soon as he entered it Hitler literally threw himself into the first chair that came to hand, on the left of the doorway, and with a vague wave of his hand he invited his guests to do the same without troubling about protocol. Schmidt sat immediately to the right of the Führer and next to him the two Englishmen. On the other side, to Hitler's left, Mussolini and Ciano took possession of a sofa. Lastly Daladier and Alexis Léger sat in the chairs directly opposite Hitler.

It was a quarter to one.

Four men held the fate of Europe and the world in their hands, although in principle they had only met to deal with one question, that of the Sudeten crisis. It was a question that each one of them knew right down to its smallest details, since they had followed – or provoked – every one of its varying phases since the beginning of that year 1938.

Hitler began to speak in his harsh voice. And even before Schmidt had started on the translation the violence of the tone and the breadth of the gestures gave his hearers to understand that this was a positive indictment. The Führer worked himself up as he spoke; he gesticulated, spreading his arms wide and hammering an imaginary rostrum with a furious fist. His voice rose and presently it reached the pitch that the radio had made familiar – it was the sound of the orator of the Nuremberg and the Sportpalast. Now everything was calm again and Dr Paul Schmidt's voice seemed wonderfully soothing after Hitler's. The interpreter translated first into French and then into English, no more, for since Mussolini prided himself on speaking to each of the heads of government in his own language it would have been pointless to lengthen this already tedious formality and repeat what Hitler had said once more in Italian.

'The Führer,' said Schmidt, 'expresses his thanks to the heads of government here present for having been so kind as to accept his invitation. He thinks it necessary to start discussing the Czech question without further delay.

'The existence of Czechoslovakia in her present form is a danger for the peace of Europe. The Hungarian, Polish and Russo-Carpathian minorities, incorporated by force into the Czechoslovak state, are revolting against the continuance of that state. Of course the Führer can only speak here in the name of a single one of those minorities – the German . . .'

After this introduction Hitler launched into a violent diatribe – still the same one – against the 'Czechs', who were inflicting dreadful sufferings upon the unfortunate Sudeten Germans, reducing them to wretchedness, massacring them, persecuting them, destroying their goods, expelling them from their homes. 'Since the Führer's last meeting with Mr Chamberlain at Godesberg,' said Schmidt, 'the number of refugees succoured in Germany has risen still higher; it now reaches 240,000 and there is no sign of the flood ever stopping.'

Hitler recalled that he had agreed to postpone his general mobilization for twenty-four hours only out of friendship for Mussolini. But to delay it still further would be a crime!

Furthermore, the difference in views was henceforward too trifling for an agreement not to be reached, and reached quickly, on the German demands. For practical purposes everyone was in agreement on the territory to be ceded. The only question was to know whether there would be agreement on the solution put forward by Germany, that is to say the plebiscite, a solution that harmonized particularly well with respect for the people's will, or whether the English and French would insist upon their 'less democratic' formula, the appointment of a commission. After this Hitler, with striking effrontery, added, 'In my speech at the Sportpalast I stated that whatever happened I should enter Czechoslovakia on October 1 at the latest. The objection was raised that this act would have a violent character. Very well, let us take advantage of the fact that we are gathered together here to remove this character from it! But it must be done quickly! With a little good will it ought to be possible to evacuate the territories within ten days, perhaps even within six or seven.'

The translation of what the Führer had to say was over. As no organization of the talks had been arranged no one was chairman, so that when silence fell there were a few moments of uncertainty. Finally Chamberlain began to speak, but it was merely to express thanks, to the Führer for his invitation and to the Duce for the steps he had taken. Perhaps when the Prime Minister had done his duty to politeness he would approach the heart of the problem. But no. Chamberlain stopped, and Daladier at once took over.

'*I know what remains for me to do*'

Not to be behind-hand, the French premier also thanked Hitler for having issued this invitation and paid a tribute to Mussolini's action in bringing it about. But these necessary preliminaries did not long prevent Daladier from making the strong intervention that he had been thinking about continually ever since he had heard Schmidt translate the Führer's last words.

'I should like Chancellor Hitler's intentions to be made perfectly clear,' said Daladier. 'If, as I have understood him, he means to destroy Czechoslovakia as an independent state and purely and simply join it to the Reich – to annex it – I know what remains for me to do. There is nothing left but for me to return to France.'

In Ciano's notebooks this statement by the head of the French government was to be summed up in the simple phrase, 'Daladier defended the Czechs' cause.'

It was Mussolini who replied. Mussolini who obviously wished, since this historic meeting was taking place and since the merit of it was attributed to him, to appear as the hero of the day, as the statesman whose authority and influence brought about better relations and allowed compromises to be reached.

'No, no,' said he to Daladier, 'there is a misunderstanding – that is not what the Führer meant to say! On the contrary, he has dwelt on the fact that apart from the Sudeten districts Germany does not claim any part of Czech territory.'

Hitler, having heard the German translation of what Daladier and Mussolini had just said, had understood the point at issue. He broke in at once to reassure the Frenchman. 'No, Monsieur Daladier, I have expressed myself badly. I do not want any Czechs! Indeed, if you were to offer me the lot, I would not accept a single one!'

The 'Italian proposal'

The atmosphere at once became less tense, and taking advantage of this Mussolini brought a sheet of paper out of his pocket. 'I have drafted a short compromise plan that I will submit to you . . .'

It was in fact the text drawn up the day before by Göring, Neurath and Weizsäcker and sent on to Mussolini through Attolico after having been seen by Hitler to be 'acceptable'.

1 Evacuation of the Sudetenland to begin effectively on October 1.

2 Guarantee to be given to Germany by France, Great Britain and Italy that the evacuation of the territory shall be finished by October 10, without any destruction having taken place.

3 The details of the questions arising from the evacuation to be looked into by an international committee on which the four powers and Czechoslovakia would be represented.

4 International supervision of the plebiscite and of the final determination of the frontiers in 'doubtful territories' and the occupation of these territories by international forces.

5 Progressive occupation by the German army of the zones with a German majority from October 1.

The first reactions to the reading of this note were favourable. Yet the proposals were to arouse a lively and immediate discussion.

What about the Czechoslovaks?

It was Chamberlain who caused the explosion.

'These proposals seem to be a very good basis of discussion,' he said. 'But they provide for a guarantee given by the powers – clause two. This clause has no meaning unless we invite representatives of the Czechoslovak government to sit with us . . . indeed, I cannot see how Great Britain can be expected to give the guarantee unless she can obtain assurances from a duly authorised representative of the Prague government.'

Daladier openly approved. But Hitler at once reacted.

'If we have to ask the Czechs for their consent to every detail we shall still be at it in a fortnight's time. Now in the present state of tension the slightest delay would be terribly dangerous ... Besides, it is not a German-Czech problem that we have to solve, but a European question ... if the Prague government are capable of calling into question an agreement based on the moral authority of our four signatures it will mean that they are determined to accept nothing but force.'

Mussolini supported his confederate with all his authority.

'We cannot wait for the arrival of an authorized representative of the Czech government before our discussions. It is for us, the great powers, to give Germany the moral guarantee that the evacuation shall take place without destruction. We will inform Prague that the Czech government must accept the demands; and that in the event of a refusal they will have to put up with the military consequences.'

Daladier supported Chamberlain as well as he could.

'I share the Prime Minister's opinion ... The presence of a Czechoslovak representative whom we could consult would be useful ... Even if it were only to prevent the disorder that can always take place when it is a question of territory being ceded.'

'It would be enough,' added Chamberlain in a conciliatory manner, 'if this representative of Prague were to remain in the next room ... at our disposition.'

In the end, as an immense concession, Hitler agreed, once it was thoroughly decided that this should mean nothing for the representative thus 'invited' but an additional humiliation.

During the afternoon the Czechoslovak minister in Berlin, Vojtech Mastny, and Hubert Masarik, a councillor in the foreign ministry at Prague, given notice by Chamberlain, came to the Führerhaus and were at once shut into a room where they were forgotten, while a few yards from them the fate of their country was at stake.

However, in the room where the conference sat there was already no further talk of Czechoslovak representation. It is of little importance whether Chamberlain had called for it more strongly than Daladier or the other way about. In the event, neither the one nor the other made it an essential preliminary condition for any discussion of the main issue. On this question there had been no more than a gun in honour of the flag, if indeed we may speak of honour in such a context.

Furthermore, Chamberlain had already turned to another subject. As a businessman for whom questions of material interest had their full weight in the scales of peace or war, he was going to do his utmost to induce Hitler to make concessions in the matter of the goods ceded by Czechoslovakia to Germany. 'Who will indemnify the Czechoslovak government for the buildings and installations belonging to the state?' he asked.

'As for these buildings and installations, it is the Sudeten Germans who have paid for them with their taxes, and nearer twice over than once ... there can be no question of indemnity,' replied Hitler angrily.

Chamberlain stubbornly brought up the indemnification of private individuals. 'How is the section of the Godesberg memorandum according to which no cattle may be taken out of the territories ceded to Germany to be understood? If the Czechoslovaks want to leave these regions and if they cannot take their cattle with them, who will indemnify them?'

For the moment Hitler lost his temper, and he coarsely made it plain enough. 'Our time is too valuable for us to waste it over trifles of this kind,' he said shortly.

The mortified Chamberlain did not go on, and that question having been settled, dealt with, eliminated, all that was left to do was to proceed with the agenda. This called for the examination of the 'Italian'* proposals, which had in principle been accepted as a basis for discussion and which now had to be looked into point by point. However Daladier asked that each member should be given a version translated into his own language so that it might be studied at leisure, and it was decided unanimously that the sitting should be suspended.

* The truth about the German origin of the proposal tabled by Mussolini (see above, p. 266) was not divulged until several years after Munich. Chamberlain died without ever knowing the truth on this point.

It was three o'clock in the afternoon. The work of the conference was not to start again for an hour and a half. Before that everybody was going to have lunch as a start. The departure of the 'big four' was watched by several journalists among the crowd, which was standing as thick as ever in front of the Führerhaus. Georges Blun, *Le Journal*'s special correspondent, describes the scene – a rather unusual one, it must be admitted.

'Hitler came out of his house first and plunged directly into his car. Chamberlain came after him and disappeared into the crowd. Then there appeared M Daladier, perhaps even a little more bearish than usual; mistaking his car he almost got into the Duce's. A black guard pointed out his mistake, and the French premier, with an imperceptible shrug, moved aside for Mussolini. Then M Edouard Daladier, lighting a cigarette with an automatic gesture, got into his own car, which had now moved up. At this moment Göring appeared; thrusting a journalist aside he came forward and sat by the French premier, laughing heartily. The crowd was amused, and clapped loudly. No doubt the fact that the marshal and the French premier were sitting side by side appeared to them a good omen.'

Hitler had invited Mussolini and Ciano to share his frugal meal in his private flat in Munich, 'a modest place in a building with several other tenants,' observed the Duce's son-in-law, turning up his nose a little, being so used to Roman palaces. Yet Ciano does acknowledge that this flat 'contained many very valuable pictures'.

The French and Germans met again at the Vier Jahreszeiten. On reaching the hotel Göring did not insist upon thrusting himself on Daladier any longer, and when Daladier walked into the dining-room with Clapier, his principal private secretary, Alexis Léger and François-Poncet, he saw the marshal already sitting at a table with his wife and some friends, while Ribbentrop, a little farther off, was there with another set of guests.

The journalists who had been clever enough to come straight from the Führerhaus to the Vier Jahreszeiten felt that they were really going to profit by it. In fact they were quite mistaken, for the French and the Germans outdid one another in discretion.

Yet Daladier could not refuse to answer Jean Thouvenin, the special correspondent of *L'Intransigeant* and *La Tribune des Nations*, who asked him, 'What are your impressions, Monsieur le Président?'

The head of the French government, weighing his words, said, 'I have no impression ... up until now we have limited ourselves to looking into the state of affairs. We know the opposing points of view; we shall have to accommodate them to one another.'

Thouvenin was insistent. 'If that reserved note is sounded in Paris, it may be misinterpreted.'

Daladier reflected. 'When I say that I have no impression, it must be understood that I do not say that I have a bad impression. On the contrary, the mere fact that we are all four here is in itself a good sign, as I see it.'

'Nothing more was to be got out of the premier for the moment,' noted the disillusioned Jean Thouvenin.

Some Italians who were half journalists, half delegates, and who because of this were treated with particular favour, had been able to stay in the Führerhaus while the talks were going on, mingling with the diplomats and the men closest to the heads of government. They took advantage of this to strut about talking importantly, and 'leak' information that the special correspondents of the world's press took up religiously. In most of the accounts published the next day there are to be found traces of these 'indiscretions' from Italian sources, which, as it were by chance, enhanced the part played by the Duce.

'Herr Hitler speaks only German, Monsieur Daladier speaks only French, Mr Chamberlain speaks only English ... only Signor Mussolini speaks the four languages. At the end of ten minutes of talking with an interpreter Signor Mussolini, who had grown impatient, suggested that the interpreter should be sent away and that they should rely upon him to translate the ideas expressed by each of the men present. And in this way it was really Signor Mussolini who directed the talks. He generally asked a question in German, Herr Hitler answered, and he summarized the meaning rather than the exact words for the French and English ...'

CHAPTER FOUR

The agreement

The examination of the 'Italian proposal' · Daladier's denial · Disorder and confusion · The Czechoslovak fortifications · Chamberlain plays a personal game · The Axis banquet · The Pope's appeal for peace · Final adjustments · The butchers' club · The reading of the verdict · Before the fall of the curtain

AT half past four everybody was back at the Führerhaus and the conference was about to begin once more. But this second session did not resemble the first in the least: the total lack of method and organization had the curious effect of inducing the participants to allow the utmost anarchy to rule over the work of the conference, however much at least two of them may have liked authoritarianism.

The anarchy began at the moment when the heads of government were returning to the room in which the first talks had taken place.

'This time,' says François-Poncet, 'I went in by reason of my office and sat down behind Daladier.'

The mere fact that so senior a diplomat as the French ambassador reached the point of taking such an initiative, at the risk of having himself put in his place in conditions wounding to his pride, says a great deal about the degree of improvisation at a meeting in which, paradoxically enough, the inviting power was the one that was always held up as an example by those who were much attached to orderliness. At all events, François-Poncet set the example: all those who had hitherto waited, as he had done, in the anteroom, rushed in after him – Göring, Henderson, Attolico, Weizsäcker, and, adds Schmidt, who watched this spectacle with amusement, 'the legal advisers, secretaries and aides-de-camp'.

The examination of the 'Italian proposal'

In front of the huge fireplace the now numerous delegations gathered

271

behind the four leaders. The English and French were opposite one another, on the left and the right, while the Germans and Italians, who separated them, remained in the middle. François-Poncet describes the scene as the curtain rose.

'The English spoke little among themselves; the Germans and Italians a great deal. Mussolini was plunged deep in his armchair. His extraordinarily mobile features were never at rest for a second; his mouth spread in a broad smile and drew in to a pout, his eyebrows shot up in astonishment and frowned in threat; his eyes had an amused and curious expression and then suddenly blazed with wrath.

'Near him, and standing, Hitler gazed fixedly at him; he was under the influence of his charm; he was as it were fascinated, hypnotized; when the Duce laughed, he laughed; if the Duce frowned, he frowned; it was a positive display of mimicry. It was to leave a lasting impression upon me and to make me believe – wrongly, it must be added – that Mussolini wielded a well-established ascendancy over Hitler. He was certainly wielding it on that particular day. At other moments it was Mussolini, of this uneasy pair, who underwent the influence of the rival who had become his accomplice.'[1]

The discussion at once began on the 'Italian plan', which had been translated into three languages and whose terms could now be appreciated by each delegation. Point one, which set the date of October 1 for the beginning of the evacuation of the Sudeten districts ceded to Germany was unanimously adopted at once, almost without discussion.

On the other hand, point two revived the argument on the advisability of obtaining the preliminary consent of the Czechoslovaks. It was still a question of this often-mentioned guarantee that Great Britain, France and Italy were to give Germany on the final date of October 10, by which time the evacuation *without any destruction* was to have been carried out.

'If we can also agree upon this point,' said Hitler, 'the question of arrangements will no longer raise any serious difficulties. I am of the opinion that we ought to fix the stages of the German occupation on the map at once. A committee could then undertake to settle the conditions of the occupation.'

272

The Chamberlains with King George VI and Queen Elizabeth after
Mr Chamberlain's return from Munich

Hitler touring the Sudetenland in October 1938

Adolf Hitler

But Chamberlain was still preoccupied by the notion of 'guarantee'. 'I am in agreement on this date of October 10, but I repeat what I have already said: the British government cannot give their guarantee so long as Czechoslovakia has not officially expressed her views.'

How was Daladier going to react?

Erich Kordt, who drew up an account for the Wilhelmstrasse, analyses what the French premier had to say thus:

'Questioned on the point of whether the giving of the guarantee provided for in the Italian plan was to be made subject to the previous approval of Czechoslovakia, as Mr Chamberlain appeared to suggest, Daladier replied that this approval did not seem to him necessary. He had earlier agreed to the principle of the cession of territory by Czechoslovakia, in spite of the Franco-Czech pact and without having previously consulted the Czechoslovak government, and he was now of the opinion that what had once been promised should also be performed. Daladier also regretted the Czechoslovak objection that had been mentioned earlier in the debate, according to which the evacuation could only take place when new fortifications had been built on Czechoslovak territory, referring to the Franco-British guarantee. The evacuation of the purely German territory could therefore be carried out rapidly.'

According to Göring, Hitler spoke of the possibility that the Czechoslovaks might not accept the occupation of the Sudetenland by the Germans: Daladier went so far as to reply, 'then we shall make them do so . . .' Still according to Göring, he added, 'that as a decision to this effect has been taken by the great powers, a decision whose aim it is to safeguard the peace, it is out of the question that the Czechs should put peace in danger by their refusal – and that furthermore, in the event of Czechoslovakia not following this advice, neither France nor England would any longer feel themselves under any obligation to that country.'[2]

Daladier's denial

But this is only Kordt's version or the even more dubious evidence of Göring.

For his part Daladier directly challenges these German reports, these 'Nazi versions of the Munich conference', which, he says, 'in no way correspond with the facts' and 'only present a false version, meant to glorify Hitler'.

The French premier is particularly vehement against the remarks that Kordt says he made on the subject of the fortifications. 'It is not true,' says Daladier, 'that I asked for the question of the building of new fortifications to be kept out of the discussion – a question that never arose, in any case.'[3]

Unfortunately Ciano cannot be relied upon to decide the issue. For although he wrote in his notebook 'Daladier defended the Czechs', the Italian foreign minister also attributes words of quite a different nature to the head of the French government – 'He said that what had come about today was caused by Benes's stubbornness.'

On another point Kordt's minute takes notice of Daladier's statements, but only in order to contrast them with the Führer's attitude. According to the minute Daladier said that since the difficulties would begin only with the linguistic enclaves it seemed to him wise to have these regions occupied by international forces – British, Italian and French. Moreover it seemed to him essential, by way of complementing the Wilsonian principle of self-determination, to take the geographical, economic and political realities into consideration.

Hitler very quickly stated that he agreed the 'doubtful regions' should be occupied by international units during the first phase; but on the other hand he was not at all in favour of the possibility of taking economic, geographical and political factors into account in the delimitation of the frontier. 'It was because of this very argument that the Czechoslovak state came into existence in 1918,' he cried. 'At the time an economically viable entity was created, but not one that was viable as a nation.'

As agreement still could not be reached on clause 2, it was decided, according to the best traditions, to entrust a drafting-committee made up of the legal advisers of the four powers with the task of proposing a fresh wording.

As for the 'doubtful regions', it was not enough to agree upon the composition and the nationality of the policing forces called in to supervise the carrying out of the plebiscite there: there still had to be agreement upon the fixing and delimitation of the zones themselves upon the map.

The agreement

Disorder and confusion

So the maps began to be unfolded, and after this there was so great a degree of confusion that henceforward the 'conference' properly so called no longer existed: there were confabulations, private conversations and even animated discussions, but with only two or three men taking part in them.

Although most of the diplomats or statesmen present added their personal contribution to this disorder and confusion, they did not fail to deplore the lack of organization and direction.

'There was no chairman,' observes François-Poncet, 'there was no methodical programme. The unguided discussion was laborious and confused, and seeing that it was hampered by the need for a double translation, it took a great deal of time. It continually changed its aim. It stopped every time a contradiction appeared. The atmosphere grew thick and heavy.'

On the German side Schmidt is no less harsh. 'As the afternoon and the evening wore on, the conference disintegrated more and more into a series of private conversations, while the legal advisers argued at length, as they usually do, to find definitive formulas.'

Yet there was one of the negotiators who was not surprised by the lack of organization: this was the ambassador Henderson, whose account of this day is singularly bare; he does no more than note complacently, 'at no stage of the conversations did they become heated'. And there was another, Count Ciano, who went even farther and attributed positive virtues to this disorder (by favour of which he was able to play a small personal part) – 'The meeting went on in the afternoon,' he says, 'but in fact it broke into so many little groups which tried to find formulas. This allowed a more intimate way of talking, and it broke the conversational ice.'

Thus Hitler had a cordial tête-à-tête with Daladier, 'as between two ex-soldiers'. Summing up the reasons that the great powers had for coming to an understanding, the Führer suddenly said to Daladier, 'There you are . . . I who love the arts, and especially architecture, I only know Paris, which is such a beautiful city, by photographs. Yet I should like to see your capital and study it and understand it.'

Daladier was all the more surprised by this declaration since Göring, an hour earlier, had said almost the same thing to him.

275

'Because of the war, you see, I have never been to Paris. And I would very much like to go.'*

According to Ciano, the French premier talked more than the others in these personal conversations. It was during one of them that the Duce's son-in-law claims to have heard the head of the French government complain of 'Benes's obstinacy', and say that 'in the course of these last months he had vainly suggested to Benes that he should give the Sudeten Germans autonomy'. Ciano adds, still claiming that he is giving an account of what Daladier said, 'He blamed the warmongers in France, who wanted to thrust the country into a ridiculous war, and one which was impossible above all because of the fact that France and England could never do anything really valuable for Czechoslovakia once that country was attacked by the troops of the Reich.'[4]

The Czechoslovak fortifications

In his account, Kordt speaks of another conversation between Daladier and Hitler, this time directly concerning the present negotiations.

'Daladier proposed the exchange of an important district with a German majority, lying on the Silesian frontier and containing some Czech fortifications, against an equal stretch of Czech territory in the Böhmerwald. He pointed out that the existence of the Czech fortifications was not the only reason that caused him to make this proposal, but that his motives were also of a psychological nature and took transport policy into account.

'The Führer rejected this proposal, having regard to the purely German nature of the district in question; but after a comparatively long discussion, he said that he was prepared to agree that a formula concerning frontier rectifications should appear in the text of the agreement.

'Daladier thanked the Führer very warmly, and stated that the acceptance of this formula considerably eased his position in France. He would let it be known in France that the Führer had made this personal gesture for him (Daladier).'

* Some days after Munich Daladier told the story of these two conversations when he was in the corridors of the Senate, and he said that at the time he thought of Parisians' expressions if he were to have brought Göring back with him in his plane – to say nothing of Hitler!

But in setting down this conversation Kordt contradicts himself, since he shows Daladier more concerned with preserving the Czech fortifications than he had said he was earlier.

The French premier's preoccupation with both Czechoslovakia's system of fortifications and her communications network* corresponded very exactly, it must be added, to the advice that General Gamelin had given the day before at Daladier's own request.

'Monsieur Daladier asked what in my opinion it would be absolutely necessary to insist upon,' says the chief of the general staff, 'if we were compelled to let Germany occupy the Sudetenland. I answered that if Czechoslovakia lost her natural frontiers she would in any case cease to be an effective military asset. At the least it would be necessary to keep all her fortified systems in her possession and to leave her railway communications from east to west intact, so that she might remain an economically viable "state". The premier added, "In any case I still hope we shall not be reduced to that." '[5]

It had indeed 'come down to that'; but Daladier did not forget what Gamelin had told him.

Chamberlain plays a personal game

Hitler displayed more coolness and reserve towards Chamberlain than he did towards Daladier. Nevertheless, the Führer willingly agreed to the Prime Minister's request when he asked that they should have a tête-à-tête meeting the next day.

In the same way the head of the British government would also have liked a personal encounter with Mussolini after the conference. But Mussolini was in a hurry to go, and he politely, though categorically, refused to postpone his time of leaving. The two men had therefore to be satisfied with having short talks during intervals in the conference. Ciano took part in them. 'We both of us said more or less the same things to him,' he writes. 'Disinvolvement with regard to Spain, coming withdrawal of the ten thousand volunteers, goodwill in the matter of putting our pact of April 16 into force. Chamberlain again alluded to the possibility of calling a four-power conference for settling the Spanish question.'[6]

* See map 3, p 216.

In fact, although the discussions went on, sometimes even with acerbity, although the British continued to urge the payment of that 'compensation' that Chamberlain had brought up at the first session and that had made Hitler lose his temper, although the French asked for the powers of the international committee to be strengthened and although Mussolini once more put forward the question of the Hungarian minorities, everyone felt that agreement was in sight and that the remaining points of friction were too unimportant to justify the failure of the conference.

The British delegation therefore considered that it was now its duty to let the Czechoslovaks know how the discussion was developing. The unpleasant mission of informing Mastny and Masarik fell to Frank Ashton-Gwatkin, one of the former colleagues of Lord Runciman, who had lent him to Chamberlain. The choice of this messenger, who throughout the whole of the Runciman mission had had more contact with the SdP than with the Prague government in itself showed a want of tact.

As for the manner in which Ashton-Gwatkin carried out his errand . . .

'A general agreement has virtually been reached,' he bluntly told the two Czechoslovaks who, during hours of anguished waiting, had been living there in a vacuum. 'I cannot give you the details yet, but you must be prepared for much harsher conditions than those of the Franco-British plan.'

'Can we not at least be heard before we are judged?' asked Hubert Masarik.

'No,' replied the Englishman curtly. 'Really, anyone would think that you did not know how difficult the position of the great powers is! If you knew how hard it has been to negotiate with Hitler . . .'

In point of fact it was more tedious and incoherent than really arduous. In front of the big fireplace the talk went on: the never-ending arguments in front of the map of Czechoslovakia continued their steady pace. For his part Mussolini had had enough, and he showed it.

'Rather bored by the vaguely parliamentary atmosphere that always comes into existence at a conference,' writes Ciano, 'the Duce strolled about the room with his hands in his pockets. From time to time he helped in the finding of a formula. Thanks to his all-embracing mind, always in advance of events and men, he already looked upon the agreement as having been reached, and while the others were still arguing about more or less formal problems, he, on the other hand, had already lost interest. His mind had gone beyond this and it was working upon other matters.'[7]

The Axis banquet

As for Hitler, he was growing impatient, for he had arranged a great banquet at the Führerhaus to terminate the conference, after the final protocol had been signed. But since half past seven the black and silver footmen had been waiting and the table had been laid, and although agreement was in sight, the discussion might very well go on for some hours still. A little after eight, therefore, the Führer very unwillingly got up and proposed that the meeting should be suspended again. He invited Chamberlain and Daladier and their colleagues with the exception of the legal advisers of the drafting-committee, who were to go on with their work during the interval, to come with him to the banqueting hall. But the French and the English refused the invitation in almost the same terms: they had to telephone, the one to Paris and the other to London – to talk with their advisers – to hear their ministers' opinions . . .

In fact, as Schmidt observes, 'they were obviously not in a mood to take part in a banquet. They had saved the peace, it was true, but at the cost of an important loss of prestige.'

So Chamberlain went back to the Regina, while Daladier, more gloomy and bearish than before, left for the Vier Jahreszeiten. In the hall of the hotel the French premier brushed the journalists aside as they swarmed about him. As he stepped into the lift he merely said 'It starts again in an hour' in an angry tone.

A few minutes later those who thought they might still glean a few scraps of news in the dining-room lost all hope of extorting the smallest detail from the members of the French delegation, for they saw trays and dumb-waiters go by – Daladier and his colleagues were having a snack sent into the rooms 42 and 44, which made up the suite reserved for the French premier.

On the other hand, the special correspondents who were waiting at the same time in the hall of the Bayerischehof, the press head-quarters, had a pleasant surprise: they saw the Nazi Hamman,

Goebbels' representative at Munich, come in; he called them together for 'an important communication'.

'The big four's discussions have been going on all day in a very friendly atmosphere. Other talks will follow them. Agreement has been reached on the chief points in question.

'Only one difficulty has arisen: it concerns the delay in transmitting the terms of the agreement to Prague.'

The Munich chief of propaganda refused to give the slightest detail as to the terms of this 'agreement', and well he might. What he did say was enough to alert all the capitals of the world, and enough to make sure that the long-expected news should be at once broadcast by all radio-stations. It was of little account that the news was untrue, or at least premature; it at once brought about such a sense of relief that it could not be undone. After this the last session of the conference could no longer be anything but a merely formal assembly.

Furthermore, this was exactly what the Germans and Italians intended as they dined at the Führerhaus, drinking champagne already. Hitler and Mussolini were at the head of the long table, round which there alternated black shirts and brown, the uniforms of the Italian fascists and those of the Nazis.

At heart Hitler was no longer sorry that the 'democrats' were not there; they would have spoiled the party. As for the Duce, he talked brilliantly, as usual. He spoke about the Western powers, the League of Nations, sanctions. 'The fools! If they had simply extended their sanctions to cover oil, in a week they would have made it impossible for me to conquer Abyssinia!'

Everyone there shook with hearty laughter. There was no doubt about it, they could get along very well without Chamberlain and Daladier.

The Pope's appeal for peace

At the close of this day a new factor made its appearance, and one which the heads of government assembled in Munich were only told about by their respective chanceries with some delay: at half past seven the Pope spoke to the world in a broadcast speech. In a voice so broken by emotion that at times it was hardly audible, the Sovereign Pontiff called to mind 'the millions of men who were living in anxiety before the imminent danger of war and before the threat of unexampled massacre and ruin', and he urged the faithful to pray 'that God, in whose hands lies the fate of the world, may sustain the trust of all rulers in the peaceful ways of fair negotiation and lasting agreement.'

Finally this moving passage in the Pope's speech aroused particular attention. '. . . for the salvation and for the peace of the world, we offer the priceless gift of a life that is already long, whether the Master of life and death chooses to take it from us or whether on the other hand He chooses to make the saddened and weary worker's days of toil still longer.'

François Charles-Roux, the French ambassador to the Vatican, explains the late hour chosen by the Pope for his intervention in this way.

'Pius XI had wind of a diplomatic move by Mussolini to decide Hitler to have the Sudetenland ceded to him without having to take it by force, and he had a feeling that England and France would be parties to forcing this sacrifice upon the Czecho-slovaks. In fact, he only broadcast on the evening of September 29, when the short Munich conference was already assembled, and scarcely more than a few hours before the four ministers finished their sorry work. He had neither wished to speak earlier nor to say more in order not to assume any moral responsibility whatever in the matter of the price that was to be paid for peace.'[8]

Final adjustments

While the Axis was already celebrating its victory in the banqueting-hall, the French and English pondered – separately, of course – over the few very small points of detail in which they might still hope to gain satisfaction from the other side.

At the Regina, where the British delegation was staying, the discussion still bore on financial and monetary problems – the business-man in Chamberlain certainly outweighed the statesman.

'During dinner,' recalls Wilson, 'we had prepared and sent in to the drafting-committee a short clause . . . providing that financial and currency questions arising out of a transfer of the territory should be referred for settlement to a German-Czech commission with a neutral chairman.'[9]

At ten in the evening Daladier once more walked across the hall of his hotel. He was as taciturn as ever, but apparently more sanguine, since this time the one observation that he granted the journalists was 'I am pleased'.

The drafting-committee had finished with the revision of the text, and the conference was going to be able to proceed to a first reading at once. At ten o'clock exactly, a few minutes before the session began again, Sir Horace Wilson managed to obtain a copy of the text worked out by the drafting-committee, and accompanied by the inevitable Ashton-Gwatkin he went to show the Czechoslovak observers the planned agreement. He even handed them a map which showed the zones that had already been agreed upon, and whose transfer to Germany had been decided. Sir Horace very stiffly cut short any request for explanation, and even more any protest. He went off to be with Chamberlain at the last session and left Ashton-Gwatkin with Mastny and Masarik.

A little after ten o'clock, then, the four heads of government, accompanied by their advisers, were once more in front of the fireplace at the Führerhaus.

'The discussion,' says Daladier, 'was rather confused and sometimes haphazard; almost all the time Hitler was silent, and stiff and pale as I had seen him in the morning when he arrived. Sometimes I was supported by Mussolini, who was proud of the role that he had given himself – that of mediator between three great powers.'

On the German side it was generally Ribbentrop who took the lead.

In fact the only two questions upon which final adjustments were necessary were those which had been stumbling-blocks since the beginning of the discussion, particularly clause 6, which dealt with the part to be played by the international commission entrusted with the settling of the frontier. The French and English asked that this commission should be able to determine the advisability of special exceptions to the rule of transfer without plebiscite of zones with a German majority. 'Hitler was against it,' says François-Poncet, 'and after a long resistance finished by giving way.'

'Giving way' is perhaps rather much; for the commission was only to have the power of 'recommending' these exceptions to the four powers.

Another point of friction was Annex 1, which dealt with the guarantee of the Czechoslovak state's new frontiers. Chamberlain and Daladier called for a guarantee by the four powers. Hitler and

Mussolini refused to bind themselves so long as the Hungarians and Poles should not have obtained satisfaction. Mussolini was in an awkward position here, in fact. Yet it was he who obtained complete satisfaction. Ciano does not conceal it in any way: '. . . as it always happens when there is one powerful will that takes the lead, the others gather round it. The question was discussed and resolved thanks to a formula that I do not hesitate to describe as very brilliant.'

Count Ciano was always charmed with himself: was he perhaps the author of the formula? Perhaps so. At all events this 'very brilliant' formula put the seal on the total success of the diplomacy of the Axis. On the one hand the French and British guaranteed the new frontiers of Czechoslovakia at once and alone; and on the other the Germans and the Italians were not to give their guarantee until after the settlement of the question of the Hungarian and Polish minorities.

And what of the clause drafted by Sir Horace Wilson during dinner? It was still causing its author anxiety.

'On returning to the Führer House,' says Sir Horace, 'I learnt that this was unacceptable to the Germans (Herr von Ribbentrop in evidence) and that all Sir William Malkin had been able to arrange was that the draft clause should come up to the conference as a separate paper. When the draft agreement came before the conference this clause was absent. (On enquiry I was told a, that it was not agreed and b, that the draft we had sent in was lost.) We took a stand on this, pointing out that there must be a number of questions – property, currency, outstanding loans, etc. – of the kind contemplated by the draft clause. Eventually a way out was found by a clause (the Supplementary Declaration) providing that all questions arising out of the transfer shall be considered as coming within the terms of reference to the International Commission.'[1]

So in spite of their stubbornness the businessmen gained no more satisfaction on this point than the diplomats had on all the others.

The butchers' club

While these everlasting discussions were in progress, and while the time dragged on and on, the journalists began to grow uneasy. Rumours that could not be checked were flying about – 'important hitch at the last moment', 'Chamberlain can decide nothing without referring to his government'.

A French journalist, an old hand at international conferences, reminded a little circle of friends of Eugène Lautier's* cruel remark at the time of the Four-Power Pact, 'It will be the butchers' club', saying, 'The butchers' club has met to carve up the Czechoslovak chicken; and no one has even thought of asking it what sauce it would prefer to be eaten with.'

At the Führerhaus the moment for signing had come. The original of the agreement had been placed on a mahogany table, next to an immense and elaborate inkpot, perhaps the only genuine specimen of the Munich style to have got into the Führerhaus. The chief assistants of the heads of government were collating the text. Ciano saw François-Poncet suddenly break off his reading and redden, and he heard him say bitterly, 'That is how France treats the only allies who remained faithful to her!'

Mussolini came up to Daladier. The Duce was smiling. 'You will be cheered when you get back to France!'

Daladier was no more than half sure of this. 'The French will be glad to hear that peace has been saved, to be sure; but they will be aware of the sacrifices that we have had to accept for it.'

'You will see, you will see,' said the Duce.

The heads of government approached the table. They were to sign in the order Hitler, Chamberlain, Mussolini and lastly Daladier.

At the moment when the Führer, with a fixed smile on his face, went to dip his pen, a ridiculous incident held up the ceremony for a second: the splendid inkpot was empty.

Finally Hitler signed the agreement and each of the annexes; and after him the three other heads of government did the same.

As soon as Daladier had signed his name the last time the members of the conference, all standing, looked at one another with an awkward air: the conference was over, but the master of the house could not decently bid his guests farewell as if this were a minor official dance in the provinces: some degree of solemnity had to be injected into the final congratulations. Hitler realized this, took a step forward and launched into a little speech, which was interrupted by the noise of private conversations from the opening words onwards. The Führer's voice, at the end of this day in which there had been so much talking, was even harsher than usual. 'I thank Your Excellencies,' he said, addressing the three statesmen, 'for having been so kind as to

---

* Under-secretary of state in Tardieu's second ministry: resigned at the time of the Oustric affair.

accept my invitation and for having come to Munich for this conversation between the four powers. I thank you too for the efforts
you have made to bring these negotiations to a happy outcome. The
German nation as well as the other nations concerned will hail these
results with the greatest joy. When I thank you, therefore, I also
thank you in the name of the German people.'

'Chamberlain,' said Kordt finally, 'replied in the name of the
foreign statesmen and associated himself with the Führer's statements on the subject of the happiness of the nations concerned with
the results of Munich. He also emphasized the importance of the
agreement for the future development of European politics.'

The reading of the verdict

As far as Hitler and Mussolini were concerned, everything was over
now. The two dictators therefore left the Führerhaus at once. One of
the journalists who watched them leaving was William Shirer, who
writes, 'I remember from that fateful night the light of victory in
Hitler's eyes as he strutted down the broad steps of the Führerhaus,
the cockiness of Mussolini, laced in his special militia uniform . . .[11]'

Chamberlain and Daladier, on the other hand, had a last disagreeable task to carry out: they had to tell the Czechoslovaks.

The chief members of the conference on the Western side are
discreet and evasive upon the conditions in which this painful interview took place. Daladier does not speak of it. Only François-Poncet
plainly expresses his feelings – those which Ciano heard him utter
before the signature of the agreement.

'If the Munich agreement is compared with the Godesberg
ultimatum it will be seen that it marks a distinct retreat in the
German claims . . . But whatever might be their value, these
reductions in no way removed the painful nature of the decisions
that have been taken. The French were fully aware of this. A
country that had always been a faithful ally to them was under-
going a serious lessening in size and an atrocious moral humiliation. It was being deprived of towns and districts which made up
a most valuable element in its wealth. It was yielding to the threat
of greater strength. It had been sacrificed to peace.

'We felt the cruelty of the event bitterly and we all of us were
sad at heart. Daladier shook his head, muttered and cursed the

state of affairs. He refused to take part in the congratulations that the other delegates were exchanging. Furthermore the most painful was not yet done. They had to go and tell the Czechs who were waiting for the result of the conference at their hotel.'[12]

At their hotel? Or in the room in the Führerhaus where they had been all day and where they had twice been visited by the Englishmen, Ashton-Gwatkin and Horace Wilson? If the very full and exact account Masarik wrote for his government is taken into consideration it will be seen that it was certainly while they were in the Führerhaus that the Czechoslovaks were invited to listen to the reading of the verdict, of the diktat, of Munich. Indeed, according to the custom in courts-martial, it was into the very place where the trial had taken place that the 'accused' were brought to hear their fate.

'We were taken into the hall where the conference had been held,' wrote Masarik. 'There were present Mr Chamberlain, M Daladier, Sir Horace Wilson, M Léger (secretary-general of the French foreign ministry), Mr Ashton-Gwatkin, Dr Mastny and myself. The atmosphere was oppressive: the sentence was about to be passed. The French, obviously nervous, seemed anxious to preserve French prestige before the court. In a long introductory speech Mr Chamberlain referred to the agreement and gave the text to Dr Mastny.'[13]

According to Kirkpatrick Chamberlain's speech was uttered in a tone 'full of sympathy and understanding', and the Englishman goes so far as to claim that this attitude on the part of the Prime Minister was in strongly marked contrast to the 'peremptory and even brutal behaviour of Daladier'. Chamberlain defended the agreement that had been reached as well as he could, but without attributing any other merit to it than that it substituted an orderly for a violent method of carrying out a decision that was no doubt unpalatable, but that had already been agreed to.

Once this little speech was over Chamberlain – it is no longer Kirkpatrick but Masarik who says this – began yawning, without making the slightest attempt at hiding it.

'I asked MM Daladier and Léger,' went on the Czech diplomat, 'whether they expected a declaration or answer of our government to the agreement. M Daladier was noticeably nervous. M

Léger replied that the four statesmen had not much time. He added hurriedly and with superficial casualness that no answer was required from us if they regarded the plan as accepted, that our government had that very day sent their representative to Berlin to the sitting of the commission, and finally that the Czechoslovak officer who was to be sent would have to be in Berlin on Saturday in order to fix the details of the evacuation of the first zone. The atmosphere, he said, was beginning to become dangerous for the whole world.

'He spoke to us harshly enough. This was a Frenchman ... Mr Chamberlain did not conceal his weariness. They gave us a second slightly corrected map. Then they had finished with us, and we could go.'[14]

During this painful scene François-Poncet came nearer to Mastny, who was not attempting to hide his tears. 'Believe me,' said the French ambassador to him, 'all this is not final! It is only a moment in a piece of history that is beginning and in which everything will soon be called into question once again.'

Before the fall of the curtain

At half past two the last cars left the Königsplatz. The delegations returned to their respective hotels.

Before going to the Vier Jahreszeiten Daladier turned aside to call in at the Regina Palace in order to take leave of the Prime Minister. In his diary William Shirer finds these few lines on the subject of this visit. 'Someone asked, or started to ask: "Monsieur le Président, are you satisfied with the agreement?" He turned as to say something, but he was too tired and defeated and the words did not come out and he stumbled out of the door in silence.'[15]

For his part François-Poncet had at once telephoned Paris to tell Georges Bonnet of the last conversations and the terms of the agreement. But it was clear that the French foreign minister attached more importance to the fact that the agreement had been signed than to its contents. He brushed the detailed explanations aside. 'The peace is saved,' he said, 'that is what counts! Everybody will be happy.'

It was perfectly plain that Göring, Ribbentrop and the Nazis in their suite were happy, as they had their cheerful supper at the Vier Jahreszeiten. Yet the same did not apply to Daladier, who did not get back to his hotel until three o'clock, worn, exhausted and literally sick at heart. The head of the French government said to the journalists in quest of a final statement, 'I believe we have done something reasonable. Were fifteen million Europeans to be killed in order to force three million Sudetens who want to be German to remain attached to Czechoslovakia?'

With the diplomatic editor of the Radio agency, Caussy, whom he knew well, Daladier did not attempt to conceal the fact that concessions had had to be made. 'But if we had not given way,' he said, 'the problem would still have been there; there would still have been Germans in Czechoslovakia.'[16]

And when another journalist urged Daladier to tell his impression of Hitler, whom he had seen for the first time that day, the premier said this, 'He is a man who knows where he is going and one who at all events speaks his mind.'

This was truer than Daladier knew: a few moments earlier Hitler, saying good-bye to Ribbentrop and Otto Abetz, had just spoken his mind, summing up his opinion on those he had been dealing with during the day. 'It is dreadful. I have nothing but nonentities before me.'*

---

* Otto Abetz himself told Paul Bringuier, the Munich correspondent of *Paris-Soir*, about this remark, which is quoted by Pierre Lazareff. During the day of the twenty-ninth and the night of the twenty-ninth to thirtieth Abetz continually looked after the French journalists, seeing to it that they neither lacked news nor, indeed, distractions.

Part Four

'PEACE FOR OUR TIME'

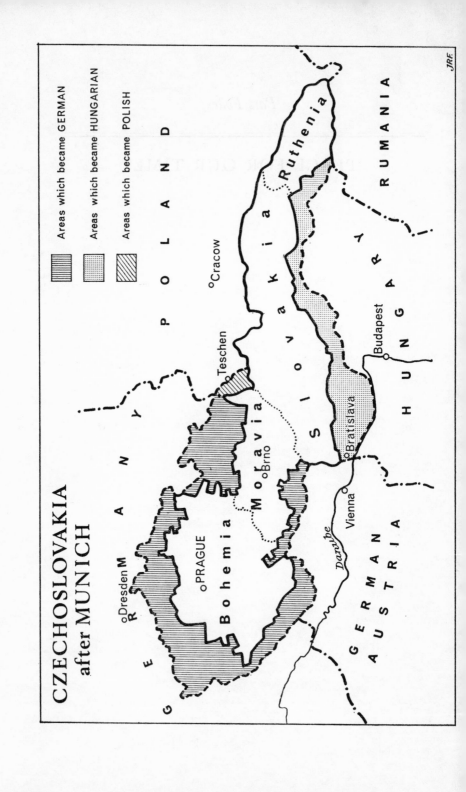

CZECHOSLOVAKIA
after MUNICH

Areas which became GERMAN

Areas which became HUNGARIAN

Areas which became POLISH

CHAPTER ONE

'If they knew what they were cheering'

Chamberlain at Hitler's flat · 'Dear little Daladier' · 'Only too heartily welcomed · Tour of France or armistice? · Surprise · 'In our present situation' · On the Prague radio · 'For he's a jolly good fellow' · First meeting in Berlin · Cabinet-meeting in Paris · Among the dictators · First international reactions · The Polish ultimatum

SPEAKING to the journalists late in the afternoon of the twenty-ninth, Hamman, the Munich propaganda chief, had pointed out that one of the Big Four's difficulties lay in informing the Prague government of the terms of the Munich agreement in time. In point of fact there was no need to be afraid of this: the Czechoslovaks were told without delay, and that in the most varied ways.

Daladier made the first move, very late that night; barely two hours after the signature of the agreement, at 3.30 am he sent Bonnet a message for immediate forwarding to the French minister in Prague. It required Lacroix to bring fresh and decisive pressure to bear on the Czechoslovak government.

Munich, September 30, 1938, 03.30 hours.

Please forward with the *utmost possible dispatch* to Prague:

The text of the agreement that has been concluded by the four powers tonight at Munich has been handed to M Mastny by the British Prime Minister and M Daladier. M Mastny will leave for Prague by plane at six this morning.

Mr Ashton-Gwatkin, who is to go with M Mastny, will give you the accompanying map at the same time as the French text of the document.

Please as a matter of extreme urgency approach M Benes to satisfy yourself that he will accept. I beg that you will tell him of all the emotion I feel in reaching the conclusion of these negotiations, in which the participation of a Czechoslovak representative did not depend upon me. However painful the sacrifices called for by the present situation may be, I have no doubt that M Benes will, as I do, understand the benefit of shielding the Czechoslovak nation from the more formidable trial of war, while safeguarding for the future the essential conditions that allow his country to keep faith with her destiny.

E. Daladier.

On their side, the German government had lost no time in informing Prague of the verdict of the four powers. As early as six o'clock in the morning the German chargé d'affaires woke Krofta, the Czechoslovak foreign minister, and handed him both the text of the agreement signed during that night at Munich and a formal invitation for the Czechoslovak representatives at the first meeting of the international commission, which was arranged for five o'clock that very day in Berlin.

At nine in the morning Mastny arrived by plane from Munich and went to see Benes at once; and Benes, after an hour's private conversation with the Czechoslovak minister to Berlin, presided over an extraordinary cabinet, held in the palace itself. This cabinet-meeting began at ten and the discussions went on until two in the afternoon; but at ten to two Prague was able to inform the chief capitals concerned that the conditions imposed by the Munich agreement were accepted.

This notification was made by means of a simple official communiqué, which was only published to the Czechoslovak nation at five o'clock, after they had heard a statement from the premier, General Syrovy.

'The government of the Czechoslovak Republic,' ran the main part of the communiqué, 'have examined all the details of the Munich decision as well as the circumstances that must influence their own decision. Having considered and examined all the urgent recommendations passed on to them by the French and British governments, and in full awareness of their historic responsibility, they, in complete agreement with the leaders of the political parties, have decided to accept the decision of the four powers at Munich.

'They have done this in the knowledge that the nation has to be safeguarded and that today it is impossible to come to any other resolution.

'In coming to this conclusion the Czechoslovak government at the same time convey to the world their protest against the decision, which has been taken in a unilateral manner and without their participation.'

In Prague, where the people were so ready to gather in crowds and go to show their feelings under the windows of the Hradschin Castle, everything was still very quiet. The morning papers had not published any comments upon the Munich conference. The midday editions had to come out before the first reactions of the press could be known. Here, for example, is that of the *Vecerni-Ceske-Slovo*:

'The agreement of the great powers has provided us with an experience that is also a warning for the small and medium-sized states lying between the Baltic and the Aegean . . . Our experience shows them that the life of the small nations is secure only if they form a bloc and make up one great power between them.

'In another connexion, if the Munich negotiations were intended to be carried on in a spirit of justice, the Serbs of Lusatia and the Czechs of Vienna should not have been forgotten.'

As may be seen, the tone was moderate; but it was far from matching the deep feelings of the mass of the people. In fact there were patriots, even among those closest to Benes, who condemned the government's capitulation policy. Thus Hubert Ripka, writing about this essential decision, says:

'For my part I was of the opinion that we should reject the four great powers' ultimatum, even if Hitler were to carry out his threat and attack our country. Many of my friends shared my way of thinking. I was sure that by ourselves alone we should be capable of holding the German attack for several weeks, and I hoped that public opinion in France and Great Britain 'would rise up against the appeasement policy and impel the Paris and London governments to come to the help of our little country.'[1]

Chamberlain at Hitler's flat

In Munich the heads of governments, ministers and diplomats, exhausted by the work of the day before, lay long abed; Henderson, François-Poncet and Weizsäcker were exceptions, however, for they took the plane early in the morning to go to Berlin, where that afternoon all three of them were to take part in the first working session of the international commission provided for in the agreement.

Yet towards eleven in the morning Neville Chamberlain reappeared: he was seen to leave the Regina Palace and get into his car, which drove him rapidly to Hitler's private dwelling – that little flat whose middle-class character had surprised Ciano.

Chamberlain was keeping the appointment that he had asked for the day before, when he spoke to the dictator under cover of the disorder. Hitler was waiting for him, still with the inevitable interpreter Schmidt by his side. According to Schmidt the Führer's attitude had changed considerably since the day before. Today he was much more sullen. 'He was pale and in a bad temper,' says Schmidt. 'Nevertheless, the Führer was secretly flattered at receiving the Prime Minister of the United Kingdom in his own place.'

At first the conversation had to do with Spain. 'I have not the slightest territorial ambition in Spain,' asserted Hitler. 'I merely want to stop this Communist infection that is threatening to overrun the whole of south-eastern Europe. And the interests that Germany is defending in this region are purely economic, not political; and from a long-term point of view they have to do with disarmament . . .'

Disarmament! That word was cleverly thrown in, and Chamberlain rose to it like a trout to a fly.

'I am oppressed myself,' said the Prime Minister, 'by the thought of the necessary burden which is being imposed upon all countries by the expenditure upon armaments, which is eating up the capital which ought to be employed on building houses, on better food and on improving the health of the people.'

'Certainly,' acknowledged Hitler. 'But there only has to be one nation that refuses to agree, all the others have to follow her example.'

In point of fact, as Schmidt observes, the Führer was really thinking about other things. Although he was so fond of discussion he let Chamberlain run the conversation, and he had the look of one whose mind is elsewhere. Furthermore, by cross-checking Schmidt finally discovered what Hitler was thinking about during Chamberlain's visit: he was in a continual state of anger as he reflected upon the demonstrations of peaceful enthusiasm by the people of Munich – and, according to reports received that very morning, the people of the whole of Germany – for the last twenty-four hours. Schmidt says that he was 'profoundly disappointed at seeing the German people react to the presence of war in a manner unlike that which was laid down in the manual of National-Socialist heroes. Instead of rejoicing at the prospect of grappling with the enemy weapons in hand, the inhabitants of Berlin and Munich had, in a manner that left no room for doubt, shown their aversion for war and their delight at seeing peace saved.'

While the Führer ruminated upon this disappointment, Chamberlain came to the true reason of his visit.

'I think it would be a pity if this meeting were to pass off with nothing more than the settlement of the Czech question, which has been agreed yesterday. What I have in mind is to suggest to you that it would be helpful to both countries and to the world in general if we could issue some statement which shows the agreement between us on the desirability of better Anglo-German relations, leading to a greater European stability. I have accordingly ventured to draft a short statement; I would like you to read it and to consider whether you would be disposed to issue such a statement over both our signatures to the public.'

And Chamberlain brought the prepared draft out of his pocket. Schmidt began his translation, and after each sentence Hitler ejaculated an encouraging 'Ja, ja!'

'We, the German Führer and Chancellor and the British Prime Minister, have had a further meeting today and are agreed in recognizing that the question of Anglo-German relations is of the first importance for the two countries and for Europe.

'We regard the Agreement signed last night and the Anglo-German Naval Agreement as symbolic of the desire of our two peoples never to go to war with one another again.

'We are resolved that the method of consultation shall be the method adopted to deal with any other questions that may concern our two countries, and we are determined to continue our efforts to remove possible sources of difference and thus to contribute to assure the peace of Europe.'

'Yes, I will certainly sign it,' said Hitler. 'When shall we do it?'

'Why not now?'

'Then let us sign!'

They both rose, went to the Führer's writing-table, and without further words appended their signature to the document.

'I thank you very heartily,' said Chamberlain, overflowing with gratitude – and no doubt in his heart of hearts rather surprised and rather disturbed at the ease with which things had gone.*

When the meeting between Hitler and Chamberlain was over, Schmidt accompanied the Prime Minister back to his hotel and profited by the occasion to take him for a drive through Munich in an open car.

'I then had a very close view of the enthusiasm with which the population greeted him,' says the interpreter. 'Since we went slowly along through the streets he was recognized at once. People cheered him and crowded round our car. Many tried to shake him by the hand.'

As soon as he was back at the Regina Palace Chamberlain, whose escape that morning had been commented upon in all manner of ways, was surrounded by the pack of journalists.

'I have always believed,' he said, 'that if a peaceful solution to the Czechoslovak problem could be found, that would be the beginning of a general appeasement in Europe. As a consequence of the conversation we had this morning, Chancellor Hitler and myself have together decided to publish an important communiqué that will be given to you very shortly.'

'What about demobilization, Mr Prime Minister?' asked a journalist.

'We did not talk about dates, but we hope that demobilization may take place almost at once.'

'Dear little Daladier'

Daladier did not hear of the existence of this Anglo-German declaration until some hours after his return to France, for the publication of the communiqué was held back in Germany until the three o'clock editions, no doubt so as to wait until the French premier should have left Munich.

But although Daladier did not go to see Hitler and although he did not leave his hotel that morning, he too received the cheers of the deliriously happy Munich crowd. Indeed, some thousands of people spontaneously gathered outside the hotel as early as eight in the

---

* A few days later Hitler sent Prince d'Assia to explain to Ciano why Chamberlain's suggestion had been agreed to in this way. When Ciano in his turn told the Duce of this démarche, Mussolini answered, 'The explanations were unnecessary. You do not refuse a glass of lemonade to a thirsty man.'

morning, under the windows of the rooms occupied by the French delegation. And Daladier had to come out on to the balcony several times.

'Great numbers of men, women and girls stopped under the windows,' says Daladier, agreeably surprised, 'they cheered peace and improvised songs or little popular rhymes.

'The French consul's secretary, a delightful girl who knew German extremely well, translated some of them for me. They were little hymns in honour of the peace that had been saved.'²

At one moment the whole crowd in unison chanted an odd little song that it repeated tirelessly. A journalist translated it. 'Be kind, dear little Daladier, and show yourself at your little window; otherwise we shall not go home.'

Daladier was not easily deceived, and turning to the consul's secretary he asked her, 'Is this not a demonstration ordered by the party or the government?'

'Not at all,' she replied. 'These are people who are going to their work. They were very frightened. They only know one thing, and that is that there will be no fighting.'

Again, for the last time, 'dear little Daladier' showed himself at his 'little window' and was wildly cheered. Then he went down into the hall, for it was nearly time to go. Göring, who was also staying at the Vier Jahreszeiten, was waiting for him to say good-bye. He was surprised by the extent of the popular demonstration and he went to the doorway of the hotel to see what was happening.

'He is cross because they do not cheer him,' whispered the consul's secretary to Daladier, with a broad smile.

By way of ultimate stylishness the marshal, who had worn the most varied and dazzling uniforms during the last twenty-four hours, was now in mufti. He mingled with the journalists. 'We can all be satisfied,' he said. And seeing some French special correspondents who were openly looking at him with an expression that was anything but pleased he went up to them and in a jovial tone said, 'Are you thinking about the Czechs? What could you do with Czechoslovakia? It was one of those foolishnesses of the post-war treaties.'

'Excuse me, Your Excellency,' retorted one of the Frenchmen. 'Was not the interest we took in Czechoslovakia rather like that which you yourself seem to take in Spain?'

It needed more than that to discomfit the brazen Göring. He smiled, and turning towards the other he replied in a confidential tone, 'You are quite right: it is the same foolishness.'

Yet when he was talking to one of the Havas special correspondents, who had asked him for an exclusive interview, Göring made a more orthodox statement.

'I am happy to see an affair that has kept Europe in suspense so long finally settled.

'The statesmen who met at Munich have just won a great victory, and the name of this victory is peace.

'As a journalist living in Berlin you have been able to see that during these last weeks of extreme tension there has been no sign of hatred or chauvinism in Germany against France. Nothing must prevent our two great nations, who esteem one another so much, from living side by side in peace.

'I am particularly glad to hear that French ex-servicemen will take part in the supervision of the international operation antici-pated in Czechoslovakia, for wherever there are ex-servicemen to be found, there also peace and justice prevail.

'I think that the four countries that have taken part in the meeting at Munich may all be equally satisfied with the results obtained.'

A stir in the hall of the Vier Jahreszeiten and Ribbentrop arrived; he too was in civilian clothes, but he still had on the brown shirt and black tie of the Nazis. He came in an official capacity, to accompany the head of the French government to the aerodrome.

Before leaving the hotel Daladier made a last statement, and this, as a gesture of courtesy, he gave to the Paris representative of the German DNB agency, as an exclusive interview.

'I think that the Munich conference may mark an historic date in the history of Europe. Thanks to the high degree of under-standing in the representatives of the Western powers war has been avoided and an honourable peace assured for all nations.

'I have had the pleasure of seeing for myself that there is no feeling of hatred or enmity for France in Germany. Rest assured that for their part the French have no feeling of hostility for Germany, and this has been the case even during the period of diplomatic tension and military preparations that we have just been through.

'The two nations must be on cordial terms with one another, and I am happy to devote my powers to this necessary and fruitful understanding.

'I have already thanked the Führer and Marshal Göring, as well as the foreign minister, Herr von Ribbentrop, for the cordiality of their welcome.

'Please convey all my thanks to the people of Munich too.'

These people of Munich were once more to give Daladier a taste of the honey of their cheers, for all the way from the hotel to the aerodrome the car with the French premier and the foreign minister of the Reich ran between pavements black with crowds overflowing with enthusiasm.

On the airfield there was a guard of honour, drawn up in perfect alignment. They presented arms while the Marseillaise was played and remained motionless as Daladier inspected them before walking over to the gangway of the *Poitou*.

The machine roared, began to move, took off. It was twenty past one.

Left there alone with the journalists, Ribbentrop came up to the Frenchman Jean Thouvenin. 'The victory that we have just won,' he said, 'is everybody's victory. There are neither conquerors nor conquered. It is the victory of peace. It has been gained thanks to the spirit of collaboration that has been shown by all. This spirit of collaboration may be useful in settling other problems. Let us hope so . . .'

Exactly an hour later precisely the same scene was re-enacted at the Oberweisenfeld aerodrome: this time Ribbentrop escorted Chamberlain, to whom General von Epp introduced an officer of the guard, who in his turn said to the Prime Minister, 'I have the honour of presenting this company to you.'

Then the band played *God Save the King* before the motionless crowd, which was making the Hitler salute. Lastly Chamberlain inspected the guard of honour before going to his plane.

A little more cordiality was observed between Chamberlain and Ribbentrop than there had been between Ribbentrop and Daladier.

'My compliments to Mrs Chamberlain, and remember me kindly to Lord Halifax,' said Ribbentrop.

'I shall not forget. Good-bye, Ribbentrop,' replied the Prime Minister with the familiarity of a friend. 'We each did our share.'

'Only too heartily welcomed'

The *Poitou* had almost reached Paris. It was half past three in the afternoon. Throughout the journey Daladier had remained gloomy and preoccupied. Was he thinking of Mussolini's prophecy about his enthusiastic reception? That is scarcely likely: or in any case if he did think of it he was still doubtful, in spite of the Duce's 'You will see, you will see.'

He was so doubtful that when the machine was immediately over Le Bourget the premier was surprised and much disturbed by the sight of a huge crowd gathered near the hangars. His first reaction was to gain a few minutes of respite.

'These thousands of people have come to boo me,' he said to one of the people with him. 'Tell the pilot to circle over the aerodrome for a few moments. I have not had the time to think about the little speech I should like to make, nor about the face I ought to put on it.'*

Between Le Bourget and the ministry of war there were indeed more than half a million Parisians who had 'come out into the streets'. But they had no intention at all of booing Daladier: they had come to cheer him. Because he was bringing back peace – and it mattered little to them whether it was a good peace or a bad one (there could not be a bad peace for them – nor, above all, a good war).

At Le Bourget itself everything was black with people, the airfield, the two-storied gallery and the roof of the airport and the area leading to the buildings. Since the beginning of the afternoon the streets leading to the airport had been filled by an uninterrupted stream of cars and bicycles and pedestrians overflowing the pavements and walking in the street. Women carrying masses of flowers gave one hand to the little children they could not leave at home. *Gardes mobiles* were strung out every ten yards: they were to do their best to clear the way when the premier's car should pass.

Gradually the officials began to arrive at the airfield. Ministers, diplomats, generals, the chairman of the Paris municipal council, the two prefects, and journalists, cinema men, radio-reporters.

One little thing, an incident rising out of a joke in rather poor taste, was indicative of the tension among these people in spite of everything.

* This remark appears in Geneviève Tabouis' book *Vingt ans de suspense diplomatique*, which was published in 1955 with a preface by J. Paul-Boncour; and as far as the present writer knows it has never been denied.

'Well, general,' said Chautemps, 'and so they are taking the bread out of your mouth?'

Gamelin changed colour. 'I have never wanted war and I never shall want it! But there are times when honour and interest require war to be made!'

'Don't be angry,' said Chautemps, 'I was only joking.'

At 15.32 hours the loudspeakers announced that the premier's plane was over Le Bourget. But minutes went by before it landed. No one on the ground knew – how could they? – the reasons why the pilot had to keep up in the air and people began to wonder whether something was wrong, something that was delaying the landing. But no . . . here at last was the Air France Bloch 220 coming in to land.

As the plane gently came to rest the guard of honour of the 34th artillery regiment presented arms and the drums and trumpets of a detachment of the air force band sounded the general salute. The gangway was wheeled up to the fuselage, the door of the plane opened and Daladier appeared; for a moment he paused, very clear against the plane, and then suddenly there was the great outburst of cheering, the delirious ovation.

Chautemps, Guy La Chambre and Bonnet were the first to greet the premier and embrace him, but very soon there was a mass of people milling round him. Everyone wanted to shake his hand in his triumph, kiss him – and above all be recognized by him.

Flowers, the Marseillaise, inspection of the guard of honour.

When the procession reached the microphones it paused; Daladier went up to them. He had an attack of stage-fright, but he did his utmost not to let it show, and almost succeeded.

'After negotiations that were difficult at times,' he said, 'agreement has been reached. I have come back deeply convinced that this agreement was essential to the peace of Europe. We reached it thanks to a spirit of mutual concession and close collaboration.

'I hope that we may very soon look forward to a general settlement of European questions. But I should also like to state that the fortunate results that have been obtained were to a considerable degree the consequences of the coolness and the understanding of the French people, who displayed calmness and resolution. That is the reason why today the French nation is esteemed by the other nations as it never has been before. Frenchmen, let us remain strong and united: it is our duty to the motherland and it is also the only means of preserving peace for the world.

Daladier was indeed forced to believe that the people who were there – not merely the officials who surrounded him, but the others – had not the least desire to boo him. Yet it needed quite some time before he was fully aware of his triumph. In a low voice he said to Gamelin, who had made his way into the front row, 'It is not very glorious, but I did everything I could. How are people taking it?'

'Oh, Monsieur le Président,' replied the general, 'you are going to be only too heartily welcomed!'[1]

No one could say better than that.

Yet Georges Bonnet, who took his rightful place next to the premier in the open Hotchkiss, beaming with joy, thought no welcome could be too hearty. From one end of the route to the other a single car stuck just behind the Hotchkiss: this was the newsreel van, in which the cameraman beat the record for consumption of film.

Tour of France or armistice?

As the Parisians had learnt of the route that the premier's car would take on the radio, the crowds were spread out along the whole length of the road. From as early as the rue de Flandres the pavements were black with people. A little group had even succeeded in climbing on to the roof of a warehouse; but the police had received the order *nobody on the roofs*. They interfered, but so clumsily that suddenly there was a dull thump and a cry: a man had been pushed and he had fallen from the roof to the pavement; he did not get up. They took him to the Lariboisière hospital and there it was found that he had broken several bones.

But the stir that this accident caused among the crowd did not last long: the cries of the wounded man were soon overlaid by the cheers for Daladier and Bonnet as they went by. 'Long live Daladier! Long live the peace! Long live Bonnet!'

The nearer the premier's car came to the centre of Paris the thicker grew the crowd.

'Anyone would think it was the finish of the tour of France,' said a bystander.

'Nothing like it since the 1918 armistice,' observed a journalist.

To judge by the lyricism and the style of some reporters it would seem that the first was by far the sounder comparison.

For his readers in *L'Ordre* (whose editor, Emile Buré, was by no means inclined to hang out flags, however) Pierre Maurice spoke of the astonishing outburst, the blossoming of flags that had broken out along Daladier's route.

'The first to put up a flag,' he wrote, 'was a little cutler in the square Montholon. Between the fans of penknives and the bristling arrays of scissors in his window he placed two minute banners with the French and British colours.

'Then it seems as though his window were darting out these colours all round it, like a prism. In a few minutes they appeared on the balcony of *Le Petit Journal*, waved at a third floor window, showed very small in the distance down by the Gare du Nord crossroads, while taking advantage of the slope they streamed towards the Galeries Lafayette.

'The fronts of the houses were a sea of tricolours and the streets a sea of closely-packed happy people who overflowed from the pavements into the roadway, taking it over and waving their little muslin flags or the bunches of flowers they had bought at the nearest stall or shop . . .

'Suddenly the crowd invaded the whole of the roadway, leaving scarcely enough room for a car to pass. And there indeed was the car, a car that was going at a walking pace, an open car in which there was standing a man in an overcoat and a navy-blue hat with his hands on the windscreen, better than anyone could have hoped for. A man you could go up to, physically touch and thank, a man who seemed to be being carried along on invisible shoulders . . .'

Surprise

What were the feelings of this man, this 'hero', at this explosion of the people's joy, at this demonstration whose spontaneity – and extent – no one could possibly call in question?

'I was astonished at this enormous crowd, delirious with joy,' says Daladier. And not without a certain sadness the premier adds, 'In point of fact I remained alone with myself, thinking over Munich again and the preceding months of negotiation when France was almost always isolated. Would the signatures of Munich be honoured? If not it would be necessary to arm and to go on arming, and that in Great Britain and the United States as well as in France. If Munich were honoured, then perhaps the nations might agree among themselves for works of humanity and good sense.'[3]

Yet there were those who said that they heard a muttered remark from the premier that shows his state of mind in a perhaps somewhat cruder light.

'The fools,' he is supposed to have said, 'if they knew what they were cheering!'*

At all events, Bonnet shared none of his premier's anxieties and he unreservedly enjoyed this triumph, in which he saw his policy's best justification – popular approval.

'For the whole of the long journey,' he says, 'we received nothing but marks of friendliness and fellow-feeling – not a hostile shout, not a disapproving gesture. The workers and the craftsmen of this whole suburb had left their work and had come to meet us. So where were yesterday's and tomorrow's "opponents of Munich" on this day of brotherly feeling when men and women and even children came running towards us to take our hands, embrace us and cover us with flowers?'[4]

Not a hostile shout, true enough. To be sure, the reporter of *l'Epoque* did hear 'those who knew how to keep faith in friendship' along the route cry 'Long live Czechoslovakia!'; but it is not impossible that this cry was uttered by people who genuinely believed that the Munich agreement had just saved Czechoslovakia.

It grew harder and harder for the premier's car to make its way through the crowd, which became steadily thicker.

'At the corner of the rue Lafayette and the main boulevards,' says Bonnet, 'there were so many people and they showed their feelings with such zeal and pertinacity that for want of police we had to rely upon unknown friends to extricate us and let us move on.'[5]

Geneviève Manceron mingled with the crowd and brought back some anecdotes.

---

* André Stibio (*La Bataille*, July 17, 1946) and Geneviève Tabouis record this remark. According to J. Debu-Bridel Daladier did not say 'the fools' but 'the cunts'. But Pierre Lazareff's version has nothing stronger than 'the idiots'.

'A very old English lady,' she says, 'had escaped from hospital with her arm in a sling, not to miss the excitement; and with the detached wisdom of the old she said, "People will put up with anything at all except war." Meanwhile a café was hanging out the French and British colours, and my neighbour, a house-painter, said to me, with his eyes filled with wonder, "And to think that today it might have started already, and there would have been some men killed already . . ." '[6]

Pierre Maurice (who was doing his job as a reporter although he had been called up) had managed to climb on to the running-board of the newsreel van, which was still following just behind Daladier's Hotchkiss. Perched there he went all the way to the rue Saint-Dominique after the premier.

'And while the cameraman was recording his page of history,' he says, 'I too was filming my historic day. I filmed it with eyes blurred with tears, but that gives a wonderful soft focus worthy of the magnificent expression of a whole people drunk with peace and gratitude.

'I saw men and women kiss our premier's hand. For he had given orders that the two policemen on either side should let the crowd do as it liked. Not that he was eager for adoration but because at that moment he was being adored. *He*, that is to say a representative of that crowd whose irresistible surge was not to be strangled or lessened by a policeman's angry interference.

'Next to him, Bonnet was weeping. And mixed with the cries of "Long live the peace!" and "Thank you, Daladier!" there was a "Bravo Bonnet!" every other moment, which made him smile through his tears. For his part Daladier did not cry; but his tense smile was even more moving.

'The bunches of flowers piled up in the car, gladioli, roses and foliage with improvised red, white and blue trimming, all devoutly handed in.

'It was a strange sight. A prime minister of France being given the appearance of one of those dictators of a totalitarian régime with whom he had just been discussing peace and war. The crowd waved flags like the Japanese, clapped as though they were at the theatre, unconsciously stretched out their hands in the fascist manner; and now from the tall buildings they were pouring out the waste-paper baskets and floating down the leaves of calendars as though they were in the United States.

At the crossing of the rue Lafayette and the boulevard Haussmann the thousands of people brought the car to a halt. A woman flung her arms round Daladier's neck and kissed him heartily on both cheeks.

'The procession began to move again, but the applause went on: they cheered us too, crying "Long live the cinema!" "Long live the press!" . . .

'The Place de la Concorde opened its vast width before us – vast, but reduced now to a mere lane. The cheering was lost in the wind. A huge bunch of Parma violets missed Daladier's car and scattered in the road. Concord! Daladier must have felt the impact of this word as we did, but he had most magnificently bought the right to pass through it as he was passing today.

'The Pont de la Concorde thundered beneath us. A blind ex-serviceman waved his white stick, shouting "Long live peace!" '

'In our present situation . . .'

'We turned in front of the empty bastion of the Palais Bourbon, and there we were in the rue Saint-Dominique. A rue Saint-Dominique that was waiting for us with thousands of people – young and old, women and children. The premier's car stopped. An immense cry of gratitude filled the little street, reverberated there, echoed and burst out again. At last Daladier was able to enter the courtyard of the ministry, where the officers of the general staff were waiting for him on the steps.

'There was a move to close the gates, but a single shout from the crowd kept them open. And as it had been in 1918, when Paris called Clemenceau to the balcony, now they called for Daladier. He appeared three times. They wanted to cheer him and thank him still more . . . but officials in black coats and stiff collars made signs that they had taken him and that they were keeping him.'

At the war ministry Daladier found Gamelin once more, the general having arrived first, as well as Reynaud and Mandel, who had not thought it necessary to go out to Le Bourget, and most of the other ministers. They had not followed the same route, and they had not taken an hour and a half to reach the rue Saint-Dominique.

Mandel and Reynaud were very distant. They followed Gamelin into the premier's room. The study was overflowing with flowers.

'I do not think,' said Daladier, 'that in our present situation anything else could have been done . . . it is the four-power pact. I was in favour of it, earlier on. General Gamelin is well aware of that: he was of the same opinion. You could talk to those people . . . Oh, if only we had ambassadors!'[7]

Reynaud merely said to Gamelin in a half-whisper, 'All you have to do now is to find twenty-five divisions.'

Several times, while the ministers and political leaders were coming with their congratulations, Daladier had to go back to the window to acknowledge the cheering of the crowd. But presently he left the rue Saint-Dominique, followed by all the members of the government; for an extraordinary cabinet-meeting was to be held at the Elysée with Lebrun as chairman.

Anatole de Monzie, one of the makers of Munich, left the war ministry with Georges Bonnet.

'Along the route people cheered the foreign minister and made friendly signs to him. Unused to popular encouragement, he felt a justifiable delight in it. He no longer knew himself, nor, I must observe, did he any longer know his friends – we who had so vigorously supported him that we had seemed to be hustling him along.'

Yet Monzie denies that he felt the bitterness that is so apparent in this last remark.

'And even if he were to give himself the airs of one who was the sole author of the peace, what should I have to say against it, seeing that I have long since been foolish enough to prefer anonymity once success has been achieved.'[8]

On the Prague radio

At half past five, just as the triumphal journey of Daladier and Bonnet through the delighted city of Paris was coming to an end, the people of Czechoslovakia could hear their national radio broadcasting the text of the official communiqué* announcing their government's surrender to the Munich *diktat*.

* See above, p. 192.

When the head of this government, General Syrovy, had read the communiqué out himself, he added these words:

'It is to you, the millions of hard-working men, the mothers and children of our country, that I am speaking.

'I have fought, and I know how hard it is at certain times to resign oneself to not taking up arms.

'As a soldier, I state that we can look forward calmly to the future.

'We have been forced to make a choice: the choice between diminished frontiers and the life of our country.

'The preservation of our existence must come first!

'It is within our power to build up a still stronger community inside our shortened frontiers, stronger because more united; and our army will still be there, as strong as it is watchful.'

After him, General Krejci, the chief of staff of the Czech army, spoke to the troops.

'Soldiers, the authorities of our republic have had to accept heavy sacrifices and conditions laid upon them from outside.

'At the head of our nation there are men who have done all that is humanly possible; and I know that they will not abandon us in the days to come.

'A soldier must be able to bear a setback with a firm mind: sometimes indeed this calls for even more courage.

'The army has not been beaten and it has preserved its splendid reputation.

'The Czechoslovak Republic will still have need of us.

'We must keep our calmness and our unity.

'We must keep ourselves prepared for even more threatening dangers. We must still be ready to make our sacrifices in the certainty that we shall emerge from these dark days.'

What struck the patriotic Czechoslovaks most of all in the official communiqué was the head of the government's reference to the 'urgent recommendations' sent by the French and English.

Everyone in Prague knew perfectly well that this was merely a diplomatic euphemism. And very soon everyone was passing on the reply of Krofta, the foreign minister, to the French minister when the latter had once more expressed these 'urgent recommendations' and had then seen fit to add some sympathetic words: Krofta cut him

short, 'Today it is our turn,' he said, 'tomorrow it will be the turn
of others.'

'For he's a jolly good fellow!'

Chamberlain left Munich an hour after Daladier, and he did not
reach Heston until thirty-eight minutes past five.

In London as in Paris the crowd had been gathering in the neigh-
bourhood of the aerodrome; they had been doing this for the last
two hours and more, although the BBC had announced neither the
time of the Prime Minister's arrival nor the route that the official
procession would follow. Thousands of Londoners took up their
positions, determined to wait as long as would be necessary. There
were hundreds of schoolboys among them, and they tirelessly waved
little Union Jacks. The traffic in the nearby roads was totally jammed,
and all movement was impossible for a radius of more than a mile.

Here too the officials had turned out in force: the members of the
cabinet, naturally, but also the entirety of the diplomatic corps,
from Dr Kordt to Corbin, the High Commissioners of the Dominions,
Sir Harry Twyford, the Lord Mayor of London, and Captain
Margesson, the government chief whip in the Commons.

As soon as the door of the plane opened Chamberlain appeared,
waving in answer to the cheers. The Prime Minister was holding up a
paper and flourishing it: this was the joint Anglo-German statement
to which Hitler had set his signature that very morning, next to
Chamberlain's.

Standing in the doorway, smiling and moved, Chamberlain heard
the ministers and the ordinary people all roaring out *For he's a jolly
good fellow* together. And as he came down the steps of the gangway
the applause was punctuated with shouts of 'Good old Neville!',
'Well done, Neville!', 'God bless you!'

Almost overwhelmed by the crowd, which the police could only
just hold back, the Prime Minister, still waving Hitler's signature
over his head, at last managed to make his way through to the
BBC's microphone. He began – and from now on this was a habit
with him – by thanking the countless people who had written to
him. He did not say very much about the Munich agreement.

'I want to say that the settlement of the Czechoslovak problem
which has now been achieved is in my view only a prelude to a wider
settlement in which all Europe may find peace.'

On the other hand the Prime Minister, with a keen sense of propaganda, made the utmost of the Anglo-German agreement. 'This morning,' he went on, 'I had another talk with the German chancellor, Herr Hitler, and here is the paper which bears his name upon it as well as mine. Some of you perhaps have already heard what it contains, and I would just like to read it to you . . .'

After this, the Prime Minister recalled Lord Beaconsfield's return from the Berlin congress of 1878, which had put an end to Russian pretensions in the Balkans: Disraeli had then said, 'I bring back peace with honour.'

'This is the second time in history,' said Chamberlain, 'that peace with honour has come from Germany to Downing Street. I think that it is peace for our time!'

The crowd cheered this comforting prospect to the echo: had not the 'peace with honour' brought back by Disraeli lasted thirty-six years?

But here was Halifax, who solemnly handed the Prime Minister an envelope: a letter from the King, who had not wanted to wait for Chamberlain's coming to Buckingham Palace to tell him of his gratitude. But this visit was not long delayed, for the Prime Minister went directly from the airport to the palace, where George VI was waiting for him. For once the sacrosanct ritual of the court was thrust aside and the whole royal family and all the members of the household, gathered in the courtyard, welcomed the head of the government with cries of joy, applause and cheers.

A little later, about six o'clock, when Mrs Chamberlain, adhering to her usual practice, came out of 10 Downing Street for her daily walk, she in turn received her share of cheers and greetings. She was surrounded, enveloped, almost crushed by the enthusiastic crowd. 'Thank you, thank you . . . I will tell him,' faltered Mrs Chamberlain, much moved.

Nevertheless, when athletic policemen had succeeded in liberating her, the Prime Minister's wife cut short her walk and hurried back to number ten after this ordeal of popularity.

Stephan Zweig, who was a witness of the British people's frenzied demonstrations, as he had been of the Commons' outburst two days earlier, had the intellectual honesty not to pretend to have been more far-seeing than he was.

'First the radio broadcast the news of peace for our time, which told our hard-tried generation that we could once more live in peace, once more live without care, once more work at building up a new and better world; and all those who, after the event, try to deny that the magic word went to their heads are lying. For who could believe that the man who had come back beaten was ready to be carried in triumph? . . .

'To this there was added the newspapers. They carried a photograph that showed Chamberlain, whose hard face usually reminded one irresistibly of a cross bird, in the act of smiling from the doorway of the plane and proudly waving this historic document that announced peace for our time and that he was bringing back to his people as the most valuable of gifts. He could already be seen at the cinema that evening, and the audience jumped from their seats, shouting and cheering: for a trifle they would have embraced one another in this new feeling of brotherliness that was about to arise in the world. For everybody who was in London, in England then, it was an incomparable day, one that unburdened all hearts.

'On historic days of this kind I like to walk about in the streets so as to absorb the atmosphere better, more sensually, to breathe the air of the time in the literal sense of the word. In the gardens the workmen had stopped digging the shelters, and people stood round them, laughing and talking, for "peace for our time" had made air-raid shelters useless . . .

'At the corner of Piccadilly someone hurried towards me. It was an English civil servant I knew, but not well, a man who was by no means demonstrative, but on the contrary distinctly reserved. At ordinary times we should have confined ourselves to a civil bow, and it would never have occurred to him to speak to me. But that day he came up to me with his eyes shining: "What do you think of Chamberlain?" he said, beaming with joy. "Nobody believed him, and yet he has done what had to be done. He has not given way, and so he has saved the peace." '9

First meeting in Berlin

As to his not having given way, that was something else again. At all events there was little chance that this idea would be shared by a single one of the members of the international commission set up by the Munich agreement, whose first meeting – no time was lost!

– was held towards the end of the afternoon of that same day at the Wilhelmstrasse. There were present André François-Poncet, Henderson, Attolico and Weizsäcker, who had all come from Munich that morning by air: Weizsäcker, as host, was the commission's chairman. The Czechoslovaks were represented by Dr Vojtech Mastny and General Husareck, who did not join the others without a certain delay, for their plane from Prague only landed at Tempelhof at nine minutes to six.

At this first sitting the commission was primarily concerned with allotting the tasks to be done among its members: yet this did not prevent the German propaganda services from announcing as early as that same evening that a detailed agreement had been reached in reference to the occupation of the 'no plebiscite' zones. This was news put out as being 'of German origin, intended for abroad and coming from a well-informed source.'

Cabinet-meeting in Paris

At the Elysée, although Albert Lebrun was delighted at Daladier's welcome by the Paris crowd (the President of the Republic would not have to worry about finding a new premier for some months), he could scarcely deceive himself as to Daladier's opinion of the real worth of the Munich agreement.

'I assure you,' said the President of the Republic at a later date, 'that his face showed neither joy nor pride. He felt that this was a painful moment in many respects and above all he felt that grave events were near.'[10]

Daladier, in the presence of his ministers, both those who saw the Munich agreement only as a victory won by the peace party – their party – and those who were uneasy about the conditions in which France had managed to unburden herself of her obligations towards Czechoslovakia, began by summarizing the talks at the Führerhaus.

He recalled Hitler's opening speech and his own immediate reaction. Then he dwelt upon the differences that he discerned between the conditions set by Hitler in the Godesberg memorandum and those that the Führer had accepted at Munich.

'The Munich agreement,' he said, 'is a compromise between Berchtesgaden and Godesberg. At Godesberg Hitler wanted to occupy the whole of the Sudetenland from October 1 without

giving the inhabitants so much as the right of option. He wanted
to organize plebiscites in the whole of the untransferred zone in
order to claim enclaves which were small in size but which would
have destroyed the union between Bohemia and Moravia.

'The "red zone", the zone with a German majority, will be
occupied progressively from October 1 to October 10, but the
international commission alone will fix the new frontiers. It is also
the commission that will say in what localities of the "green zone",
the untransferred zone, plebiscites will take place.'

Daladier then urged the importance of the guarantee given by
France and Great Britain – in spite of Chamberlain's reserves about
committing himself before the Germans and Italians – and that of the
promise of guarantee as soon as the problems set by the Polish and
Hungarian minorities should be settled that Hitler and Mussolini
had given.

Finally the premier spoke at length upon the atmosphere in which
the conference had taken place, upon the German people's welcome,
and upon Göring's and even Hitler's cordiality. 'Both of them,' said
he, 'would like to come to Paris. Hitler longs to see the Louvre . . .'

There was no debate after the premier had given his account.
Lebrun spoke in order 'to congratulate Daladier warmly upon the
fortunate outcome of his mission', and Chautemps, as vice-premier,
did the same.

'Daladier,' says Bonnet, 'returned thanks and associated me with
all that had just been said to him.'

At the end of the cabinet-meeting a communiqué was issued to
the press, and it stressed the government's unanimity in congratulating their chief.

When Daladier was back at the rue Saint-Dominique he continued
to see visitors, particularly Bullitt, the American ambassador, whom
he told of his doubts about the manner in which Germany would
keep her word – which was one way of expressing reserves as to the
value of the Munich agreement.

The latter part of the day provided Daladier with another and
equally important subject for bitterness, or at least of anxiety:
Franco-British solidarity. This had scarcely shown much during the
Munich conference, but at least it could be supposed that the French
and English had preserved its appearance; yet now there was a
telephone call from Bonnet and Daladier learnt of the signature of

the joint statement of Hitler and Chamberlain, a document that Bonnet himself had only heard of from the evening papers.

When Chamberlain was questioned through diplomatic channels about this step which had been so carefully hidden from the head of the French government he answered with what Bonnet calls 'his usual sincerity'.

What did such a sincere reply consist of?

'The statement,' said the Foreign Office, Chamberlain's mouthpiece, 'had not been thought out beforehand: during their last conversation, Herr Hitler's remarks to Mr Neville Chamberlain on the subject of Anglo-German relations were of such a reassuring nature that it seemed sound policy to the British Prime Minister to record them in writing at once ...'

It is really difficult to know which to relish more, Neville Chamberlain's 'sincerity' or the French foreign minister's gullibility. At all events, Bonnet was not at all well informed, for the premeditated character of the diplomatic operation that Chamberlain had successfully carried out on the morning of the thirtieth – appointment made the day before, the text of the agreement drafted in advance – was particularly marked.

'In conclusion,' observes Bonnet without the least embarrassment, 'Mr Neville Chamberlain urged us to enter into negotiations with Germany to obtain a non-aggression declaration from her, of the same nature as that which he had signed with Hitler.'[11]

Among the dictators

While Chamberlain and Daladier were returning home as conquering heroes, what was happening to the two confederates whose solidarity had been confirmed by Munich and whose power had been demonstrated?

The Führer delayed his journey to Berlin for twenty-four hours. After the mental strain of that day and night of talks he went to Eva Braun. (Although the whole world paid the closest attention to the Führer's smallest words and deeds, no one knew the part that she played in his life.)

In her private diary the Führer's mistress wrote, 'Three of the Big Four have gone. The fourth, and without any sort of doubt the most important, has stayed. He talked about the negotiations for more than three hours. "It is only now that I see how weak the West is," he said to me, "and now I shall make the war I need to impose my ideas upon the world. The difference that there is at present between Mussolini and me will grow more and more obvious. He wants his peace; I want my war." '[12]

In Berlin this day of respite was none too long for Goebbels and Wilhelm Frick to give the town the appearance they wanted for the Führer.

The proclamation of the minister of propaganda left nothing to chance.

> People of Berlin, come out into the streets. You will line the pavement from the Anhalt station to the Reich Chancellery. It is in this way that we wish to show the Führer our gratitude for the historic decisions taken at Munich.
>
> Hang flags from the houses!
>
> Decorate the streets of the city!
>
> Long live the Führer! Long live the National-Socialist nation! Long live the Great German National-Socialist Reich!

And in his diary General Jodl drew this logical conclusion from the Munich conference – the same conclusion that was drawn by all Germans that evening.

> 'The Munich pact has been signed. As a power, Czechoslovakia no longer exists . . . The Führer's genius and his decision to stand firm even in the face of a world war have once more won the victory without the need for fighting. There is still hope that unbelieving, weak and doubtful people have been converted and will remain converted.'

As for Mussolini, after a whole day of travelling, he once more tasted the intoxicating delight of a Roman triumph. 'From the Brenner to Rome, from the king to the peasant,' noted Ciano with a yet-untarnished poetic enthusiasm, 'the Duce received such a welcome as I have never seen. He himself told me that he had only felt such zeal on the evening the empire was proclaimed.'

The little king, who feared nothing so much as a war in which Italy should find herself on Germany's side against England, made a spectacular move: he left his residence at San Rossore and went specially to Florence in order to be on the station as the Duce's train went through.

'Peace for our time'

In Rome Mussolini travelled through the city in an open car and reached the Piazza di Venezia by way of the via Nazionale, passing under a triumphal arch of leaves and branches 'adorned', says the French diplomat Blondel, 'with the absurd alliteration "*Roma doma*" '. (Rome tames.)

The crowd had gathered in the Piazza di Venezia according to the invariable ceremonial of the régime's great demonstrations: the fascist organizations, from the adults to the *balillas* by way of the youth formations and the GUF,* arrived in good order and grouped themselves under the palace balcony; the ex-servicemen occupied the open space at the foot of the war-memorial. On the steps there were flags, among them the British Legion's Union Jack. And lastly those who belonged to no organization appeared, coming in well-ordered ranks, by district, street, house.

They sang *Giovinezza*, and by the time the far side of the square had reached the chorus, those who had begun were already dealing with the next verse. Laughter, shouting: and now suddenly the crowd, organized and yet at the same time chaotically turbulent, had no more than a single voice. In a quickening, vibrating, hammering rhythm, something like that of a railway engine, every throat uttered the same cry, 'Du-ce! Du-ce! Du-ce!'

On and on, tirelessly the fascist crowd called for its chief. For his part he took care not to appear until this demonstration of mass hysteria should have had its effect – a kind of trance that would change into an unending roar as soon as the tall French windows giving on to the famous balcony should open, showing the massive, thickset form of the Duce.

For a long while he stood there, patiently, savouring the full taste of the ovation and waiting until a lull should allow him to utter his first word and thus obtain an immediate total silence. At last he spoke. 'Comrades! You have lived through memorable hours. At Munich we have worked for peace in justice. Is not that the ideal of the Italian people?'

The cheers, alternating with the *Du-ce, Du-ce*, the equivalent of encore, went on and on long after Mussolini had returned to his own quarters.

If he cast a balance, now that these forty-eight hours were over, the result could not fail to be in his favour: his intervention in the matter of calling the conference had been decisive; he had so managed

* The fascist university groups.

affairs at Munich that he had appeared to one and all as the leading figure; everybody agreed in considering this peace, which had been obtained without his German partner's having had to make the slightest concession, as his work; France, who for such a time had refused to recognize the empire, was quite certainly about to regularize her relationships with Rome and to accredit an ambassador to the 'king and emperor' at last; and finally Germany, speaking through Ribbentrop (Ciano had told his father-in-law of this during the journey), had just proposed a three-handed alliance between Italy, the Reich and Japan. When the Berlin-Rome-Tokio axis was a fact and a power 'it would be the greatest thing in the world' said Ribbentrop – always given to hyperbole, as Ciano pointed out.

First international reactions

By the end of the day on the thirtieth the most important international reactions to the Munich agreement were all known.

In Washington Cordell Hull had made an unenthusiastic statement. The American secretary of state chose to welcome only 'the immediate results obtained in favour of peace'; and he was primarily concerned with expressing the hope that 'whatever the circumstances the upholders of the principles that govern international relationships in peace and order and of the application of these principles should not relax but rather redouble their efforts at maintaining order in the respect for law.'

In Moscow *Izvestia* headed the news of the Munich conference 'Fresh Anglo-French surrender'. And in the body of the article there appeared this observation, 'The war has merely been postponed, and France and England are occupying a weaker position than they did before.'

As for the Pope, he received Charles-Roux, the French ambassador to the Vatican, but it was to speak to him in a manner that the diplomat, as he admits himself, had not expected at all.

'I was received by the Holy Father on September 30, at Castelgandolfo,' says the ambassador. 'Supposing that he was more concerned with the peace than with its conditions, I expected to find him relieved, almost happy. This was not the case. He told me of his astonishment at the fact that Czechoslovakia should have been disposed of without her consent; he gave me to understand that there had been a certain amount of bluff in the attitude of Germany and Italy; and he displayed much anxiety for the future. Three Italians were received after me, Mgr Costantini, Senator Cini and an architect, who came to present the model of a church that had been planned, the Church of the Missions, for the universal exhibition that was to take place in Rome in 1941. They thought they were doing the right thing in congratulating Pius XI on the fact that during the very night before their visit to him peace had been preserved. They were unfortunate. "A very fine thing," he replied, "this peace botched together at the cost of a weak country that was not even consulted! A peace that has been negotiated without all those concerned having been called together is an unjust peace. You may tell the head of the Italian government so from me." '13

The Polish ultimatum

But yet that day, that triumphant day of September 30 which saw the delight of Paris answering that of Berlin, and London's joy echoing Rome's, was not yet over.

For the only nation that could have no feelings that day but sadness and anger, for the Czechoslovak nation, there was still another trial to undergo before the ill-omened month was done.

A quarter of an hour before midnight a message from Warsaw reached Prague. Not without difficulty, for as Colonel Beck himself, who wrote it, admits, it had been necessary 'to make use of every means of communication, telephone, radio, air-borne courier' because of the break in communications between Poland and Czechoslovakia. The message was an ultimatum, and Beck describes it thus:

> 'An ultimatum with a twelve-hour* time-limit in which, referring to our earlier exchange of diplomatic notes and to the events that have just taken place (Munich), I demanded that the territories of Trans-Olzan Silesia, unquestionably inhabited by a Polish majority, should be ceded to Poland, and that there should be minor rectifications of the frontier in places where we thought it justifiable.'

* And not twenty-four hours as Georges Bonnet says.

The 'earlier exchange of diplomatic notes' to which Colonel Beck refers took place between September 21 and 26.

On September 21, learning that Czechoslovakia was yielding to Franco-British pressure and agreeing to submit to the requirements expressed by Hitler at Berchtesgaden, Beck sent a 'warning' to the Prague government. The Polish foreign minister officially denounced 'that part of the 1925 liquidation agreement which dealt with minority problems' – which amounted to the same thing as insisting upon the transfer of the zones with a Polish majority to Poland, that is to say, Trans-Olzan Silesia. The French ambassador in Warsaw, Léon Noël, was to play a personal and subtle game at this juncture. He felt that he was required to do this not only because of the post he held but also because of the strong friendships that he had formed in Prague some years before, when he had been head of the French diplomatic mission.

The Polish warning was ill-received by the Czechoslovak government, which, as Léon Noël puts it, 'having agreed to submit to the imperious pressure of the Western powers as to the fate of the Germans in Bohemia, had for the time being exhausted their capacity for making concessions'.

It was at this difficult conjuncture that Léon Noël, who thought that the threat of conflict between his country's allies of Prague and Warsaw obliged him to interfere, 'acted with passion to keep the peace between them'.[14]

In spite of instructions from the Quai d'Orsay requiring him 'to arrange with Beck that Poland should renounce her demand for annexation and be content with limited satisfaction', Léon Noël at once made personal approaches to induce Benes to accept the Polish claims. Lacroix, the French minister in Prague, willingly helped in the manoeuvre and immediately told Benes of the advice that Léon Noël gave him.

'President Benes, who up until then had been determined to resist the Polish demands,' says the ambassador to Warsaw, 'paid attention to what he said, reflected, showed that he was shaken, and finally told my colleague that seeing that this advice came from one whose sentiments he knew, he would follow it. A few hours later the president sent a personal message by plane to President Moscicki* to inform him that Czechoslovakia accepted

* The head of the Polish state.

319

the basis of the Polish demands and agreed to immediate negotiations with a view to seeing that they were satisfied.'

This letter from Benes was handed to Moscicki on September 26.

Beck claims that in fact this message was dated September 22. It is quite clear that this was materially impossible, since after the sending of the Polish warning to Prague on the twenty-first, Léon Noël had to have the time to tell the Quai d'Orsay, receive Bonnet's reply, make up his mind to intervene personally in Prague and lastly to persuade Lacroix to undertake the necessary démarche.

Why then did Beck make this 'mistake' about the date of Benes' message? Simply because the Polish foreign minister wanted to justify his action against Prague a posteriori, and therefore wished to provide himself with an alibi. Between September 22, the date upon which Beck says the letter was written, and the twenty-sixth, the date upon which it was handed to Moscicki, Poland had received a threatening note from Moscow pointing out that the Soviet-Polish non-aggression pact would lapse if Poland were to attack Czechoslovakia.

According to Beck Benes kept his reply to President Moscicki by him for three days; from this he deduces that Benes instigated the Soviet move and that he waited for it to take place before displaying his good intentions. What is more, Josef Beck does not merely insinuate this; he asserts it. 'There was an obvious link,' he says, 'between the delivery of M Benes's letter and the date of the Soviet intervention. This detail also had its importance from the point of view of the attitude we were to adopt with regard to the intervention of the President of Czechoslovakia.'[15] And Beck goes on to say that 'President Benes's belated letter contained exceedingly vague promises'.

Léon Noël was aware of all this: he knew the contents of Benes's letter (he had been behind the writing of it), and he knew about Jozef Beck's scheming.

'I had told Jozef Beck that a favourable reply from Czechoslovakia could be expected, and he should have been satisfied,' he writes. 'But he was not like that. Prague's acquiescence was not enough for him; he meant to make his success stand out and to give it as spectacular an appearance as he possibly could. What he wanted from Czechoslovakia was something in the nature of a formal surrender that should be seen as a great event and be useful to the prestige of his policy. To begin with he needed an ultimatum. When he was faced with the letter from the President of the Czechoslovak Republic he pretended to have legal scruples of a constitutional nature that one would hardly have expected in one of Pilsudski's disciples: this was only a personal communication from the head of the Czechoslovak state; what worth did it have? Was it a valid document? There had been no governmental communication to confirm it. President Benes had in this way intended to give the acceptance of the Polish demands a greater value by expressing it personally; and now Beck was pretending to consider that the acceptance did not have enough value because it came from him ... This was neither particularly genuine nor particularly elegant. It was perfectly obvious to anyone with the slightest idea of what was going on in Prague that in this matter President Benes had not taken up an official attitude without in the first place having made sure that he was in full agreement with his government.'[16]

But, as Léon Noël points out, Beck wanted his ultimatum. Munich gave him the opportunity of flourishing it without running any very grave danger.

CHAPTER TWO

Munich, the last instalment

Pacifist euphoria · Review of the French Press · . . . and the British · Duff Cooper resigns · Parliamentary sanction in London and Paris · Benes withdraws · The first cracks · The international commission at work · The Bonnet-Ribbentrop agreement · The last act · The last scene

WOULD the Polish ultimatum, which was contrary to the letter and the spirit of the Munich agreement and which was delivered less than twenty-four hours after the signing of that agreement, put a sudden end to the wild euphoria that had seized upon the nations and their rulers?

Jozef Beck had set noon on October 1 as the limit of the delay that Poland 'granted' Czechoslovakia.

Czechoslovakia could make use of this time to make an immediate trial of the guarantee that Daladier's France and Chamberlain's Britain had given her new frontiers. She had the right to do so, as Léon Blum proved the very next morning in his implacably logical leader in *Le Populaire*. Indeed, having recalled the wording of the annex to the Munich agreement on the subject of the Franco-British guarantee and that of the supplementary declaration,* Léon Blum concluded:

'The result of the combination of these two texts is therefore:

'That as far as the Polish minority is concerned, the Munich agreement looked forward to and in set terms advised a friendly understanding between Poland and Czechoslovakia; that if the negotiations were not to end in agreement, the four powers should meet again to look into the matter; and that if in the meanwhile Czechoslovakia were the object of an unprovoked attack by Poland she might call upon the Franco-British guarantee, which was immediate and unconditional.'

* See the supplementary declaration, p. 399.

Here, then, was the first test that the Munich agreement had to meet.

It is true that the test was rendered nugatory beforehand, not only by the French and British proof to the whole world of their desire for 'peace at any price', but also by the untimely activities of a diplomat whose judgment [did not equal his good intentions. It was Noël that Blum was referring to when he added, 'It may be that the Czechoslovak government feel themselves bound by earlier, and quite recent, engagements taken with regard to Poland. It may be that these engagements were urged upon them with a view to strengthening their position with regard to Germany and that now they are suffering from it.'

What is more, Léon Noël, this counsellor whose advice had been 'quite recently' attended to, was to repeat his offence. On the morning of October 1,* having learnt that the Czechoslovak government, 'indignant at the conduct of the Poles', thought of rejecting Beck's ultimatum, the French ambassador in Warsaw examined the situation that would arise from this rejection: he could see only two outcomes – either a fresh capitulation by the Western powers and the immediate invasion of Czechoslovakia by the Germany army, or else a sudden change of public opinion in France and England that would bring about a change of front and induce the Western powers to intervene, basing themselves upon the Munich agreement. But in this second case Poland would find herself on the same side as Germany, a state of affairs not at all well calculated to show the diplomatic abilities of the French ambassador in Warsaw to their best advantage. 'The thing to do,' says Léon Noël, 'was at any cost to avoid both the one eventuality and the other. I at once got into touch with the Quai d'Orsay and our minister in Prague for this purpose.'[1]

These efforts to bring the Czechoslovaks to agree to another sacrifice were not in vain: during the morning Prague gave way, merely asking that the time-limit set by the Polish ultimatum should be changed from noon to one o'clock.

Prague gave way: but the Czechoslovak papers drew a bitter lesson from these successive capitulations forced upon Czechoslovakia but agreed to, in fact, by France.

'France's international importance has lessened,' wrote the Paris correspondent of the *Pravo Lidu*, an extreme left wing paper.

---

* And not September 30, as he says in his book *L'agression allemande contre la Pologne*.

'France has lost her positions in central Europe ... France's security now depends solely upon England's good will. A service of this kind costs money, and in Paris people are wondering what the price of this protection will be.'

The semi-official *Lidove Noviny* dealt with exactly the same subject.

'France is no longer what she was in 1914 and 1918. She has become a second-rate power, protected by a kind of British tutelage.' The article went on to reach this conclusion, 'If it is no longer right that is to rule in the world but might, then our place is where that might is greatest. There is nothing left for us to do but to come to an understanding with Germany.'

It would be exceedingly difficult to argue that these reactions were not well based, since not forty-eight hours after the signing of the Munich agreement the emptiness of the Franco-British guarantee had been proved – and proved at the instance of the French diplomats posted to Warsaw and Prague. It was indeed an activity that was all the more unseasonable since upon this very question there was by no means a total agreement between the two members of the Axis. Ciano's diary bears witness to the fact.

'This Polish impatience was not justified. They had waited twenty years and they could very well wait another few days and avoid an incident that might make the situation difficult again. I telephoned this to our ambassador in Warsaw and told him to make an approach to Beck. France and England also stirred themselves. On the other hand Ribbentrop, who was not really at all pleased that things had gone off so easily, telephoned to tell me that he should make no démarche whatever in Warsaw, and he almost urged the Poles to attack.'

It goes without saying that Colonel Beck took very little notice of these diplomatic moves, knowing very well that they would remain merely verbal. The Polish foreign minister, writing on this subject, observes, not without effrontery, 'As almost always happens in time of serious tension, we received various appeals to keep the peace, in particular one from President Roosevelt: I was able to reply after Czechoslovakia had accepted our note, which settled the matter. The same thing happened with the French and British interventions.'[2]

On the afternoon of that October 1, therefore, while the Wehr-

macht was occupying the Sudetenland, the Polish forces under
General Bortnowski entered Silesia.

Beck triumphed: his policy made Poland the equal of the Third
Reich, which up until then had always succeeded in increasing its
territory by intimidation, without ever having had to fight so much
as a skirmish.

And the Polish minister expresses his contempt for the pusillani-
mity and the want of decision of the Hungarians, who, unlike himself, did not grasp the chance offered by Munich.

> 'The Hungarians,' he says, 'could not make up their minds to
> take forceful steps. Our talks with them were extremely difficult,
> for their government passed from total defeatism (according to
> them any violation of Czechoslovakia by Germany must inevitably
> set off a world war) to the most extraordinary plans – for example,
> they asked us to undertake the military occupation of Subcar-
> pathian Ruthenia and Slovakia in order to cede them back again to
> Hungary. It was really hard to get them to speak reasonably.'[3]

Indeed, the Hungarians did not join the rush for the spoils until
some days had gone by.

Pacifist euphoria

To be sure, the London and Paris papers did give a decent amount of
space to the Polish ultimatum. But it did not appear that anyone
seriously thought that such a side-issue could endanger the 'new
balance in Europe' that had arisen from the Munich conference.

Besides, as they had been too thoroughly persuaded that there
would be war, people would now believe only in peace. And they
were not sparing of their gratitude to the men who had 'saved the
peace' on September 29 and 30.

In a single day Daladier received more than thirty thousand
messages. Everywhere there were the most preposterous schemes for
thanking the statesmen who had gone to Munich or who had arranged
the meeting.

One is absolutely bound to acknowledge – though without taking
much pride in it – that France and Paris beat all records in this field
by miles. In the Paris municipal council Taittinger proposed that
during their lifetime the names of Daladier and Bonnet should be
given to important streets in the city; and at the same time another

councillor said that there should be simply an Avenue du 30-Septembre. Furthermore others suggested that this historic date should become an 'international holiday'. But there were some cross-grained souls who protested that September 30 meant nothing: it was on the twenty-ninth that the agreement had been reached, although for technical reasons the signing had taken place early on the morning of the thirtieth.

As soon as *Paris-Soir* put out the idea of a subscription to buy a country house as a present for Chamberlain – 'the house of Peace on the soil of France' – it made headway. Some could already see it in the Dordogne: the Prime Minister was a great fisherman – and he would have Georges Bonnet as a neighbour. The names of Henry Bernstein and Louis-Louis Dreyfus appeared at the top of the subscription-list, which reached a hundred thousand francs the first evening.

The *Petit Parisien* undertook a less costly venture: this was the opening of a visitors' book in which all those who wished publicly to show their approval of Munich could come and sign their names. Presently the count reached a million.*

The reactions in the provinces were quite up to those of Paris. Here too there were moves to rename streets and squares after Chamberlain and Daladier. Here too motions were passed and resolutions carried, and here too there were thanksgiving ceremonies.

Some activities, though carried out by private individuals, made quite as much noise. This was the case when it was learnt, on October 1, that Flandin had just sent a telegram to Hitler.† 'I beg you to accept my hearty congratulations on the preservation of peace, with the hope that from this historic act there may arise a cordial and trusting collaboration between the four great European powers assembled at Munich.'

* Georges Bonnet is perfectly right in saying, 'Many of these enthusiasts, for-getting that their names and addresses are clearly to be seen in the book, were unwise enough, after the liberation of France, to boast that they had been "anti-Munich" from the very first.'

† P.-E. Flandin did in fact send the same telegram to Hitler, Mussolini and Chamberlain; for Daladier had received the text of a motion passed by the central committee of the *Alliance Démocratique*. Furthermore Flandin has very justly pointed out, with regard to this telegram, '(a), that Roosevelt, for his part, had sent one in almost the same terms to the same men. (b) That this telegram was by no means a congratulatory telegram on the dismemberment of Czechoslovakia but one in which I expressed the wish that agreement between the great powers might con-tinue, so that it might safeguard peace.' (P.-E. Flandin.)

Munich, the last instalment

The day after Munich the great majority of the papers reflected the pacifist euphoria that enveloped the country.

In *L'Action française* Léon Daudet exulted openly under the headline *We shall not have to fight for the Czechs.*

'Israel and Moscow may wring their hands. We are not going to fight for the Czechs, nor out of love for M Benes, nor for the "splendid memory" of Briand, that consecrated pimp, nor for the depraved memory of the baleful Philippe Berthelot, the father of the present mess, and one who was certainly very well paid for having prepared it.'

In *Le Petit Bleu* Philippe Henriot began by abusing the 'warmongers'.

'Now that the peace is saved we still hear the recriminations of those whose war has been snatched away from them.' And he went on to analyse the crisis that had just been solved in his own way. 'Again and again I have had the impression that for many worthy, short-sighted people the conflict that has been poisoning the atmosphere in Europe amounted to a struggle for prestige, a match, France versus Germany. Why did the attitude of the Communist party not enlighten them about another match, that of the Soviets versus civilization?'

In *La République* Emile Roche drew up a list of the 'good ministers' and chose to forget the others.

'The whole of Europe, suddenly recovering its wits, has seen how great would be the folly of a conflict. Will Europe also understand the imperative reasons which make an understanding essential? This understanding has been begun by good workmen; and those on our side, those whose ideology we share, are called Daladier, Bonnet, Chautemps, Monzie, Marchandeau, Pomaret . . . and the others I forget.'

Edouard Pfeiffer moved over to the attack in the same paper.

'After Roche, after Frot, after Déat, I too wish to write "The time for settling scores has come".'
'Even more than the leaders of the Communist party, who have openly urged a clash, the guilty men are those few who, in agree-

ment with the Communists, wanted war and have done everything to thrust the country into it.'

The leader in *Le Temps* also blamed the 'war party', but in more dignified terms, as was fitting.

'In short, it is the feeling of the people, clearly discerned and well interpreted by a few far-sighted and courageous leaders, that has just overcome what may be termed "the war party".'

And Jean Prouvost, the chief of *Paris-Soir*, discovered a formula which outdid Disraeli's and which had its popularity.

'Our premier and our foreign minister have kept the peace for us.

'They have preserved for us peace with honour and with dignity. That is even better.'

Yet there were some discordant notes to spoil the concert, and these came both from the right and the left. Blum's 'historic remark' comes to mind at once, for it was one that set its seal upon this time. 'I feel myself divided between a cowardly relief and shame.'

Yet these words, which are so often quoted, were not written the day after Munich. They are to be found in a leader which appeared in *Le Populaire* of September 20, 1938, the day after Benes accepted the Franco-British plan. On September 30 *Le Populaire*'s leader was more balanced.*

But there was also an article by André Tardieu which caused a great deal of comment: in this, having admitted that 'joy in having avoided a war whose beginnings would have been terrible was legitimate,' he wrote,

'The first act is over. We have yet to see the others, which, assuring Germany's supplies of corn, meat, oil and metallic ore, will make her unconquerable for the next war. There is no longer any barrier against the eastward march.

'We have been told, "It is the beginning of a new Europe". No! It is the resurrection, in a worse form, of the Europe of 1914 – that Europe from which the war arose. It is the Europe of the revision of the treaties – that revision of which M Briand said, in 1930, that it would mean war and revolution.

'The Allies did not create Czechoslovakia for her own sake. They

* The text of this article is given in Appendix III, p. 395.

saw in her a vanguard against Germanism. That is why Germany wanted to destroy her, and why the destruction has begun. From now on it is the European problem as a whole that is set before us. For Germany Czechoslovakia was only a pretext and only a first stage.

'The Munich agreement is the finest German success since the war.'[4]

Emile Buré also experienced this double emotion of relief and uneasiness: he wrote in *L'Ordre*,*

'I have too much human feeling not to have been moved yesterday by the happiness of mothers who had bravely parted with their children and who are about to have the joy of seeing them again, the horror of the war having retreated. Like them I would like to be sure, that it has retreated for ever. But I should be lacking in intellectual honesty if I were to disguise the fact that I am still uneasy about that Munich agreement which they, in the relaxation of their feelings, have hailed with such trustfulness.'

Henry de Kérillis was more direct.

'Those who advised firmness were right. Firmness at the beginning meant peace, peace with security. The Munich pact, born of a belated firmness, brings us peace without security . . .

'This Munich peace leaves us less strong than we were yesterday, since we have lost an ally and since more than thirty German divisions, with no cares in the west† any more, are going to turn towards us. So if in the past when we were stronger we were unable to stand up against formidable intimidation and a formidable threat from Germany, how shall we stand up to it the next time, when we shall be weaker?'

As for Gabriel Péri, in *L'Humanité*, he dreaded not only the consequences of Munich but also those of the new Anglo-German agreement.

'At Munich France lost allies. But Germany secured the complaisant neutrality of certain countries. The aggressor is protecting his rear.

* Michel Clemenceau had written an article meant for *L'Ordre* in which he protested vehemently against the triumphal welcome of Paris for Daladier. But, Paul Reynaud points out, 'Pétain, with whom the Tiger's son was on good terms at that period, advised him not to publish it.'

† Clearly this should read 'in the east'.

'Peace for our time'

'M Daladier was told of the Chamberlain-Hitler declaration at nine o'clock yesterday evening, as he was relishing his triumph! The Nazi press has reproduced it in huge letters. The *Deutsche Allgemeine Zeitung* explains that "the Führer's will, as it is expressed in *Mein Kampf*, has been accomplished".

'The policy of *Mein Kampf*? Isolate France, the chief enemy, in order to make war on her.

'Rejoice, prime minister Daladier!'

... and the British

Most of the English papers, though they showered the Prime Minister with laurel, spoke in a more reserved manner – and expressed more reservations – than the majority of the French.

To be sure *The Times*, which had been the first to ring Czechoslovakia's death-knell, expressed a smug satisfaction.

'By the agreement concluded at Munich, the most dangerous threat of war in Europe has been done away with, and by the declaration signed by Herr Hitler and Mr Chamberlain there is hope that the other dangers will be peacefully eliminated.

'We owe this double achievement by common consent first and foremost to the Prime Minister. If the government of the United Kingdom had been in the hands of a less determined man, it is certain that war, with its incalculable consequences, would have broken out against the wishes of all the nations concerned.'

But the leader-writer of the *News Chronicle* began by thinking of the Czechoslovaks.

'The last blow inflicted upon the Czechoslovak nation, which but a few days ago was assured of Great Britain's support against attack* . . . has been that the conditions submitted to it by the British Prime Minister insisting upon fresh concessions, had to be accepted within the space of a few hours.'

And the Liberal journalist also regretted that Russia should have been 'overlooked'.

'From the point of view of the Czechs' security, the fact that

* Obviously an allusion to the Foreign Office communiqué, which was still regarded as a forgery in France.

Russia is not yet to be one of the parties to this new guarantee is a vitally important omission.'

The Labour Party journalists of the *Daily Herald* also had objections to put forward, particularly on the subject of the Chamberlain-Hitler declaration.

'Great Britain has not the least desire to fight against any nation whatsoever. But that is not a practical basis for European peace. On the contrary, if there is to be any kind of hope of genuine European appeasement, it cannot be by a bilateral agreement. It can only be reached by a conference of all the powers.'

Lastly, the leader-writer of the *Daily Telegraph* did not hide his scepticism with regard to Hitler's assurance when he asserted that he had no further territorial claims to make in Europe.

'It is impossible to forget that after the return of the Saar to the Reich, and after the reoccupation of the Rhineland, he made the same kind of promises, whose practical result has been so strongly impressed upon our minds during the present year.'

Duff Cooper resigns

These reserves and this want of satisfaction expressed by a section of the leader-writers in the British press were to find an additional justification in a resignation that was to resound not only throughout Great Britain but throughout the whole world – that of Alfred Duff Cooper, the First Lord of the Admiralty.

The reasons for this resignation were given in a letter whose traditional and (to put it in a nutshell) essentially British tone had the ultimate effect of emphasizing its severity.

My dear Prime Minister,

I find it extremely painful, at the moment of your great triumph, to be obliged to sound a discordant note. For reasons which you know and which I intend to explain to the House of Commons in due course I am profoundly distrustful of the foreign policy that the present government are pursuing and that they seem to intend to go on pursuing.

As I feel this very deeply, it seems to me that honour and straightforwardness require me to send you my resignation. I do this with great regret, because I have been very proud to hold my present office, which I valued more than any other in the state; and because I am so grateful to you for having had such confidence in me and for always having shown me so much friendship and patience.

Yours very sincerely,

Duff Cooper.

No less traditional, and no less British, was the Prime Minister's reply, which did no more than record the divorce.

My dear First Lord,

I have received your letter in which you resign your office in the government with great personal regret.

But knowing that you are sincerely convinced that the foreign policy of the present government is mistaken, I agree with you in thinking that it would not be fitting for you to remain a member of the government.

Before submitting your resignation for the approval of His Majesty the King, I should like to thank you for your work in the important office that you are leaving, and to express the conviction that differences in matters of public policy will lead to no break in our personal relations.

Sincerely yours,

N. Chamberlain.

Towards ten o'clock in the evening of October 1 Duff Cooper telephoned Georges Mandel in Paris to tell him about his decision. At first Mandel was somewhat tempted to follow his example; but in the end he came to the opinion of Paul Reynaud and Champetier de Ribes: their gesture would obviously be completely against the trend of public opinion, so not only would it initiate no sympathetic movement but it would neither be understood by the country nor approved in parliament.

Mandel was convinced of this, and later he said to Paul Reynaud,* 'A resignation is only justified when it is of some use. Ours would have been of no use at all.'

And for his part Coblentz heard him say. 'It is better to keep one's ring-side seat to serve as a witness to history.'[5]

Daladier was growing steadily more and more persuaded of the

---

* When they were both imprisoned in the Fort du Portalet (P. Reynaud).

merits of the agreement he had signed at Munich and he had now taken up his definitive attitude: he was still quite unaware of the threat of crisis that had hung over his government and at the end of the day he went, together with Champetier de Ribes, the minister of pensions, to relight the flame at the Arc de Triomphe. White barriers, huge tricolour and the army's searchlights – all the usual arrangements for July 14 were hurriedly set up. Ex-servicemen, demobilized or indeed still mobilized, in greatcoats and without belts, turned out in force to shout 'Vive Daladier!'†

As the evening came on the last news items of the day came in one after another on the Havas tickers.

Tomorrow, Sunday, October 3, the bells will be rung throughout the Reich, from 2 pm to 2.30, to mark the Evangelical Church's participation in the happenings of these last days and to give thanks for the work of peace and liberation.

Chancellor Adolf Hitler has appointed Herr Konrad Henlein commissioner of the Reich for the Sudetenland.

General Franco has sent the Führer a congratulatory telegram on the occasion of the success of his efforts, which have allowed the Sudetenland to be reunited to the Reich.

Prince Konoye has sent the Führer a telegram congratulating him upon the happy settlement of the Sudeten question.

Parliamentary sanction in London and Paris

One formality still remained for both the democracies: the ratification of the Munich agreement had to be obtained from their respective parliaments.

The debate in the House of Commons and in the House of Lords began as early as October 3 and lasted three days. Labour members, Liberals and Conservatives who sympathized with Churchill and Eden spoke one after another, and their criticisms were severe.

'The Prime Minister will presently explain in what the details of the Munich conditions differ from the Godesberg ultimatum,' said Duff Cooper bitingly. 'There are noteworthy and important differences. And it is a great triumph for the Prime Minister to have

† Cardinal Verdier was asked to have the bells of Notre Dame rung upon this occasion 'as for the armistice of 1918': he replied to this unseemly request with a firm and dignified refusal.

been able to obtain them. I spent most of Friday in trying to persuade myself that these conditions ought to satisfy me. I tried to swallow them; but they stuck in my throat.'

Attlee, following him, observed that 'France and Great Britain have suffered the greatest diplomatic defeat in their history'. And Eden asserted, 'There cannot be many among us who, however great their relief, do not feel a certain humiliation, if they really understand the decisions of Munich.'

Lastly Winston Churchill. 'We are in the midst of a disaster of the first magnitude . . . If we want to see the decadence of British and French foreign policy, today we have only to look at the facts.'

Certain of his majority, and certain too of the popular approval that had been lavished on him in Great Britain and throughout the Empire since his triumphal return from Munich,* Chamberlain listened unmoved to his critics and stood up to them bravely. 'I am not ashamed of anything!' he said, at the end of the debate.

Yet if the Prime Minister did not feel, or did not choose to feel, any shame, he does at least appear to have regretted some imprudent words – the famous phrase about 'peace for our time'.

'I hope,' he confessed, 'honourable members will not be disposed to read into words used in a moment of some emotion, after a long and exhausting day, after I had driven through miles of excited, enthusiastic, cheering people – I hope they will not read into those words more than they were intended to convey. I do indeed believe that we may yet secure peace for our time, but I never meant to suggest that we should do that by disarmament, unless we can induce others to disarm too . . . I realize that diplomacy cannot be effective unless the consciousness exists, not here alone, but elsewhere, that behind the diplomacy is the strength to give effect to it.'

The debate in the French parliament did not attain the same proportions. It nevertheless provided the occasion for Henry de Kérillis to make a speech that was in no way inferior to the strongest attacks of the British opposition.

'Let nobody come and tell us,' he cried, addressing Daladier directly, 'as some have done, that the French army condemned

---

* 'I was almost expelled from my club because I spoke against Chamberlain, who was thought of as a god at that time,' said Randolph Churchill later. (High Court of Justice, Flandin's trial, hearing of July 5, 1946.)

us to this political disaster, for I should reply that the premier knew the state of the French army, for which he has been the minister responsible for the last three years and a half, when he was continually renewing the promises that you know about before the whole world.'

But it was all over now, and the vote that ended the debate in the French Chamber brought into evidence an even greater majority than in the Commons: 535 votes against seventy-five. It was only the Communists who voted against the motion and two isolated members, Kérillis and the Socialist Jean Bouhey. On the other hand the bill for giving the government full powers won only 331 votes against seventy-eight and 203 abstentions.

Benes withdraws

Herriot proclaimed the ratification of the Munich agreement by the Chamber of Deputies at ten in the evening of October 4. The next day Paris received the news of Benes's resignation, which was announced in a broadcast message from General Syrovy.

The Czechoslovak premier began by describing the new attitudes his government would adopt.

'The government mean to apply the decisions taken by the four powers at Munich fairly. The principles of our foreign policy are clear – friendly relations with everybody and particularly with our neighbours, for if we want to live in quiet we must collaborate with them.'

Then after a long silence General Syrovy went on,

'With all the pain that can be felt by a former member of the Legion and one who has helped in the building up of this state, I carry out the most repugnant task that exists, that of announcing to you that the President of the Republic, Eduard Benes, has renounced his office. remaining even in this act a most shining example of abnegation. This decision of the president's is so painful to us that words would be only a pale reflection of what we feel.'

After this the premier himself read out the letter of the resigning president.

'I was elected,' wrote Benes, after he had spoken of 'the happenings of the last days', 'in fundamentally different conditions: I cannot forget it. The state of affairs has changed to such a degree that I myself might be an obstacle to the work of adaptation that is essential for our country in the international field; I might also stand in the way of rapidly obtaining the necessary tranquillity in the whole of the region that surrounds us, and of collaboration with our neighbours . . .

'For my part I have judged it necessary to draw the consequences from the present situation and to resign my office. This does not mean that I am thinking of abandoning the storm-tossed ship: my sole intention is to make the future development of our country and our nation easier, both at home and abroad.'

The next day Léon Blum commented upon this resignation.

'The wheel goes on turning. Eduard Benes has just resigned the presidency of the Czechoslovak Republic. For a long while he was the incarnation of the country in its democratic aspirations and its spirit of national unity. Now Czechoslovakia's national unity is broken and the days of democracy there are numbered. For the last five months he personified it in its determination to withstand Hitlerite penetration. Now desertions have rendered this determination powerless.

'Eduard Benes no longer represented anything in his country but a defeat, a cause for mourning, something in the past.

'Added to all this, the Führer-Chancellor's hatred for him has been expressed with too public a violence for him to be able to be unaware of it, and he sacrifices himself again for the peacefulness of his country.'

And Léon Blum added these bitterly sad words,

'I knew him for twenty years. I do not know whether he will still allow me to call him my friend.'[6]

The wheel went on turning indeed, and it was not Benes's going that would stop it. Not content with being able to offer Hitler the resignation of the man the Führer hated more than any other man on earth, Syrovy rearranged his government and gave the ministry of foreign affairs to Chvalkovsky. When Blondel, the French chargé d'affaires in Rome, where Chvalkovsky had been minister, heard of this promotion, he remembered a shameless remark uttered by Chvalkovsky in his presence. 'Do not worry about us . . . we shall very easily turn into the Germans' servants again.'[7]

As far as he personally was concerned, it was something that had already been done. But one would have had to be very simple to suppose that this sudden docility was going to earn Czechoslovakia preferential treatment.

Yet Chvalkovsky very quickly showed his new masters just how far his servility could go.* Many Czechs thought they could see an intrigue between Chvalkovsky and Osusky, the Czechoslovak minister in Paris and a notorious opponent of Benes, in Osusky's request for the setting up of a committee of inquiry 'to find those responsible for Czechoslovakia's misfortunes'. Their suspicions were aroused because the news was published shortly after Osusky and Chvalkovsky had met in Prague.†

At the same time the senator Matousek drew up the same request, appending to it a questionnaire which was obviously inspired by Chvalkovsky and Osusky, if not written by them, and which implicated Benes at every turn. Most of the questions, furthermore, referred to the warnings vainly given to the head of state by the Czechoslovak ministers in Rome and Paris – that is to say by Chvalkovsky and Osusky.

The first cracks

And now, while in Prague Benes's enemies were thus at the same time settling old scores and giving pledges to the Germans, the Czechoslovak state began to fall apart, as though the presence of Benes in the Hradschin Castle had up until then been the sole link that maintained an apparent cohesion between elements that were clearly not adapted for life together.

The resignation of the head of the Czechoslovak state was made public on October 5. A few hours later all the leaders of the Slovak parties met at Tsilina, urgently summoned by Mgr Tiso, the vice-president of the Populist party. In his invitation Mgr Tiso said that 'the Slovak nation was claiming for itself the right of determining its

---

* Chvalkovsky, received by Hitler on January 21, 1939, pushed sycophancy to the point of 'earnestly begging the Führer to address a kind word to the Czech nation from time to time', adding 'that might work miracles'. (Nuremberg, hearing of February 9, 1946.)

† See Appendix Six for further details about this inquiry.

own fate'. The various tendencies in Slovak nationalism very quickly agreed to profit by the situation: they merged with the Populists and voted in favour of a manifesto in which, having stated that 'the Munich agreement had profoundly altered political and state relations in central Europe', the Slovaks demanded that 'the right of nations to self-determination' should apply to them, and insisted that 'governmental and executive power in Slovakia should be placed in the hands of a Slovak government without delay'.

Mgr Tiso, chosen president of this government, informed Prague of these decisions the same evening; and as early as October 7, with the consent of General Syrovy, the autonomous state of Slovakia came into existence. In addition to Mgr Tiso there were four ministers in the Slovak government, Durcansky, Cernak, Teplansky and Lichner, the last two being former members of parliament belonging to Hodza's Agrarian party.

The Slovak example was at once followed by the Ruthenians, who met at Uzhorod on October 8. They too easily persuaded Syrovy to grant autonomy to the Carpathian Ukraine.*

The international commission at work

As for the ambassadors of the four powers who, together with the Czechoslovak minister, made up the international commission in Berlin provided for in the Munich agreement, they completed the 'work' of the Big Four in a few days.

With a certain ingenuity Nevile Henderson sums up the labours of this branch of the 'Butchers' Club'.

'The Munich protocols were vaguely worded, and the first [major crisis] arose out of the question as to the extent of the areas to be handed over without plebiscite to Germany, and as to the meaning of the fifty-per-cent-majority provision. The German attitude towards the latter was, as it happens, in accordance with the text of the Munich Agreement and the Anglo-French proposal which had preceded it, but the Czechs refused to accept it. Hitler retorted with an ultimatum, demanding occupation up to the language line drawn in the Austrian maps of 1910. There was no

* On November 18 the Prague parliament, by 144 votes against twenty-five (the Czech Communists), ratified the transformation of the Czechoslovak Republic into a federal state made up of three member-states.

map showing the racial areas between that year and 1923, by which time the pre-war position had been considerably modified. My French and Italian colleagues, on direct instructions from their Governments, both accepted the German standpoint, and, when they came to see me at the British Embassy to tell me so, I was left to decide whether to do so also or to say that I could not do so without prior reference to His Majesty's Government. I decided on the former course mainly because I hoped thereby, firstly, to avoid plebiscites, secondly, to pin the Germans down to a line of their own choosing, which they would find it difficult to modify again to their own renewed advantage, and thirdly, because the German contention was actually, in my opinion, the better founded of the two theses.'

And the British ambassador, delighted with having got out of it so well, concludes,

'The acceptance of the 1910 boundary rendered plebiscites superfluous, and by October 10 direct co-operation and negotiation between Czechs and Germans were sufficiently advanced for the meetings of the political section of the International Commission to be adjourned *sine die*. Act II was over.'

What with the concessions thus made by the international commission (Hitler having issued an ultimatum) and the additional satisfactions obtained by the Germans in their 'direct negotiations' with the Czechoslovaks, the settlement that followed the Munich agreement amounted to the transfer of eleven thousand square miles of territory to Germany; and in these zones thus attached to the Reich without plebiscite there lived *800,000 Czechs*,* in addition to the 2,800,000 Sudeten Germans.

Of course, the entirety of the system of fortifications, whose importance had so rightly been emphasized by the French general staff, was included in the territory ceded to Germany.†

And yet in spite of what Henderson says the second act was not yet over: Hungary had not had her share. She had nevertheless asked for it, and that in a far more subtle manner than Poland; for

* See map 4, p 290.
† Appendix V gives the text of an unpublished letter dated October 8, 1938, from the Czechoslovak minister Neczas to O. Rosenfeld: it concerns the work of the international commission.

having found that friendly negotiations did not answer, the Hungarians submitted themselves to the discretion of the great powers. Not the four of Munich, but the only really great powers, Germany and Italy. It was this double arbitration that Hungary proposed to Czechoslovakia – an arbitration that the Prague government were already in no condition to refuse.

Here once more was an open violation of the Munich agreement. But above all it must be seen as a confession of powerlessness, an abdication.

On November 2, at the Belvedere Palace in Vienna, Prince Eugene's summer residence, Ribbentrop and Ciano gave their decision. Although it gave the Hungarians the most ample satisfaction, by poetic justice this was at the cost of the Slovaks and the Ruthenians, who had just turned the misfortunes of the Czechs to their advantage. Furthermore, the English and French would have been ill-placed to argue against the arbitration of Vienna (it must be added that they seemed to have no desire to do so), for the decision of the German and Italian foreign ministers was based upon the ethnographic maps of 1910 – the same as those whose use had been agreed to by the British and French ambassadors at the Berlin commission.

According to the terms of the judgment of Ciano and Ribbentrop 3,981 square miles of territory and 853,670 inhabitants were ceded to Hungary by Slovakia; and in this last number there were 272,145 Slovaks. As for the Subcarpathian Ukraine, 625 square miles were lopped off it; and of the 190,768 people who lived there by no means all were Magyars, either.*

Mgr Tiso was present in Vienna when the two foreign ministers made their decision known: he did not conceal his bitterness. 'We can only bow our heads,' he said, 'and go back to our work. But no one can prevent us from declaring to the world that the Slovak nation has just been the victim of a great injustice.'[8]

But Ribbentrop was not to be moved. 'Munich,' he replied, 'has saved Slovakia from the catastrophe of total dismemberment.'[9]

Besides, the Germans pretended to believe that the Vienna arbitration was only a compromise. In his official comments on German foreign policy Freytagh-Loringhoven defended this point of view.

'Although this decision did not fail to cause regret in some

* See map 4, p. 290.

quarters, the two parties accepted it. The Hungarians complained that they were not given the town of Pressburg (Bratislava), while the Slovaks and the Ukrainians bitterly felt the loss of Kassa (Kaschau) and Ungvar (Uzhorod) respectively. Here, *mutatis mutandis*, we once more come across the old saying in jurisprudence, which states that any judgment can only satisfy fifty per cent of the parties. This logical necessity can never be made to vanish . . .

'Although not all wishes were fulfilled, it nevertheless cannot be denied that the Vienna solution answered the most stringent requirements of justice.'[10]

Coming after Munich, after the Polish violence, after the autonomy granted to the Slovaks and Ruthenians and after the surrender of the French and British on the Berlin international commission, the 'Vienna solution' completed the dismemberment of Czechoslovakia.

To be sure, the republic of Masaryk and Benes had been handicapped by the diversity of its ethnic elements. Yet no one denied the value of this balanced construction in the economic field; for its prosperity was unequalled in central Europe. Nor could anyone doubt the importance of its fortifications or the quality of its army.

From this time on nothing of all this remained except a caricature – an illusory federal government, divided between member-states which looked upon autonomy merely as a stage towards independence; an economy that was henceforward dependent upon powerful neighbours; a system of fortifications handed over unharmed to the aggressor against whom it had been built; a hurriedly demobilized army.

In order to make the powerlessness of this ghost-state even greater and to cut short any attempt at national revival, it still remained to change all the political figures. A further step in this direction was made on November 30, when Dr Emile Hacha, a member of the supreme court, was elected to succeed Benes by 272 votes out of 312. Syrovy was at once replaced by Beran at the head of the government, though he kept the ministry of defence; Chvalkovsky, of course, remained foreign minister.

This time the second act was over indeed.

The Bonnet-Ribbentrop agreement

It was to be followed by the short entr'acte during which Georges Bonnet won a 'diplomatic success' all by himself, without needing

Daladier's help this time – a success in every respect comparable to that won by Chamberlain at Munich on September 30.

In Paris, from as early as the day after the conference the circles that favoured not only peace at any price but also and above all improvement in relations, 'collaboration'* with Nazi Germany, undertook a campaign to carry the Munich policy on to its logical completion and consequences – that is to say, that a Franco-German agreement should appear as the counterpart to the Hitler-Chamberlain declaration.

In addition to and outside her official diplomatic representatives, Germany had semi-official agents in France; and at the head of these there was a young and still comparatively unknown German, Otto Abetz, whom Jean Luchaire and Bertrand de Jouvenal introduced to ministers and influential politicians.

'After the Munich conference,' said Jean Luchaire at a later date, 'M Georges Bonnet asked me to keep in contact with Abetz for semi-official soundings as to the reactions of M von Ribbentrop, and even of Chancellor Hitler.'†

Abetz had funds at his disposal and he spread them about with an open hand: he managed to secure some assistance, particularly in the newspaper world.

Fernand de Brinon's *Comité France-Allemagne* was also in a position to hand out envelopes, or simply invitations to go to Germany with all expenses paid.

All these agents, who were working in direct and permanent liaison with the Wilhelmstrasse, found an unusually favourable climate in France after Munich. From Georges Bonnet to Paul Faure, by way of Monzie, Bergeret and Montigny, all these leaders of the 'peace party' knew, since Daladier's return, that they could rely upon the support of the immense majority of the people. They also knew since the parliamentary vote on the Munich agreement that the reaction of public opinion had for the time being neutralized all the opponents of the 'appeasement' policy, with the exception of the Communists.

* This is no anachronism; the word was used currently as early as 1938 by those who advocated a Franco-German rapprochement.

† During the trial that ended in Jean Luchaire's being condemned to death, the president of the court, Ledoux, stated among other things, 'In 1938 your magazine *Notre Temps* became somewhat *persona grata* at the Quai d'Orsay with M Georges Bonnet, then foreign minister. The Munich crisis arose. You supported the policy of this foreign minister who then paid you a subsidy of twenty thousand francs a month.' (Hearing of January 21, 1946.)

It was therefore a particularly well chosen moment to make a spectacular improvement of relations with Hitler's Germany go down with the France of the Front Populaire.

Furthermore it was the Führer himself who particularly wished that the merit of this step in favour of peace should be attributed to him. He made the first move on October 17, when he received François-Poncet, who was taking his leave, at his Obersalzburg eagle's nest. The ambassador at once sent an account of his démarche ? to the Quai d'Orsay.

> 'As regards the hypothesis of a written recognition of their respective frontiers by France and Germany and of an undertaking that there should be reciprocal consultations in any event affecting the relations of the two countries, he (Hitler) states that he is ready to agree immediately; and fundamentally it is this that attracts him most.'

For a short while it was thought that the murder of Ernst von Rath, a third secretary in the German embassy in Paris, by the young Jewish refugee Herschel Grynszpan would disturb Franco-German relations and compromise the negotiations that were going on.

But this was not the case. Indeed, the murder of Ernst von Rath was too useful to Hitler and the Nazis for them to feel very angry with the country in which the crime had chanced to take place. For the murder of the third secretary (who, it should be said in passing, was anti-Nazi and opposed to anti-Semitism) served as a pretext for the most appalling pogrom ever begun by the Nazis. Not only in Germany itself but in Austria and all the districts that had recently come under the control of the Reich, the night of November 10–11 saw the massacre of thousands of Jews, the destruction of shops, the pillaging and burning of houses.

The coolness that appeared in Franco-German relations arose not from the fact that a German diplomat had been murdered in the heart of Paris but because this brutal unleashing of anti-Jewish fury caused the French leaders to slow down the negotiations.

Indeed, when Georges Bonnet triumphantly brought the cabinet the text of the Franco-German declarations on November 23 and announced that Ribbentrop would presently come to Paris for the exchange of signatures, his enthusiasm was not shared by many there. Jean Zay, the minister of education, summarized the cabinet debate in his diary.

'Several ministers regretted the untimeliness of this declaration, in view of Germany's isolation since the anti-Semitic outburst. Daladier pointed out that the negotiations had begun well before that and regretted that it had not been made public earlier.

'Ribbentrop's coming to Paris in the next few days was generally opposed, and the premier certainly seemed to be of this opinion: Bonnet urged his point.

'I observed that it was easy to see that it was very much in Germany's interest to have herself rehabilitated by France. But were we no longer free? We were going to cause the most lamentable effect in England and America.* There would be great feeling among the people in France. The journey should be put off.

'Bonnet said that Germany's interests were not concerned and that she was consenting to the agreement solely to please us.

'Campinchi was afraid of demonstrations if Ribbentrop were to come to Paris. Monzie suggested Strasburg.

'I asked whether the agreement could not be signed by the ambassador. Mandel called for the postponement of the journey. So did Reynaud. Campinchi asked whether Ribbentrop would be received in London. As Daladier pointed out in the end we were all in agreement on the text. As for the journey it was agreed that Bonnet should receive the ambassador and tell him frankly that it could only be thought of in a calmer atmosphere.'†

Georges Bonnet does not agree with this, however.

'This account,' he says, 'is based upon imperfect recollection; this is proved by diplomatic documents and the papers of the time. In the first place it was impossible to approve the Franco-German declaration and refuse to let the German minister come and sign it. Daladier never did take up this attitude, which would have been ridiculous. Furthermore it was he who told the English

---

* After the anti-Semitic violence of November the United States ambassador in Berlin was recalled to Washington.

† The *Carnets secrets de Jean Zay* were published in 1942 by Les Editions de France. They were 'issued with comments by Philippe Henriot'. Jean Zay for his part was then in prison – a prison that he was to leave only to be murdered. Nevertheless he did not disavow these documents, which had been stolen from him. 'There is not a line I regret,' he wrote in his prison (in *Souvenirs et solitude*) on April 28, 1941, when 'selections' from his notebooks were appearing in *Gringoire*. Jean Zay merely observes that Philippe Henriot and his friends had 'cut, shuffled out of sight, summarized ... everything that might be awkward for the Hitlerite doctrines.' What is left is therefore all the more convincing.

ministers, they being then in Paris, of Ribbentrop's coming arrival, the day after the cabinet, on November 24.[11] In the second place it was not at the last moment that Ribbentrop's visit was publicly announced, since *Le Temps* gave the news of it as early as November 26 and 27; and it was in all the other papers, which even gave the hour-by-hour programme of his stay in Paris, on December 2.'

It must be said that Georges Bonnet's denial in no way proves that the debate in the cabinet did not follow the course that Jean Zay describes in his diary, which he filled in every day. It merely shows (and the facts confirm it) that whatever reservations may have been expressed at the cabinet meeting, the foreign minister did not swerve from the path he had set himself, and the invitation, which in any case had perhaps already been sent, was not cancelled.

So on December 6 Paris saw the arrival of Joachim von Ribbentrop. His journey was something of a disappointment for the France-Allemagne propagandists. Indeed, not only did the German foreign minister's car travel through a deserted Paris that morning, but in the evening there were people who did not come to the reception given at the German embassy in the rue de Lille – absences that were remarked upon.

As to the substance of the diplomatic talks before or after the official signing ceremony in the salon de l'Horloge, there are once more two opposing versions.

According to the interpreter Schmidt, who of course travelled with Ribbentrop, the two ministers had an interview in his presence 'in another room in the foreign ministry' *after the signature of the declaration*. There, says Schmidt,[12] 'Bonnet, who a little while before had said that France's intentions were to devote herself to the development of her colonial empire, stated at one point that she had shown her lack of further interest in the east at the Munich conference.'

On his side Ribbentrop later wrote Bonnet[13] a personal letter in which he called these talks to mind and said, 'On this occasion I explicitly observed that eastern Europe was a German sphere of interest and upon this you on your side emphasized that a radical change had come about in France's attitude towards the problems of eastern Europe since the Munich conference.'

By way of reconciling the two, Schmidt 'interprets' both Bonnet's words about 'lack of further interest in the east' and the meaning that Ribbentrop gave them. 'Ribbentrop,' he says, 'saw a pointer to France's future attitude towards Poland in Bonnet's remark, which, when all is taken into account, only really concerned Czechoslovakia; and Ribbentrop felt this to be the case all the more since Bonnet was urging that a Polish-German agreement on Danzig and the corridor should be sought.'

But these explanations do not satisfy Bonnet, who not only strongly denies ever having said that France had no further interest in the east but also asserts that Ribbentrop 'did not in any shape or form ask for a free hand in the east, any more than Hitler had required it from François-Poncet during the earlier talks.'

He goes much farther, adding, 'It is . . . completely untrue that the interpreter Schmidt was present at our conversation* . . . M Schmidt was never brought into my office at any time whatever.'

So if the matter is looked into a little more closely it appears

(1) that Georges Bonnet situates his interview with Ribbentrop *in his office* and *before the official signing of the Franco-German declaration,*

(2) that Schmidt, far from ever having claimed that he went into the French foreign minister's office, speaks of a conversation at which he was present and which took place *after* the signature, *in a reception-room* at the Quai d'Orsay.

Were there, as it has been said, two conversations that day, one before the signature and the other after, one in the minister's office and the other in a reception-room?

Bonnet refers to the testimony of Alexis Léger, who for his part speaks of only one conversation – yet without asserting that there was only one.

> 'During the interview in question,' he says, 'I never heard the foreign minister assert or in any way give it to be understood that France might be expected to have the inclinations that the German minister subsequently put forward. On this point I never had the impression that there was the slightest danger of misunderstanding . . . M Georges Bonnet's *Mémoires* correspond, as to the substance, to all that I remember of the conversation at which I was present.'

After all, the text of the declaration that was signed on December 6

---

* Yet although Schmidt is aware of Georges Bonnet's denial he holds to what he has said. 'These words', he writes, 'were indeed said, although they have been disputed on the French side.'

clearly takes into account the obligations contracted by France with regard to 'third powers' in clause three.

1 The French government and the German government fully share the conviction that peaceful and neighbourly relations between France and Germany constitute one of the prime elements in the consolidation of the European situation and the mainten- ance of general peace. The two governments will therefore use all their endeavours to ensure that the relations between their countries develop in this direction.

2 The two governments observe that there is no question of a territorial nature still unsettled between their countries and they solemnly recognize as definitive the frontier between their countries as it stands at present.

3 The two governments are determined, subject to their special relations with third powers, to remain in contact on all questions concerning their two countries and to consult one another should the subsequent development of these questions run the risk of leading to international difficulties.

The last act

The Franco-German interlude was over. The curtain (to borrow Sir Nevile Henderson's theatrical expression) might now rise on the third act, which, as far as the Czechoslovak crisis was concerned, was the last.

The year 1938 came to an end with the first striking displays of the new Czechoslovak government's meekness in the face of Hitler's demands.

On December 16 General Faucher left Czechoslovakia.*

On December 23 a decree authorized the Czechoslovak govern- ment to order the dissolution of political parties. And on the twenty- eighth this decree was first put into application: the Czechoslovak Communist party was dissolved.

On January 30, 1939, addressing the Reichstag, Hitler openly took pride in having managed the Czechoslovak affair as he chose. Raising the veil (but only partly) on Operation Green he said, 'In January 1938 I took the final decision to win the right of self-determination for the six and a half million Germans of Austria in one way or

* The French military mission that he headed ceased to exist on December 31.

another . . . On May 28 last I gave the order to prepare for military action against Czechoslovakia, with October 2 as the final date.'

On the other hand the Führer took care not to say that the military preparations for the next phase, which still concerned the wretched Czechoslovakia, were already in motion.

A week after Munich he had questioned the OKW upon the means required 'to break all Czech resistance in Moravia and Bohemia', and on October 21 he sent his army chief this ultra-secret directive.

'It must at any time be possible to crush what remains of Czechoslovakia in the event of her adopting a hostile policy with regard to Germany.

'The preparations that the armed forces are to make for this eventuality will have considerably less scope than those for Operation Green; yet they must be far more exact, since the usual mobilization measures have been done away with. Organization, order of battle and the state of preparedness of the units intended for these operations must all be arranged in peace-time for a surprise-attack, so as to deprive Czechoslovakia of any possibility of organized resistance. The operations' objectives will be the rapid occupation of Bohemia and Moravia, after which Slovakia will be detached from the rest of the country.'

On December 17 Keitel in his turn distributed a 'supplement to the directive of October 21'.

'Top Secret.

'With reference to the "liquidation of the rump-state of Czechoslovakia" the Führer has given the following orders:

'The operation is to be prepared on the assumption that our troops will encounter practically no resistance.

'With regard to foreign opinion, the operation must have the obvious appearance of a peaceful action and in no way that of a warlike undertaking.

'The operation must therefore be carried out *solely* with peacetime effectives, without their having been strengthened by mobilization.'

So everything was ready for the 'liquidation of the rump-state', although her new frontiers had been guaranteed by France and Britain at Munich.

And now, on February 8, London and Paris suddenly began to worry about the question that had been raised at Munich – that of the German and Italian guarantee. It is not fair to say* that neither the British nor the French had troubled about it for the past four months. Georges Bonnet had indeed raised the point at the time of Ribbentrop's visit to Paris on December 6, and had urged that the matter should be dealt with, though without any result, it is true.

On February 8, therefore, a joint 'verbal note' was delivered to Ribbentrop by the two ambassadors.

'According to the terms of Annex 1 of the agreement signed at Munich on September 29, 1938, the German and Italian governments stated that they were prepared to associate themselves with an international guarantee of the new boundaries of the Czechoslovak state against any unprovoked aggression, when the question of the Polish and Hungarian minorities in Czechoslovakia should have been settled.

'Referring to this declaration and to the statements recently made in Rome by M Mussolini to the British Prime Minister as to the preliminary conditions that the Italian government, as far as they were concerned, would think necessary before considering the grant of this guarantee, the French government, anxious to give effect to all the provisions of the Munich agreement, would be very happy to learn the views of the government of the Reich on the question of the guarantee alluded to in the above agreement.

'The French ambassador would be grateful if the foreign ministry of the Reich would be so kind as to put him in a position to satisfy the wishes that his government has thus expressed as soon as possible.'

Three weeks were to go by before a reply reached London and Paris from the Wilhelmstrasse. Three weeks during which Hitler allowed the situation in Czechoslovakia 'to go bad'. Furthermore the 'rot' was to be attributed entirely to the activities of the Nazi agents in Slovakia and Ruthenia, who set themselves to stimulate and increase the separatist movements in order to produce a crisis inside the country within a short period that should justify German intervention.

However on March 2 Coulondre, François-Poncet's successor at

* As W. L. Shirer does.

349

the French embassy in Berlin, was able to send on to Paris a German note dated February 28. This note had in fact been drafted by Hitler personally. It recalled that the German and Italian guarantee could only be given when Czechoslovakia's relations with all her neighbours should have been rendered normal; it questioned whether this was the case, and even pretended to believe that the Vienna arbitration was not yet accepted by those concerned. But the most important passage – most important because in fact it required the French and English not to interfere in that part of Europe any longer – was this: 'The German government are fully sensible that in the last analysis the general development of this part of Europe primarily belongs to the sphere of the Reich's most essential interest, and that not only from the historical but also from the geographical and above all economic point of view.'

As Coulondre pointed out, 'Decoded, this message means that the Western powers no longer have any right to look in the direction of central Europe.' And the ambassador concluded, 'At first sight this document is therefore far from reassuring as to the immediate views of Nazi policy with regard to Czechoslovakia.'[14]

Although he was so trustful of the Germans' word and so anxious to say or do nothing that might endanger the good relations between Britain and the anti-Bolshevik Germany, even Henderson displayed a certain uneasiness.

'My first indication of imminent trouble was at the annual banquet which Hitler gave to the diplomatic corps, somewhat later than usual, on March 1st. After dinner Hitler used to remain standing in the drawing-room, and would speak for some five or ten minutes in turn to each of the Heads of Missions in the order of their precedence. The apparent friendliness which he had shown at the motor exhibition* was notably absent at this dinner. At the exhibition he had shaken me by the hand not once, but three times. On this occasion he carefully avoided looking me in the face when he was speaking to me: he kept his eyes fixed over my right shoulder and confined his remarks to general subjects, while stressing the point that it was not Britain's business to interfere with Germany in Central Europe.'[15]

In fact during this first fortnight in March events were to follow one another in very rapid succession. And paradoxically it was the Prague

* Less than a fortnight earlier.

government that helped to increase the speed of the machine that was to crush them.

On March 9, with the intention of putting an end to separatist intrigues, Hacha decided upon the dissolution of the Slovak government and ordered the arrest of its head, Mgr Tiso. But with no great difficulty the latter managed to 'escape' from the monastery in which he had been placed under house-arrest.

For Hitler this was the moment for action. On March 11, the anniversary of the Anschluss, while Prague was appointing Karol Sidor as the new head of the Slovak government, the Wehrmacht was given orders to get ready to carry out the directive of October 21.

On March 13, leaving Karol Sidor at grips with Seyss-Inquart and the gauleiter Bürkel, who had come 'as neighbours' from Austria to summon the new Slovak government to proclaim its independence, Mgr Tiso took the train for Vienna, and at Vienna the plane for Berlin. The next day he returned to Bratislava with the title of prime minister, the bearer of a declaration of independence that was at once accepted by the Slovak parliament.

Hitler, by way of exactly reproducing the setting that had succeeded so well the year before, had also given Tiso a telegram that he was to send as soon as he was in office 'informing the Führer of Slovak independence' and asking for the protection of the German army.

On the same day, Tuesday, March 14, Ruthenia too proclaimed her independence.*

At twenty to eleven that night a special train reached the Anhalt station in Berlin: Hacha and Chvalkovsky were coming to beg for the Führer's 'protection'.

The last scene

Berlin, March 15, a quarter past one in the morning.

Passing between the double row of SS paying the compliment due to a head of state, 'a little old man with sad eyes and his face red with emotion' arrived at the new Chancellery, which had scarcely yet been finished. It was Dr Hacha; and behind him came his minister, Chvalkovsky, who was a little man too, dark-complexioned, with a

---

* But the 'Independent Republic of the Subcarpathian Ukraine' asked for the protection of the Germany army in vain. Hitler had already made a present of this territory to Hungary, and the Regent Horthy had warmly thanked him on March 13. At dawn on the fifteenth the Hungarian army took possession of the region, simply annexing it.

Czech accent that amused the German diplomats and irritated Hitler.

The Führer received his two late-coming visitors in his new study, which Schmidt describes with his usual exactness.

'It was a high room with brown panelling. Hitler's desk stood at one of its ends. In the opposite corner an area had been arranged for deep armchairs and sofas standing in a square about a low round table. In front of the window there was a long table which nevertheless gave no impression of heaviness. The middle of the room was open, with a very thick carpet – this was brown too. The only light came from a few bronze standard-lamps which because of the panelling and the dark carpet only gave a hint of the pictures and the little bust of Frederick the Great that stood on the table: it was a fit setting for the tragic scenes that took place there that night.'

Tragic scenes: that indeed was the only word to use. Several characters appeared on the stage – Göring, Ribbentrop, Schmidt, Hacha, Chvalkovsky, Dr Morell – but as the Wilhelmstrasse interpreter points out there was only one real actor: Hitler.

At the very beginning, without giving Hacha time for a single word, the Führer broke into an impassioned monologue, rehearsing the list of his 'complaints' against Czechoslovakia, as though he had Benes and Krofta in front of him rather than Hacha and Chvalkovsky. However Hitler did acknowledge that Germany was not displeased with the new head of the Czechoslovak state; she had confidence in his good faith. And it was because Hacha, in spite of his good faith, had not been able to root 'the Benes spirit' out of his country that Germany had to intervene.

'It is necessary for the security of the Reich,' ended Hitler, 'that Germany should extend her protection over what remains of Czechoslovakia, in order to see that her rights are respected there.'

'Hacha and Chvalkovsky,' says Schmidt, 'sat in their chairs as though they were turned to stone. Only their eyes remained alive. It must have been an extraordinary shock for them to learn from Hitler's mouth that the existence of their country was coming to an end.* They had left Prague with the hope of being able to

* No doubt Hacha and Chvalkovsky had little contact with public opinion in their country, for according to the French minister, Lacroix, 'all the Czechoslovaks knew that Hitler would enter Prague on March 15'. (Parliamentary commission of inquiry, 1933–45, session of March 16, 1948.)

negotiate. At the Anhalt station, even before Hacha had reviewed the guard of 'honour' under a sudden flurry of snow, Mastny, the Czech ambassador in Berlin, had told him that German troops had already crossed the Czech frontier at Ostrav!'

During Hitler's diatribe Hacha was overcome by a kind of numbness, an amazement; but coming out of it at last he tried to plead his cause. He did so in the most humiliating, the most abject manner possible. He abandoned all dignity, and hoping to mollify by a display of servility, the head of the 'rump-state' of Czechoslovakia grovelled at the Führer's feet.

'Not only have I never had anything to do with politics, as you know, but I never had any liking for Benes or Masaryk: I always found their government repugnant . . . I am entirely convinced that Czechoslovakia's fate is in the hands of Germany and her Führer. Her safety depends on this. But it is impossible that you should not understand that we want to exist as a nation . . . I know very well that in Czechoslovakia there are still supporters of the Benes régime, but give us time and we shall put a stop to them – we shall reduce them to silence . . .'

It was wasted effort: the Führer had taken his decision and dismal complaints could do nothing to alter it. Hitler merely replied with a few curt remarks, pointing out the kind of destruction that was waiting for Czechoslovakia if she did not yield voluntarily.

'At six in the morning my troops will thrust into Czechoslovakia from all sides at once. The Luftwaffe will occupy the airfields. If we meet with resistance we shall crush everything that lies before us, and at the end of two days the Czech army will have ceased to exist . . . I am almost ashamed to say so, but for every Czech battalion there is a German division . . . Six in the morning . . . the hours are fleeting by. I advise you now to withdraw with your foreign minister so that you can decide between you what you are to do.'

'What is the use?' faltered Hacha. 'It would be madness to resist . . . But between two and six in the morning I cannot possibly send orders to the whole Czech nation! Unless there is an interval . . .'

'The orders have been given; the machine is on the move;

nothing can stop it now,' interrupted Hitler. 'Try to telephone Prague.'

Having reduced the Czechs to this state Hitler left them to Göring and Ribbentrop, who pitilessly told them of the fate of Prague, which could be wiped out in a few hours by hundreds of bombers.

Meanwhile Schmidt was vainly trying to get Prague on the telephone. Suddenly a door opened on to the corridor and he heard Göring calling for Dr Morell, the charlatan who was Hitler's private physician: Hacha had been taken ill.

'If something really happens to Hacha,' thought Schmidt, still struggling for his line, 'tomorrow the whole world will say that he was killed in the Chancellery tonight.'[16]

But Morell's injections did wonders, and when at last Prague was on the line Hacha was in a state to make himself understood.

At five to four in the morning everything was over. The Czechoslovaks were brought into Hitler's study once more and he handed them an already prepared text that they had to sign without changing a single word.

'At their request the Führer received Dr Hacha, President of Czechoslovakia, and Dr Chvalkovsky, the Czechoslovak foreign minister, in Berlin today, in the presence of Herr von Ribbentrop, the Reich foreign minister.

'During this meeting ... there was a very frank examination of the exceedingly grave situation that has developed in the course of the last weeks in what was hitherto the territory of the Czechoslovak state. Both sides agreed in declaring that the goal of all their efforts must be to preserve calm, order and peace in this part of central Europe. The President of Czechoslovakia declared that in order to attain this end and reach a final pacification he confidently placed the fate of the Czech nation and its country in the hands of the Führer of the German Reich. The Führer accepted and stated that he should take the Czech nation under the protection of the Reich, at the same time allowing it to follow the autonomous evolution of its national life, in accordance with its own character.'

Two hours later German troops invaded Bohemia and Moravia without meeting resistance, and that night, having made a conqueror's entry into Prague and having gone through the town in his open Mercedes (the same that had been used in Vienna a year before), Hitler slept in the Hradschin Castle, in Benes's bed.

'Czechoslovakia has ceased to exist.' These were the words Hitler used in his triumphant proclamation to the German people before he left Berlin.

As for the Munich 'peace', the 'peace for our time', who thought about that any more?

Chamberlain was the first to make an official statement: referring to the proclamation of Slovak independence on March 15 he said, 'This proclamation puts an end, by internal dissolution, to the existence of the state whose boundaries we guaranteed. His Majesty's government therefore no longer consider themselves bound by this obligation.'

Under the pressure of public opinion the Prime Minister had to retract this a few days later, and on March 17 at Birmingham he spoke of aggression, defiance . . .

In Paris, on the other hand, Bonnet himself denounced the 'flagrant violation of the Munich agreement' from the first day and 'refused to recognize the legitimacy of the new situation that the Reich's action had created in Czechoslovakia.'*

But whether the reactions were spontaneous or slow in coming and whether or not Coulondre made his representations in an energetic manner and Henderson with a conniving want of zeal, in either case it was only a question of formal protest. For paradoxically it was henceforward only those who had been opposed to the policy of Munich who insisted that the September agreement should be respected.

Léon Blum analysed this paradox in a subtle and undeniable argument.

'So what is a "man of Munich" today? Taking these present happenings into consideration, what is the meaning of this term –

* 'I no longer had any reason for staying at my post,' said the French minister, Lacroix, at a later date. 'In the end I decided to play the part of a sort of consul, by trying to protect the French residents in Prague. These were to be repatriated, and I entered into contact with the Germans to obtain the necessary exit visas.

'The German civil servant who was acting as foreign minister thereupon asked me what I intended to do with the Czechs who had taken refuge in the legation. I answered that if he would agree to give them exit visas I should send them to France at once. On the pretext of making sure that there were no people wanted by the Czechoslovak police for criminal offences among them, he asked to know their names. I of course refused to give them.'

one which, by the way, I do not use, for I dislike it. By definition the "man of Munich" is he who approves of the Munich agreement, who at least stands up for it and justifies it, and who thinks its execution favourable to France's interests. It cannot mean anything else. In this present moment of time, therefore, the genuine "man of Munich" would be the man who insists upon the fulfilment of the four powers' guarantee to preserve the integrity of the new Czechoslovak state, who reminds Germany and Italy of their undertakings, and who at least calls upon Great Britain and France to honour theirs. For Great Britain and France duly took upon themselves obligations, and short of hiding behind a most pitiful quibble – which in any case would deprive treaties of mutual assistance and guarantee of all meaning – an ultimatum based upon the threat of force and supported by the display of force amounts to unprovoked aggression. But everyone has the impression that if the question were put to him in this form the "man of Munich" would on the contrary at once become "anti-Munich", whereas on the other hand it would be the uncompromising opponents of Munich that would today be found to be in favour of calling for the execution of the agreement.'[17]

But it was already too late to call for the carrying out of the Munich agreement: the time to do that was when it was first violated, as early as the Polish ultimatum of September 30.

On March 15, while the heavy boots of the Wehrmacht soldiers were thumping in the streets of Prague and the windows of the Hradschin Castle rattling as the Panzers went by, Munich was already no more than a memory.

The balance-sheet

The international obligations · The fifth column · The campaign against Czechoslovakia · Hitler's word · 'A free hand in the East' · The 'realists' · The Russian attitude · The refusal of military co-operation · The relative strength in the East · . . . and in the West · The 'respite'

So between the Anschluss and Hitler's entry into Prague, between Göring's 'word of honour' given one festive evening and the liquidation of the Czechoslovak state, only one year elapsed.

These twelve months from March 1938 to March 1939 were divided with singular precision into two equal periods of time. And the dividing mark was 'that day', September 29, which came six months after the Anschluss and preceded Hitler's annexation of the whole of Czechoslovakia by the same time. Of this whole period, rich in sudden dramatic changes, it was rightly the Munich conference that remained the most characteristic moment in the minds of those who lived through it: henceforward 1938 was 'the year of Munich' for history. Still more, the Munich conference very soon became one of those comparatively few events which not only stand as landmarks in history but which also take on an exemplary meaning. The word, the name Munich is loaded with a strongly pejorative significance. Since the overwhelming but quickly forgotten popular consent of September 30, how many times has one not heard people dreading or denouncing 'another Munich'?

This 'another Munich' is of the same nature as 'another Sedan' or 'a diplomatic Dien-Bien-Phu' – the expression evokes an image and there is no need for a long explanation. In the same way the description 'man of Munich' which so rightly shocked Léon Blum's natural good taste has become part of the language – or at least of political jargon. And it too has a pejorative meaning.

It seems then that in the absence of history's verdict (for history takes longer in passing judgment) public opinion has long since condemned Munich and the spirit of Munich.

Is this condemnation just? Is there to be no appeal from it?

It is for the reader, who has all the evidence before him, to decide.

Yet without encroaching upon this decision or trying to suggest the reasons that should be adduced, we think it allowable to draw up a balance-sheet, by way of conclusion. This is all the easier today, since a quarter of a century has passed since Munich, and the strong feelings of the time, although they may not have died quite away, are henceforward confined to the justifications of the parts they played by the last of those who took a leading role at the conference.

In the course of this book their attitudes, their own interpretation of their actions and the motives that they allege have been dealt with and compared with the facts and the opposing points of view. There is no point, therefore, in going over them again. On the other hand it is the historian's acknowledged privilege to take the scales and place on one side those aspects that are favourable and on the other those that are somewhat less so.

The international obligations

To begin with we must go back to a short analysis of the legal situation as it was in the first place, since it was the obligations that her allies undertook with regard to Czechoslovakia that were at the origin of the international tension which culminated in Munich.

In 1938 Czechoslovakia's security and the integrity of her boundaries were guaranteed by international agreements. France had signed one of these. The USSR for its part had consented to another; but this contained a suspensive clause which laid down that the agreement should be operative only after the Franco-Czechoslovak treaty should have come into effect. People have too often forgotten to point out that this suspensive clause was only inserted into the Russo-Czechoslovak pact in 1935 *at the express request of the French government,* justifiably anxious to avoid a position in which Russia could set off a war by her own motion.

France had therefore reserved to herself the right to be the first, and practically the sole, judge of when these obligations that had been undertaken by herself and the USSR should have to be fulfilled. This right of selecting the proper moment was all the more readily accepted by the leaders of the Czechoslovak Republic since it was to be exercised by France, a country whose international prestige was then based upon a long and splendid tradition of scrupulous respect for obligation assumed, for the given word, and for the signature at the bottom of a contract.

On her side Czechoslovakia had already had an occasion for showing that she attached even more importance to the spirit of international engagements than to their letter – and of showing this to France!

'I cannot forget,' wrote Albert Sarraut,[1] 'that on March 7, 1936, the day Germany violated the treaty of Locarno and committed her aggression in the Rhineland, while all the countries which had signed this treaty and had guaranteed that it should be respected, starting with England, the chief guarantor, coldly turned their backs on us and refused to hear our call to resist, courageous Czechoslovakia alone turned towards us, *and although she had not signed the treaty*, offered to mobilize to bring us her support.'

However, as the months went by, and the Nazi threat to Czechoslovakia became clearer and with it the risk of war greater, a current of opinion in France that favoured a 'restrictive interpretation' of the Franco-Czechoslovak pact came into being and increased in strength. This did not happen all at once. On February 26, 1938, Yvon Delbos, the foreign minister, stated in parliament that 'France's engagements towards Czechoslovakia would be faithfully fulfilled in case of need.' The next day the premier, Camille Chautemps, confirmed this.*

A few weeks later, on March 14, immediately after the Anschluss, Paul-Boncour, who had just succeeded Delbos at the Quai d'Orsay, in his turn made the same statement.

But in the foreign affairs committee of the Chamber P.-E. Flandin reproached Paul-Boncour for taking up this attitude, asserting that 'the collapse of the treaty of Locarno, to which our last treaty with Czechoslovakia was bound, it being signed the same day and as one of its consequences, rendered the latter null and void.'[2]

Shortly afterwards Joseph Barthélemy expressed the same point

---

* This clear statement takes on its full meaning when one knows that a messenger had come from Hodza to say to Chautemps 'If in the end you have to abandon us it would be better to say so at once – we shall adapt ourselves to the situation.'

of view in his well-known article in *Le Temps*,* doing his utmost to provide it with a juridical basis. The tracts printed in Germany but written in Czech that took up Barthélémy's 'proof' were at the origin of the bloody frontier incident at Cheb.

Professor René Cassin demolished these juridical excuses as early as August, 1938,[3] by showing that if Czechoslovakia owed France assistance in the event of Germany's violating the Rhineland pact or the Franco-German arbitration treaty, then France was bound to come to the help of Czechoslovakia in the event of the violation of the arbitration convention between Germany and Czechoslovakia, which was still in force. And René Cassin ended, 'The nations must be warned against the persuasion that even the plainest of treaties is not binding once the execution of it entails certain risks. Civilization can continue to exist only if treaties are respected.'

Nevertheless Flandin's and Barthélémy's thesis gained many adherents, the first being Jean Montigny, the deputy from the Sarthe and Laval's friend and mouthpiece, who on September 19, 1938, published an 'open letter to the President of the Republic, the members of the government and of parliament' entitled 'Should France go to war for Czechoslovakia?' He quoted Flandin, Barthélémy, Bergery, Emmanuel Berl, Emile Roche and Paul Faure, and ended, 'Legally and morally, France will therefore be free to act or not to act, to act to the degree that she sees fit, even if unhappily the Germans were to enter the Sudetenland.'

And going as far as naming his own country as the aggressor in advance, Montigny added, 'If she made up her mind to attack Germany it would therefore be for political motives and not by reason of any legal or moral obligation.'

There were ministers within Daladier's government who shared this point of view: on September 13 Anatole de Monzie also made a laborious juridical survey, by which he established that in the event of a German attack upon Czechoslovakia, at the most France would be required (and only after the League of Nations had intervened) to take economic sanctions against Germany. Since the Abyssinian affair everyone knew what 'economic sanctions' amounted to.

In justice it must be said that neither Daladier nor even Georges Bonnet openly adopted this argument during the first six months of the German-Czechoslovak crisis, that is to say, from the Anschluss to Munich.

* See above, p. 34, note ‡.

In London Daladier even went so far as to emphasize the engagements undertaken by France. And in his speech at La Pointe de Grave Bonnet, alluding to the Czechoslovak affair directly, said, 'In any event France will remain faithful to the obligations she has contracted.'

It is true that an expression of this kind has a meaning only if the extent of these obligations is clearly defined. Now according to Georges Bonnet he spoke on that occasion with a deliberate ambiguity; he meant to impress Germany, yet without giving Czechoslovakia any illusory hopes. Here is his own interpretation of the Pointe de Grave speech. 'It was particularly directed at Germany and it could not create any misunderstanding in Prague since we were continually pointing out the extent of our obligations to the Czech government, and as early as the next day the French minister, M de Lacroix, once more repeated his counsels of prudence.'[4]

Nevertheless Léon Noël, himself a witness of the events, formally denies that the Czechoslovaks could have doubted Bonnet's expressed intention of standing by all the engagements that arose from the treaty of 1925. The interview that he speaks of took place on his return from Czechoslovakia, after the semi-official mission of inquiry that the government had entrusted to him.

'I came back to Paris,' he writes, 'and said to M Georges Bonnet, "It is war or surrender." These were the very words that I used in the conclusion of a note that I gave him; and as the foreign minister's conversation seemed to give the impression that the government to which he belonged had now made up their mind to abandon Czechoslovakia, I added that if this were to be the case, the most elementary decency required us to warn the Czechoslovak government and to tell M Benes for example that up until a given date our diplomatic assistance could be fully relied upon but that we were absolutely determined not to help Czechoslovakia by force of arms if she should be attacked by Germany. The fate of this piece of advice is known; and in fact, M Bonnet never did speak to Czechoslovakia in this manner, although he has often maintained the contrary, particularly in his book that was published in Switzerland. He quibbled and he played upon words, firmly resolved for his part not to keep to our engagements to Czechoslovakia to the end, that is to say not to keep them to the point of military intervention.

'Like Alexis Léger, the secretary-general at the Quai d'Orsay, he was convinced that we should fulfil our engagements towards Czechoslovakia with enough good faith and enough efficacity by mobilizing, without going into action, in the event of Germany's attacking that country – for I stress the point that that was the doctrine of the chiefs of the Quai d'Orsay. So almost until the day before Munich he let the Czechoslovak leaders believe that France would support their unhappy country by force of arms.'[3]

It is difficult not to agree with Léon Noël here: as it happened, both Georges Bonnet and after him Daladier adopted an attitude that carried with it far graver consequences than if they had frankly admitted their intention of limiting the scope of France's engagements.

There was an ever-increasing disparity between their words and their deeds, for while they spoke of the obligations that France had undertaken they never stopped acting in such a manner that they would not have to fulfil them. They carried on this course of action with remarkable perseverance, particularly in their attempts at causing it to be understood that it was impossible for France to intervene physically unless she was assured of British support; yet Great Britain was not bound to Czechoslovakia by any pact of the nature of the Franco-Czechoslovak treaty of 1925.

However, the French government were basing themselves upon the attitude taken up by the British when, on September 20, they brought pressure to bear on the Czechoslovak government to induce them to accept a 'Franco-British plan' that reiterated all the requirements that Hitler had laid down at Berchtesgaden on September 15. And the only way in which this pressure could be made effective was by the threat of not keeping the promises that had been made.

And when, after the Godesberg ultimatum, Great Britain nevertheless agreed at last that she might come in on the French side (though she was not obliged to do so), the Quai d'Orsay set the most discreditable machinery in motion to try to conceal this change of front from French public opinion. As a last resource Georges Bonnet's people even went so far as to accuse what others considered a victory for French diplomacy of being a forgery.

The fifth column

The responsibility for this development of French policy, for this

withdrawal from the possible consequences of engagements undertaken, must of course fall primarily upon the government. Yet one
must not underestimate the part played, both in France and England,
by a public opinion that carried fear of war to the point of mass
cowardice.

It is true that public opinion, particularly in times of extreme
tension, can be influenced. What is more, it can be misled.

'People of France, you are being deceived!' proclaimed Flandin in
his poster of September 28. And as we have seen he then, with
virtuous indignation, denounced 'the hidden forces that have set
cunning machinery in motion to make war inevitable'.

It can scarcely be denied that hidden forces did operate and that
cunning machinery was set in motion. Yet one has but to leaf
through the files of the main daily and weekly papers to see that the
pressure exerted on public opinion was brought to bear by the 'peace
at any price' party and not by the 'war party'.

The pacifists, or more exactly the defeatists, did their utmost to
carry out their policy and they did so with some degree of unity;
yet their origins were very varied and their motives were sometimes
contradictory: there were genuine idealists, ex-servicemen haunted
by the terrible slaughter of Verdun and committed to a pacifist
campaign with no ulterior motives; unscrupulous journalists drawing
on secret funds like Luchaire; fascists who wanted to see France fall
into line with Hitler's Germany or Mussolini's Italy. These scattered
'men of good will' quickly found work for themselves behind the
scenes, thanks to important support from outside from which they
sometimes profited without knowing it – that of the German agents
in France. Whether they were already called the fifth column or
not is of little importance: what matters is their influence of French
public opinion in 1938, and this was certainly brought to bear in all
fields – press and politics of course, but also arts, letters and all other
circles from the top bankers to the proletariat, without forgetting the
government.

Their activities took on the most varied aspects. Some were perfectly open, such as the 'France-Allemagne' committee of Fernand
de Brinon, Jean Goy and Scapini, or the 'Grand Pavois', where
Hitler's admirers went in the evening, and which operated in a
building in the Champs Elysées. Anyone in the political circles of
Paris could make a list of such people as René Brunet, the
'Sudeten Germans' defender', who frequented the German embassy

and who were at the same time intimate with Georges Bonnet.*

Furthermore, by way of facilitating matters, the German embassy had set up 'cultural' services whose official task was to distribute books and pamphlets, and which in fact handled quite important sums of money with which to pay for the services of newspapermen and politicians.

The chief press officer at the foreign ministry, Pierre Comert,† gave evidence about this corruption.

'I learnt that Claude Jeantet was receiving money from a Nazi propaganda centre set up by the Germans in the Boulevard Saint-Germain. The same applied to Brinon. I can say nothing about Stéphane Lauzanne.

'At that time the methods of the German agents consisted not of buying the newspapers, but certain newspapermen. It was cheaper and it worked better. In any case, Germany had men ready to serve her in some Paris editorial offices.'

And Pierre Comert added, 'Certain Germans were the first to despise the Frenchmen who took their money in this way.'[6]

The activities of a centre of this kind could not go unnoticed. But it was no good hoping that the French government would put an end to it. Here again we have Pierre Comert's evidence.

'An important anti-Nazi German had told me that the Boulevard Saint-Germain propaganda service distributed money to a certain number of Frenchmen every month by means of envelopes which a person on a bicycle took to their homes. I was given the name of this cyclist, and I learnt that he had just left his job to go

* Count Welczeck, the German ambassador to Paris, wrote to Ribbentrop on June 17, 1938, to give him an account of an interview with Georges Bonnet. 'Quite recently too he (Georges Bonnet) took the occasion to strengthen his compatriots who had been invited to the Comité France-Allemagne meeting in their intention of making the journey to Baden-Baden.' During the same conversation it seems that Bonnet also said that he 'would speak louder, if need be, should the Czechs display stubbornness in the settlement of the Sudeten question'. Lastly there are the remarks reported by Welczeck on the subject of Spain. 'In this context Bonnet observed that the Communists living in what is called the red zone round Paris, and who are foreigners for the most part, had provided a very considerable number of volunteers for the Spanish civil war. According to the information that he had received almost eighty per cent of these volunteers had been killed or had died, which had had the fortunate result of thinning out the population of the zone a great deal.'

† Because of his hostility to the policy of Munich Pierre Comert was superseded by Georges Bonnet shortly after the conference.

and do his military service in a certain town in the east. It would have been possible, by questioning this man, to find out the names of many of these precocious collaborators. I sent in my information. Nothing whatever was done about it.'

To whom was this information sent?

'To the Quai d'Orsay authorities,' replied Pierre Comert, who added, 'It must have reached the minister: it was the minister who made the decision.'[7]

Many more instances could be given. When it was a question of reaching figures to whom one could not in decency send an envelope by a man on a bicycle, more 'dignified' means were used. Another French diplomat, M L. Tarbe de Saint-Hardouin, described them exactly.

'The German tactical approach, which I saw develop and which was largely the work of Abetz, who usually carried it out, consisted of this kind of manoeuvre. Take the Kiel regatta for example. A certain number of Frenchmen, usually chosen from a variety of circles, received invitations to be present. They were told that their whole journey would be paid for – that all their expenses would be met. Generally some kind of a contact was found so that they knew something about the invitation before it came. People were not often surprised at receiving invitations of this sort. They went off charmed, saying inwardly that they had been asked because of their position. They were always very well looked after during the journey and very well entertained. They were told of France's dreadful misunderstanding with regard to Germany, of the need for reconciliation and of the fact that Germany's claims were perfectly natural. By the end of a few days they were sincerely won over, and as they had been so kindly received they felt themselves called upon to make a speech. They were taken to the German war memorial. I have seen it happen again and again. In this way they were trapped without being aware of it. From the moment they had made this journey they had entered into relations with Germans, who often came to see them in Paris and who asked them again the next year. So a circle of Germanophiles was gradually and very cleverly built up, without people being aware of it at first.

'In the literary world the Germans also behaved very astutely.

They bought the German translation rights of the works of a great many French authors, but they never published their works. From that time on these writers dared not write a word against Germany; and on their side the publishers concerned would refuse any book unfavourable to the Germans.

'People were thus at peace with their consciences, the more so as their vanity played a part in the business. They found it perfectly natural that they should be invited, in view of their position, and that the translation rights of their books (which were not translated) should be bought. But little by little they passed into the service of the German propaganda, without even knowing that they did so.'

By these varied means, from the monthly envelopes to the Kiel regatta, by way of translation rights for books that were never published, Nazi Germany had succeeded, between 1934 and 1938, in building up a solid body of consciously or unconsciously hired propagandists in the 'opinion-forming' circles of Paris. During the period in which public opinion was being prepared, the period that came before the Munich conference, these people were able to work all the more efficiently since they found powerful supporters in the heart of the government itself, and especially at the Quai d'Orsay.

Jacques Debu-Bridel lists a certain number of journalists who gravitated about the foreign minister. 'M Georges Bonnet,' he writes, 'whose intimates and authorized mouthpieces, F de Brinon (*L'Information*), Claude Jeantet (*La Liberté* and *Je Suis Partout*), Luchaire (*Les Nouveaux Temps*), Alfred Mallet,* J.-L. Le Boucher (*L'Action Française*), Prété (*Le Peuple*), M. A. Piétri (*Le Jour*) were all violently hostile to Czechoslovakia.'[8]

The campaign against Czechoslovakia

One of the chief themes of pro-German, and 'pacifist', propaganda between March and September 1938 was indeed a systematic denigration of Czechoslovakia, her rulers and her army. This campaign, reinforced by every new speech of Hitler's, consisted of spreading the most impudent lies and the coarsest slanders against Benes, his government and his nation, by the newspapers or the radio.

* Alfred Mallet, who edited *Le Petit Journal* for a long while, was Laval's intimate friend and colleague.

General Faucher emphasizes the way the French foreign minister believed, or pretended to believe, the most fantastic stories, even when they had only come out in the German papers. Above all, anything that could make Czechoslovakia look like the vanguard of Bolshevism met with willing ears at the Quai d'Orsay.

One day, for example, Lacroix asked the head of the French military mission to come to the legation with all haste.

'The Quai is asking me for an explanation of the following event,' said the minister to General Faucher. 'The German papers report that a Soviet detachment in the garrison of N . . . has mutinied, killed the colonel of the Xth regiment, seized army lorries and left for an unknown destination. You will have to make an inquiry.

'I will make the inquiry,' replied the general, 'but I can give you the result of it right away, and you can wire the minister, without fear of error, that the whole thing is utterly untrue, since as we have often said there has never been any Soviet detachment in Czechoslovakia, and the only Soviet soldiers here are the military attaché in Prague and his assistant.'

'Another day,' says General Faucher again, 'the German papers said that Russian officers, whose names were given, were going to teach in the war school in Prague. Now there never were any Russian teachers in any Czechoslovak schools whatever.'

But the German papers were not the only ones to publish false news of this kind.

'The campaign against Czechoslovakia,' goes on General Faucher, 'was supported by a section of the press in France and by various publications. I pointed out to the general staff that certain articles in *Je Suis Partout*, signed by French contributors, were obviously put together with material supplied from abroad, for the author did not know what he was writing about and he had left the trade-mark showing. There was no doubt that he was getting his documents from abroad.'*

* In 1939, shortly after the mobilization, General Faucher asked that Ferdonnet should be arrested, giving proof of the German origin of the documentation used in his book *La crise tchèque*. In spite of the exact information that General Faucher provided the answer was 'cannot be found'. Two or three weeks later Ferdonnet began his career on Radio Stuttgart.

In the same way the head of the French military mission in Prague had to call attention to the part played in the campaign of denigration by certain military circles – the people who were close to Pétain or Georges. On various occasions General Faucher even had to point out to the French high command that there were untrue and slanderous articles about Czechoslovakia in such military publications as *La France militaire* or the *Bulletin des armées étrangères*, which was issued by the intelligence department of the general staff.

At the same time certain left-wing papers, taking part in the 'pacifist' campaign conducted by a section of the SFIO and the trade union movement, also published articles hostile to Czechoslovakia on the subject of the alleged persecution of the minorities or the Bolshevization of the country; these articles were well enough written to set a part of the French working class against the Czechoslovak Republic.

Hitler's word

It was in this atmosphere, carefully prepared by German propaganda and by the 'pacifists' in the newspapers, parliament and government both in London and Paris, that the first decisive conversations with Hitler took place – Berchtesgaden, Godesberg and finally Munich.

At first Chamberlain alone and then the two heads of the Western governments, Chamberlain and Daladier, deliberately took an important risk during these negotiations. Agreeing to be parties to a settlement that must necessarily, because of Hitler's requirements, lead to the dismemberment of Czechoslovakia, they consented to the dismantling of the system of defences that the Prague government had erected at great expense. This meant reducing Czechoslovakia's military potentialities almost to nothing and placing her economy under the complete domination of the most powerful of her neighbours. In fact they were relying upon Hitler's word for the survival as a state of a country to which France had given her guarantee, a guarantee very close to protection.

This being so we may ask – and this calls the very basis of the Munich conference into question – whether the French and English heads of government had any sound reason to believe that Hitler would keep his promises? And was this presumption of good faith enough in Daladier's eyes to justify the sacrifice of our ally's possibilities for defence; for it was he who was the more direct guarantor of the Czechoslovak state?

A historical survey will provide the material for an answer to the question.

On May 17, 1933, Hitler stated in the Reichstag, 'Germany will follow no other path than that drawn up by the treaties ... The German nation has not the least idea of invading foreign countries.'

On February 1, 1934, still in the Reichstag, 'The allegation that Germany intends to violate the borders of the Austrian state is absurd and devoid of any foundation.'

On March 13, 1934, in a note to the French government, 'The German government had never called the validity of the treaty of Locarno in question.'

On March 7, 1936, after the violation of that treaty by the reoccupation of the Rhineland, Hitler spoke again before the Reichstag. 'At the end of three years I think I may consider that the struggle for equality of rights for Germany has reached its end today. We have no territorial claims to make in Europe.'

On May 1, 1936, in the Reichstag, 'People are spreading a rumour that Germany would like to invade Austria or Czechoslovakia. It is all lies! Who spreads the rumour? A little circle of interested parties, people who do not want peace.'

On July 11, 1936, at Berchtesgaden, he signed the German-Austrian agreement with Schuschnigg. 'The government of the Reich acknowledge the full sovereignty of the federal Austrian state. Each of the two governments considers the political structure existing in the other country, including the question of Austrian National-Socialism, as an internal affair concerning the other country and one in which they will interfere in no way, directly or indirectly.'

On January 30, 1937, in his speech to the Reichstag, 'The time of surprises is over from now onwards.'

On March 14, 1938, two days before the Anschluss, Chamberlain could tell the House of Commons:

'Marshal Göring has given the Czechoslovak minister in Berlin a general assurance, an assurance that was later expressly renewed in Chancellor Hitler's name, that the German government publicly wished to improve their relations with Czechoslovakia ...

'The same day [March 12] Baron von Neurath assured the Czechoslovak minister that Germany considered herself bound by the German-Czechoslovak arbitration agreement of October 1925.'*

Daladier and Chamberlain, Georges Bonnet and Halifax were all aware of these successive declarations made by Hitler or by his closest colleagues speaking in his name. When the engagements thus entered into by Hitler were compared with his subsequent actions was the result such as to justify the sacrifice of the Czechoslovak bastion by the French premier, and did it allow Chamberlain to promise the English 'peace for our time' as he waved a sheet of paper with Hitler's signature upon it?

Yet after Munich Daladier does not seem to have been fully aware of the nugatory character of the signature that Hitler had set to the agreement reached at the Führerhaus. At the most there was that little doubt which spoilt the premier's happiness when he arrived at Le Bourget: 'Would the Munich signatures be honoured?'

'A free hand in the east'

It was not long before Daladier knew the answer to the question that he had asked himself while the Paris crowd was cheering him without either shame or restraint.

That very evening the Polish ultimatum was to bring about the first violation of the Munich agreement.

A few days later, in Berlin, the work of the international commission provided the Führer (who no doubt regretted not having been the first to break the agreement of September 29) with the occasion for making fools of his partners. As soon as the first difficulty arose over the delimitation of the zones he stepped in with his usual brutality: he replied to the Czechs' argument with an ultimatum. And the French and British ambassadors received orders from their governments not to cross the master of the Reich in any way.

After this there came the German-Italian arbitration on Hungary's claim – a third stroke against the Munich agreement. This time the French and English were finally relegated to the class of nonentities; they were no longer even asked to the meetings of the butchers' club.

The fourth violation of Munich was the insolent note written by Hitler in reply to the Franco-British démarche that timidly reminded

* At the Nuremberg trial the British prosecutor reproached Hitler and his accomplices with the violation of sixty-nine treaties, pacts or agreements—the Munich agreement among them.

him that the promised German-Italian guarantee to Czechoslovakia had not yet materialized.

And lastly the downright annexation of Czechoslovakia provided the final and complete liquidation of all that still remained of the Munich agreement. Six months were all that was needed to reach this point.

Daladier, an incorrigible optimist where Munich is concerned, wrote (although he had had plenty of time to see these six months in perspective, and what followed after), 'The Munich agreement put a check on the war. To a certain degree it limited the expansion of Germanism.'[9]

But for this to be true the signatories of the agreement, beginning with Daladier, would have had to insist that it was honoured; and they would have had to do so, of course, at the very first violation.

For if the Western leaders had taken a heavy responsibility upon themselves, first by letting things reach such a state that they had to go to Munich, then by going there and surrendering almost everything, they increased the weight of this responsibility tenfold by accepting the repeated violations of the agreement even before the ink on the signature was dry.

As we have seen, Georges Bonnet disagrees with Ribbentrop over the notorious phrase in which he is supposed to have agreed to Hitler's request for 'a free hand in the east'.

It does not really matter much whether the words were uttered or not. What does matter is that both on the French and the English side everything was done, from as early as the days immediately following Munich, so that Hitler should in fact have a free hand not only 'in the east' but in the whole of central Europe.

It is impossible to forget Coulondre's observation on March 2, when he was sending Bonnet Hitler's refusal to the request for a guarantee of the Czechoslovak frontiers: 'Decoded, this passage means that the Western powers no longer have any right to look in the direction of central Europe.'

The 'realists'

The hysterical crowds that welcomed Daladier at Le Bourget and Chamberlain at Heston on September 30 did not regard the Munich agreement as a last resource, a makeshift.

Yet apart from the paid agents of the fifth column none of those

who defended the Munich agreement immediately after its signature, nor any of those far fewer people who continued to defend it
later, claimed to see it as anything but a lesser evil.

The defenders of Munich and of the 'Munich spirit' made use of
the doctrine that was Hitler's golden rule, the reason for his success
and for his fall: they attributed to the provisionally peaceful settlement that was reached on September 29, 1938, one essential 'virtue',
that of being realistic.

Clearly when it was a question of Munich it was easier to see it as a
display of realism rather than the application of those moral rules
that give both the nations and the private persons who observe
them a clear conscience.

It would be tempting to enter into a discourse upon the merits of
political realism and to inquire how far it absolves a nation from very
dishonourable conduct; but this is not the place to do so.

One might also, with Albert Sarraut,[10] emphasize the singular
coincidence 'of realism and feeling' in the Czechoslovak affair.

'. . . for the engagement that we entered into with regard to
Czechoslovakia,' he wrote, 'and which was repeated by M Bonnet
in his speech at La Pointe de Grave was not entered into for ideo-
logical or humanitarian reasons, nor from sentimentality. We
entered into it out of an interest that was quite as realistic as personal interest; we entered into it for the effective support that it
would guarantee us in case of danger. We were not indulging in
delicate feelings nor in fraternity; we were making a strategic
speculation. We did not simply wish to please a friend: our
essential aim was to secure a defender and an ally . . .'

Nevertheless, since these are important factors in the balance-sheet
of Munich, we must look for the arguments upon which those who
still look upon realism as the justification for the agreement can base
themselves.

These arguments fall into three categories, and they may be
objectively summarized thus:

1. It was necessary to see that peace was kept in September 1938
because of the attitude of the USSR, which, though Czechoslovakia's
ally, produced nothing but good advice and did nothing to overcome
the diplomatic obstacles to an eventual military intervention.

2. The proportion of the opposing forces, both in central Europe
and in a possible western theatre of operations, was so favourable to

the Axis in September 1938 that it was impossible for France, even if it were granted that England would come in on her side, to engage in a conflict.

3. Finally, the Munich peace, however precarious it may have been, did provide the democracies with a respite that allowed them to alter this proportion so that it was to their advantage.

Each of these three points, diplomatic isolation, military weakness and respite, deserves to be looked into and discussed.

The Russian attitude

The Soviet Union, allied with France since the signature of the Franco-Soviet pact of May 2, 1935, which was negotiated by Laval, and with Czechoslovakia by the terms of the Russo-Czechoslovak treaty concluded a fortnight later on May 16, was the only counter-poise in eastern Europe that could, by opening an eastern front, make Hitler hesitate.

It still had to be known whether on the one hand the USSR would honour its signature in the event of open conflict and come in on the side of its allies, and on the other whether the Red Army would, in spite of the absence of a common frontier between Czechoslovakia and Russia, be physically capable of intervening.

According to Georges Bonnet and Daladier the reply to the first question was, in a theoretical and grudging manner, affirmative; but there was no possible doubt that the answer to the second was negative. In other words Russia was all the freer in declaring herself ready to stand by her engagements since she was sure of having a valid excuse for not having to keep them.

This interpretation is based on the negative result of a series of approaches undertaken by French diplomats, and even by Georges Bonnet in person on several occasions, particularly behind the scenes at the League of Nations – approaches to the Rumanians and Poles to ask them to let the Red Army go through their territories in the event of a German aggression against Czechoslovakia.

It is certain that these démarches took place. Nor is there any question that they met with a flat refusal on the part of Beck or his colleagues and with a more delicately shaded refusal from Comnenus.

But it is far less evident that the USSR would have used these difficulties as a pretext if Czechoslovakia had been attacked.

In point of fact the Western powers, and more particularly Chamberlain and his personal advisers in England and Bonnet and his 'pacifist' associates in France, had only one fear – that of finding themselves engaged in a European war against Nazi Germany and fascist Italy, the two countries 'of order', and on the same side as Bolshevik Russia, the centre of disorder and subversion. What is more the example of the Spanish war was there before their eyes, to increase their dread; they could not feel sympathy with the 'reds', supported by Moscow. How could they contemplate becoming in their turn part of the 'red' camp?

In order to get rid of this untimely and compromising alliance it was necessary to prove, at any cost, that the USSR had very little desire to keep its international engagements, and could not do so, in any case. And this, by the bye, at the very moment when France, while repeating solemn assurances that she should remain faithful to her own obligations, was getting ready not to keep them.

No doubt the French government hoped that by keeping systematically in step with Great Britain (who was in no way bound to Czechoslovakia) and by taking care not to reply to the Soviet offers of military co-operation they would discourage the Russians.

But the trap was far too obvious for a diplomat of Litvinov's quality to fall into it. Far from it, for all through the six months that preceded Munich the Soviet statesmen reiterated their assurances, renewed their overtures and with increasing clarity expressed not only their intention of standing by their engagements but also of their attachment to the policy of collective security and indivisible peace.

As early as March 17, immediately after the Anschluss, Litvinov defined his government's position in a statement to the press.

'The Soviet government bears in mind the obligations that devolve upon them in virtue of the League covenant, the Briand-Kellog pact and the treaties of mutual assistance entered into with France and Czechoslovakia.

'I am therefore able to state in their name that they are ready, as they have always been, to take part in a collective action of such a scope that it could aim at stopping the further development of aggression and at eliminating the increasing danger of another world-wide slaughter.

'The Soviet government are ready to give immediate consideration, with the other states belonging to the League of Nations or outside it, to the practical measures that are called for by the present circumstances.

'Perhaps tomorrow it will be too late; but today the moment is not yet past if all states and particularly the great powers adopt a firm and unambiguous attitude towards the problems of safeguarding the peace.'

Chamberlain replied to this specific offer of an international conference open to all nations, even those 'outside the League', with a flat refusal: why think of preventive action? Let the disaster happen first. 'The Soviet proposal,' said the British premier, 'seems to lead less to a meeting for reaching a settlement than to an agreed action to guard against an eventuality that has not yet occurred.'[11]

On May 11, the height of the crisis and the time when 'the eventuality' looked as though it were about to happen, President Kalinin emphasized the contribution that the great resources of the USSR would provide for those who might be called upon to resist the aggressor, and he added, 'If our country is asked to do so, it will honour its obligations towards Czechoslovakia to the full.'

Two days earlier, at Manchester, Churchill had addressed a solemn warning to the democracies. 'What a mad lack of foresight on our part, at a time of great danger, to put obstacles on the road of the general association of the huge Russian mass with the resistance to a Nazi act of aggression.'

Yet the game of the Western statesmen did consist of piling up these 'useless obstacles', and, when they were found to be not only useless but inefficient, of drawing gloomy conclusions from the Soviet leaders' clear declarations. This was particularly the case when Georges Bonnet at last made up his mind at Geneva to question Litvinov on the steps that the USSR thought of taking to come to Czechoslovakia's assistance. Bonnet retained only that part of Litvinov's reply which referred to the legal scruples of the People's Commissar, who did not want his country to have the appearance of an aggressor by forcing a passage through Poland or Rumania.

Yet when Litvinov and Bonnet were discussing the chances of obtaining a right of passage from Rumania more easily than from Poland, and when Litvinov urged Bonnet to make an urgent approach to Bucarest, he proved that he was in no way concerned with a convenient excuse.

In the same way when Litvinov replied to Payart, the French chargé d'affaires, 'that in view of the negative attitude adopted by Warsaw and Bucarest he saw only one practical way out, an appeal to the League of Nations',[12] he did so, as he pointed out immediately afterwards, with the intention of obtaining a mandate from the majority of the council which should give the USSR the possibility of coming to the help of the victim in the event of a German attack upon Czechoslovakia.

But Bonnet and even Daladier pretended to see nothing but a means of evasion in this proposal, which was nevertheless in conformity with the traditional conception of collective security.

In fact, as Odette Merlat points out, 'The first reserves did indeed appear to have been on one side alone, and in Litvinov's answers Bonnet seems to have found what he really wanted to find, so repugnant was it to him to be obliged to turn to Soviet help for what he called his defence of the peace.'[13]

Her interpretation is confirmed by this incident, which is described by Jean Champenois, a French journalist who was working in Moscow at the time of Munich.*

'Here again is something that I was told by M Payart, counsellor at the French embassy in Moscow before the war: M Coulondre, the ambassador in Moscow, was in Paris, and he was conferring with M Georges Bonnet when Bonnet was brought a dispatch in which M Payart, chargé d'affaires in his chief's absence, gave an account of the assurances he had received from the Soviet foreign ministry, assurances which left no doubt as to the Soviet Union's fidelity to its engagements.

'This did not answer M Bonnet's purposes at all, for he was in the act of asserting that the contrary was the case. He glanced at the paper and said, "I knew it! These Russians will not march!" Coulondre asked to see the telegram and protested. Bonnet got out of it by saying something like this, "Oh, your Russians, you know, you can never tell what they mean." '[14]

So Bonnet stubbornly kept to the letter as far as the 'technical' possibilities of a Russian intervention were concerned, and pretended to deplore Soviet formalism. And in the same way Daladier, in the

* Jean Champenois stayed at Moscow as AFP's correspondent after the Allied victory until 1947.

matter of a possible appeal to the League, merely decried the 'ramshackle machinery of Geneva', just as Hitler and Mussolini did.

It is pleasant to hear another note in a statement upon these two basic aspects of Franco-Soviet relations in 1938. Coulondre, the French ambassador in Moscow, gives particularly exact information on the Russian military preparations in liaison with the Czechoslovaks which proves that they genuinely intended to intervene. Speaking of the démarches undertaken in Moscow by Zdenek Fierlinger, the head of the Czechoslovak diplomatic mission, he writes,

'He has obtained the immediate delivery of sixty bombers. Twenty have already landed at the airfield of Uggorod in Slovakia. It is thus proved that Russian planes can land in the less immediately threatened part of the country. On their side the Russians have laid out a great airfield at Vinnitza, considerably nearer the frontier west of Kiev. The Uggorod airfield, where the work had to be held up because of a German press campaign, is not yet finished and it still has to be supplied with the spare parts and petrol storage needed for the Soviet planes.'[15]

Furthermore, on September 15 the Rumanian government gave up their opposition to having their territory flown over and informed Thierry, the French minister in Bucarest. Shortly after General Delmas, the French military attaché in Rumania, noticed a significant incident: a Soviet plane made a forced landing on a Rumanian airfield and when it was repaired it was allowed to fly on to Czechoslovakia. At the time of Munich, therefore, it was possible to count roughly two hundred Soviet aeroplanes delivered to Czechoslovak airfields.

It is worth knowing the opinion of Winston Churchill on this double problem, military and diplomatic. For not only did the English statesman follow the evolution of the 1938 crisis with the utmost attention, hour by hour, but on this occasion as on so many others during the whole of his long career he displayed a far-sightedness that can very easily bear comparison with that shown by Georges Bonnet or Edouard Daladier.

'I have heard it suggested that it was geographically impossible for Russia to send troops into Czechoslovakia and that Russian aid in the event of war would have been limited to modest air support. The assent of Roumania, and also to a lesser extent of Hungary, to allow Russian forces to pass through their territory was of course necessary. This might well have been obtained from Roumania at least, as indicated to me by M Maisky,* through the pressures and guarantees of a Grand Alliance acting under the aegis of the League of Nations. There were two railways from Russia into Czechoslovakia through the Carpathian Mountains, the northerly from Czernowitz through the Bukovina, the southerly through Hungary by Debrezcen. These two railways alone, which avoid both Bucarest and Budapest by good margins, might well have supported Russian armies of thirty divisions. As a counter for keeping the peace these possibilities would have been a substantial deterrent upon Hitler, and would almost certainly have led to far greater developments in the event of war. Stress has also been laid upon Soviet duplicity and bad faith. Anyhow, the Soviet offer was in effect ignored. They were not brought into the scale against Hitler, and were treated with an indifference – not to say disdain – which left a mark on Stalin's mind.'[16]

Only a few days before Munich, on September 23, the USSR provided a fresh proof of its desire to help Czechoslovakia by sending Poland a note that warned her of the consequences of aggression.

But the more evident the determination of the Russians became, the stronger grew Georges Bonnet's reserve. How could it have been otherwise, once the French foreign minister had finally made up his mind to the policy of appeasement?

Later, and the paradox was only apparent, he openly complained that France was reduced to defending Czechoslovakia by herself (which led him to do nothing of the kind out of 'realism') while at the same time he was using every way of hiding the firmness of the Soviets and the stiffening of the British attitude from French public opinion.

The business of the Foreign Office communiqué of September 26 illustrates this duplicity: not only was the communiqué, which pointed out the support given to France by Great Britain and the USSR, at once described as a forgery, but the dispatches that confirmed its official origin mysteriously vanished as soon as they reached

---

* During a conversation at Chartwell on September 2 – a conversation which left no doubt as to the Soviet Union's desire to intervene. Churchill sent on account of it in a personal note to Halifax on September 3 (see above, p 92).

the Quai d'Orsay, and the authenticity of the document was finally acknowledged only on September 30 – after Munich.

This fear of seeing the Russians concerning themselves with the Czechoslovak affair and upsetting the contemplated 'peaceful' settlement induced Daladier and Bonnet to agree that the Munich conference should be held without the USSR, although Russia was France's ally.

Yet some days before Russia had let it be known that she would agree to be represented at a conference of the great powers and the states concerned: Litvinov had stated this at Geneva to Mr Butler, the Under-Secretary of State at the Foreign Office, and Lord De La Warr, the Lord Privy Seal, who had asked him the question in the presence of Maisky, the Soviet ambassador in London.

This 'overlooking' of Russia at the time of Munich is severely criticized by so experienced a diplomat as Coulondre.

'Certain documents,' he says, 'particularly a note taken by Schmundt, the Chancellor's aide-de-camp, lead one to think that the allies might perhaps still have been able to deal with the situation immediately before Munich if they had had the courage and the common sense to insist that the USSR and Czechoslovakia should take part in the conference.

'By Munich itself France and Great Britain had lost the essential part of the game. Yet at least with a little energy they might have secured that the amputation of the Sudetenland should take place in less disadvantageous conditions, and above all that the remaining Czechoslovak territory should be guaranteed without reserves or conditions by the four signatory powers. Czechoslovakia would have been mutilated and neutralized, but not sacrificed.

'By the end of the summer of 1938 the peace-loving powers could scarcely avoid going to Munich. The mistake was to go there without Russia and with the "Munich spirit".'[17]

The American ambassador in Moscow, in 1938, Davies, was one of the first to foresee the dramatic consequences of this mistake. On January 18, 1939, that is to say seven months before the signature of the German-Soviet pact, Davies wrote to Harry Hopkins:*

'Chamberlain's policy, which is pushing Italy, Poland and Hungary into Hitler's arms, may end by disgusting the Soviets to

---

* From Brussels, his new post, which he had just reached.

379

such a degree that it will induce Russia to come to an economic agreement and a political truce with Hitler. This is not beyond the range of possibility nor even of probability – for ten years it was a fact.' And Davies added, 'The reactionaries in England and France will presently, in their despair, beg for the Soviets' support, but perhaps it will be too late, if between now and then the Soviets grow utterly disgusted by their attitude.'[18]

It was indeed to be too late, and that for a series of reasons: Pierre Comert certainly seems to have detected one of the most important, and this must be set on the debit side of the Munich balance-sheet.

'Litvinov,' he stated, 'was in favour of co-operation with France and England. He backed this policy with his entire career, perhaps even with his life. If instead of smothering the British communiqué we had strongly approved of it, thus supporting those who had put it out in London, and if we had supported Litvinov by words and deeds, thus proving that he was right in following this policy, and if we had refused to go to Munich without the Russians, then perhaps the course of events would have been different. After Munich Litvinov vanished; and in Moscow that was the end of the policy of understanding between France and Russia.'[19]

The refusal of military co-operation

So far from being a voluntary withdrawal, as Georges Bonnet would have it, Russia's diplomatic isolation at the time of Munich was in fact the result of the Western powers' systematic mistrust and of those 'useless obstacles' that Churchill denounced in his speech at Manchester.

This mistrust and these obstacles are to be found again in another field, and one no less important – that of military co-operation.

Georges Bonnet has stuffed his brief with evidence to prove that on several occasions he did question the Russians as to what they could do to intervene in the event of a German attack upon Czechoslovakia. But each time the French foreign minister contented himself with hearing the reply he expected, that is to say, that the crossing of Poland or Rumania by the Red Army would set delicate diplomatic problems.

Yet there was a way of getting over, or getting round, this obstacle in procedure: it was to go straight to the concrete aspect of things and

to set the general staffs (which would have to carry out the operations, after all) the task of planning a joint strategy and of comparing the ends to be achieved with the means at their disposal. It is
easy to guess the objection: what would be the point of staff-talks,
since the Russians could not bring a single soldier into the field?

It may seem an attractive argument for a moment, but it will not
bear examination. In the first place it should be observed that talks
of this kind had been carried on with the British, although their
contribution to a possible European campaign could only be a token
force, and that for a long while. And then again it is not true to say
that even if the passage of Russian troops through Rumania or
Poland were deliberately excluded, direct Soviet military assistance
to Czechoslovakia would necessarily have been trifling. In the field of
aviation alone Russian intervention would have been enough to
take the control of the air from the Luftwaffe – to say nothing of the
effect on the German population of raids as reprisals for the
bombing of Czech towns.

Besides, why was George Bonnet so insistent that the Soviet intervention could only come about by means of a passage through
Rumania or Poland, arranged on a 'friendly basis'?

Surely in such a case it was the general staffs' duty to seek and
find alternative solutions – for example, that diversion in East Prussia
which, as it later appeared, was for a long while the chief anxiety of
the German general staff. And did not the Quai d'Orsay also know
that Poland was ready to combine with Germany in the event of an
attack upon Czechoslovakia, and that in this event Russia intended
to go into action against Poland – without asking for her authoriza-
tion?

Lastly, the mere fact of beginning talks of this kind would have
given a clearer view of the real intentions of our possible partner and
at the same time it would, in case of need, have made it possible to
overcome any remaining reserves by making use of the soldiers to
overcome the civilians.

But all this would have called for a desire to act on the part of the
French leaders (and of the British, if in the event they had chosen to
come in), and not the a priori exclusion of any possibility of a clash.

Georges Bonnet has assumed the task of proving that France was
alone in meaning to go as far as war in order to stand by her engagements. In fact there were others, that is to say, Czechoslovakia and
the USSR, who considered this risk. But he, on the contrary, so

completely excluded it that he told Daladier of his intention to resign if a war should break out over the Czechoslovak affair.

Furthermore it was because he had taken his decision and made his choice that he never stopped minimizing the desire to intervene on the part of France's possible partners or their possibilities of doing so.

The staff-talks that were called for by the Russians, the Czechoslovaks and those Frenchmen such as General Faucher* who did not share the opinions of the foreign minister would have brought both desire and possibility into evidence. They had therefore to be avoided. And in fact, despite the imminence of war, despite the general mobilization measures, and despite the fact that France's safety and the outcome of the possible conflict depended in a large measure upon Czechoslovakia's resistance and Russia's intervention, no military co-operation between France, Czechoslovakia and Russia was even begun during the six months that preceded Munich. Yet this was not for want of strong representations that it should take place.

At the time of the May crisis Coulondre came to Paris to urge the necessity for opening military talks upon Georges Bonnet.

'Surely it is normal and even necessary,' he said, 'that before committing all our strength against Germany, the government should wish to know not only what military assistance the Soviet Union can give Czechoslovakia, but also what it may be able to give France? It is therefore not enough that the military talks should be carried on between Prague and Moscow. They should at once be extended to include the examination of ways of co-ordinating the military activities of the three countries for the defence of Czechoslovakia.'[20]

But for this to have been quite sound, the French government would have had to intend 'to commit all its strength against Germany'.

A little earlier, at the beginning of 1938, Benes received General

* In volume III of their *Histoire de la Diplomatie*, edited by the academician Vladimir Potemkin, the official Soviet historians speak of an interview that General Faucher is supposed to have had with 'certain Prague politicians' during which the former head of the French military mission said, 'We do not want to intervene against Hitler with the Bolsheviks as our allies.' General Faucher, whose attitude both before and after the 1938 crisis forms the best denial of these tendentious allegations, a few months before he died, authorized us to say that he never said anything of the kind. But are the Soviet 'historians' who handed out praise and blame in 1947 still thought of as historians in the USSR today?

Faucher, who was just about to go to France, and expressed the same anxieties.

'The question of military co-operation with the Soviets has to be taken up again,' he said. 'Since we have a pact we must try to get the most out of it from the military point of view. You may say in Paris that I shall take no initiative whatsoever; that is to say I shall do nothing from the military point of view except in agreement with your government. Then you must ask whether the government do not think that the time has now come for us to consult, as we formerly thought we should, about what attitude we could adopt with regard to the Moscow general staff and what proposals we could make them, after we, Paris and Prague, have jointly concerted our action.'[21]

Furthermore in his memoirs the Czechoslovak statesman has, with an understandable bitterness, listed the fruitless démarches that were undertaken to obtain this essential co-ordination of military effort.

'After the mobilization of May, 1938,' writes Benes, 'I agreed that the chief of our general staff, General Krejci, should enter into direct contact with General Gamelin to settle the steps to be taken to co-ordinate French and Czechoslovak mobilization. General Gamelin replied that he had no instructions upon this subject. We received no other response and none of our generals was invited to come to Paris. It was in this way that, a little before the Munich crisis, we reached the conclusion that the French were unwilling or were unable to institute joint preparations . . .

'Czechoslovakia and the Soviet Union found that they were completely isolated in the camp among those who were on principle openly and determinedly anti-fascist and anti-Nazi . . . On several occasions the Soviet diplomats made serious attempts to organize conferences at which there could have been an exchange of views on the joint defence of eastern and western Europe against a fascist attack. We were always ready to take part in conferences of this kind. Yet until the end of September 1938 the Soviet efforts came up against the negative attitude of the French and the English.'*

* Yet it should be noted that Benes had been deceived at the time of the Tukha-chevsky affair to the extent of warning Léon Blum, who wanted military co-opera-tion between France, Czechoslovakia and the USSR, against the Soviet general staff, which was 'partly rotten'.

The relative strength in the east . . .

Yet Russia's military potentialities were not trifling. To refuse contacts that would have allowed the beginning of a fruitful collaboration between the general staff of the Red Army and those of the Western powers could only mean that in Paris there was a determination to put up with all Hitler's exigencies in advance and to avoid war at all costs.

In the field of aviation – that which was worrying the French general staff most since General Vuillemin's depressing trip to Germany – Russia alone possessed an air force that was enough to outmatch the Luftwaffe. As Daladier said on several occasions, the Russian air force was the most numerous in Europe. But in addition to this, since the spring of 1938 the Soviet government had put forty-five motorized divisions on a war footing and had gathered them all on her western frontier.

For their part the Czechoslovaks amounted to an important military force in central Europe. The responsibility for this estimate again falls upon Daladier: 'The mobilized Czech army represented a considerable force, well-equipped and well-officered, of thirty-five divisions.* Its fortifications were partially outflanked by the annexation of Austria. But in spite of that the army intelligence reckoned the Czech resistance at one month at the least "on condition that she should have Germany alone to deal with".'

Furthermore the necessary steps had been taken, immediately after the Anschluss, to re-order the Czechoslovak troop dispositions in the light of this new situation.

'The concentration of Czechoslovak strength,' states General Faucher, 'was greater in Slovakia than in Bohemia, even in peacetime. It is quite certain that while Bohemia was not to be abandoned, the Czechoslovaks were taking good care not to be surrounded there. Furthermore, very extensive and very strong fortifications in the north of Moravia were there for the very purpose of allowing movement from west to east.'

As for the Czechoslovak air force ('excellent', according to Daladier), it was, as the head of the French military mission points out, quite remarkably powerful.

'It might amount to between one thousand and fifteen hundred

---

* According to the military experts the Czech army only had between thirty and thirty-two divisions.

machines.* The Czechoslovaks were quite well supplied with fighters; they had very good pilots who distinguished themselves during the war. In France, in 1939–1940, we had nearly a thousand Czechoslovak airmen, nearly all of them pilots, and they fought very well. The machines were not bad, either. There were a few medium bombers that came from Russia; they were the best in the world, and that was why they had been ordered from Russia. The Czechoslovaks had a highly-developed aircraft industry, but it was behind-hand in the matter of bombers: they were looking for a medium bomber, and they found it in Russia.'

It is understandable that General Faucher, who was one of the chief causes of this success, should have added with legitimate pride,

'Czechoslovakia made a continuous effort for her national defence: it was an outstanding, remarkable effort that went on from 1933 to 1938. Czechoslovakia honourably made ready to take her place beside her allies in case of war. She was as straight-forward in the preparation of her national defence as she was politically: this was not the case everywhere.'[22]

Germany did dispose of a certain superiority in the eastern theatre of operations in the case of an attack upon Czechoslovakia and before any Russian intervention, for she had more than forty divisions, including a fairly high proportion of armoured units.

Yet this superiority was not so great that the 'four days' that Hitler gave for the Czechoslovak army's resistance were to be taken seriously. And even the estimate of a month made by the French army intelligence did not by any means correspond with the pessimistic forecast of the German general staff. Later Keitel, the chief of the OKW, stated, 'We had always considered that our means for an attack on the Czech frontier fortifications were insufficient. From a purely military point of view we did not have the requisite means for launching an attack which would have allowed us to breach the defences.'[23]

Mannstein, who did not belong to the same set, confirmed this. 'There is no doubt that if Czechoslovakia had resisted we should have been stopped by her fortifications, for we did not possess the means of getting through them.'[24]

And Hitler himself said, 'What we were able to see of the military

* The French air force had eight hundred planes: this is a figure quoted by Daladier.

strength of the Czechoslovaks greatly disturbed us; we had run a serious danger.'[25]

... and in the West

If the relative strength of the opposing forces in the eastern theatre in September 1938 made the German generals doubtful about the outcome of a war, the situation in the west, on the French frontier, filled them with dismay.

It was no longer a matter of calculating the comparative inadequacy of their superiority in numbers: for while the mobilized French army could range close on a hundred divisions against Germany and Italy, the commander-in-chief appointed to the western theatre, General Wilhelm Adam, had only twelve at his disposal, and of those, as we have seen, only five were regular divisions; and his strength in the air was reduced to this barest minimum, since the mass of the German air force was assigned to Operation Green. As for the Siegfried line fortifications they were as yet nothing more than 'a building-site', as Jodl put it, not only devoid of military value, but of such a kind that they would in fact hinder the defenders in their task.

In these conditions it was of little consequence that Great Britain should not, for a fairly long time, be able to send more than a single army corps to the continent.

It is wholly understandable that the German generals, all the German generals without exception, were opposed to the war.

On the other hand it is harder to comprehend the mystery which still 'envelopes the Munich affair' and which William L. Shirer rightly dwells upon – that is to say, the reason why, both in London and Paris, the notion of inferiority was allowed to grow up – a notion that has provided the 'men of Munich' with their best excuse. The only valid explanation lies in Germany's intelligent use of propaganda and deception. There is no sort of doubt that Munich was one of the first great victories won by the German specialists in psychological warfare.

Yet it is difficult to believe that even if the intelligence services did over-estimate the German strength, perhaps out of prudence, they could possibly have made so huge an error as to reverse a proportion that was in the nature, as far as the western theatre was concerned, of twelve to a hundred.

And in addition to this, the English, both the soldiers and the statesmen, had, as we know, been told by several messengers of the serious crisis through which the German high command was passing and its causes, as well as of the military plot that had arisen from it.

On September 20, therefore, at the time when the French and English were forcing Prague to accept the conditions that Hitler had dictated to Chamberlain at Berchtesgaden and at Munich a fortnight later, when they went there (without the Russians or the Czechoslovaks) in order to bow down before the Godesberg ultimatum, not only did the balance of forces show a distinct superiority on the part of the Western powers, but the discontent among the leaders of the German army made it particularly vulnerable.

A strange 'realism', that which led the stronger side to give in, at the cost of its honour and its security.

Does this mean, as it has often been said, that all through the 1938 crisis Hitler was only bluffing, as he had been in March 1936 at the time of the remilitarization of the Rhineland, and that he would have withdrawn at the first shot across his bows?

Certainly not. Now, particularly since all the documents concerning the preparation of Operation Green have been seen at Nuremberg, no one can doubt that the Führer had firmly taken his decision in 1938: if there had been no Munich war would certainly have broken out, on October 1 or 2.

Furthermore it was because they knew that this time Hitler was not bluffing that the German generals (who were genuine realists) wanted nothing of this war, which was lost before it was begun.

It is even true, and Daladier points it out with great pride, that after the signature of the Munich agreement Hitler was far from pleased. Was he displeased, because, as he said to Schacht, he had missed making his entry into Prague, although this was only put off until later? No doubt he was. But above all he was displeased at the sight of the German people so openly showing their peaceful feelings.

The 'respite'

At all events there was one point upon which Hitler had no room for displeasure – the famous 'respite' that Munich granted peace. For he knew better than anyone that he would be not only the first but indeed the only person to benefit from this respite. Yet this is the argument, the third in the list, that is most often advanced by those who defend the Munich agreement.

There is almost no point in demolishing it, because it is known, alas, how much in favour of the Western powers was the balance of strength in September 1938, and it is known how the war that broke out after a year of respite did in fact develop. Nevertheless, since it is a factor in the balance-sheet, we must show the consequences of this year that was 'gained'. It does not appear that anyone goes so far as to claim that the French and the English were able, on the moral plane, to derive any sort of advantage from Munich, particularly when it was seen in perspective: loss of prestige and an uneasy conscience – that was how the result of the meeting of September 1938 may be summarized as far as this aspect is concerned.

On the military plane, which is said to be that upon which the 'respite' was worth most, what the Allies lost in that year was incalculably great.

To begin with there was the Czechoslovak bastion. That is to say a well trained, well equipped army of more than a million men; an air force of between a thousand and fifteen hundred planes (including one French reconnaissance and one bomber group based in Czechoslovakia); and ultra-modern war material worth three hundred million Czechoslovak crowns (particularly the Skoda heavy artillery mortars of a 305 regiment).

At that time Czechoslovakia represented a holding-force: with its disappearance the Danube valley and the way to the Balkans was open to the Germans, thus allowing them to secure the essential forward bases for a subsequent action against Russia. Germany was now less than two hundred miles from Ploesti and the Rumanian oil; and being the dominant power in the great corn-growing area of central Europe, she could make what use she chose of this granary.

Furthermore Hitler, carrying out the plan whose main lines he had explained to Mussolini in his carriage on September 29, could disengage thirty divisions and move them back to the western front. And Germany now had the time needed to finish the fortification of this western front, to pour the concrete and to fill it with steel.

Can it at least be said that these few months of respite provided by Munich allowed the Western powers to catch up with the lag in production of their war factories?

No, it cannot. As Pertinax observes, 'Day by day Germany drew ahead, because in that country the war industry was in motion, because her mass-production was in full swing, while our engineers were still struggling with the choice of prototypes and with the laborious setting up of assembly-lines.'[26]

The air forces, then?

It is quite possible that the British aircraft industry, which was only just beginning the mass-production of the Hurricane (five squadrons in service in September, 1938) and which was getting ready to bring out the Spitfire, might have moved faster than the German factories. But making up for the planes that were captured intact on the Czechoslovak airfields and at once taken over by the Luftwaffe was something else again.

Finally, and there is no doubt that this was far from the least grave of the consequences of this 'pause for thought', Davies's clear-sighted and pessimistic forecast was to be proved true.

Before Munich, when she had proposed staff-talks, and at the time of Munich, when she saw her ally France taking part without her in a conference that was to determine the balance of power in Europe, Russia could see that in the mind of the French government the Franco-Soviet pact was henceforward considered a dead letter.

After Munich the USSR had only to observe the repeated violations of the agreement and France's passive conduct to be sure that Bonnet and Daladier would from then on leave Hitler 'a free hand in the east'.

Lastly, after the annexation of the 'rump state' of Czechoslovakia the direct threat was too near for Stalin not to think of showing that he too was a 'realist' – but not merely in words.

There remained Poland.

For the Poland of the colonels, the first vulture to come down on the corpse of Czechoslovakia, was now, thanks to Munich, France's last hope, her last ally in central Europe – the ally for whom many 'pacifists' would agree to go to war – the same men who would not fight when it was a question of honouring the promise given to the democratic Czechoslovakia.

So in the end we are obliged to agree with Churchill's summing up. 'For all the above reasons, the year's breathing-space said to have been "gained" by Munich left Britain and France in a much worse position compared with Hitler's Germany than they had been at the Munich crisis.'

It is impossible to give a clearer definition of what was – as this balance-sheet has just shown and as the subsequent events were to prove – one of the most wretched of diplomatic failures.

Yet it would be wrong, as we recall the facts in the perspective of history, and with the assurance of hindsight, to forget that in September 1938, virtually the entire population of France, with a greater or lesser degree of thoughtless exuberance, restraint or shame, but with an equal degree of relief, approved of Munich or accepted it.

A few months later and there was scarcely anyone, apart from the chief actors at the conference (and not even all of them), who could find any excuse for it.

So true it is that the natural way of putting an error right, when it has been committed by an entire nation, will always be a collective loss of memory.

Appendix One

Joint declaration of the British and French Governments to the President of the Czechoslovak Republic, September 19, 1938.

1. The representatives of the French and British Governments have been in consultation today on the general situation, and have considered the British Prime Minister's report of his conversation with Herr Hitler. British Ministers also placed before their French colleagues their conclusions derived from the account furnished to them of the work of his Mission by Lord Runciman. We are both convinced that, after recent events, the point has now been reached where the further maintenance within the boundaries of the Czechoslovak State of the districts mainly inhabited by Sudeten-Deutsch cannot in fact continue any longer without imperilling the interests of Czechoslovakia herself and of European peace. In the light of these considerations both Governments have been compelled to the conclusion that the maintenance of peace and the safety of Czechoslovakia's vital interests cannot effectively be assured unless these areas are now transferred to the Reich.

2. This could be done either by direct transfer or as the result of a plebiscite. We realise the difficulties involved in a plebiscite, and we are aware of your objections already expressed to this course, particularly the possibility of far-reaching repercussions if the matter were treated on the basis of so wide a principle. For this reason we anticipate in the absence of indication to the contrary that you may prefer to deal with the Sudeten-Deutsch problem by the method of direct transfer, and as a case by itself.

3. The areas for transfer would probably have to include areas with over 50 per cent of German inhabitants, but we should hope to arrange by negotiations provisions for adjustment of frontiers, where circumstances render it necessary, by some international body including a Czech representative. We are satisfied that the transfer of smaller areas based on a higher percentage would not meet the case.

4. The international body referred to might also be charged with

questions of possible exchange of population on the basis of right to opt within some specified time limit.

5. We recognise that if the Czechoslovak Government is prepared to concur in the measures proposed, involving material changes in the conditions of the State, they are entitled to ask for some assurance of their future security.

6. Accordingly His Majesty's Government in the United Kingdom would be prepared, as a contribution to the pacification of Europe, to join in an international guarantee of the new boundaries of the Czechoslovak State against unprovoked aggression. One of the principal conditions of such a guarantee would be the safeguarding of the independence of Czechoslovakia by the substitution of a general guarantee against unprovoked aggression in place of existing treaties which involve reciprocal obligations of a military character.

7. Both the French and British Governments recognise how great is the sacrifice thus required of the Czechoslovak Government in the cause of peace. But because that cause is common both to Europe in general and in particular to Czechoslovakia herself, they have felt it their duty jointly to set forth frankly the conditions essential to secure it.

8. The Prime Minister must resume conversation with Herr Hitler not later than Wednesday,* and earlier if possible. We therefore feel we must ask for your reply at the earliest possible moment.

Appendix Two

A personal letter from General Faucher to General Gamelin, sent on September 5, 1938.

General,

Last night General Krejci showed me a telegram in which M Osusky gave an account of an interview that he had had with the [French] premier on the subject of the military measures that the

* i.e. September 21.

Prague government has just taken. It appears that the premier was uneasy at the far-reaching nature of these measures and that he expressed astonishment at not having been consulted beforehand.

Here we have an example of the interference of Paris in the Prague government's activities.

General Krejci did not disguise from me that it was impossible to understand that steps that did appear and that still do appear essential and urgent in Prague should have caused a reaction of this kind in Paris. It is feared that this may arise from a view of Czecho-slovakia's position that does not have much to do with reality.

Here are further details to supplement the telegram I sent last night after my interview with General Krejci.

The measures in question have only one aim: to give a hope that mobilization will be possible in the event of a German attack.

It would be misunderstanding the situation to suppose that with the army on its peace-time footing, increased only by the graduated calling-up of reservists in the manner provided for in normal times, it would be possible to deal with mobilization effectively. And there are more than two thousand kilometres of common boundary with the Reich.

These measures have been taken with the utmost discretion. There is no question of putting a covering plan into operation as there was on May 21, with the stopping of communications, preparation for destruction and so on. They could not be put off.

The extraordinary augmentation of the German military prepara-tions will, according to information here, reach its height just during these present days as far as the numbers of men and the setting on foot of reserves and Landwehr units are concerned. In the view of our general staff itself it is a question of a camouflaged mobilization.

The still ambiguous attitude of Henlein's party has become more than suspect during these last days. The serious disturbances that broke out after Hitler's speech provide solid reasons for believing that there was the intention of creating a pretext for intervention by the Reich. And it is obvious that this danger has not disappeared.

In these conditions it is no longer the moment for discussion and negotiation. To be sure, there are circumstances in which a pre-liminary agreement would be in the highest degree desirable. This is not the case here, as I see it, because of the limited nature of the steps taken and the circumstances in which they were taken – circumstances that called for an immediate decision.

I may add that I have every reason to believe that the decision was in no way taken in a moment of panic. There is no doubt that there would be some degree of disturbance among the soldiers if there were nervousness at the top; but I see an exemplary calmness at the ministry of national defence and at the army general staff, and I know it does not arise from indifference or want of comprehension.

May I remind you, General, as regards the agreement that the prime minister would have liked, that it seems that some months ago General Krejci sent you a letter containing proposals for a joint study of appropriate steps for ensuring the co-ordination of the two allies' decisions. You passed this letter on to M Daladier, the premier. No answer has reached Prague except for yours, which only amounted to a provisional reply or even to an acknowledgment.

Finally, General, may I put two questions:

1 Do the essential precautionary measures taken in Prague increase the risks of a clash, or may it not on the contrary be supposed that it would be the lack of these precautions that would increase the risk?

2 Is it considered that French public opinion would be more unanimous if, at the moment mobilization was proclaimed in France, it was learnt that the soldiers of the Reich were at the gates of Prague?*

Appendix Three

Léon Blum's leader in *Le Populaire* of September 20, 1938.

I am summing up the situation in a few dry phrases, but each one of them could be expanded and justified.

Mr Neville Chamberlain, who left to negotiate 'an honourable and fair' settlement, has come back from Berchtesgaden carrying an ultimatum from the Führer-Chancellor.

---

* 'This was a personal letter to General Gamelin,' points out General Faucher, 'but in a postscript I added that General Gamelin might make any use of it that he thought fit.'

The British government have given way before this ultimatum.

The French government, if one is to go by their official communiqué, have purely and simply acquiesced. If one is to trust certain rumours they have made a mental reserve, and they are keeping back their final consent until Prague's reply should be known.

The French government have therefore considered that they were in no condition to bring about a change in the British attitude. This powerlessness is the result of the inner divisions and pressures that have been showing themselves obscurely for some months and which have been obvious both to Berlin and London for the last week; and which furthermore their authors have taken care to make public. It is not impossible that the British cabinet's yielding may in some degree be set down to this state of affairs in the French cabinet and in certain French political circles.

The Prague government were informed at the beginning of the afternoon, after the meetings of the English and French cabinets; and they in their turn have considered the matter. Mr Chamberlain went to Berchtesgaden: no one has invited M Benes or M Hodza to come to London. They have been informed of a plan that has been discussed in their absence and settled in their absence, a plan that maims the territory of the Czechoslovak state, amputates its sovereignty and consequently breaks and repudiates its alliances.

As I write this I do not know Czechoslovakia's reply. But whatever it may be, Hitler's match against England and France is won. His plan has become theirs. It is they who have presented it to Czechoslovakia. There is nothing wanting in his success, since he has even managed to make them agree that the USSR should be excluded from the system of powers that are to guarantee the territory of the mutilated Czechoslovakia, and no doubt to the breaking of the Czech-Soviet pact as well.

Come what may, it will have far-reaching consequences both in Europe and in France. War has probably been averted. But in such conditions that I, who have never ceased struggling for peace and who for these many years have offered up my life for it in advance, can feel no joy and that I find myself divided between a coward's relief and shame.

LÉON BLUM

Appendix Four

THE MUNICH AGREEMENT

Germany, the United Kingdom, France and Italy, taking into consideration the agreement which has been already reached in principle for the cession to Germany of the Sudeten German territory, have agreed on the following terms and conditions governing the said cession and the measures consequent thereon, and by this agreement they each hold themselves responsible for the steps necessary to secure its fulfilment:

1 The evacuation will begin on the 1st October.

2 The United Kingdom, France and Italy agree that the evacuation of the territory shall be completed by the 10th October, without any existing installations having been destroyed, and that the Czechoslovak Government will be held responsible for carrying out the evacuation without damage to the said installations.

3 The conditions governing the evacuation will be laid down in detail by an international commission composed of representatives of Germany, the United Kingdom, France, Italy and Czechoslovakia.

4 The occupation by stages of the predominantly German territory by German troops will begin on the 1st October. The four territories marked on the attached map [not reproduced here] will be occupied by German troops in the following order: The territory marked No. I on the 1st and 2nd October, the territory marked No. II on the 2nd and 3rd October, the territory marked No. III on the 3rd, 4th and 5th of October. The remaining territory of preponderantly German character will be ascertained by the aforesaid international commission forthwith and be occupied by German troops by the 10th of October.

5 The international commission referred to in paragraph 3 will determine the territories in which a plebiscite is to be held. These territories will be occupied by international bodies until the plebiscite has been completed. The same commission will fix the conditions in which the plebiscite is to be held, taking as a basis the condi-

tions of the Saar plebiscite. The commission will also fix a date, not later than the end of November, on which the plebiscite will be held.

6 The final determination of the frontiers will be carried out by the international commission. This commission will also be entitled to recommend to the four Powers, Germany, the United Kingdom, France and Italy, in certain exceptional cases minor modifications in the strictly ethnographical determination of the zones which are to be transferred without plebiscite.

7 There will be a right of option into and out of the transferred territories, the option to be exercised within six months from the date of this agreement. A German-Czechoslovak commission shall determine the details of the option, consider ways of facilitating the transfer of population and settle questions of principle arising out of the said transfer.

8 The Czechoslovak Government will, within a period of four weeks from the date of this agreement, release from their military and police forces any Sudeten Germans who may wish to be released, and the Czechoslovak Government will, within the same period, release Sudeten German prisoners who are serving terms of imprisonment for political offences.

	Adolf Hitler
	Neville Chamberlain
Munich,	*Edouard Daladier*
September 29, 1938	*Benito Mussolini*

Annex to the Agreement

His Majesty's Government in the United Kingdom and the French Government have entered into the above agreement on the basis that they stand by the offer, contained in paragraph 6 of the Anglo-French proposals of the 19th September, relating to an international guarantee of the new boundaries of the Czechoslovak State against unprovoked aggression.

When the question of the Polish and Hungarian minorities in Czechoslovakia has been settled, Germany and Italy for their part will give a guarantee to Czechoslovakia.

	Adolf Hitler
	Neville Chamberlain
Munich,	*Edouard Daladier*
September 29, 1938.	*Benito Mussolini*

Appendix Four

Declaration

The Heads of the Governments of the four Powers declare that the problems of the Polish and Hungarian minorities in Czechoslovakia, if not settled within three months by agreement between the respective Governments, shall form the subject of another meeting of the Heads of the Government of the four Powers here present.

Adolf Hitler
Neville Chamberlain
Munich, *Edouard Daladier*
September 29, 1938. *Benito Mussolini*

Supplementary Declaration

All questions which may arise out of the transfer of the territory shall be considered as coming within the terms of reference to the international commission.

Adolf Hitler
Neville Chamberlain
Munich, *Edouard Daladier*
September 29, 1938. *Benito Mussolini*

Composition of the International Commission

The four Heads of Government here present agree that the international commission provided for in the agreement signed by them to-day, shall consist of the Secretary of State in the German Foreign Office, the British, French and Italian Ambassadors accredited in Berlin, and a representative to be nominated by the Government of Czechoslovakia.

Adolf Hitler
Neville Chamberlain
Munich, *Edouard Daladier*
September 29, 1938. *Benito Mussolini*

Appendix Five

A personal letter from the Czechoslovak minister Neczas to Oreste Rosenfeld.

Prague, October 8, 1938

I beg you to communicate the following to the president of the party* at once.

1 The present new frontier, the result of a simple diktat against all protests, is far more unfavourable for our republic than the frontier proposed at Godesberg, which was distinctly refused by France and England at the time.

Some purely Czech communes and regions will fall to Germany. Minorities are being created in central Europe. The railway and the most important roads are destroyed. Centres of great economic and strategic importance, such as Pilsen, Ostrau, Brno, etc., are condemned to stagnation. A million Czechs will be allotted to Germany.

The republic becomes impossibly crippled.

2 The French and English representatives on the international commission have given their consent to the use of the 1918 census, or that of 1910, as a basis, to correct the faults of the Versailles conference. But in 1910 that census was made under the pressure of the former Austrian and Hungarian government against the Czechs and the Slovaks. Purely Czech and Slovak communes were Germanized or Magyarized and merely nominal German or Magyar majorities were thus built up. The French and English representatives have therefore given their consent to the correction of the mistakes of Versailles; but they have forgotten that the official figures of 1910 are making them commit an even greater injustice against an allied state.

3 It is absolutely essential that the French and English representatives in Berlin should support at least the Czechoslovak representatives' most important desiderata. Up until now this has not happened once.

* This refers to Léon Blum, president of the SFIO Socialist party.

4 Since Berchtesgaden our state has merely been dictated to. Only a conquered, completely beaten state can be treated in this way.

If there is a desire to help us in our darkest hour (not merely with Platonic words and sympathy) and if there is still a desire to save good relations with France, this is how it must be done: the president of the party must speak to Daladier at once and demand that Poncet in Berlin should receive orders to support the Czechoslovaks' most important and just desiderata at Berlin.

Yours ever

Neczas

Appendix Six

Further details about the committee of inquiry (see pages 336–7) received from the Czechoslovak minister Osusky.

After publication of the French edition of this book Stefan Osusky, now resident in Washington, wrote to the author making some interesting points. An article written by Professor Horacek and widely quoted in the Czechoslovak papers accused 'diplomatic representatives in the most responsible positions' of failure to keep the Government in Prague 'sufficiently informed of the policies of the Governments to which they were accredited'.

Osusky sent Chvalkovsky two telegrams from Paris asking him to deny this accusation. When no dementi appeared he asked for an inquiry.

'A little later', writes Osusky, 'I visited Prague officially in connection with the Franco-British loan. Chvalkovsky asked for my resignation in the interests of better relations with Germany. My long years of collaboration with the French made things difficult so long as I remained in Paris. I refused to resign unless and until Professor Horacek's accusation had been denied. After consulting General Syrovy, Chvalkovsky told me that the former preferred to deny the accusation rather than order an inquiry. I agreed and we drafted the text of the dementi.

'After several days Chvalkovsky told me that General Syrovy had changed his mind and preferred an inquiry to a denial.

'On my return to Paris Chvalkovsky informed me that the Council of Ministers had decided to open an inquiry into my responsibility for the events leading to Munich. I protested immediately that this was unjust since public opinion would assume that the accusations against me were based on fact if the Government was holding an inquiry into my conduct and mine alone. I suggested that the inquiry should deal with four ministers: the Czechoslovak representatives in Paris, London, Berlin and Rome. In the end I reluctantly agreed that the inquiry should be directed solely against me.

'Nothing whatever happened in the end. The Government took no action at all. The inquiry never took place and no dementi was ever published. These are the facts.'

Notes

Part One

Chapter One · The Austrian dress-rehearsal

1 Nuremberg, the hearing of March 14, 1946
2 *French Yellow Book*, Hutchinson (London) 1940. Dispatch of André François-Poncet of March 12, 1938
3 *Ibid*
4 Nuremberg, the hearing of March 14, 1946
5 Joseph Paul-Boncour, *Entre deux guerres, Souvenirs sur la IIIe République*, vol III, 1935–1940, Brentano (Paris and New York) 1946
6 Joseph E. Davies, *Mission to Moscow*, Simon and Schuster (New York) 1941; Victor Gollancz (London) 1942
7 Davies, *op cit*

Chapter Two · Czechoslovakia in 1938

1 G. M. Gathorne-Hardy, *A Short History of International Affairs, 1920–1939*, fourth edition, Oxford University Press for the Royal Institute of International Affairs, 1950
2 Quoted in Joseph A. Mikus, *La Slovaquie dans le drame de l'Europe*, Les Iles d'Or (Paris) 1955
3 Roman Fajans, *Douze ans dans la tourmente*
4 Quoted in Mikus, *op cit*
5 Fajans, *op cit*
6 *Ibid*
7 Walter Schellenberg, *The Schellenberg Memoirs*, André Deutsch (London) 1956. *The Labyrinth*, Harper (New York) 1957
8 Fajans, *op cit*
9 *Ibid*
10 General Faucher's statements on Czechoslovakia's military potentialities at the beginning of 1939 are taken from his evidence, given on July 20, 1948, before the parliamentary commission of inquiry into the events that occurred in France from 1933 to 1945, presided over by Gérard Jaquet

Chapter Three · The vice tightens

1 Paul-Boncour, *op cit*
2 *Ibid*
3 Pierre-Etienne Flandin, *Politique Française, 1919–1940*, Les Editions Nouvelles (Paris) 1947

Notes

4 J. Debu-Bridel, *L'Agonie de la IIIe République, 1929–1939*, Editions du Bateau Ivre (Paris) 1947

5 General Gamelin, *Servir, vol 2. Le prologue du drame, 1930–August 1939*, Librairie Plon (Paris) 1947

6 Jean Zay, *Souvenirs et Solitude*, René Julliard (Paris) 1945

7 Churchill, *The Second World War: The Gathering Storm*, Cassell (London) 1948

8 Edouard Benes, *Memoirs*, Allen and Unwin (London) 1954

9 Letter written by Daladier to the president of the parliamentary commission of inquiry into the events that occurred in France between 1933 and 1945. (The letter is dated May 21, 1951, but it is annexed to the minutes of the meeting of May 18, 1951)

10 Pierre Lazareff, *De Munich à Vichy*, Brentano (New York) 1944

11 Nuremberg, hearing of March 14, 1946

12 Gamelin, *op cit*

13 *Ibid*

14 Iain Macleod, *Neville Chamberlain*, Frederick Muller (London) 1961

15 Daladier published long extracts from these official minutes in the weekly *Minerve*, April 1946. He omitted a good deal from that part of Chamberlain's statement which is printed here. A full (British) account of this Anglo-French meeting is given in *Documents on British Foreign Policy, 1919–1939*, Third Series, vol II, pp 198–234

16 This conclusion was not printed in Daladier's *Minerve* article. A similar version, however, can be found in the British record

17 Article by Daladier in the magazine, *Le Nouveau Candide*, September 1961

18 Georges Bonnet, *Défense de la Paix, vol I. De Washington au Quai d'Orsay*, Les Editions du Cheval Ailé (Geneva) 1946

19 Paul Schmidt, *Hitler's Interpreter*, Heinemann (London 1950)

20 Davies, *op cit*

21 Léon Noël's testimony before the parliamentary commission of inquiry into the occurrences that took place in France between 1933 and 1945. (Before being sent to Poland, Léon Noël had been head of the French diplomatic mission in Prague.)

22 Document USSR 268, quoted at the Nuremberg trial, hearing of February 8, 1946

23 Churchill, *op cit*

24 Bonnet, *op cit*

Chapter Four · The May crisis

1 Taken from Nevile Henderson, *Failure of a Mission*, Hodder (London) 1940

2 Schmidt, *op cit*

3 Henderson, *op cit*

4 *Documents on British Foreign Policy 1919–1939*, Third Series, vol I, p 341. Halifax to Henderson, May 22, 1938

5 *Documents on German Foreign Policy 1918–1945*, Series D, vol II, p 319. Minute by Weizsäcker, May 22, 1938

6 *British Documents*, 3, vol I, p 346. Halifax to Phipps, May 22, 1938. Quoted also in Bonnet, *op cit*

Notes

Chapter Five · Lord Runciman appears

1 *German Documents*, D, vol II, p 358, Directive for 'Operation Green'
2 Bonnet, *op cit*
3 Robert Coulondre, *De Staline à Hitler*, Hachette (Paris) 1950
4 *British Documents*, 3, vol I, p 418. Halifax to Newton, May 31, 1938. Quoted in Bonnet, *op cit* p 157
5 Bonnet, *op cit*
6 *German Documents*, D, vol II, p 412. Memorandum by Ribbentrop, June 11, 1938
7 *German Documents*, D, vol II, p 473. General Strategic Directive
8 Nuremberg. Hearing of October 1, 1946
9 *cf* German Documents, D, vol VII, Appendix III, H (iii)
10 *German Documents*, D, vol II, p 539. Hencke to the German Foreign Ministry, August 6, 1938
11 Coulondre, *op cit*
12 *German Documents*, D, vol II, p 521. Eisenlohr to the German Foreign Ministry, July 28, 1938
13 *Ibid*, Welczeck to the German Foreign Ministry, August 10, 1938
14 *British Documents*, 3, vol II, p 79. Memorandum by Halifax, August 11, 1938

Chapter Six · Priority for Operation Green

1 *British Documents*, 3, vol II, p 79. Halifax to Henderson, August 11, 1938
2 Quoted in Jodl's Diary
3 *German Documents*, D, vol II, p 611. Minute by Weizsäcker, August 23, 1938
4 Gamelin, *op cit*
5 Account telegraphed by Payart; quoted in Bonnet, *op cit*
6 *German Documents*, D, vol II, p 578. Letter from Friedrich Bürger to the German Foreign Ministry, August 17, 1938
7 Shirer, *op cit*
8 *German Documents*, D, vol II, p 715. German chargé d'affaires in Prague to the German Foreign Ministry
9 Telegram from M de Lacroix; quoted in Bonnet, *op cit*
10 Anatole de Monzie, *Ci-devant*, Flammarion (Paris) 1942
11 Bonnet, *op cit*
12 *German Documents*, D, vol II, pp 722–3. Theodor Kordt to the German Foreign Ministry, September 8, 1938

Part Two

Chapter One · The road to Berchtesgaden

1 Schmidt, *op cit*
2 *German Documents*, D, vol II, p 729. Notes by Schmundt on conference at Nuremberg, September 9, 1938
3 Shirer, *op cit*

4 *German Documents*, D, vol II, p 735. Selzam to the German Foreign Ministry, September 10, 1938
5 *Ibid*, p 739. Bräuer to the German Foreign Ministry, September 10, 1938
6 *Ibid*, p 744. Memorandum by von Selzam, September 12, 1938
7 *British Documents*, 3, vol II, p 303. Letter from Halifax to Phipps, September 12, 1938
8 *German Documents*, D, vol II, p 742. Kordt to the German Foreign Ministry, September 12, 1938
9 *Ibid*, p 752. Memorandum by Altenburg, September 13, 1938
10 *Ibid*, p 754. Kordt to the German Foreign Ministry, September 13, 1938
11 Schmidt, *op cit*
12 Gisevius, *To the Bitter End*
13 Lazareff, *op cit*
14 Keith Feiling, *Neville Chamberlain*, Macmillan (London) 1947. Letter by Chamberlain to his sister, Ida, September 19, 1938
15 Schmidt, *op cit*
16 *Ibid*
17 Feiling, *op cit*

Chapter Two · *The first surrender*

1 Edouard Daladier, article in *Le Nouveau Candide*, September 1961
2 French parliamentary commission of inquiry into the events occurring in France between 1933 and 1945; evidence of Léon Blum
3 Bonnet, *op cit*
4 French parliamentary commission; evidence of M de Lacroix
5 de Monzie, *op cit*
6 Gamelin, *op cit*
7 de Monzie, *op cit*
8 P. L. Bret, *Au feu des événements*
9 French parliamentary commission; evidence of Albert Lebrun
10 J. Szembek, *Journal, 1933–1939*, Plon (Paris) 1952
11 Churchill, *op cit*

Chapter Three · *Dramatic events at Godesberg*

1 Macleod, *op cit*
2 Henderson, *op cit*
3 *Ibid*
4 Shirer, *op cit*
5 Henderson, *op cit*
6 Schmidt, *op cit*
7 Henderson, *op cit*
8 Paul Reynaud, *In the Thick of the Fight*, Cassell (London) 1955
9 The version given by de Monzie, *op cit*
10 *British Documents*, 3, vol II, p 489, British Delegation (Godesberg) to Viscount Halifax, September 24, 1938
11 Henderson, *op cit*
12 Schmidt, *op cit*

Notes

Chapter Four · The great September manoeuvres

1 Daladier, *op cit*
2 *Ibid*
3 Conversation reported in a telegram from Lacroix to Bonnet, quoted in Bonnet, *op cit*
4 Quoted in Vladimir Potemkin, *Histoire de la Diplomatie*, vol III, 1919–1939, Librairie de Médicis (Paris) 1947. (Translated from the Russian)
5 Gamelin, *op cit*
6 Bonnet, *op cit*
7 Adapted from the account in *British Documents*, 3, vol II, p 536. Record of Anglo-French conversations held in Downing Street, September 26, 1938
8 *Memoirs of Cordell Hull*, Macmillan (New York) 1948
9 *German Documents*, D, vol II, p 958, Roosevelt to Hitler
10 *British Documents*, 3, vol II, p 541, Chamberlain to Hitler, September 26, 1938
11 Schmidt, *op cit*
12 Daladier, *op cit*
13 *German Documents*, D, vol II, p 939, Rothermere to Ribbentrop, September 26, 1938
14 Bonnet, *op cit*
15 Shirer, *op cit*
16 Gamelin, *op cit*
17 *German Documents*, D, vol II, p 943, statement by the British Prime Minister, September 26, 1938
18 Bret, *op cit*
19 French parliamentary commission: evidence of Pierre Comert
20 Bonnet, *op cit*
21 Henderson, *op cit*
22 Quoted in Hugh Thomas, *The Spanish Civil War*, Eyre and Spottiswoode (London) 1961
23 Henderson, *op cit*
24 Shirer, *op cit*
25 Gisevius, *op cit*
26 Debu-Bridel, *op cit*
27 Bonnet, *op cit*. Halifax' exact instructions to Phipps are given in *British Documents*, 3, vol II, p 602
28 Bonnet *op cit*
29 Gamelin, *op cit*

Part Three

Chapter One · The race against the clock

1 Daladier, *op cit*
2 Bonnet, *op cit*
3 *Ibid*
4 Chamberlain to his sister, Macleod, *op cit*

5 A. François-Poncet, *Souvenirs d'une ambassade en Allemagne*
6 *Ciano's Diary, 1937–1938*, Methuen (London) 1948
7 *Ibid*
8 *Ibid*
9 Henderson, *op cit*
10 *Von Hassel's Diary*
11 *Ibid*
12 Schmidt, *op cit*
13 The chief part of this account of the interview is taken from Schmidt, *op cit*, corroborated by François-Poncet, *op cit*
14 Henderson, *op cit*
15 *Ibid*

Chapter Two · *The invitation to the journey*

1 Stefan Zweig, *The World of Yesterday*
2 Bret, *op cit*
3 J. W. Wheeler-Bennett, *Munich, Prologue to Tragedy*, Macmillan (London) 1948
4 Ciano, *op cit*
5 Nuremberg; hearing of March 14, 1946

Chapter Three · *The four great powers*

1 Schmidt, *op cit*
2 Nuremberg: evidence of Luftwaffe general Bodenschatz.
3 Ciano, *op cit*
4 *Paris-Soir*, September 30, 1938
5 Daladier, *op cit*
6 *Ibid*
7 Ciano, *op cit*

Chapter Four · *The Agreement*

1 François-Poncet, *op cit*
2 Nuremberg: hearing of March 18, 1946
3 Daladier, *op cit*
4 Ciano, *op cit*
5 Gamelin, *op cit*
6 Ciano, *op cit*
7 *Ibid*
8 F. Charles-Roux, *Huit ans au Vatican*
9 Quoted in Macleod, *op cit*
10 *Ibid*
11 Shirer, *op cit*
12 François-Poncet, *op cit*
13 Shirer, *op cit*
14 *Ibid*
15 *Ibid*
16 Article by Caussy in *Le Populaire*, March 3, 1948

Notes

Part Four

Chapter One · 'If they knew what they were cheering'

1 Hubert Ripka, *Le Coup de Prague*, Plon (Paris) 1949
2 Daladier, *op cit*
3 *Ibid*
4 Bonnet, *op cit*
5 *Ibid*
6 G. Manceron, *L'Ordre*, October 1, 1938
7 Gamelin, *op cit*, and Reynaud, *op cit*
8 In *Ci-devant*, the book from which these lines are taken, Anatole de Monzie adds, in reference to this sentence, the note 'I stand by this remark. April 20, 1941.'
9 Zweig, *op cit*
10 French parliamentary commission: evidence of President Lebrun
11 Bonnet, *op cit*
12 Eva Braun, *Journal Intime*
13 Charles-Roux, *op cit*
14 Léon Noël, *L'aggression allemande contre la Pologne*, Flammarion (Paris) 1946
15 Josef Beck, *Final Report*, Robert Speller (New York) 1958
16 Noël, *op cit*

Chapter Two · Munich, the last instalment

1 Noël, *op cit*
2 Beck, *op cit*
3 *Ibid*
4 This article appears, with all those Tardieu wrote in 1938, in his book *L'Année de Munich*
5 Paul Coblentz, *Georges Mandel*, Editions du Bélier (Paris) 1946
6 *Le Populaire*, leader on October 6, 1938
7 J-F. Blondel, *Au fil de la carrière*
8 Quoted in Mikus, *op cit*
9 Hubert Ripka, *Munich, before and after*, Gollancz (London) 1939
10 Freytagh-Loringhoven, *La politique étrangère de l'Allemagne*, Fernand Sorlot (Paris) 1942. (French translation of *Deutschlands Aussenpolitik 1933–1939*, Otto Stolberg (Berlin) 1939
11 Page 3 of the minute of the Franco-British talks (Bonnet's note)
12 Schmidt, *op cit*
13 French Yellow Book, No 163, July 13, 1939
14 The Wilhelmstrasse's note and Coulondre's accompanying message, dated February 28, and March 2, 1939, respectively, are to be found in the French Yellow Book (No 51).
15 Henderson, *op cit*
16 Schmidt, *op cit*
17 *Le Populaire*, leader of March 15, 1939

Notes

Chapter Three · The balance-sheet

1 Unpublished personal notes of Albert Sarraut
2 Paul-Boncour, *op cit*
3 René Cassin, *Les traités d'assistance entre la France et la Tchécoslovaquie*, in *Politique Etrangère*, no 4, August 1938
4 Bonnet, *op cit*
5 Noël, *op cit*
6 French parliamentary commission: evidence of Pierre Comert
7 *Ibid*
8 Debu-Bridel, *op cit*
9 Daladier, *op cit*
10 Sarraut, unpublished notes
11 Speech in the House of Commons, March 24, 1938
12 Daladier quotes Payart's telegram giving an account of this interview in *Minerve*, April 19, 1946
13 *La Revue Socialiste*, no 13, July, 1947, 'Le Chemin de Munich'
14 Jean Champenois, *Le peuple russe et la guerre* (Paris) 1947
15 Coulondre, *op cit*
16 Churchill, *op cit*
17 Coulondre, *op cit*
18 Davies, *op cit*
19 French parliamentary commission, evidence of Pierre Comert
20 Coulondre, *op cit*
21 French parliamentary commission, evidence of General Faucher
22 *Ibid*
23 Nuremberg: hearing of April 4, 1946
24 Nuremberg: hearing of August 9, 1946
25 Pertinax (André Géraud), *The Gravediggers of France*, Doubleday (New York) 1944
26 *Ibid*

Index